OECD Tax Policy Studies

Taxation and Skills

No. 24

OECD
BETTER POLICIES FOR BETTER LIVES

This work is published under the responsibility of the Secretary-General of the OECD. The opinions expressed and arguments employed herein do not necessarily reflect the official views of OECD member countries.

This document and any map included herein are without prejudice to the status of or sovereignty over any territory, to the delimitation of international frontiers and boundaries and to the name of any territory, city or area.

Please cite this publication as:
OECD (2017), *Taxation and Skills*, OECD Tax Policy Studies, No. 24, OECD Publishing, Paris
http://dx.doi.org/10.1787/9789264269385-en

ISBN 978-92-64-26937-8 (print)
ISBN 978-92-64-26938-5 (PDF)
ISBN 978-92-64-26939-2 (ePub)

Series: OECD Tax Policy Studies
ISSN 1990-0546 (print)
ISSN 1990-0538 (online)

The statistical data for Israel are supplied by and under the responsibility of the relevant Israeli authorities. The use of such data by the OECD is without prejudice to the status of the Golan Heights, East Jerusalem and Israeli settlements in the West Bank under the terms of international law.

Photo credits: Cover © selensergen/Thinkstock.

Corrigenda to OECD publications may be found on line at: *www.oecd.org/publishing/corrigenda*.

Foreword

Higher skill levels lead to higher wages and better employment prospects for individuals, higher productivity and profits for businesses, and higher growth rates and tax revenues for governments. While there is broad consensus about the importance of skills for inclusive growth, sharing the costs of skills investments equitably and efficiently between governments, individuals, and businesses is a matter of continued debate. This report analyses how taxes impact the costs and returns of skills investments. The tax system is a key means through which the returns and the costs of skills are shared between governments and students.

Understanding the role of the tax system in the investment in human capital is important for both tax and skills policy makers. The impact of the tax system on physical capital is extensively studied and can be a significant factor in shaping tax policy reform. Similar consideration should be given to the impact of taxes on human capital. This study provides insights into the influence of tax systems on skills in 29 OECD countries: Australia, Austria, Belgium, Canada, Chile, the Czech Republic, Denmark, Estonia, Finland, Greece, Hungary, Iceland, Ireland, Israel, Italy, Luxembourg, Mexico, the Netherlands, New Zealand, Norway, Poland, Portugal, the Slovak Republic, Slovenia, Spain, Sweden, Switzerland, Turkey, and the United Kingdom.

Taxation and Skills *finds that for a typical 17-year-old individual in OECD countries, a tertiary education is one of the best investments available. A tertiary degree more than pays for itself in terms of future expected after-tax income even before accounting for additional employment, health and well-being benefits. On average, a student's earnings after education must rise by 15% to break even on the costs of education. In fact, they rise by 48% on average. Governments generally recoup the costs of their investment in tertiary education through higher income tax revenue. Estimates suggest that, on average, the extra income tax revenue gained from educating a typical student at the tertiary level amounts to 118% of government education costs across the OECD. This does not incorporate the wide variety of other returns to skills investments for governments.*

Tax expenditures that encourage skills investments exist in many OECD countries. However, they may be poorly designed, regressive, and can have mixed impacts on education outcomes. Direct support for skills and financing through student loans encourages skills investments by both targeting support to those who need it most, while at the same time mitigating the risk of skills investments by providing a form of insurance against such risk.

Creating incentives to invest in skills across society is a key component in lifting wage and productivity levels across OECD economies, and in ensuring that growth in the coming years is inclusive and sustainable. Taxation and Skills *demonstrates that tax and spending policies need to be designed in a coherent manner in order to encourage skills investments. The analysis contained in this report can help policy makers to compare their countries with other OECD countries, to design effective skills policies and to create inclusive growth across the OECD.*

Acknowledgements

This study was prepared under the guidance of Working Party No. 2 of the OECD Committee on Fiscal Affairs and was approved for publication by the OECD Committee on Fiscal Affairs. Comments and information provided by Delegates to both the Working Party and the Committee and by other national officials is gratefully acknowledged. Input provided by the Delegates to Working Party No 2. of the Committee on Fiscal Affairs in response to the 2011 questionnaire on Tax and Skills and in verifying the models and results presented in this study is particularly appreciated. The support of the Education Directorate and the OECD Young Professionals Programme is also gratefully acknowledged.

The study was prepared by Pierce O'Reilly and Bert Brys of the OECD's Centre for Tax Policy and Administration (CTPA). Chapters 1, 2, 4 and 5 and Annexes B,C and D of the study were prepared by Pierce O'Reilly and supervised by Bert Brys, while the methodological Chapter 3 as well as Annex A was prepared by Pierce O'Reilly and Bert Brys. The methodology has been developed by Bert Brys together with Pierce O'Reilly and Carolina Torres. Previous versions of the methodology were presented in Brys & Torres (2013). The 2011 questionnaire on Tax and Skills on which the models are based was carried out by Carolina Torres and supervised by Bert Brys. Axelle Magnier provided excellent research assistance. The project was carried out under the guidance of David Bradbury. Early guidance on the project was provided by Pierre LeBlanc and Stephen Matthews.

The project also benefitted from extensive collaboration with the OECD Education Directorate, and in particular from the help of Deborah Roseveare, Joanne Caddy, Andrew Bell, Soumaya Maghnouj and Corinne Heckmann. Comments on various drafts and other assistance were provided by David Bradbury, Pierre LeBlanc, Anna Milanez, and Alastair Thomas, as well as by seminar participants at the Centre for Tax Policy and Administration's seminar series, and the OECD Skills Strategy Advisory Group. Dominique Paturot provided helpful support regarding *Taxing Wages*. Michael Sharratt provided helpful support on many modelling and graphical issues, and prepared country notes for the project. Carrie Tyler assisted with the production of the publication and associated brochure. Violet Sochay provided invaluable administrative assistance.

Table of contents

Tables

Figures

Follow OECD Publications on:

http://twitter.com/OECD_Pubs

http://www.facebook.com/OECDPublications

http://www.linkedin.com/groups/OECD-Publications-4645871

http://www.youtube.com/oecdilibrary

http://www.oecd.org/oecddirect/

This book has...

StatLinks

A service that delivers Excel® files from the printed page!

Look for the *StatLinks* at the bottom of the tables or graphs in this book. To download the matching Excel® spreadsheet, just type the link into your Internet browser, starting with the *http://dx.doi.org* prefix, or click on the link from the e-book edition.

Abbreviations and acronyms

AETR	Average effective tax rate
ARCR	Average returns to costs ratio
AW	Average wage
BEI	Breakeven earnings increment
CTPA	Centre for Tax Policy and Administration
DC	Direct education costs
GDP	Gross domestic product
IMF	International Monetary Fund
METR	Average effective tax rate
MRCR	Marginal returns to costs ratio
OECD	Organisation for Economic Co-operation and Development
PIT	Personal income tax
SG	Scholarships and grants
SME	Small and medium enterprise
SSC	Social security contribution
TFE	Tax rate of foregone earnings
TEI	Tax rate on earnings increment
VAT	Value added tax

Executive summary

Ensuring that all individuals can develop the skills needed to productively participate in the economy is necessary for inclusive economic growth. Investing in skills can expand the productive capacity of the economy and at the same time reduce inequality by ensuring that all members of society have the opportunity to fulfil their productive and creative potential. Improving the level of skills across the economy has positive impacts for individuals and society as a whole. For many individuals, human capital represents the most valuable asset they will possess in their lifetime.

The tax system impacts the ability of individuals to develop skills in a variety of ways. The revenues that taxes raise can be used to finance direct investments in skills. The tax code can treat labour and capital income differently, which can create incentives to invest in physical instead of human capital. Equally, the tax system can impact the financial incentives of individuals to develop, activate and use their skills efficiently in the labour market.

Better skill levels lead to higher wages and stronger employment prospects for workers, higher productivity and profits for businesses, and higher growth rates and tax revenues for governments. However, financing this spending is challenging for many OECD countries, especially in the context of high levels of public and private debt, and debate continues about how the costs of skills investments should be equitably and efficiently shared between governments, individuals, and businesses. A principal mechanism for this sharing of costs and benefits is the tax system.

This study assesses the way that taxes and other policy levers impact skills investments. While the effects of the tax system on investment in physical capital have been widely studied, investment in human capital has received less attention. This study presents indicators that measure the impact of tax and spending policy on individuals' incentives to invest in skills. These indicators take into account the financial costs of skills investments for individuals such as lost after-tax earnings and tuition fees, as well as the costs borne by governments such as grants, scholarships, lost taxes, and skills tax expenditures. The indicators also incorporate the returns to skills investments for individuals and governments through higher after-tax wages and higher tax revenues respectively.

The first indicator measures how much an individual's earnings need to increase before they recover the costs of a skills investment over their remaining years in the workforce. The second indicator is an effective tax rate on skills, which measures how much taxes raise or reduce the net returns to skills investments for an individual. The third indicator measures the returns to skills investments for governments, comparing the government's costs of educating an individual to the government's expected returns in the form of higher tax revenues. These indicators are developed for individuals who will just break even on a skills investment, and for individuals who will earn a larger return. Investments financed with both debt and savings are examined.

These indicators are modelled for a series of hypothetical skills investment scenarios, including a young university student and a mid-career worker. Results are presented for 29 OECD countries. The results in the study do not incorporate the impact of social security contributions; only personal income taxes are incorporated. Some of the key insights of the study include:

- **Tertiary education is a financially attractive investment for individuals**: Based on the current tax, scholarship, and tuition policy mix, the results show that the wage premium earned by a university student in the current labour market is above – often well above – what is required to break even on the costs of tertiary education.
- **Governments recoup the costs of their investment in tertiary education on average through higher tax revenues on higher wages from more highly skilled workers**: The extra income taxes paid over the lifetime of an average student more than cover government costs of educating that student. For some countries – though not all – the results suggest that increasing tertiary education spending would be self-financing in terms of income tax revenue alone.
- **For individuals whose returns to skills are lower, future expected income tax revenue may not cover governments' costs of tertiary education**: This is especially true where government spending on tertiary education is currently high. For governments to break even financially from increased skills spending, this spending should be targeted to encourage those skills investments where returns will be highest.
- **The effective tax rate on skills depends on how much the individual's wage rises after the skills investment**: For a tertiary student who just breaks even on the costs of their investment over their lifetime, tertiary education is comparatively lightly taxed; the tax system accounts for about 4% of the amount of extra earnings needed to break even on a skills investment. High-return skills investments are taxed more heavily than low-return skills investments. For an average rate of return on a tertiary education in the OECD, the tax system reduces the net returns by 19% on average.
- **Governments provide many tax expenditures to support investment in skills, such as tax deductions of skills expenses, or tax exemptions for scholarship income**: The study argues that a careful case-by-case analysis of these provisions is needed, and suggests that good design is important in ensuring their effectiveness. Skills tax expenditures often provide larger benefits to those with larger taxable incomes, and to those in secure employment relative to those in casual employment. They may provide less assistance to those who are credit constrained, who are more likely to be from lower income households. Moreover, evidence of their impact on wages and employment is mixed.
- **Some design aspects of skills tax provisions may reduce labour market flexibility, exacerbate skills mismatches and represent a drag on productivity**: Existing skills tax expenditures are often only available for training connected to a workers' current employment, and may be ineffective in assisting workers who need or want to change careers.
- **Tax policies that encourage skills development and activation are complementary**: Those who are more likely to develop skills are more likely to use them in the labour market, and those who work more and for longer have higher incentives to invest in skills. Tax

policies that increase both skills investments and skills activation levels pay double dividends, particularly for groups with lower labour market participation such as women and older workers.

- **Ensuring access to skills for those who are credit constrained is crucial**: Skills are unlike physical capital because they cannot be used as collateral to finance an investment. This may mean that skills investments with positive returns are not undertaken. Income-contingent loans may be an efficient and equitable approach to addressing these issues.

The study provides a number of important messages for governments and policy makers. First, the study demonstrates the importance of coherent policy mixes to encourage skills investments. Where governments tax away the returns to skills through higher taxes, it is important that public expenditure in support of skills is used to make skills investments sufficiently attractive. Where spending on skills by governments is lower, it is important that high taxes do not act as a large disincentive to invest. In all cases, the burden of the tax system on human capital investment should be considered by both tax policy makers and skills policy makers. Finally, the study presents a clear message to governments that the costs of failing to invest in skills will have consequences in the years ahead. A failure to invest in skills today will not only impede the economic participation of individuals and restrain productivity growth, but will reduce future expected tax revenues, increase future expected levels of social expenditure, and jeopardise future inclusive economic growth prospects.

Chapter 1

Introduction: Tax, skills, and inclusive growth

This chapter places this study in the context of OECD work on productivity and inclusive growth, as well as the broader literature on the public finance of education. The importance of skills for growth and productivity, as well as for equality and inclusive growth are all discussed. The impact of the tax system on skills is briefly summarised, and an outline of the study is also provided.

The statistical data for Israel are supplied by and under the responsibility of the relevant Israeli authorities. The use of such data by the OECD is without prejudice to the status of the Golan Heights, East Jerusalem and Israeli settlements in the West Bank under the terms of international law.

1.1 Skills, growth, and productivity

Skills are the cornerstone of building productive economies and inclusive societies. In a world of increasing globalisation and rising inequality, increasing the quality of and access to education has never been a higher priority for policy makers. This study considers how the tax system can affect skills by building indicators that measure the impact of income tax and spending policy on individuals' incentives to invest in skills.

The nexus between tax, productivity, growth and equity has been the subject of significant study at the OECD in recent years (OECD, 2015a, 2016). Recent work has investigated how tax policy can be used to raise growth levels in the OECD, by shifting the tax mix towards growth-friendly taxes (OECD, 2010b). Other research has also focused on how the tax system can do more to encourage equity and inclusiveness, by examining the whole tax system from a distributional perspective, by improving tax administration, and by removing tax expenditures that mainly benefit those on higher incomes (Brys et. al. 2016; OECD, 2014b). Often, however, tax policies that improve efficiency of the economy run counter to equity considerations, and policies that increase the equity of the tax system may reduce growth. Optimising the tax system for skills investments offers tax policy makers the opportunity to increase both equity and efficiency, to foster growth that offers benefits for all.

Raising skill levels is crucial for increasing economic growth rates and building economies that can provide employment and prosperity. Economic growth will increasingly depend on improvements in productivity (OECD, 2015a). Scare resources, slow population growth, and low levels of investment in physical capital have led to concerns about the future sources of growth across the OECD. Increasing skill levels and boosting productivity is an important response to these concerns: higher productivity means that even in the context of slowing rates of growth of the capital or labour stock in the economy, growth can continue to improve well-being and raise living standards in the OECD (OECD, 2016).

Over recent decades, productivity growth has been slowing. This is a key concern given the importance of productivity growth for improving well-being. Figure 1.1 shows the decline in factor productivity growth across selected OECD countries over the last decade compared to previous decades. Ninety per cent of OECD countries experienced a decline in the trend of labour productivity growth after the turn of the millennium (OECD, 2016). The ability for technological developments to continue to provide strong productivity growth across the OECD is increasingly being called into question, and concerns about a period of secular stagnation across the developed world have been expressed by some policy makers (Summers, 2014). The decline in the growth in productivity raises questions about whether the countries can continue to raise living standards in years to come. There are also questions as to whether future increases in living standards will accrue to a broad spectrum of workers or whether only certain groups will benefit.

Raising skill levels can help policy makers meet these challenges. Adequate investment in skills can ensure that all individuals can both contribute to and benefit from productivity growth. While this is true for all workers it is especially vital among those demographics and communities that currently have lowest skills levels. Workers with higher skills are more likely to help firms innovate, to participate in global value chains, and increase the knowledge spillovers from more productive sectors to less productive sectors.

Figure 1.1. **Multifactor productivity in long run comparative perspective**

Annual average growth

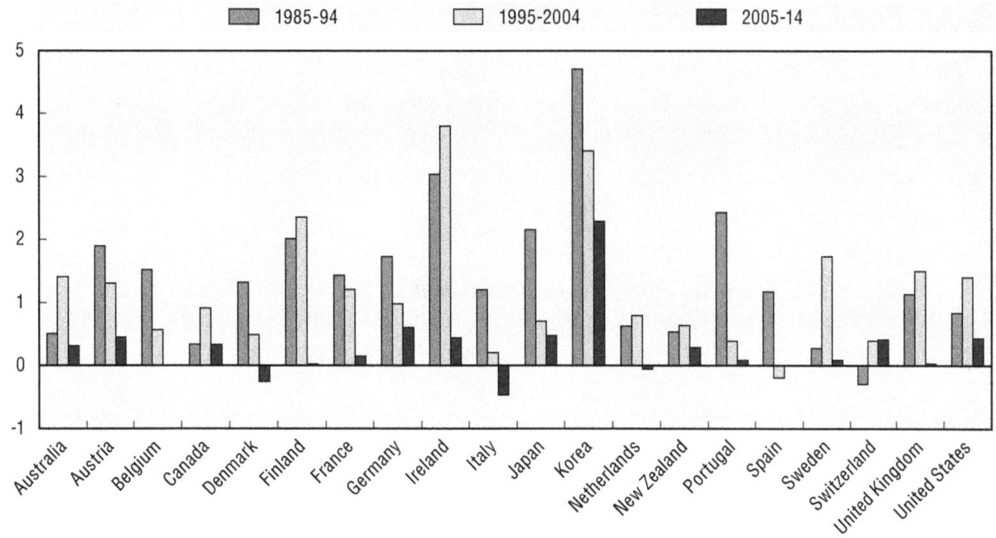

Notes: Multifactor productivity growth rates for the period ranges are the annual averages.
Source: OECD Dataset on Growth in GDP per capita and productivity

The link between skills and productivity is strengthened by the continuing integration of the global economy. Those who are left without skills are less likely to work in the kinds of industries and companies that participate in global value chains (OECD, 2016). This in turn hampers prospects for future skills development and productivity gains for these individuals; participation in global value chains is a means by which productivity gains in the form of innovations in work practices are passed from firm to firm and from worker to worker. Without adequate skills investment, certain demographics, sectors, and even countries may be increasingly left out of global value chains and may fall further away from the productivity frontier.

Though improving workers' skills is important for growth, raising the amount of human capital in the economy is about more than just increasing participation in education and lifelong learning. Individuals must develop the kinds of skills that are in demand in the labour market, reducing mismatches between those fields of study chosen by students and those that will yield benefits in the labour market. Individuals must also develop soft skills such as communication and teamwork that are necessary in the modern workplace. Skills that are developed must be activated in the labour market by raising labour market participation. This is especially true among marginalised groups where participation rates are comparatively low, including women, migrants, the elderly, and the disabled. Finally, workers' skills must be used effectively in the workplace. The right skills must be paired with the right jobs so skills are not under-utilised. There is thus a strong need for better alignment between workers' skills and those skills demanded in the economy.

1.2 Skills, tax, and inclusive growth

The centrality of skills in the current policy environment does not just stem from their important role in boosting productivity and growth; it also stems from the increasing importance of reducing inequality for policy makers (OECD, 2015b). Raising skill levels can make growth fairer, more inclusive, and more durable. Increasing skills across the workforce allows more individuals to participate in the economy and to transition into higher-quality jobs with higher wages.

Figure 1.2 shows that inequality in disposable income has increased in most OECD countries over the last three decades. The Gini coefficient of income inequality stood at 0.29 on average across OECD countries in the mid-1980s. By 2013, it had increased by about 10% or 3 points to 0.32, rising in 17 of the 22 OECD countries for which long-time series are available (Brys et al., 2016).

Figure 1.2. **Income inequality increased in most OECD countries**

Gini coefficients of disposable income inequality, mid-1980s and 2013, or latest date available

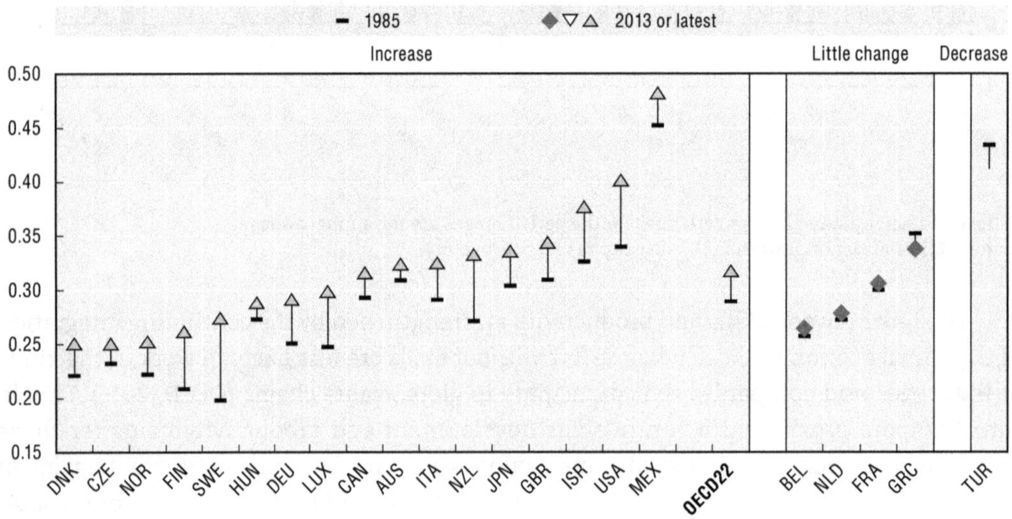

«Little change» in inequality refers to changes of less than 1.5 percentage points. Data year for 2013 (or latest year).
Source: OECD Income Distribution Database (IDD) *www.oecd.org/social/income-distribution-database.htm.*
Source: In It Together - Why Less Inequality Benefits All (OECD, 2015b).

Previous trends in inequality have been exacerbated by the economic crisis. In many OECD countries, the crisis most affected those who had low savings levels, less secure employment, and low skills: those people who were most vulnerable to economic shocks. Widespread job losses and wage stagnation over this period compounded modest wage growth over previous decades.

The crisis and its aftermath also resulted in straitened public finances across the OECD. Addressing budget deficits in many OECD countries resulted in reductions in the generosity of transfer payments to those on low incomes. In these and other ways, the negative impacts of the crisis were visited most heavily on those with low incomes. Figure 1.3 shows the decline in household real disposable income in the post-crisis period. Across 33 OECD countries, disposable income fell for those with low incomes, median incomes, and for those with high incomes. But on average those with low incomes saw their incomes fall most. By comparison, top earners' incomes fell on average across the OECD, but by a smaller amount. Indeed, in 15 countries, the real disposable income of the top 10% rose during the crisis period. So the crisis has exacerbated decades-long trends in inequality.

Figure 1.3. **Changes in household disposable income by income groups**

Annual percentage changes between 2007 and 2011 by income groups, total population

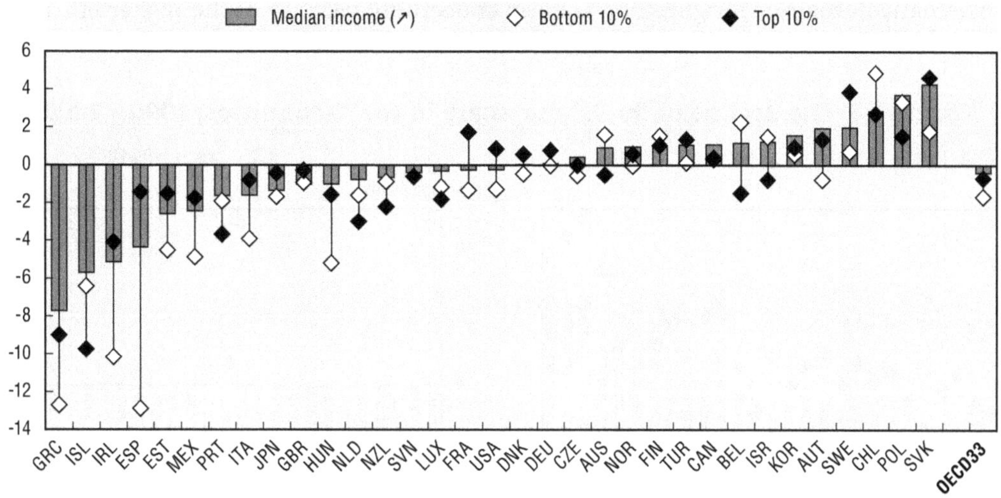

2007 refers to 2006 for Chile and Japan: 2008 for Australia, Germany, Finland, France, Israel, Mexico, Norway and Sweden. 2011 refers to 2009 for Japan; 2010 for Austria, Belgium, Ireland and the United Kingdom and 2012 for Australia, Hungary, Korea and United States; Switzerland is not available. OECD33 refers to the unweighted average.

Source: OECD Income Distribution Database (IDD), *www.oecd.org/social/income-distribution-database.htm*.

Recent policy debates have also focused on increasing inequalities between capital and labour income. For the vast majority of individuals, wages are by far the largest component of income. However, those on higher incomes earn more of their income from capital: from dividends, capital gains and other forms of business income.

Capital's share of income has been rising. Figure 1.4 shows changes in labour's share of total income across OECD countries from 1990 to 2009. While significant heterogeneity across countries exists, on average labour's share of income has fallen. This means that inequalities have been driven not just by increasing differences in wage levels, but also by divergence in the returns to different factors of production. Those who earn their income from their human capital have seen their share of total income fall relative to those who earn their income from physical capital. Many individuals receive income from both their human capital (through wages) and physical capital (through income from savings). Those with higher incomes have a higher share of physical capital and so have benefited more from the rise in capital's share of total income. This means that shifts in the returns to different factors of production have exacerbated trends in inequality that are present with respect to wage income.

These increases in inequality present a combination of challenges for policy makers. Increasing inequality generates more pressure on governments to engage in redistributive spending, to reduce market inequalities using the tax and transfer system. While this can reduce disposable income inequalities, redistribution using the tax and transfer system can have efficiency costs (Brys et al., 2016). High taxes on labour income can reduce work effort and reduce labour market participation. High degrees of welfare spending put pressures on limited government resources at a time of high debt levels. Moreover, increased spending on poverty alleviation and social benefits can create poverty traps. These factors demonstrate that shrinking the gap between market income inequality and disposable income inequality can be costly. The larger the amount of market inequality, the larger those costs can be. This means that inequalities in wages and between capital and labour income are not only problematic in their own right; they are also concerning because of the higher efficiency and growth costs of policy efforts to address them.

Figure 1.4. **The decline of the labour share in OECD countries, 1990 – 2009**

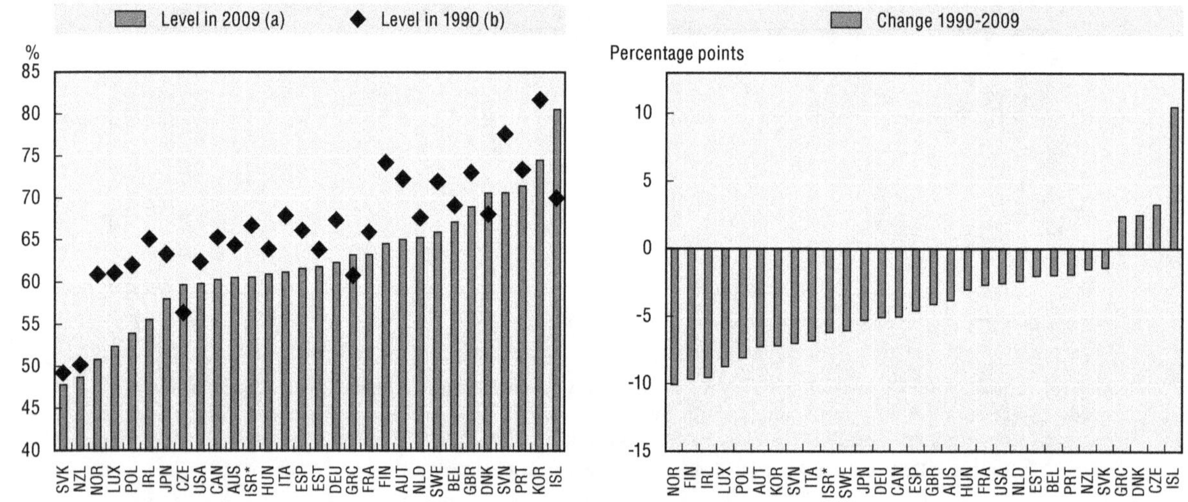

Notes: a) Germany and Iceland: 1991; Estonia: 1993; Poland: 1994; Czech Republic, Greece, Hungary, Slovak Republic and Slovenia: 1995; Israel: 2000. b) Portugal: 2005; Canada and New Zealand: 2006; Australia, Belgium, Ireland, Norway and Sweden: 2007; France, Iceland, Israel, Poland and the United Kingdom: 2008.

Source: OECD calculations based on OECD STAN and EUKLEMS.

Source: OECD Employment Outlook 2012 (OECD, 2012).

One factor that has contributed to the decrease in labour share of income is the favourability with which capital income is taxed relative to labour income across the OECD. Part of the reason for this is the highly mobile nature of capital income. This makes capital income harder to detect, and capital taxes harder to enforce. High taxes on capital income can also negatively impact on savings and investment in physical capital.

In part due to these policy challenges, the increase in inequality across the OECD has taken place at the same time as an overall reduction in the amount of redistribution being undertaken by OECD governments. Figure 1.5 shows the percentage difference between pre- and post-tax Gini coefficient for a selection of OECD countries, as well as the OECD average. This functions as a proxy for the total amount of redistribution occurring in OECD countries. Overall, the reduction in the estimated Gini coefficient caused by the tax and transfer system fell from 29.6% to 26.3% in 2008, before rising slightly to 27.6% in 2012. For a variety of reasons, OECD member states are redistributing less using their tax and transfer systems than was the case in 1999.

Increasing skills can potentially address inequality while at the same time raising growth rates. Recent research has suggested that gaps in human capital may be seen as the most important worldwide determinant of inequality (Blöndal et al., 2002; Sequeira et al., 2014).

Figure 1.5. **Redistribution became weaker in most countries until the onset of the crisis**

Percentage difference between inequality (measured by the Gini coefficient) of gross market income and inequality of disposable income, working age population

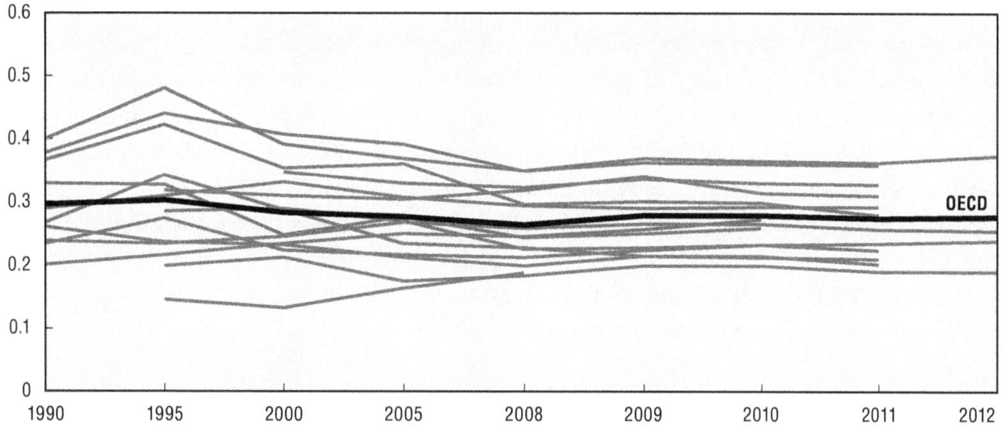

Note: OECD average: un-weighted and based on 10 countries for which data are available at all points (Canada, Denmark, Germany, Israel, Italy, Netherlands, New Zealand, Sweden, United Kingdom and United States).

Source: OECD Income Distribution Database, *www.oecd.org/social/income-distribution-database.htm.*

Raising skill levels can reduce inequality through a number of channels. Those with high skills are more likely to earn higher wages and to participate in the labour market. Raising wages and employment through higher skills is a key inclusive growth oriented policy goal; it can raise efficiency with modest efficiency costs. Reduced market inequality will also reduce the pressure on governments to undertake redistributive spending, and mean that existing redistributive spending can go further in reducing inequality than might otherwise be the case.

Increased skill levels can also reduce the extent to which inequality is passed down through the generations. Reducing inequality can raise the incomes of low-income families who are most likely to be credit constrained with respect to skills investments, which may make them more likely to invest in skills and in the skills of their children (OECD, 2015b). OECD research suggests that inequality may be associated with greater variation in educational outcomes: an increase in inequality of around six Gini points lowers the probability of poorer people graduating from university by around four points (OECD, 2015b). Similarly, as inequality rises, people from poorer families face much weaker job prospects while there is little change for those from better-off families (OECD, 2015b). More equal societies may by themselves increase education prospects of future generations.

Better skills policies can also make productivity gains more inclusive through the diffusion of innovation. OECD studies on productivity have highlighted gaps between the developments at the productivity frontier and behind the frontier: the gap between those workers, firms and sectors that are highly innovative and have high productivity and those that do not (OECD, 2015a). A key means by which high-performance work practices pass from the frontier to the rest of the economy is through movement of workers through churn in the labour market. However, existing skills policies may hamper this movement. As will be discussed in Chapter 5, many OECD countries currently provide tax support for skills investments that are related to current work, but do not provide similar support for skills investments for workers seeking to change career. In doing so, they may reduce the amount of churn of workers through the labour market. This in turn may reduce the diffusion of skills, raising mismatch levels and reducing spread of innovation.

The positive impacts of higher skills on inequality are part of the reason why access to education and training has undergone a dramatic expansion over the last sixty years. More recent years have seen access to education continue to expand, especially in countries where education rates are low (see Figure 1.6). Some research suggests, however, that expansion in education has resulted in a decline in educational quality (OECD, 2016). In spite of the expansion of educational opportunities, skills gaps remain even among younger cohorts. Even amongst those with ready access to education, the pace of technological change raises concerns of a 'digital divide' between those who have the skills to participate in a digitalised knowledge economy and those who do not.

Figure 1.6. **Trends in enrolment rates of 15-19 and 20-29 year-olds (2005-2013)**

Students in full-time and part-time programmes, in both public and private institutions

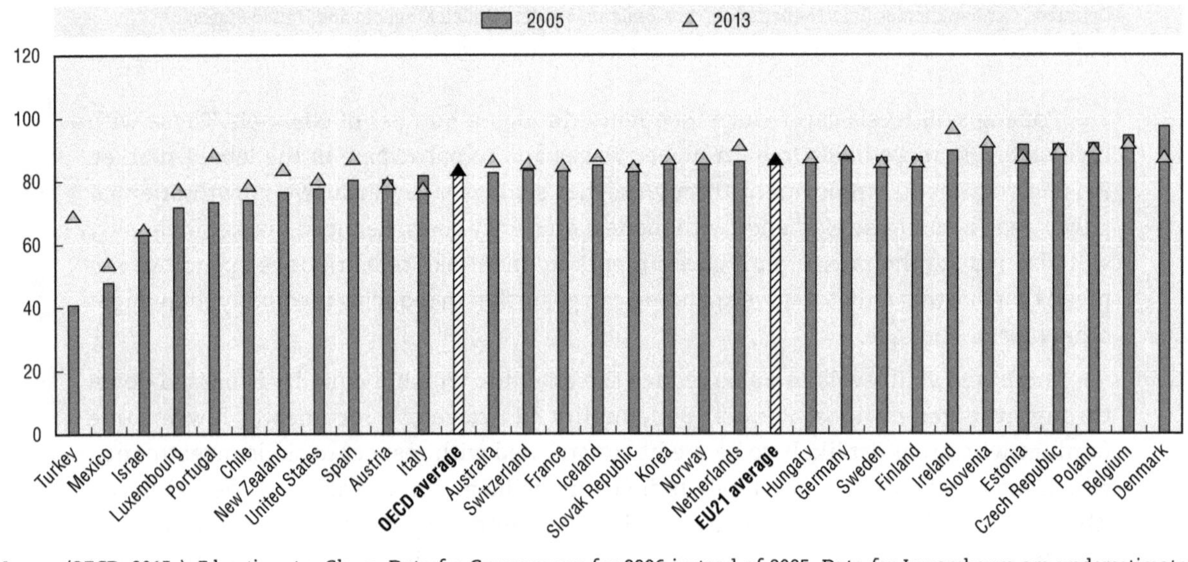

Source: (OECD, 2015c), *Education at a Glance*, Data for Germany are for 2006 instead of 2005. Data for Luxembourg are underestimated because many resident students go to school in the neighbouring countries.

In addition, education outcomes for children are still strongly associated with the education levels of their parents: those with more educated parents are more likely to be educated themselves. Educational advantage and disadvantage are propagated throughout the lifecycle – the education systems in many countries are not reducing intergenerational replication of inequality as much as they could be. Figure 1.7 shows the shares of students in OECD countries who match, exceed, or do not exceed the education level of their parents. In most countries, the levels of upward mobility are low: more than half of students achieve the same or a lower level of education than their parents.

Figure 1.7. **Intergenerational mobility in education (2012)**

Survey of Adult Skills, educational attainment of 25-34 year-old non-students compared with their parents

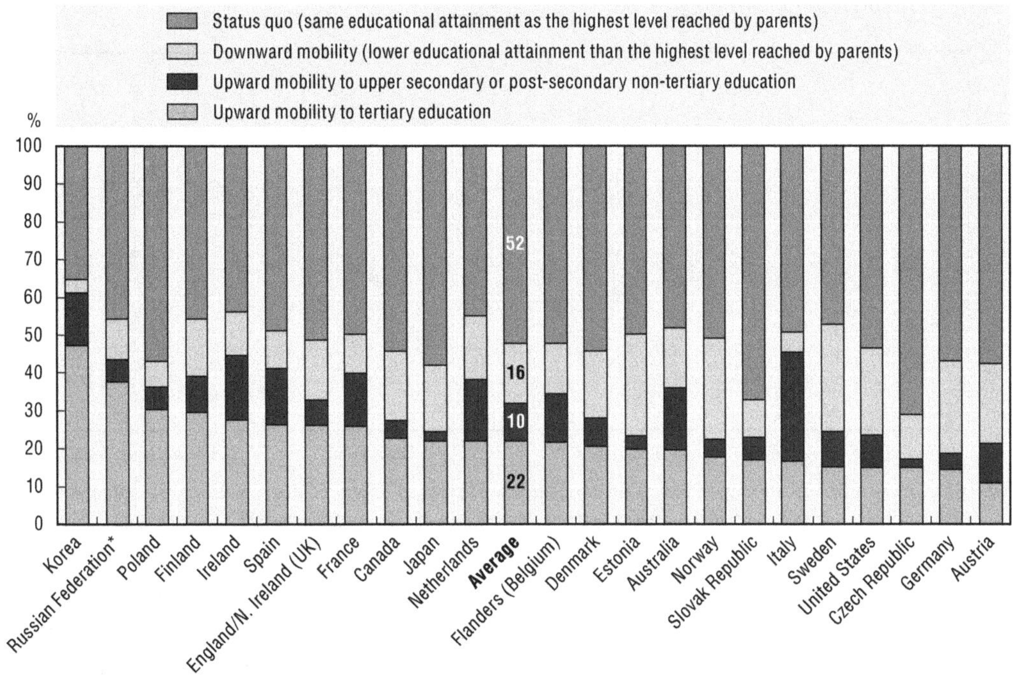

Source: (OECD, 2015c), *Education at a Glance*. Countries are ranked in descending order of upward mobility to tertiary education among tertiary-educated 25-34 year-old non-students.

1.3 The returns to skills

Increasing skills are a vital mechanism to address important policy challenges in OECD countries: lower productivity and higher inequality. However there remains much debate in the academic community and in the policy literature regarding what constitutes the right tax and spending policy mix when it comes to education and training. It is not clear what the optimal amount of total spending on skills should be, or how this spending should vary with existing skill levels and with economic development. In addition, the mix of spending between the public and private sectors is the subject of much debate. Not all skills investments are equal: the extent to which skills spending should focus on soft skills is debated, as is the extent to which spending should focus on early childhood education, lifelong learning, or tertiary, secondary or primary education. Debates also exist about the extent to which government spending on skills should encourage skills investments in certain areas such as STEM skills, and how the risks of skills investments should be shared between individuals, governments and firms.

Choosing the right skills policies requires a comprehensive assessment of the costs and benefits of skills investments. A key return to skills is higher wages. Those with better skills are more productive in the workplace and can demand higher wages from their employers. Recent OECD work based on the Survey of Adult Skills has shown that not only are wages higher for those who have spent more years in education, but they are also higher for those with better literacy, numeracy and problem solving skills. Figure 1.8 shows the distribution of wages by literacy proficiency level. There is a seven USD hourly wage gap between the wage levels of those with a literacy level in the lowest of five literacy categories compared to those with a literacy level in the highest category.

Figure 1.8. **Distribution of wages, by literacy proficiency level**
Hourly wages at 25th, 50th and 75th percentiles of the wage distribution, USD PPP

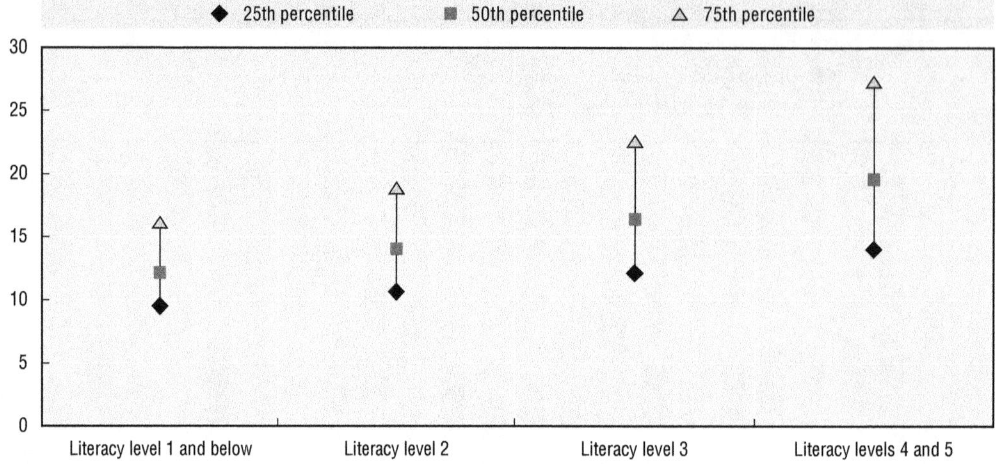

Notes: Employees only. Hourly wages, including bonuses, are expressed in purchasing-power-parity-adjusted USD
Source: (OECD, 2013) *OECD Skills Outlook – First Results from the Survey of Adult Skills (PIAAC)*, Table A6.4 (L).

While the data on the current wage premium earned by those with higher skills is clear, assessment of the future path of wages is more challenging. Some research suggests that the returns to skills investments may be lower than what is suggested by current wage levels. For example, in some OECD countries, those with tertiary degrees earn a significant earnings premium over those without tertiary degrees, pointing to a significant skills shortage in these countries. This suggests that the returns to skills investments may be high in these countries. However, as more and more people become educated and skills shortages are reduced, this wage premium may fall. Indeed, some of the OECD countries with the lowest wage premiums for tertiary education are countries where tertiary education is most widely available. So a dynamic approach to assessing the returns to skills investments may yield lower estimates than a static approach such as the one taken in this study (Heckman and Jacobs, 2010).

At the same time, there is a large economic literature debating the extent of skill-biased technological change across the OECD. This literature suggests that technological advances have raised the wage premium for certain kinds of skills while reducing the wages available in the labour market for many low-skilled workers. Jobs requiring routinised activities that formerly would have been undertaken by low-skilled workers have been automated, leading to a decline in wages for these workers. Figure 1.9 shows the evolution of employment across occupations of various skill levels (OECD, 2013). These results suggest that availability of low and medium-skilled jobs may continue to decline, suggesting in turn that the returns to high-skilled work relative to low-skilled work may continue to rise. This highlights the complexity of assessing the future returns to skills in the form of wages.

The returns to skills may change over time due to the depreciation of skills assets. OECD research has suggested that skills level rise over time before beginning to sharply depreciate as workers approach their mid-40s (OECD, 2013). This depreciation of skills that are not kept up-to-date, especially in technology rich-environments, may see wage levels fall as workers grow older. On the other hand, there is evidence that more highly skilled workers not only earn higher wages immediately after upskilling, but also see their wages increase at a faster pace compared to their low-skilled counterparts (Hanushek et al., 2013). This means that assessing the impact of skills on the future path of wages is subject to a significant degree of uncertainty.

Figure 1.9. **Evolution of employment in occupational groups defined by level of education**

Percentage change in the share of employment relative to 1998, by occupational groups defined by workers' average level of education

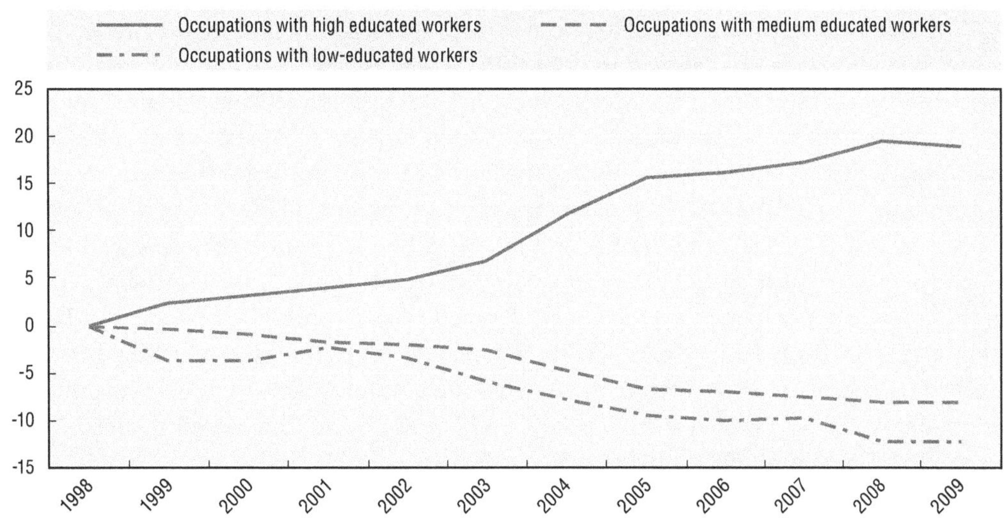

Notes: Only the 24 OECD countries available in the 1998 LFS database are included in the analysis. High level of education refers to tertiary level or more than 15 years of schooling; medium level of education refers to no tertiary but at least upper secondary education or around 12 years of schooling; low level of education refers to less than upper secondary education or 11 years of schooling. Occupations with high-educated workers: legislators and senior officials; corporate managers; physical, mathematical and engineering science professionals; life science and health professionals; teaching professionals; other professionals; physical and engineering science associate professionals; life science and health associate professionals; teaching associate professionals; and other associate professionals. Occupations with medium-educated workers: managers of small enterprises; office clerks; customer services clerks; personal and protective services workers; models, salespersons and demonstrators; extraction and building trades workers; metal, machinery and related trades workers; precision, handicraft, craft printing and related trades workers; stationary plant and related operators; and drivers and mobile plant operators. Occupations with low-educated workers: other craft and related trades workers; machine operators and assemblers; sales and services elementary occupations; and labourers in mining, construction, manufacturing and transport.

Source: (OECD, 2013) *OECD Skills Outlook – First Results from the Survey of Adult Skills (PIAAC).*

There is also significant heterogeneity in the returns to education in the form of future wages. The returns to education may be higher for individuals with higher natural abilities. Returns may be higher for individuals who are already well-educated, or for those who are poorly-educated. The returns to education in subjects such as science and engineering may be higher than the returns to other fields. The returns to education may be higher at a younger age than at older ages. The literature suggests that the returns to early childhood education in the form of future incomes are very high, in part due to higher abilities to learn new skills at very young ages (Heckman and Jacobs, 2010). At older ages, abilities to learn new skills may be diminished. In addition, skills investments in later life have fewer years to earn returns compared to skills investments earlier in life. For example, those who are near retirement may not see sufficient returns to their skills investments to make these investments worthwhile.

The returns to skills investments are also not confined to wages and employment prospects. This study focuses on higher wages as a measure of the returns to skills investments. However, many other forms of financial and non-financial benefits also result.

Those with higher skills are likely to work longer, raising their lifetime income and reducing the demographic pressures on pension systems. Those with higher skills are also less likely to leave the labour market or become unemployed, further increasing the returns to skills investments. There are also other non-financial benefits to investing in skills. Those with higher skills are more likely to report being in good health, potentially reducing the pressure on public health systems. Skills can have positive impacts on other aspects of well-being as well (Hanushek et al., 2013; OECD, 2013).

The value of these various benefits from skills on government finances, on the economy, and for individuals is challenging to quantify. Estimates of the positive impact of skills investments that rely on wages alone such as those in this study likely underestimate the true benefits of these investments (de la Fuente and Jimeno, 2008).This study takes a step towards such an assessment by examining the financial costs and benefits of certain stylised skills investments in the OECD. In assessing the returns to skills investments, the study focuses on tertiary education and lifelong learning. The key return to tertiary education considered is higher wages. Consideration of the impacts on employment and labour market participation is not factored into the analysis, nor are the broader impacts on trust, health, crime and well-being. From a government's perspective, estimates of the future revenue impacts are confined to increases in income tax revenue; other positive economic impacts are not analysed. Much more work in this area is needed, and so the results presented in this study should be carefully interpreted.

1.4 Public finance of education

The previous discussion has outlined that the returns to governments, firms and individuals from skills investments are substantial. However, a cost-benefit analysis of skills policies also requires a discussion of the costs of investment in skills, and who bears these costs. Figure 1.10 outlines how the direct costs of education from primary to tertiary level (i.e. costs excluding lost earnings) are apportioned between governments and individuals in OECD countries. Education spending as a share of GDP varies substantially. So too does the share of spending accounted for by governments and by private actors such as firms and individuals. On average, direct education spending comprised 5.3% of GDP in the OECD in 2012. On average spending comprising 4.6% of GDP was carried out by governments, and 0.7% by private actors. The largest amount of private spending is in Chile, where 37% of all education spending is carried out by private actors. In some European countries, however, very little direct education spending at primary to tertiary level is undertaken by private actors.

Given the large private benefits from skills investments, government subsidies for skills investments are substantial. There are two principal motivating factors behind government intervention into the provision of public capital goods such as education. The first is the presence of market externalities. As discussed in Section 1.3, the returns to skills investments go far beyond the narrow returns to individuals in the form of wage increases or even broader individual returns such as increased well-being and life expectancy. There are social returns as well, in the form of increased growth, increased innovation, and reduced crime. Given that these benefits are not internalised by individuals making skills investment decisions, they may underinvest in skills relative to the socially optimal level. Extra government spending resolves this externality raising the incentives to invest in skills through subsidies (Dur and Teulings, 2003; Heckman and Jacobs, 2010).

Figure 1.10. **Spending on primary-tertiary educational institutions as a share of GDP**

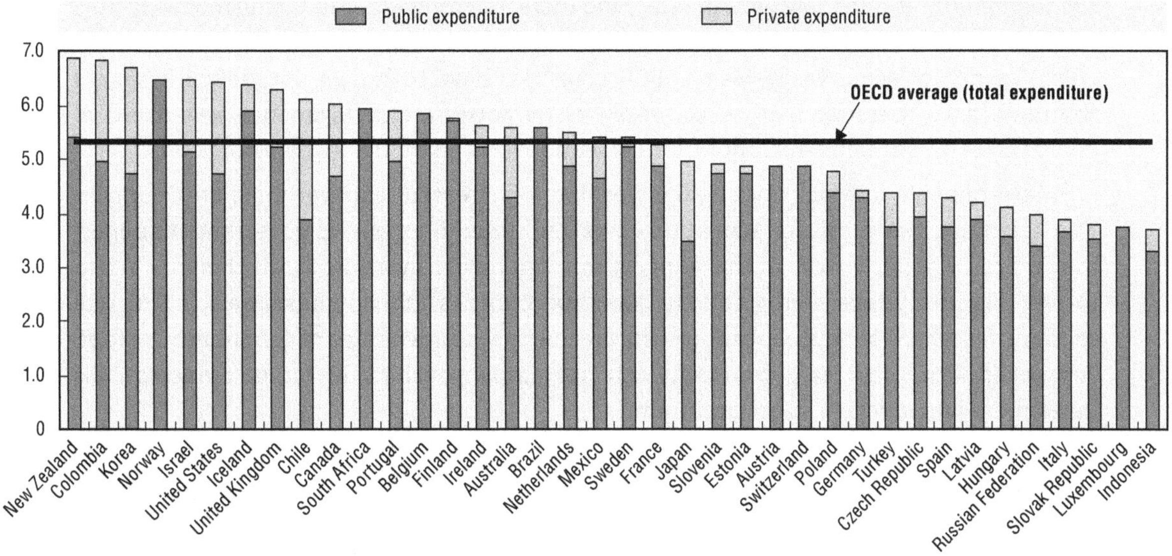

Source: (OECD, 2015c), *Education at a Glance*. Public expenditure only (for Switzerland, in tertiary education only; for Norway, in primary, secondary and post-secondary non-tertiary education only). Countries are ranked in descending order of expenditure from both public and private sources on educational institutions.

The second principal motivating factor behind government intervention into the provision of education relates to imperfections in the capital market for education. Human capital is different from physical capital in that human capital is not transferable from person to person. Physical capital assets can be sold by their owners, the costs of transferring them from person to person is low. This means that physical capital assets can be offered as collateral on debt to finance such investments. The same is not true for human capital investments; if a debt is incurred to finance a skills investment, the skills cannot be recouped in the event of non-repayment of the debt. This may make lenders reluctant to provide financing for human capital investment, in turn meaning that profitable human capital investments do not proceed for lack of finance (Dur and Teulings, 2003; Lochner and Monge-Naranjo, 2002).

These particular features of skills investments mean that financing skills investments presents challenges for individuals, firms and governments. For individuals, skills investments may be difficult to finance because it may be difficult or impossible to use skills as collateral. Capital markets do not function as effectively for human capital investment as they do for physical capital investment. This means that profitable skills investments are more likely to not occur compared to physical capital investments.

Firms face financing pressures as well. Skills investments by business are a key form of spending on lifelong learning. However firms may underinvest in the skills of their employees because of concerns that newly-skilled employees may leave or be poached by rival firms. It is difficult for firms to account for the depreciation of their human capital assets in the same way that they usually account for the depreciation of their physical capital assets. Many tax systems attempt to counteract these difficulties by allowing skills expenses to be immediately deducted from the personal and corporate tax bases, but such provisions are of benefit mainly to firms that are highly profitable: firms with low profits may not benefit from such provisions. In addition, investments in skills may require significant sunk costs for firms, which may be challenging for credit constrained firms, especially SMEs.

In addition, governments face financing challenges in providing support for skills. Demographic pressures, low growth rates, and increased difficulties in taxing mobile factors of production including labour and capital all have increased the financial pressures facing governments in recent years. Many OECD countries have high debt and deficit levels. At the same time, there are increasing pressures for governments to finance new forms of educational investments in early childhood education and in lifelong learning.

Governments may also face challenges due to increased taxpayer mobility. Countries that attempt to keep private education costs low through extensive government support may try to recoup the costs of this support through higher taxes. However this may result in well-educated workers emigrating to lower tax countries. Individuals may also immigrate to countries where private education costs are low to take advantage of generous education support. In such instances, governments can face similar poaching dilemmas, reducing skills investments relative to a social optimum.

This study analyses the ways in which the costs and benefits of skills investments are shared across society. A key conclusion in the study is that in many cases the market for financing skills investments does not work. This may mean that risks and returns for skills investments are not shared in proportion to costs. Risky skills investments may not be undertaken due to lack of access to finance for skills, or lack of insurance against skills outcomes. This in turn reduces the positive impacts that skills can have on inequality, on productivity, and on growth.

1.5 Tax, skills, and financial incentives

A key policy lever by which the government intervenes in skills financing decisions is through the tax system. The tax system is widely regarded as a key lever in affecting many important objectives of OECD governments: raising physical capital investment, reducing inequality, raising employment, increasing R&D activity. However the impact of the tax system on human capital investment has not been at the centre of tax policy making.

Tax and education spending policies need to be examined in a holistic way. Education policy makers cannot rely on education spending levels alone to assess the skills-friendliness of their system from a financial perspective. Nor can tax policy makers examine their tax system solely from a revenue-raising perspective, or even simply from a combination of revenue-raising, labour market activation, and redistribution perspectives. Instead, the efficiency and equity consequences of tax policies from a skills perspective are a key aspect of tax policy and tax design.

Optimising the tax system from a skills perspective could positively affect economic and social outcomes through a number of channels. It may reduce the need for redistribution through the tax system by reducing the inequality of market income. In doing so, raising skill levels can alleviate the distortions that come with trying to reduce inequality through the tax and transfer system (Bovenberg and Jacobs, 2005). Better tax and skills policies can also potentially reduce the need for costly education spending by governments. In addition, raising the stock of human capital may increase the growth-friendliness of the tax system overall.

The impact of the tax system on skills investments is complex. The first and most obvious impact is that progressive income taxation reduces the returns to skills investments from the perspective of an individual because their wages – their returns to skills investments – are taxed away. As taxpayers earn higher and higher returns from their skills investments, progressive tax systems reduce the returns to skills investments at an increasing rate (Cameron and Heckman, 1999).

The tax system also reduces the costs of skills investments for the individual. A key input into a skills investment is the individual's time: while studying individuals' earning capacity is diminished. Foregone earnings are for many individuals a larger cost component of a skills investment than direct costs such as tuition fees. But as individuals earn less their tax liability falls in progressive income tax systems. This reduction in tax liability offsets lost earnings: in this way the tax system reduces the cost of skills investments. The tax system can also reduce the costs of skills investments through tax expenditures that reduce an individual's tax liability in proportion to the direct costs of education, as is discussed further below. Taxes also impact the financial incentives to invest in skills by influencing the costs of the financing of skills investments. Many OECD countries allow financing costs to be deducted from the tax base, and so the tax system can provide added support to skills investments financed with debt. All of these channels through which the tax system impacts the costs of skills investments are modelled in this study.

This study focuses on the ways in which the tax system affects the financial decision to invest in skills through the personal income tax (PIT) and social security contribution (SSC) system. But other parts of the tax system may matter for skills investments as well. For example, countries may provide VAT relief to education providers or educational institutions. Skills expenditures by firms are generally deductible from the corporate income tax base. Taxes on savings can reduce the opportunity costs of skills investments by making physical capital investment less attractive (D'Andria and Mastromatteo, 2012; Jacobs and Bovenberg, 2010). These and other non-PIT and SSC provisions to encourage skills investments are discussed further in Torres (2012).

Taxes also affect the supply of skills through their impact on work effort and labour market participation and the demand for skills, which will impact the level of unemployment. The impact of the PIT and SSC systems modelled in this study focuses on the ways in which increased taxation can reduce incentives to invest in skills by taxing away higher wages. But high taxes on labour may result in reduced labour market participation. This in turn reduces the incentives to invest in skills and may reduce skills investment.

All taxes distort economic activity. The challenge for tax policy makers is to design the tax system in a way that minimises these distortions as much as possible. The literature on optimal taxation has argued that reduced taxation of physical capital encourages investment and raises growth (Chamley, 1986; Judd, 1985). The effective tax rates discussed in this tax policy study are based on the effective tax rate methodology for physical capital developed by Devereux and Griffith (2003). Concerns about the negative impacts of physical capital investment have seen statutory tax rates on physical capital fall over recent decades (Brys et al., 2016).

In recent years however, attention in the theoretical literature on optimal taxation has increasingly turned to how optimal taxes should be considered in light of investment in human capital (Brys and Torres, 2013; Gottardi et al., 2014; Krueger and Ludwig, 2013; Stantcheva, 2015; Torres, 2012). This literature has argued that the taxation of physical and human capital should be more closely aligned. Many of these recent studies recognise the differences between physical and human capital; including that human capital cannot be offered as collateral, and that it may be difficult to design efficient contracts that insure against the risks of human capital investment. Given the centrality of skills for policy outcomes such as productivity and inclusive growth, it is important that the impact of taxes on skills is taken into account by policy makers.

This study provides empirical grounding for many of the theoretical insights from this literature, and highlights how the details of tax systems in different countries can result in variation in the incentives to invest in skills depending on the taxpayers' age, income, and family status, as well as on the duration, nature and costs of a skills investment. In doing so, the study aims to nuance the discussion of the impact of taxes and skills relative to the theoretical academic literature, and place consideration of skills investments at the centre of the design of tax systems for policy makers.

1.6 Plan of the study

The study proceeds as follows. Chapter 2 outlines tax expenditures used to support skills investment (skills tax expenditures, or STEs) in the 29 countries examined in this study. The year of analysis is 2011. Incorporating these STEs into a broader analysis of the overall impact of the tax and spending system on skills is a key innovation of this study. There is a substantial body of research on the impact of education spending on skills outcomes. However, government spending on skills that occurs through the tax system has not been studied in a comparative way.

There are several kinds of STEs. Some countries provide tax credits and tax allowances that allow tax liability to be reduced in proportion to skills expenditures. Some countries reduce the amount of labour taxation levied on student wage income, or on student scholarship income. Student wage income or scholarship income can also be subject to relief regarding social security contributions. Some tax systems can also offer tax relief in proportion to the amount of debt individuals incur as part of their skills investment. These tax expenditures are all discussed in Chapter 2.

Chapter 3 outlines the core methodology for designing the tax and skills statistics developed in this study. Three main indicators are developed:

- A Breakeven Earnings Increment (BEI); which measures how much earnings need to increase for an individual after their skills investment so that they earn back the costs of that investment over their remaining years in the workforce.
- An Effective Tax Rate on Skills, which measures how much taxes increase or reduce the net returns to skills investments for an individual. Effective tax rates are developed for different estimates of the returns to education. The Marginal Effective Tax Rate on Skills (METR) examines the case of an individual just breaking even on a skills investment. It measures the extent to which the BEI is increased by the tax system: how much it rises compared to a world without taxes. The Average Effective Tax Rate on Skills (AETR) examines the case of an individual who earns a higher-than-breakeven return. This indicator measures the difference in the net present value of education between a world with and without taxes.
- The third indicator measures the returns to skills investments for governments, comparing the government's costs of educating an individual to the government's expected returns in the form of higher future tax revenues. This indicator is referred to as a Returns to Costs Ratio (RCR). As with the Effective Tax Rates on Skills, break-even and higher-return scenarios are considered, so a Marginal Returns to Costs Ratio (MRCR) and Average Returns to Costs Ratio (ARCR) are both developed.

The chapter also describes how to interpret the indicators, how they relate to each other, and how they change in response to changes in educational spending, student income, and tax rates before education, during education and after education.

Chapter 4 outlines the main results for the BEI, METR, AETR, MRCR, and ARCR for four stylised skills investment scenarios: a 17-year-old student undertaking a four-year degree, a 27 year-old undertaking a one-year degree, a 32-year old undertaking a short course of job-related training, and a 50-year old undertaking a one-year degree. These examples are chosen to be representative of the different kinds of post-secondary skills investments commonly undertaken in the OECD. This chapter also discusses how these different indicators depend on the returns to education, on the countries concerned, on the individual's income level, on the individual's age, and on how the skills investment is financed.

Chapter 5 features an analysis of the specific STEs outlined in Chapter 2. The overall value of these STEs in some of the example cases in Chapter 4 is considered. Chapter 5 also examines the impact of these STEs on the results presented in Chapter 4. The chapter also discusses the relative impacts of tax-based means of encouraging skills investment compared to non-tax means of encouraging skills investment such as reducing tuition fees, expanding loan support to students, and increasing scholarships and grants. The chapter concludes with a discussion of the overall impact of the tax system on skills investment.

Four annexes are provided. Annex A outlines in greater detail the methodology behind the indicators: a formalised version of Chapter 3. Previous work by Brys & Torres (2013) outlined a formal methodology for defining the BEI and the METR on Skills. This Annex expands on their work, extending the discussion of the METR and also showing how the same approach can be used to define the AETR on Skills as well as the MRCR and ARCR. The Annex also outlines how the Brys and Torres methodology can be expanded to include consideration of student debt.

The remaining three annexes provide country-specific tables and information. Annex B provides cross-country comparisons of the key indicators, the BEI, the METR, the AETR and the MRCR for the stylised skills investment examples outlined in Chapter 4. Annex C outlines key details of the STEs modelled for each country. This section is based on the discussion in Torres (2012). Annex D provides tables of the key tax and skills results for the stylised education scenarios in Chapter 4, as well as selected other results on a country-by-country basis. Extensive details of the various factors making up the indicators are provided, corresponding to the equations outlined in Chapter 3 and Annex A.

References

Blöndal, S., S.Field, and N. Girouard, (2002), "Investment in human capital through upper-secondary and tertiary education", *OECD Economic Studies*, Vol. 2002/1, OECD Publishing, Paris, *http://dx.doi.org/10.1787/eco_studies-v2002-art3-en*.

Bovenberg, A.L. and B. Jacobs, (2005), "Redistribution and education subsidies are Siamese twins", *Journal of Public Economics*, Vol. 89, pp. 2005–2035.

Brys, B., S. Perret, A. Thomas, and P. O'Reilly, (2016), "Tax Design for Inclusive Economic Growth", *OECD Tax Policy Working Papers*, No. 26, OECD Publishing, Paris, *http://dx.doi.org/10.1787/5jlv74ggk0g7-en*.

Brys, B. and C.Torres, (2013), "Effective Personal Tax Rates on Marginal Skills Investments in OECD Countries: A New Methodology", *OECD Taxation Working Papers*, No. 16, OECD Publishing, Paris, *https://doi.org/10.1787/22235558*.

Cameron, S. V. and J.J. Heckman, (1999), "Can Tuition Policy Combat Rising Wage Inequality", in Kosters, M.H. (Ed.), *Financing College Tuition: Government Policies and Educational Priorities*, The AEI Press, Washington, D.C.

Chamley, C. (1986), "Optimal taxation of capital income in general equilibrium with infinite lives.", *Econometrica*, Vol. 54, pp. 607–622.

D'Andria, D. and G. Mastromatteo, (2012), "Fiscal Policy Impacts on Growth: an OECD Cross-Country Study with an Emphasis on Human Capital Accumulation", *CEIS Tor Vergata Research Paper*, Vol. 10 No. 217.

Devereux, M.P. and R. Griffith, (2003), "Evaluating Tax Policy Decisions for Location Decisions", *International Tax and Public Finance*, Vol. 10, pp. 107–126.

Dur, R.A.J. and C.N. Teulings, (2003), "Are Education Subsidies an Efficient Redistributive Device?", in Agell, J., Keen, M. and Weichenrieder, A. (Eds.), *Labor Market, Institutions and Public Regulation*, M.I.T. Press, Cambridge (MA).

Gottardi, P., A. Kajii, and T. Nakajima, (2014), "Optimal Taxation and Debt with Uninsurable Risks to Human Capital Accumulation", *Federal Reserve Bank of Atlanta Working Paper Series*, No. 2014–24.

Hanushek, E.A., G. Schwerdt, S. Wiederhold, and L. Woessmann, (2013), "Returns to Skills around the World - Evidence from PIAAC", *NBER Working Paper*, No. 19762.

Heckman, J.J. and B. Jacobs, (2010), "Policies to Create and Destroy Human Capital in Europe", *NBER Working Paper*, No. 15742.

Jacobs, B. and A.L. Bovenberg, (2010), "Human capital and optimal positive taxation of capital income", *International Tax and Public Finance*, Vol. 17, pp. 451–478.

Judd, K. (1985), "Redistributive taxation in a simple perfect foresight model", *Journal of Public Economics*, Vol. 29, pp. 59–83.

Krueger, D. and A. Ludwig, (2013), "Optimal Progressive Labor Income Taxation and Education Subsidies When Education Decisions and Intergenerational Transfers are Endogenous", *American Economic Review: Papers & Proceedings*, Vol. 103 No. 3, pp. 496–501.

de la Fuente, A. and J.F. Jimeno, (2008), "The Private and Fiscal Returns to Schooling and the Effect of Public Policies on Private Incentives to Invest in Education: a General Framework and Some Results for the EU", *Barcelona Graduate School of Economics Working Paper*, No. 342.

Lochner, L. and A. Monge-Naranjo, (2002), "Human Capital Formation with Endogenous Credit Constraints", *NBER Working Paper*, No. 8815.

OECD (2010), "Tax Policy Reform and Economic Growth", *OECD Tax Policy Studies*, No. 20, OECD Publishing, Paris, *http://dx.doi.org/10.1787/9789264091085-en*.

OECD (2012), *Employment Outlook 2012*, OECD Publishing, Paris, *http://dx.doi.org/10.1787/empl_outlook-2012-en*.

OECD (2013), *OECD Skills Outlook 2013 - First Results from the Survey of Adult Skills*, OECD Publishing, Paris, *https://doi.org/10.1787/9789264204256-en*.

OECD (2014), *The Distributional Effects of Consumption Taxes in OECD Countries, OECD Tax Policy Studies*, No. 22, OECD Publishing, Paris, *http://dx.doi.org/10.1787/9789264224520-en*.

OECD (2015a), *The Future of Productivity*, OECD Publishing, Paris, *http://dx.doi.org/10.1787/9789264248533-en*.

OECD (2015b), *In It Together: Why Less Inequality Benefits All, OECD Publishing*, OECD Publishing, Paris, *https://doi.org/10.1787/9789264235120-en*.

OECD (2015c), *Education at a Glance 2015: OECD Indicators*, OECD Publishing, Paris, *http://dx.doi.org/10.1787/eag-2015-en*.

OECD (2016), *The Productivity-Inclusiveness Nexus*, OECD Publishing, Paris, *http://dx.doi.org/10.1787/9789264258303-en*.

Sequeira, T., M. Santos, and A. Ferreira-Lopes, (2014), "Income Inequality, TFP, and Human Capital", *Unpublished Working Paper*.

Stantcheva, S. (2015), "Optimal Taxation and Human Capital Policies over the Life Cycle", *NBER Working Paper*, No. 21207.

Summers, L.H. (2014), "U.S. Economic Prospects: Secular Stagnation, Hysteresis, and the Zero Lower Bound", *Business Economics*, Nature Publishing Group, Vol. 49 No. 2, pp. 65–73.

Torres, C. (2012), "Taxes and Investment in Skills", *OECD Taxation Working Papers*, No. 13, OECD Publishing, Paris, *http://dx.doi.org/10.1787/5k92sn0qv5mp-en*.

Chapter 2

Tax and skills policies in OECD economies

This chapter outlines the specific tax expenditures aimed at encouraging skills investment in OECD countries. Four main kinds of skills tax expenditures are considered, tax allowances and credits to reduce tax liability based on skills expenditure, reduced tax rates for scholarship income, interest deduction of student debt, and reduced tax or social contribution rates on student income.

The statistical data for Israel are supplied by and under the responsibility of the relevant Israeli authorities. The use of such data by the OECD is without prejudice to the status of the Golan Heights, East Jerusalem and Israeli settlements in the West Bank under the terms of international law.

2.1 Introduction

This chapter outlines skills tax expenditures (STEs) designed to increase investment in skills modelled in this Tax Policy Study. The chapter is based on the information in Torres (2012) which is in turn based on a survey of OECD delegates carried out in 2011. Individuals' decisions to invest in skills are based on a wide variety of financial incentives and other factors. Factors impacting skills investment decisions include the direct costs of education, the lost earnings in the labour market while studying, the cost of financing, and the available returns in the labour market for those with high skill levels. The tax system has an impact on all of these factors either through the general personal income tax (PIT) and social security contribution (SSC) system or because of specific STEs in the tax system. This chapter reviews the specific STEs designed to encourage skills investments that can be found in 30 OECD countries.

In addition to specific STEs, the impact of the tax system on incentives to invest in skills also depends on the overall level, general characteristics and progressivity of the PIT and SSC systems. The overall tax system governs the extent to which the returns to skills are taxed away, a key component of the indicators developed in this study. In addition, the tax system reduces the cost of making a skills investment by reducing pre-tax foregone earnings. Information on the general PIT and SSC systems is not included here but can be found in the *OECD Taxing Wages* report (OECD, 2016).

The tax system also impacts incentives to invest in skills through a wide variety of other measures outside of the PIT and SSC systems, which are not included in the calculations underlying this Tax Policy Study. Investments by firms in the skills of their employees are often deductible from the corporate income tax base and some countries implement R&D tax provisions linked to the researchers wage bill, for example. Some countries implement special STEs to stimulate savings for future skills investments. General tax rules on savings, which have an impact on the after-tax opportunity return for an investment in skills, are not covered. Skills investments are often exempt from VAT, and sometimes are zero-rated. Universities and other educational institutions may also benefit from reduced property taxation.

For the purposes of this study, specific 'tax and skills' policies that are modelled are only those policies in the PIT and SSC systems that partially or fully offset the costs of investing in skills. OECD countries do not implement specific tax rules beyond the standard progressive PIT rate schedule, such as graduate taxes, that increase the tax burden on the return on skills.

As mentioned previously, a wide variety of other drivers beyond the tax system impact individuals and firms decisions to investment in skills, as well as influencing the decisions of firms and other organisations to supply training and education, and the decisions of banks and other institutions to aid in financing skills investments. The other impacts of the tax system on financial incentives to invest in skills are treated as beyond the scope of this study; which confines itself to the individual's financial incentives.

This chapter proceeds as follows. Section 2.2 discusses tax allowances that allow the costs of skills to be deducted from taxable income. It also discusses tax credits that allow the costs of skills to offset tax payable. Section 2.3 discusses policies that reduce the taxation of scholarship and grant income. Section 2.4 discusses polices that allow the cost of student debt to reduce a student's tax liability. Section 2.5 discusses STEs that reduce the taxation of the labour income of students. A summary of the tax and skills policies available in each country is provided Table 2.1. A country-by-country outline of the STEs available can be found in Section 2 of Annex D.

Table 2.1. **Summary of Tax and Skills Expenditures**

	Tax Allowance	Tax Credit	Special Student Debt STEs	Special Student Income STEs	Scholarship Income STEs
Australia	Yes	No	Yes	No	Yes
Austria	Yes	No	No	No	Yes
Belgium	Yes	No	No	Yes	Yes
Canada	Yes	Yes	Yes	No	Yes
Chile	No	No	No	No	Yes
Czech Republic	Yes	No	No	No	Yes
Denmark	Yes	No	Yes	No	No
Estonia	Yes	No	No	No	Yes
Finland	Yes	No	Yes	No	Yes
Greece	Yes	No	No	No	Yes
Hungary	No	No	No	Yes	Yes
Iceland	Yes	No	No	No	No
Ireland	No	Yes	No	No	Yes
Israel	Yes	Yes	No	No	Yes
Italy	No	Yes	No	No	Yes
Luxembourg	Yes	No	No	No	Yes
Mexico	Yes	No	No	No	Yes
Netherlands	Yes	No	No	No	Yes
New Zealand	No	No	No	No	Yes
Norway	Yes	No	Yes	No	Yes
Poland	No	No	No	Yes	Yes
Portugal	Yes	Yes	No	No	Yes
Slovak Republic	No	No	No	No	Yes
Slovenia	No	No	No	No	Yes
Spain	No	No	No	No	Yes
Sweden	Yes	No	No	No	Yes
Switzerland	Yes	No	No	No	Yes
Turkey	Yes	No	No	No	Yes
United Kingdom	Yes	No	No	No	Yes
United States	Yes	Yes	Yes	No	Yes
Number of Countries	21	6	6	3	28

Source: National Delegates. Results are as of 2011.

2.2 Tax treatment of educational spending

In most OECD countries, some part of an individual's direct spending on skills investment can be used to reduce tax liability. This is true of 25 of the 30 countries discussed in this Tax Policy Study. The exceptions are Hungary, New Zealand, Poland, Slovenia, and Spain. For Spain, some tax reliefs for the direct costs of skills investments exist at the regional level, but not at the national level.

Tax allowances

For most of the countries that do provide tax relief for the direct costs of skills investments, the relief comes in the form of tax allowances (i.e. deductions from taxable income) for skills spending.[1] 21 of the 30 countries in this study have such provisions, including Australia, Austria, Belgium, Canada, the Czech Republic, Denmark, Estonia, Finland, Greece, Iceland, Israel, Luxembourg, Mexico, the Netherlands, Norway, Portugal, Sweden, Switzerland, Turkey, the United Kingdom, and the United States.[2] In most of these countries, the deduction is only available where the training concerned is related to, or even necessary for a worker's current employment; this is the case for 19 of the 21 countries listed. The exceptions are the Czech Republic and the Netherlands. The stringency of these provisions differs; in some countries training need only be 'related' to current employment to be eligible for a tax deduction, in some countries such as the United Kingdom the training must be necessary for the worker's current employment for the worker to be eligible for a tax allowance.

In 7 of the 21 countries with tax allowances for skills expenditures, caps exist which limit the amount of skills expenditure that can be deducted from taxable income. In Estonia, the cap is set at EUR 1 920 (USD 2 670). In Greece, the deductibility is limited to EUR 100 (USD 72). In Mexico, this cap depends on the kind of training the worker is engaged in. In this study, the cap used is that for technical professional education, which is set at MXN 17 100 (USD 2 229). In the Netherlands, deduction of skills expenses cannot exceed EUR 15 000 (USD 18 036). In Portugal, the cap is set at 3% of 12 times the SBI (an indexed minimum wage). For 2011, this value was equal to EUR 171 (USD 272).[3] In Turkey, the maximum deductible amount is 10% of declared income of the taxpayer. While in Turkey the cap is defined with respect to the income of the taxpayer, other OECD countries implement a deduction which is a lump-sum amount or a fraction of the costs of a skills investment. Finally, for the United States, the maximum eligible amount of the deduction is the lesser of qualifying expenses less related scholarships and a fixed threshold. This threshold is USD 4 000 when taxpayers have incomes of USD 65 000 or less (USD 130 000 for married filing jointly). The threshold is USD 2 000 if income does not exceed USD 80 000 (USD 160 000 if married filing jointly).

In 2 of the 21 countries with tax allowances for skills expenditures, thresholds also exist below which skills expenditures cannot be deducted from taxable income. In Denmark, a minimum threshold of DKR 5 500 (USD 931) is required. In the Netherlands, this threshold is EUR 500 (USD 695).

Certain other restrictions on the use of skills deductibility also exist in some OECD countries. In both the Czech Republic and in Estonia, the deduction is only available for taxpayers 26 years old or younger.[4] In Sweden a taxpayer is required to be receiving full or close-to-full payment from their employer during periods of education to be eligible for deductibility of training costs.

Tax credits

The second way in which expenditure on skills can be used to reduce tax liability is through tax credits. Seven countries in the sample examined in this study have such credits. These countries are Canada, Ireland, Israel, Italy, Portugal, and the United States.[5] These STEs vary in their targeting, and tend to be used to offset the costs of university or basic education more than they are used to reduce the costs of career-related education.

In Canada, 15% of the cost of tuition is creditable against tax payable. In Ireland, a tax credit is offered at the lower marginal tax rate of 20%. In Israel the credit is limited to a fixed value of ILS 2 508 (USD 700). In Italy, a 19% credit is offered for the costs of education. In Portugal a credit is offered for 30% for education and training expenses. In the Slovak Republic the credit has a fixed value of EUR 243.18.

As with tax allowances, a variety of thresholds and caps apply to the available tax credits. A limit on the value of education tax credits is set in Ireland and Portugal. In 2011, this limit was set at EUR 7 000 (USD 9 736) in Ireland; in Portugal it was EUR 475 (USD 661) in 2011. Thresholds also apply. In Canada, claims must be higher than CAD 100 (USD 101). In Ireland, claimed relief is only available for fees above a threshold. In 2011, this threshold was EUR 2 000 (USD 2 782) for full-time students and EUR 1 000 for part-time students (USD 1 391).[6]

In the United States, the eligibility for tax credits depends on a taxpayer's income; above a certain threshold, the size of the available credit begins to shrink; high income taxpayers become ineligible (see Annex D for further details). These thresholds vary depending on the credit and family status of the taxpayer concerned.

A key difference between tax credits and tax allowances is that tax credits can be more readily made non-wastable, so that taxpayers who do not have sufficient tax liability to exhaust the full value of a tax provision can receive a refund. This can help increase the value of these STEs to taxpayers on low incomes. Skills tax credits are non-wastable in full or in part only in the United States; they are wastable in Ireland, Israel, Italy, and Portugal; Canada allows the value of credits to be transferred (up to a dollar limit) to a supporting individual such as a parent, and/or carried forward for use in subsequent years. Taxpayers in these latter countries who do not have sufficient tax liability to exhaust the value of the credit will pay no tax, but will not receive a refund. This is discussed further in Chapter 5 of this study. Key differences between tax credits and tax allowances are also discussed further in OECD (2011).

2.3 Tax treatment of scholarship income and grants

In most OECD countries, scholarship income and grants are subject to some form of tax relief. Of the 30 countries discussed in this study, tax relief is available in 28 of them. The exceptions are Denmark and Iceland, where this income is treated as ordinary income. In general, the tax relief in these countries comes in the form of a straightforward exemption from taxation, subject to various restrictions.

There are exceptions to this. In Italy, scholarship income is exempt from PIT but not from SSCs; it is subject to a reduced SSC schedule but not exempted entirely. In Finland, scholarship income is exempted (up to a cap) from PIT and from some SSCs, but a health insurance contribution is still payable.

In most OECD countries an unlimited amount of scholarship income can be exempted from taxation if the income qualifies for exemption. However in some countries a cap on the amount of income that can be exempted exists. In Canada, the amount is limited to the value of tuition and other programme costs if the student follows part-time education. In Finland, a tax allowance is granted for student grant income, but this allowance is capped at EUR 2 600 (USD 3 616). In Israel, the cap is ILS 92 000 (USD 25 713). In Mexico a ceiling of MXN 148 344 (USD 11 941) exists on the amount of scholarship income that is exempt from taxation. In Slovenia, scholarship income is tax exempt up to EUR 8 977 (USD 12 485), the level of the minimum wage. In Spain, the cap is EUR 3 000 (USD 4 172), for undergraduate education, and EUR 15 000 (USD 20 833) for graduate education. In the remaining 20 countries, no caps exist. These countries include Australia, Austria, Belgium, Chile, the Czech Republic, Estonia, Greece, Hungary, Ireland, Luxembourg, the Netherlands, New Zealand, Norway, Poland, Portugal, the Slovak Republic, Sweden, Switzerland and Turkey. In the United Kingdom, no caps exist except where the scholarship is paid by an employer to an employee.[7]

Other restrictions are placed on the tax exempt status of scholarship income besides caps on the amount that can be exempted. In general, scholarship income eligible for an exemption from taxation must not be related to a student's current job (if the student has one). In Australia, the exemption does not apply to payments received by a student on condition that the student will become or continue to be an employee of the payer.

Other restrictions also exist. In the Czech Republic, the exemption applies only to the scholarships received from the state budget. In the Netherlands, scholarships are given as loans conditional on timely completion of university education. They are tax exempt if a course of study is completed on time. In the Slovak Republic, only public scholarships are exempt. In Turkey, scholarship income is exempt except where this income is earned by apprentices. In the United States, scholarship income that is not a payment for research or teaching is normally taxed as ordinary income, with two exceptions for degree candidates, including where the income is used to support studies abroad, and where it is spent on documented educational expenses such as tuition fees and books and materials.

2.4 Tax treatment of student debt

The most common provision in the tax systems with respect to student debt is the tax deductibility of interest payments on student debt. This is similar to the tax deductibility of business interest income, and is particularly important where debt-financed education is widespread. Interest deductibility on student loans is available in five OECD countries: Belgium, Denmark, Finland, Norway, and the United States.

In the United States there is a cap on this interest deductibility of USD 2 500 per year. As with the tax credits to offset direct costs of education, there are also phase-out provisions; the interest deduction are not available when a taxpayer's annual income passes over a certain threshold. This is discussed in more detail in Annex D.

Two countries offer relief for student debt that does not come in the form of interest deductibility. In Canada, interest paid on student loans approved under the Canada Student Loans Program and similar provincial or territorial programs is eligible for a 15% non-refundable tax credit. Australia has a system of income contingent loans. Students can borrow to finance the cost of their education. Students below a specific threshold (USD 51 309 in 2011) do not have to repay the balance of their loan, or pay any interest, though their loan is indexed by CPI each year. Students above this threshold begin to repay.

2.5 Tax treatment of student income

Finally, some countries allow students to reduce their foregone earnings during educational periods by reducing the tax burden on student income. Three countries provide these STEs. In Belgium, students who work less than 23 days per year are subject to reduced SSC rates. In Hungary, employers SSC rates are reduced when a worker is below 25 years of age. In Poland, income from contracts of mandate – commonly used by students – are exempt from social contributions where the student's age is less than 26.

Notes

1. The provisions by which the tax system offsets the costs of skills investments are also discussed elsewhere in this study. They are briefly discussed as a component of the overall costs of a skills investment in Chapter 3. Chapter 5 discusses STEs from efficiency and equity perspectives. In Annex A, these policies are summarised as the parameter χ. In Annex B, the tables of country results, these effects are summarised as the "Value of Education Tax Credits % of Direct Costs".
2. Canada predominantly provides tax assistance for expenses related to post-secondary education and skills training through tax credits. Where a deduction is available, it is generally with respect to financial assistance provided to the unemployed for the purpose of skills training. As discussed in the Annex, this deduction is not modelled for Canada.
3. In 2013 onwards, this deduction was abolished from the PIT system.
4. In the Czech Republic, this threshold is 28 in the case of PhD students.
5. Certain other countries, such as the Slovak Republic, have tax credits that reduce parent's tax liability for their children's education, but these are not modelled in this study. Further discussion of these provisions can be found in Torres (2012).
6. This threshold has been increased steadily: in 2016 it was available for EUR 3 000 (USD 4 173) for full-time students and EUR 1 500 for part-time students (USD 2 086.5).
7. Where a scholarship is paid by an employer to an employee, and certain conditions are met, a cap of GBP 15 480 applies in the United Kingdom.

References

OECD (2011), *Taxation and Employment, OECD Tax Policy Study*, No. 21, OECD Publishing, Paris, *http://dx.doi.org/10.1787/9789264120808-en.*

OECD (2016), *Taxing Wages 2016*, OECD Publishing, Paris, *http://dx.doi.org/10.1787/tax_wages-2016-en.*

Chapter 3

Methodological approach to tax and skills statistics

This chapter outlines an approach to estimating the financial incentives for individuals and governments to invest in individuals' skills, and the effect of the tax system on these incentives. Specifically, it outlines the key indicators developed to examine the impact of the tax system on skills. These indicators include Marginal Effective Tax Rates (METRs) and Average Effective Tax Rates (AETRs) on Human Capital Investment, as well as Marginal Returns to Costs Ratios (MRCRs) and Average Returns to Costs Ratios (ARCRs) of Government Investment in Human Capital. The chapter cites the data sources used to develop results for these indicators, and explains how the results presented in Chapters 4 and 5 of the study should be interpreted.

The statistical data for Israel are supplied by and under the responsibility of the relevant Israeli authorities. The use of such data by the OECD is without prejudice to the status of the Golan Heights, East Jerusalem and Israeli settlements in the West Bank under the terms of international law.

3.1 Introduction

This chapter outlines the methodology used in this study to estimate the key indicators of the financial incentives surrounding skills investments. Specifically, it outlines the approach used to estimate the earnings necessary to breakeven on a skills investment (the Breakeven Earnings Increment or BEI). It also outlines the effects of the tax system on the incentives individuals face to invest in skills, both for a marginal student (the marginal effective tax rate or METR on skills), and for an average student (the average effective tax rate or AETR on skills).

The chapter also discusses the indicators developed that analyse the government's net financial returns from investing in skills of students. Two indicators are developed from the government's perspective, analogous to those for individuals. Specifically, an indicator is developed for a marginal student (the marginal returns to costs ratio or MRCR) and another for an average student (the average returns to costs ratio ARCR).

The study draws on the approaches used in the literature on the taxation of physical capital, in particular the succession of models by King and Fullerton (1984), Devereux and Griffith (1998), Devereux (2003) and Klemm (2008), which outline effective tax rates on physical capital investments in a net present value (NPV) framework. Marginal Tax Rates similar to those derived in Devereux and Griffith (1998) are provided, and equivalent AETRs as derived in Klemm (2008), but for human instead of physical capital.

All of these indicators have been built within the OECD's *Taxing Wages* country models (OECD, 2016). This chapter, and the accompanying Annex A to this study, outline the methodology behind these additions to the *Taxing Wages* models. The chapter also discusses the data sources used, some of the assumptions made in the analysis, as well as some important caveats that need to be considered when interpreting the results.

The chapter proceeds as follows. Section 3.2 outlines the various cost components of education, and the data sources used to derive them. Section 3.3 discusses the costs that may be incurred when students must borrow to finance their skills investment. Section 3.4 outlines the various components of the necessary breakeven earnings level, and how it differs from the BEI. Section 3.5 outlines how the BEI differs in the presence and absence of taxes, and how it is used to calculate the METR on skills within the country models. Section 3.6 outlines how assumed post-education earnings levels are used to calculate the AETR on skills. Section 3.7 outlines some differences between the METR and AETR, and how they are both a function of two key tax rates: the tax rate on foregone earnings and the tax rate on the earnings increment. Finally, Section 3.8 outlines the average and marginal returns to costs ratio of government investment in education.

3.2 The costs of education

The main financial costs of a skills investment considered in this study for a student are:

- Direct costs: tuition fees, books, computers, materials and other similar costs for students.
- Foregone earnings: the reduction in earnings that takes place while a student is studying.

These costs are offset by:

- Scholarship and grant income provided to the student by the government. The study abstracts from scholarship and grant income provided to students by other non-governmental entities.
- Reduced taxes: as the students' earnings decrease, they will pay less in tax. This offsets the cost of their skills investment, compared to a world without taxes where their foregone earnings would be larger.
- Skills Tax Expenditures (STEs): special tax provisions that may offset the direct costs of skills, such as tax allowances and credits for tuition.

These separate factors are combined to calculate the overall cost of an education investment. In addition, it may be that a student is unable to finance their education with savings and so may have to incur debt to finance their education. These extra costs related to debt financing of education are discussed in Section 3.3. For the remainder of this section, it is assumed that a skills investment is financed with savings for ease of exposition.

Foregone earnings

Education is time-intensive. With many courses of study, full-time work and even part-time work cannot be continued. These lost earnings constitute a major barrier to education, especially for adults. In this study, a variety of assumptions about lost earnings during education are examined. Generally it is assumed that a student can earn 25% of their previous wage while they are in full-time education. In this way, the model captures the situations of older workers who may be able to continue to work part-time during education. In the case of 17-year-old university students, it is assumed that they can earn 25% of the average wage in their country during schooling, which is taken as an estimate of the earnings available from part-time low-skilled work.

Foregone earnings are affected by the tax system. The way in which this occurs depends on the tax system concerned. In a proportional tax system, foregone earnings will be reduced at the student's statutory tax rate. In a progressive tax system a taxpayer may drop to lower tax brackets as they earn less during education. This will reduce the taxpayers' foregone earnings even more. This means that while progressive tax systems discourage skills investments by taxing away the returns they also encourage investments in skills by reducing foregone earnings.

This is a key issue for the design of tax systems. Highly progressive tax systems are generally thought to discourage skills investment, but this progressivity can also encourage skills development if tax progressivity moderates the amount of foregone earnings during education. If taxes are progressive, income net of taxes will fall at a lower rate than income gross of taxes, reducing the cost of skills investments.

The fact that many countries provide benefit support for those on low incomes may mean that those investing in skills may not see their incomes fall when they invest in skills – their incomes may be subsidised by social benefits of different kinds. In such countries income during a skills investment does not fall as much as it would in the absence of the tax-benefit system. If after-tax income does not fall much over the range over which pre-tax income falls during the skills investment, then the tax system raises the incentives to invest in skills.

The importance of reducing lost earnings as a form of support for skills is even more important when social benefits are considered. In some countries, students on low incomes can avail of a variety of social benefits such as housing benefits, medical benefits, or other social transfers. These benefits can further reduce forgone earnings and thus provide a significant extra incentive to invest in skills by reducing lost earnings. These social benefits are not, however, captured in the results presented in this study which focuses mainly on the tax system.

Direct private costs

Direct costs include costs directly paid by the student to acquire skills such as tuition fees, books and materials, computers, registration fees, transportation costs of attending school, and so on. In this model, estimates of the costs of education are taken from the OECD's *Education at a Glance* data (OECD, 2014).[1] Further details are provided in Box 3.1. Figure 3.1 shows the estimates of direct costs for OECD countries of tertiary education. Due to data limitations, the calculations in this study use tertiary education costs as a proxy for costs of lifelong learning, workplace training, and so on.

Box 3.1. **Calculating BEI and ETR inputs from Education at a Glance**

To calculate the Effective Tax Rates (ETR) on Skills and other skills indicators discussed in this study, three key data points are required regarding education spending in each country examined. These are:

The direct spending by each student on their education (DC_W).

The direct spending by the government on the education of each student (DC_G).

The scholarship and grant income received by each student (SG).

Detailed data at an individual level are not currently available. The approach taken in this study is to estimate average levels of spending on DC_W, DC_G, and SG, as proxies for spending by individuals.

It is also important to note that estimates of DC_W, DC_G, and SG are based on OECD *Education at a Glance* (EAG) figures for third-level education. These spending estimates are used as proxies for educational costs for graduate education, for continuing mid-career education, and for spending on life-long learning. An exception to this is in-work training, where the assumption is that no scholarship and grant income is received from the state, and so set SG = 0. Future editions of EAG should contain more detailed data on costs of these different types of education, in which case these figures could be revised. In this study, the latest data available is from EAG 2014 which contains data for 2011. This data is combined with the *Taxing Wages* 2011 models, to ensure conformity between estimates of education spending and the tax system.

Direct spending by each student on their education (DC_W)

The formula used is as follows

$$DC_W = Cur * \text{Total Spending} * \text{Private Fraction}$$

- **Total spending** is total spending on third level education, expressed in equivalent PPP USD. It is taken from EAG Table B1.1a, "Annual expenditure per student by educational institutions for all services". The column used is Column 9, "all tertiary education".
- **Private Fraction** is the fraction of total spending that is undertaken by households. It is taken from EAG Table B3.1, "Relative proportions of public and private expenditure on educational institutions, by level of education". The column used is Column 12, "household expenditure". This omits non-household non-government private education spending, such as spending by firms or NGOs.
- **Cur** is a currency adjustment factor, converting the amount spent by each student in PPP USD to 2011 national currency units.

These data sources are used for Australia, Austria, Belgium, Canada, Chile, the Czech Republic, Estonia, France, Iceland, Ireland, Israel, Italy, Japan, Korea, Mexico, the Netherlands, New Zealand, Norway, Poland, Portugal, the Slovak Republic, Slovenia, Spain, Sweden, and the United Kingdom. For some countries in the analysis, data omissions from EAG require other data sources to be used.

Box 3.1. **Calculating BEI and ETR inputs from Education at a Glance** *(cont.)*

- For **Denmark**, separate data on household spending as distinct from private spending are not available. Data on all private spending is used. This means that total costs to the individual of educational spending are possibly inflated compared to other OECD countries.
- For **France**, separate data on household spending as distinct from private spending are not available. Data on all private spending is used. This means that total costs to the individual of educational spending are possibly inflated compared to other OECD countries.
- For **Germany**, separate data on household spending as distinct from private spending are not available. Data on all private spending is used. This means that total costs to the individual of educational spending are possibly inflated compared to other OECD countries.
- For **Greece**, 2011 data on the share of public and private investment in total educational spending are unavailable. The shares of public and private spending used are from 2008.
- For **Hungary**, 2011 data on the share of public and private investment in total educational spending are unavailable. The shares of public and private spending used are from 2000.
- For **Luxembourg**, data on both the share of private spending in total spending, as well as on the total educational spending per student are unavailable for the entire EAG time series. Data for Belgium are used to proxy for educational costs in Luxembourg.
- For **Switzerland**, 2011 data on the share of public and private investment in total educational spending are unavailable. The shares of public and private spending used are from 2000.
- For **Turkey**, 2011 data on the share of public and private investment in total educational spending are unavailable. The shares of public and private spending used are from 2006.

Direct spending by the government on the education of each student *(DC_G)*

The formula used is as follows

$$DC_G = Cur * TotalSpending * PublicFraction$$

- **Total spending** is total spending on third level education, expressed in equivalent PPP USD. It is taken from EAG Table B1.1a, "Annual expenditure per student by educational institutions for all services". The column used is Column 9, "all tertiary education".
- **Public Fraction** is the fraction of total spending that is undertaken by governments. It is taken from EAG Table B3.1, "Relative proportions of public and private expenditure on educational institutions, by level of education". The column used is Column 11, "public sources".
- **Cur** is a currency adjustment factor, converting the amount spent by each student in PPP USD to 2011 national currency units.

These data sources are used for Australia, Austria, Belgium, Canada, Chile, the Czech Republic, Denmark, Estonia, Finland, France, Germany, Iceland, Ireland, Israel, Italy, Japan, Korea, Mexico, the Netherlands, New Zealand, Norway, Poland, Portugal, the Slovak Republic, Slovenia, Spain, Sweden, Switzerland, and the United Kingdom. As with DC_W, for some countries in the analysis, data omissions from EAG require other data sources to be used.

- For **Greece**, 2011 data on the share of public and private investment in total educational spending are unavailable. The shares of public and private spending used are from 2008.
- For **Hungary**, 2011 data on the share of public and private investment in total educational spending are unavailable. The shares of public and private spending used are from 2000.
- For **Luxembourg**, data on both the share of public spending in total spending, as well as on the total educational spending per student are unavailable for the entire EAG time series. Data for Belgium are used to proxy for educational costs in Luxembourg.

Box 3.1. **Calculating BEI and ETR inputs from Education at a Glance** *(cont.)*

- For **Switzerland**, 2011 data on the share of public and private investment in total educational spending are unavailable. The shares of public and private spending used are from 2000.
- For **Turkey**, 2011 data on the share of public and private investment in total educational spending are unavailable. The shares of public and private spending used are from 2006.

Scholarship and grant income received by each student (SG)

The formula used is as follows

$$SG = Cur * \frac{SchSpending\ \%Total * TotalSpending\ \%GDP * GDP}{\#of\ Students}$$

- **Sch % Total** is total spending on scholarships and grants, expressed as a % of total spending on third level education, expressed in equivalent PPP USD. It is taken from EAG Table B5.4, "Public support for households and other private entities for tertiary education". The column used is Column 2, "Scholarships and other grants to households".
- **Total Spending % GDP** is total spending on tertiary education, expressed as a % of GDP. It is taken from EAG Table B4.1, "Total public expenditure on education". The column used is Column 7, "Tertiary education".
- **GDP** is simply a measure of GDP in PPP USD, taken from the OECD National Accounts.
- **# of Students** is a measure of the total number of full-time students in a given year. It is calculated by dividing total education spending at third level by total spending per student at third level. The measure of total education spending is taken from EAG Table B4.1, "Total public expenditure on education". The column used is Column 7. The figure for total spending per student is taken from EAG Table B1.1a, "Annual expenditure per student by educational institutions for all services". The column used is Column 9, "all tertiary education". Dividing these two figures yields an estimate of the number of students in third-level education.
- **Cur** is a currency adjustment factor, converting the amount spent by each student in PPP USD to 2011 national currency units.

These data sources are used for Australia, Austria, Belgium, Canada, Chile, the Czech Republic, Denmark, Estonia, Finland, France, Germany, Iceland, Ireland, Israel, Italy, Japan, Korea, Mexico, the Netherlands, New Zealand, Norway, Poland, Portugal, the Slovak Republic, Slovenia, Spain, Sweden, Switzerland, and the United Kingdom. As with DC_W, for some countries in the analysis, data omissions from EAG require other data sources to be used.

- For the **Greece**, 2011 data on scholarship levels are unavailable. The shares of public and private spending used are from 2008.
- For the **Luxembourg**, data on scholarship levels are unavailable for the entire EAG time series. Data for Belgium are used to proxy for educational costs in Luxembourg.
- For the **Turkey**, 2003 data on scholarship levels are unavailable. The shares of public and private spending used are from 2008.

Scholarship income

Scholarship and grant income reduces the cost of education, and so is a key component of the net costs of investment in skills. Data on scholarship income is also taken from *Education at a Glance* (OECD, 2014).[2] Details of scholarship income calculations are discussed in Box 3.1. It is assumed that scholarship income is available to university students, graduate students and to those engaged in lifelong learning. It is assumed that it is not available to those mid-career training. The amounts of scholarship income used for each country are shown in Figure 3.2.

Figure 3.1. **Direct private costs of skills investment for individuals**

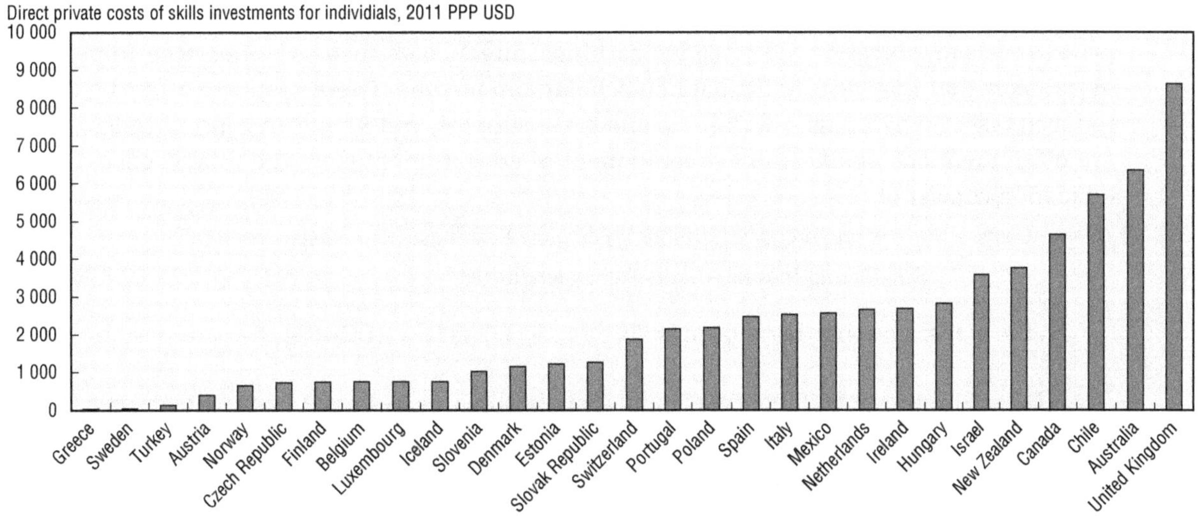

Source: (OECD, 2014) *Education at a Glance 2014*. Data are expressed in 2011 PPP USD. Data for Luxembourg are not available, so data for Belgium are used in the Luxembourg case as a proxy.

StatLink http://dx.doi.org/10.1787/888933446254

Figure 3.2. **Average scholarship income for tertiary education students**

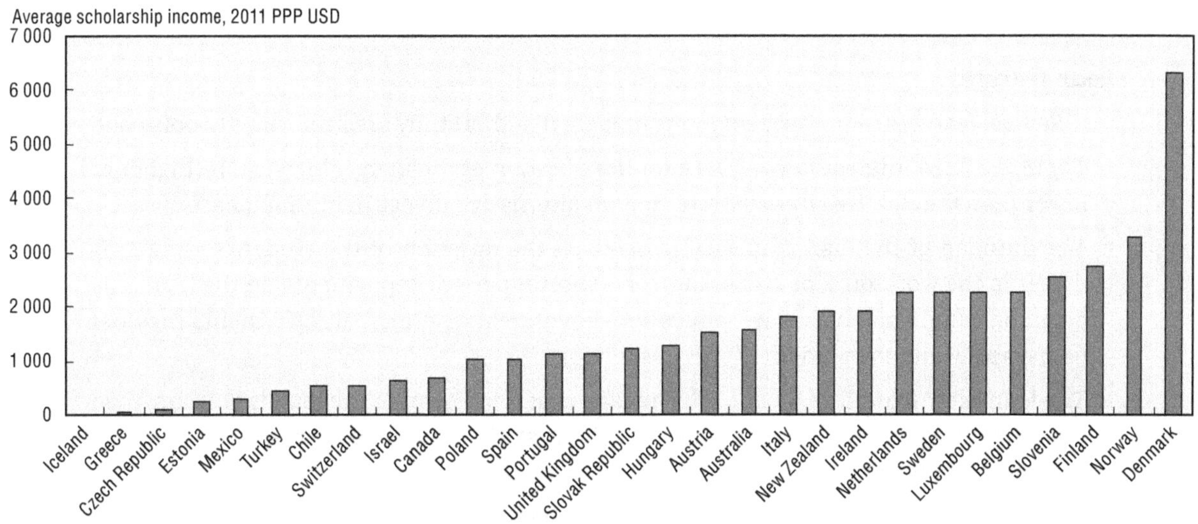

Source: (OECD, 2014) *Education at a Glance 2014*. Data are expressed in 2011 PPP USD. Data for Luxembourg are not available, so data for Belgium are used in the Luxembourg case as a proxy.

StatLink http://dx.doi.org/10.1787/888933446267

Special tax expenditures for education spending or scholarship income

STEs are also included as a component of the "costs" of education, for the same reason as scholarship income. That is, tax expenditures that reduce the costs of education are a form of financial benefit that only accrues to someone pursuing a course of study (they would not be given to someone not pursuing such a course). These STEs can come in the form of reductions in taxable income by the amount spent on education, or reductions in tax liability in some proportion to education spending. They can also come in the form of tax benefits that reduce or exempt scholarship income from taxation. Finally, in some countries student wage income is subject to lower levels of income taxation or social security contributions. These tax expenditures are discussed in greater detail in Chapter 2.

The total costs of education

The previous sections have outlined the key cost components of education. Key private costs of education are foregone earnings, direct costs such as tuition fees, and extra taxes that may need to be paid on scholarship income. These costs are offset by reduced taxes on earnings, scholarship and grant support, and STEs. Foregone earnings are often the most significant cost component of education. In sum, the total costs of education consist of:

$$\begin{aligned} Costs = & (1 - Tax\ on\ Foregone\ Earnings) * Foregone\ Earnings(FE) + Direct\ Costs(DC) \\ & - Scholarship\ Income - Skills\ Tax\ Expenditures \end{aligned}$$

In the model, the shorthand used is: $TC = (1 - T_{FE})FE + (1 - \chi)(DC - SG)$

$(DC - SG)$ represents Direct Costs minus Scholarships and Grants. χ represents the net impact of STEs. This equation is discussed in more detail in Annex A of this study. The value and impact of STEs is discussed in more detail in Chapter 5.

3.3 The financing of the student's education costs

The student's education can be financed in different ways. This study considers just two options: that the student finances a skills investment either with retained savings or with a loan from the government.

Loan features

Several features of the student loans modelled in this study are important to point out.

- There is a **fixed interest rate** in place for the duration of the loan, which can be higher or lower than the risk-free interest rate that an alternative investment might earn.
- The **duration of the loan** may vary, it may last the duration of the students remaining career in the workforce, or it may last for a shorter period. Repayments on the loan only begin once the student has left education (so interest or principal repayments may not be payable while the student is still upskilling).
- The **loan is structured as a bond.** This means that if the term of the loan is β years, then the student pays interest on the loan for the first $\beta - 1$ periods. In the final period an amount of interest is paid, and the principal is repaid.
- Both the amount of the interest payable in each period as well as the principal to be repaid at the end of the loan term are **fixed in nominal terms.**
- **Debt write-offs may exist**; that is, some fraction of the principal to be repaid can be written off by the government in the final period. The effects of increases in income from loan write-offs on tax liability are not modelled.
- The **interest paid on the loan in each period after education may be set against tax liability** (depending on the provisions in a given country's tax system). This may take the form of deductibility of interest from taxable income. Other similar provisions can also be incorporated.
- **Loan repayments can be made dependent on income after education.** This means that if a taxpayers' income does not pass a certain income level, their repayments may be smaller, or they may not have to make any repayments at all.

Modelling loans

To model the impact of these loans on the incentives to invest in skills, the costs of education are weighted upward or downward depending on the specifics of the loan concerned. For example, if the interest rate on a loan is higher than the risk free rate which a student could earn on savings, then debt financing increases the costs of education compared to financing education with savings. By contrast, if loans are subsidised such that the interest rate is below the risk-free rate, then debt financing reduces the cost of education. The total costs of education incorporating these financing costs are referred to as Total Financing Costs, or *TFC*. If a fraction *TFC* of the total costs of education TC are borrowed, then TFC is expressed as follows:

$$TFC = TC\left[(1-a)+a(1-F)\right]$$

Where the term F is a composite term of the different ways that

- The value of the loan write-offs spread over the duration of the loan.
- The value of the differential between the real interest rate at which the student can borrow r^*, and the risk free interest rate which he can earn interest on savings r. In the absence of capital taxes, this value is simply $r-r^*$, where r^* is the rate at which the student borrows.[3]
- The value of any tax deductibility of interest payments.

The overall value of F is

$$F = Value\,of\,Loan\,Writeoffs + Value\,of\,Interest\,Subsidy + Value\,of\,Interest\,Deductibility$$

F is then multiplied by the total costs of education, the fraction of these costs that are borrowed, and appropriate discount factors, to arrive at the correct weighting of the true costs of education. This is discussed further in Annex A to this study. All in all the TFC measures the total cost of education accounting for how the education is financed. As outlined, government policies can reduce these costs to the individual directly, by reducing tuition fees or increasing scholarship income, or by reducing financing costs, by subsidising loans or expanding loan write-off provisions.

3.4 The returns to education and the breakeven earnings increment

In order to recoup the costs of education, the student expects to earn higher wages after education. The returns to education for the individual come in the form of higher after-tax wages. Increases in the probability of employment after education, increases in the pace of wage gains, and other benefits to education are not modelled. In this study, it is assumed that wages rise once post-education, and then continue to rise linearly with inflation thereafter. The term "breakeven earnings level" is used to describe the level of pre-tax earnings that must be earned after education in order to make the skills investment worthwhile. The previously-discussed BEI is the difference between the breakeven earnings level and income before the skills investment. It is helpful to think about the breakeven earnings level as being made up of several components. This is another way of asking what must a student earn to make a skills investment worthwhile?

First, earnings after education must be at least as much as earnings before education. The methodology assumes that wages rise naturally with inflation, but do not rise otherwise unless a skills investment is made. In the absence of education, a worker's real wage will stay constant until retirement. For a skills investment to break even, workers must earn at least this level of income after education.

The second component that must be earned for a skills investment to break even is a return that allows the worker to recover the costs of the skills investment. Physical capital investments can be sold at the end of the period of use to recoup initial costs of the investment.[4] Human capital cannot be readily sold; retirees cannot sell off their talent or knowledge when they retire. In other words, a skills investment depreciates entirely upon retirement. This means that, in contrast to a physical capital investment, a human capital (skills) investment must earn enough to repay these initial costs over the course of the investment. This raises the amount of earnings needed for a skills investment to break even relative to a physical capital investment.

The third component of the required return for a skills investment to breakeven pays for the opportunity cost of spending on skills. If a student or worker had not made a skills investment, they could have invested the cost of the skills investment in an alternative capital asset which would have yielded a return. The opportunity cost of such an alternative investment must also be recouped in order for a skills investment to break even.

Finally, a skills investment must earn enough to recoup whatever extra taxes are owed as a result of any extra earnings. This tax rate is referred to in this study as the tax rate on the earnings increment, T_{EI}. There is an element of endogeneity to this process; as a taxpayer must earn more after education, their tax rate will rise. This means that the component of the required return to pay for the taxes will rise also –students must earn even more to break even, increasing their tax liability even further and so on. This is illustrated in Figure 3.3.

Figure 3.3. **The relationship between income after education and taxes paid after education**

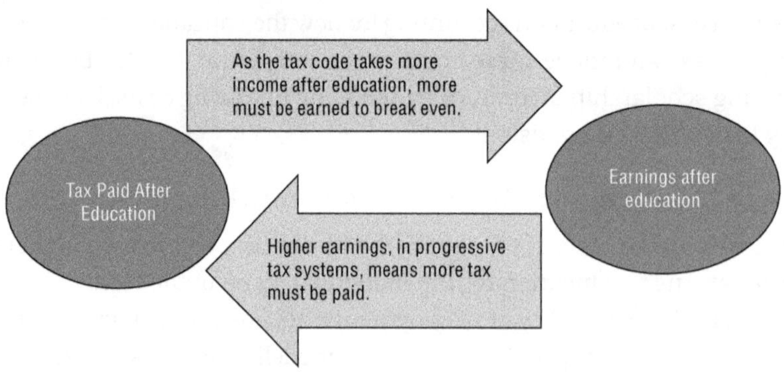

In the taxation and skills model, the required level of earnings is calculated such that the pre-tax earnings are enough to break even. The total picture of costs and returns is illustrated in a simple way in Figure 3.4; post-tax income, flat before education, falls during a period of education; due in part to foregone earnings, and in part to direct costs. Wages then increase after education to break even on the investment. The necessary size of this increase has several components: the necessary amount to recover the initial costs of education, the necessary amount to recover the returns to an alternative investment, and the extra earnings needed to pay for the extra taxes incurred. The latter component is referred to as the skills tax wedge.

Figure 3.4. **The costs and benefits of education**

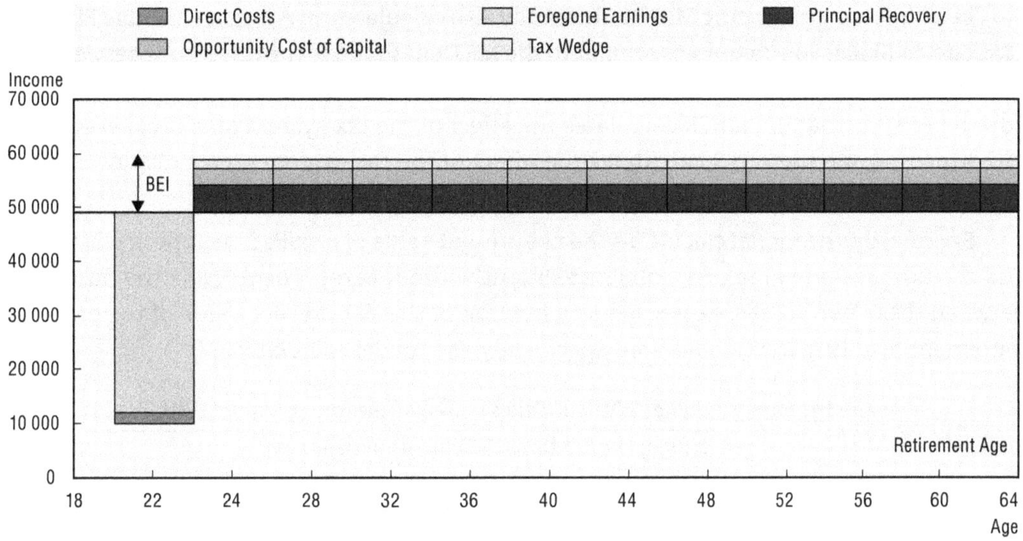

3.5 The marginal effective tax rate

The METR is the effect of the personal income tax system on the incentives of a "marginal" student to undertake a skills investment. Specifically, it is the difference between the BEI in a world with taxation and the BEI in a world without taxation, divided by the BEI in a world with taxation. It answers the question of whether a student would need to earn more after education to break even in a world without taxes compared to in a world with taxes.

$$METR = \frac{BEI(With\,Taxes) - BEI(Without\,Taxes)}{BEI(With\,Taxes)}$$

The METR on skills calculated in this study is marginal in the sense that it is the effect of taxes on a person who is just indifferent between making a skills investment and not making one. In the same way that a METR on labour is the tax rate on the return of the last unit of labour a person is supplying, so the marginal tax rate on skills is the tax rate on a person who is just considering making a skills investment. This is why the level of earnings at which the tax rate is calculated is the breakeven earnings level.[5]

The METR calculation procedure can be summarised as follows. First, the three elements of what a worker would need to earn to pay for a skills investment are calculated. The extra amount needed to pay for taxes on these higher earnings is then added. This means the model must find an equilibrium solution because the tax rate that is paid on these extra earnings changes as earnings rise, requiring yet more earnings to pay for extra taxes. The model finds a point where the worker is just indifferent between making the investment and not. Once the BEI has been found, it can be expressed as a share of previous earnings. The increase in the BEI as a result of the tax system can then be calculated by subtracting the BEI in the absence of taxes from the BEI in the presence of taxes. The share of the extra earnings that is necessary solely because of taxes, as a share of the earnings increment needed to break even on a skills investment in the presence of taxes, is called the METR.

3.6 The average effective tax rate

In addition to calculating METRs, this study also calculates an AETR, an Average Effective Tax Rate on Skills. This tax rate is similar to the METR in that it is the difference between the returns to skills in a world with taxes and a world without. The difference between the METR and the AETR is that the METR calculates the effect of the tax system on a breakeven skills investment, while the AETR calculates the effect of the tax system on a skills investment in a more general way.

Specifically, the model calculates the net present value of a skills investment with taxes, and the net present value of a skills investment without taxes. The AETR is the difference between these two values, expressed as a fraction of the net present value of the earnings increment resulting from education. Specifically, the model calculates:

$$\text{AETR} = \frac{\textit{Skills Investment Value}(\textit{Without Taxes}) - \textit{Skills Investment Value}(\textit{With Taxes})}{\textit{NPV of the Earnings Increment}(\textit{with Taxes})}$$

To find the AETR, it is necessary to calculate the value of an average skills investment. This is calculated in a similar way to the marginal skills investment; the costs come in the form of foregone earnings and direct costs, offset by taxes on foregone earnings, scholarship income, and tax provisions for skills investment. On the returns side, however, an important difference is that the breakeven earnings level is not calculated. The AETR is instead based on a fixed return, which may be higher or lower than the breakeven earnings level.

For the estimation of the returns to undergraduate education, data on the actual tertiary education premium for 15-64-year-olds from Education at a Glance are used (OECD, 2011). Unfortunately the data on the earnings returns for graduate education, for lifelong learning and workplace training are not as extensive as for undergraduate education. Instead, an assumed 15% return on a year of education is used in these cases. Estimates of the tertiary education premium are given in Figure 3.5. In most cases, the average return to a tertiary education available in the labour market is well above the required BEI calculated in the tax and skills models. Chapter 4 discusses this point further.

Figure 3.5. **The labour market premium for tertiary education**

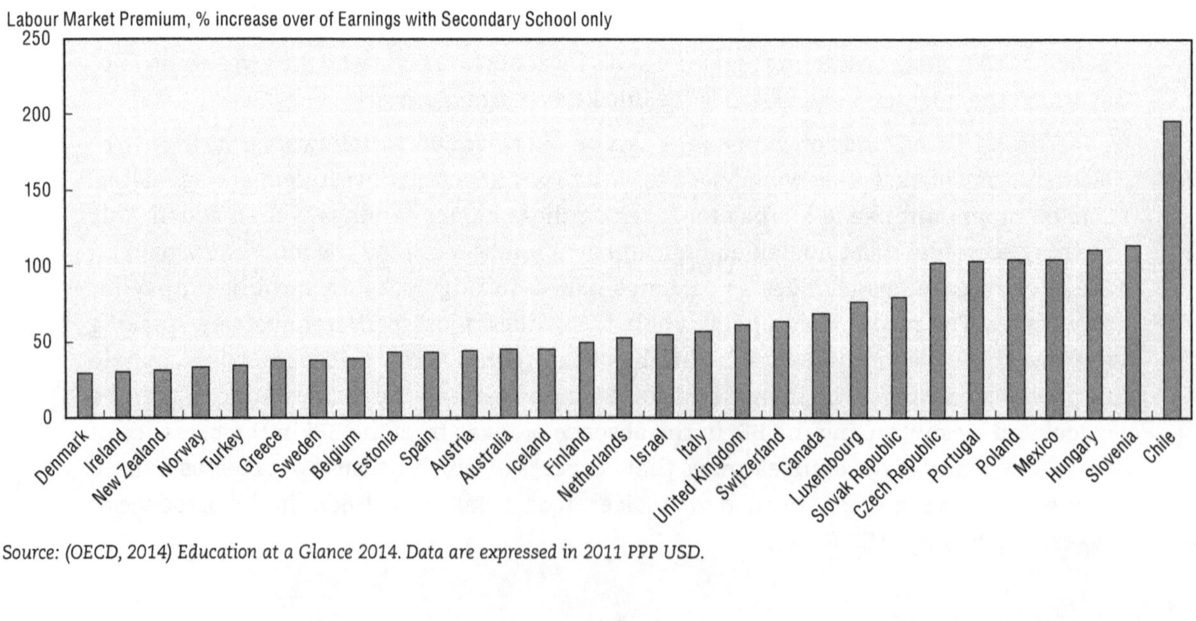

Source: *(OECD, 2014) Education at a Glance 2014. Data are expressed in 2011 PPP USD.*

Using these returns, the model calculates the net present value of a skills investment with and without taxes. The difference between these two values, expressed as a fraction of the net present value of the returns to education with taxes, is the AETR.

3.7 Understanding the results

The effect of the tax system on a skills investment, as discussed, is the difference between the returns to skills without and with taxes. In the METR case, this difference is measured at a breakeven earnings level; in the AETR case, this difference is measured at some other (usually higher) earnings level, or at the earnings level based on labour market data where available.

In practice, the two tax rates are a function of how the tax system reduces the cost of an investment in skills, and taxes away the returns to skills. As mentioned, the PIT system reduces the cost of upskilling by reducing foregone earnings; the amount of income foregone during education is offset by the fact that a student also foregoes the taxes which would have been paid on these earnings. In addition, tax liability can be reduced in some proportion to the direct costs of education. The tax system reduces the cost of skills in these two ways. As these two subsidies (the tax rate on foregone earnings and the subsidies for skills costs and scholarship and grant income) increase, the METR and AETR will fall.

On the returns side, the tax system reduces the returns to skills by taxing them away; as a worker earns more after education, tax progressivity often means that they pay taxes at a steadily higher rate. Higher taxes, and tax progressivity, tax away the earnings increment after a skills investment. Increasing this tax rate on the earnings increment will increase the METR and AETR.

The tax system affects the financial incentives to invest in skills both positively and negatively. It reduces the costs of skills but also reduces the returns; the former through the Tax Rate on Foregone Earnings and the Tax Expenditures for Direct Costs and Scholarship Income, and the latter through the Tax Rate on the Earnings Increment.

The relative size of the TFE and the TEI is a function of the PIT and SSC tax schedules. In a proportional tax system, the marginal tax rate is the same regardless of the income level. This means that necessarily the TFE and the TEI will be the same. If direct costs are fully tax deductible, then the tax system should be neutral with respect to skills: the METR on skills will be zero. This is because the costs of a skills investment are being subsidised by the tax system at the same rate at which the returns to skills are being taxed away. Moreover, this will be the case whether the tax rate is low or high. At a high tax rate, the TEI and TFE will both be high. At a low tax rate, the TEI and the TFE will both be low. In both cases, where the rate at which the tax system reduces costs is the same as the rate at which it taxes away returns, the tax system is neutral with regard to the skills investment. In such instances skills investments that would be profitable from the individual's perspective in the absence of taxes will be profitable in the presence of taxes (Brys and Torres, 2013).

In progressive tax systems, the tax rate rises with income. As wages after a skills investment will typically be higher than wages during a skills investment, the TFE will be less than the TEI in progressive tax systems: the tax system will tax away the returns to skills at a higher rate than it subsidises the cost. In these cases the METR will be positive. In this way progressive taxation can act as a disincentive to invest in skills, holding other factors equal.

In instances where the TFE and TEI are not equal, the overall impact of the tax system depends on the size of the returns to skills. Where returns are very low; the tax rate on the earnings increment does not matter as much; low returns means that the impact of the tax system through the way these returns are taxed is comparatively small. The effect of the tax system on the costs of upskilling predominates. Where returns are high, the tax rate on these returns is usually also high, and so this effect dominates the overall METR and AETR; the tax rate on returns matters more. These details are summarised in Table 3.1.

Table 3.1. **Components of the METR and AETR**

Name	Effect on METR and AETR	Dominates the METR and AETR when:
Tax Subsidy for Direct Costs	Decreases	Direct Costs of Skills are High
Tax Subsidy for Scholarship and Grant Income	Decreases	Scholarship Income Is High
Tax Rate on Foregone Earnings	Decreases	Foregone Earnings are High
Tax Rate on Earnings Increment	Increases	Returns to Skills are High

Figures 3.6 and 3.7 illustrate these dual effects of the tax system on incentives to invest in skills using concrete data. The example used here is that of a 32-year-old worker investing in one year of education, earning 25% of their earnings before education while doing so. Income before education (and thus foregone earnings) varies along the x-axis. The y-axis shows three key tax rates in both figures. In Figure 3.6, the top line shows the marginal tax rate on the earnings increment; the rate at which the returns to skills are taxed away. It is also a measure of how the METR is being increased by the tax system. The bottom line is the negative of the tax rate on foregone earnings; it is a measure of how the tax system is subsidising skills investments. It is also a measure of how the METR is being reduced.

The line in the middle of Figure 3.6 is the METR on Skills. For each country, it is a weighted average of the tax rate on the returns to skills investments, and the tax subsidy of the costs. Where the tax rate on the earnings increment (the top line) rises sharply, the METR rises as well. Where the tax subsidy of the cost rises (where the bottom line falls) the METR falls as well. This clearly shows the overall impact of the tax system is a weighted average of its positive effects (by reducing the costs in terms of foregone earnings) and its negative effects (by reducing the returns in terms of the earnings increment).

Figure 3.7 shows AETRs, instead of METRs in Figure 3.6. As with Figure 3.6, The AETR is the line in the middle, with the tax rate on the earnings increment and the tax rate on foregone earnings being the lines above and below respectively. As mentioned above, the earnings level with which the AETR is calculated is usually higher than the breakeven earnings level. This means that skills investment usually makes enough to pay for itself and more; the breakeven earnings level is reached and then passed. This means that the returns to skills are higher in Figure 3.6 than they are in Figure 3.7, while the costs remain the same.

This can be seen by comparing the top and bottom lines in each figure. The costs remain the same in both cases; so the effect of the tax system on the costs of upskilling is the same. This is why the bottom line is the same for each country.

Figure 3.6. **The tax rate on foregone earnings, the tax rate on the earnings increment and the marginal effective tax rate on skills**

Tax rate by income level as % of average wage

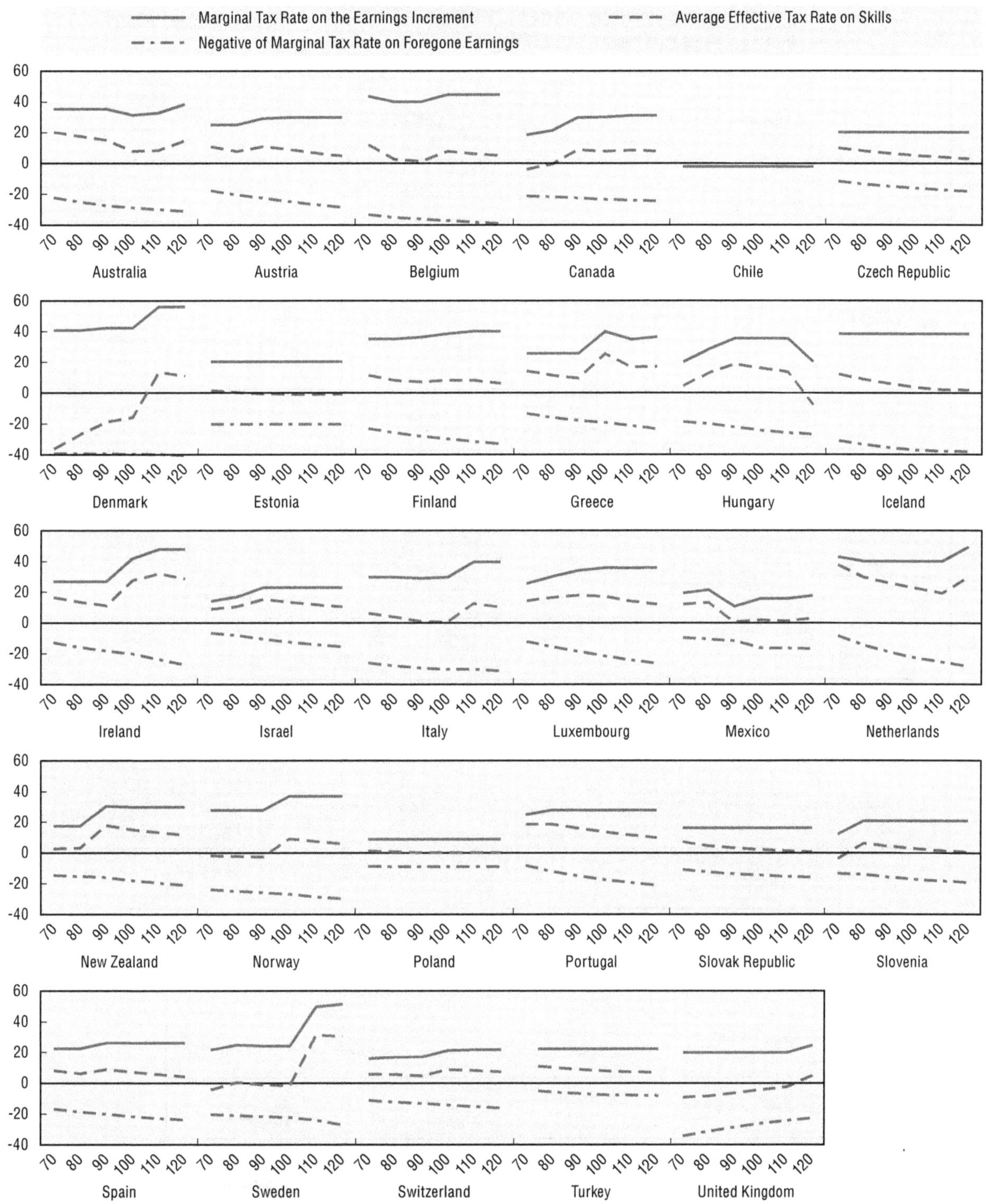

Note: Data are for a 27-year-old single taxpayer with no children, who undertakes a 1 year course of non-job-related education, earning 25% of the average wage during schooling. This figure shows results that incorporate tax deductions and tax credits for direct costs, tax exemptions for scholarship income, and reduced taxes on student wage income. Tax incentives in the personal income tax system are incorporated, but not the social security contribution system. They do not incorporate STEs that subsidise parental spending on education or that subsidise firm spending on education. It is assumed that the skills investment is financed wholly with savings: students do not incur any debt to make a skills investment.

StatLink http://dx.doi.org/10.1787/888933446273

Figure 3.7. **The tax rate on foregone earnings, the tax rate on the earnings increment, and the average effective tax rate on skills**

Tax rate by income level as % of average wage

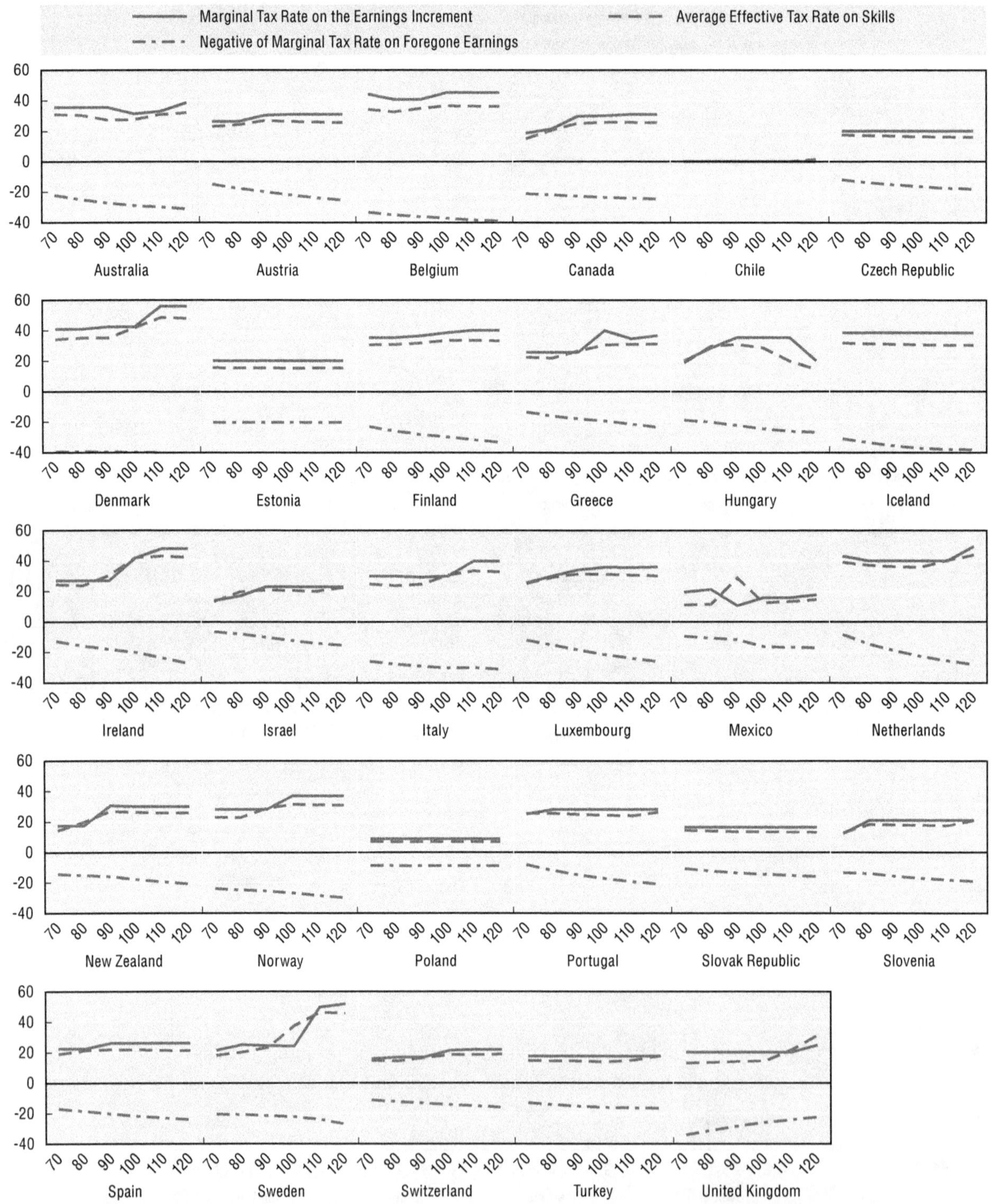

Note: Data are for a 27-year-old single taxpayer with no children, who undertakes a 1 year course of non-job-related education, earning 25% of the average wage during schooling. This figure shows results that incorporate tax deductions and tax credits for direct costs, tax exemptions for scholarship income, and reduced taxes on student wage income. Tax incentives in the personal income tax system are incorporated, but not the social security contribution system. They do not incorporate STEs that subsidise parental spending on education or that subsidise firm spending on education. It is assumed that the skills investment is financed wholly with savings: students do not incur any debt to make a skills investment.

StatLink http://dx.doi.org/10.1787/888933446283

What changes is the estimation of the returns to skills, and the tax rate on these returns. In Figure 3.6, the model examines a METR, based on a breakeven return. In Figure 3.7 it examines an AETR, based on an assumed return that is higher than the breakeven earnings level. Post-education earnings are higher in the average case than they are in the marginal case; the tax rate on this earnings increment is higher as well. This is clear as the top line is higher in most country cases.

The difference between these two graphs also illustrates that both the AETR and METR are weighted averages of the positive and negative effects of the tax system on incentives to invest in skills. The weight is the earnings increment; where returns are high, the tax rate on the earnings increment is a larger determinant, where returns are low, the tax system on foregone earnings is a larger determinant. In Figure 3.7 returns are higher; the AETR (the line in the middle) is closer to the tax rate on the earnings increment than in the marginal case.

The impact of taxes on skills investment is a function of the subsidies the tax system gives to skills investments that reduce their costs and the taxes on the returns to skills investments that reduces these returns. Moreover, for low-return skills investment, it is the subsidies on costs (both directly and as foregone earnings) that have the largest effect. For high return skills investments, it is the tax rate on returns (not subsides of costs) that matters most. This can be seen in the below formula which describes the relationship. This result is derived in Annex A.

$$AETR = \left(\frac{BEI}{EI}\right)METR + \left(1 - \frac{BEI}{EI}\right)T_{EI}$$

This result shows that as the return to skills grows large, the tax rate on the earnings increment, T_{EI}, has a higher weight in the AETR. When the returns to skills fall to the breakeven level, the AETR falls to the METR. This is the same result that can be seen in Figures 3.6 and 3.7.

3.8 The returns to costs ratio of investment in education

In addition to examining the financial costs and returns to education from the perspective of the individual, this study also explores the financial costs and returns to investment in skills from the perspective of the government. This is done through the MRCR and ARCR, the Marginal and Average Returns to Cost Ratios. These are measures of the ratio of the returns to education to the costs of education for the government.

Costs of education for government

On the cost side, the government's cost of education has six main components.

- The first is the government's direct spending on education; on teacher salaries, grants to private universities, public universities and so on. As with the data on private educational costs and scholarship income, estimates of government direct educational spending are taken from Education at a Glance 2011. These estimates are shown in Figure 3.8. This is discussed further in Box 3.1.
- The second is the scholarship and grant income that is provided by the government to the student. Note that the model assumes no private scholarship income; it is assumed that all scholarship income received is received by the student from the government.
- The third component is lost taxes while a student is working. This is exactly the converse of the after-tax foregone earnings component of costs to the student. While the student loses their after-tax earnings when they are in school instead of working, the government

loses the tax revenue it would have earned had the student continued working instead of educating themselves.

- The fourth component is the lost tax revenue that results from STEs. The government may lose tax revenue if STEs exist that defray the costs of education for the student of the kind outlined in Section 3.1.4.
- The fifth component is lost taxes that may result from deductibility of interest payments from workers as they repay student debts.
- The sixth component is fiscal costs that may accrue to the government if it lends to students to finance education at rates lower than it can borrow, or from the government writing off student loans, including in systems when repayment of these loans is contingent on a worker's income. By contrast, if the government is able to earn real returns on student loan provision, these returns may offset government costs elsewhere.

Figure 3.8. **Direct costs of skills investment for governments**

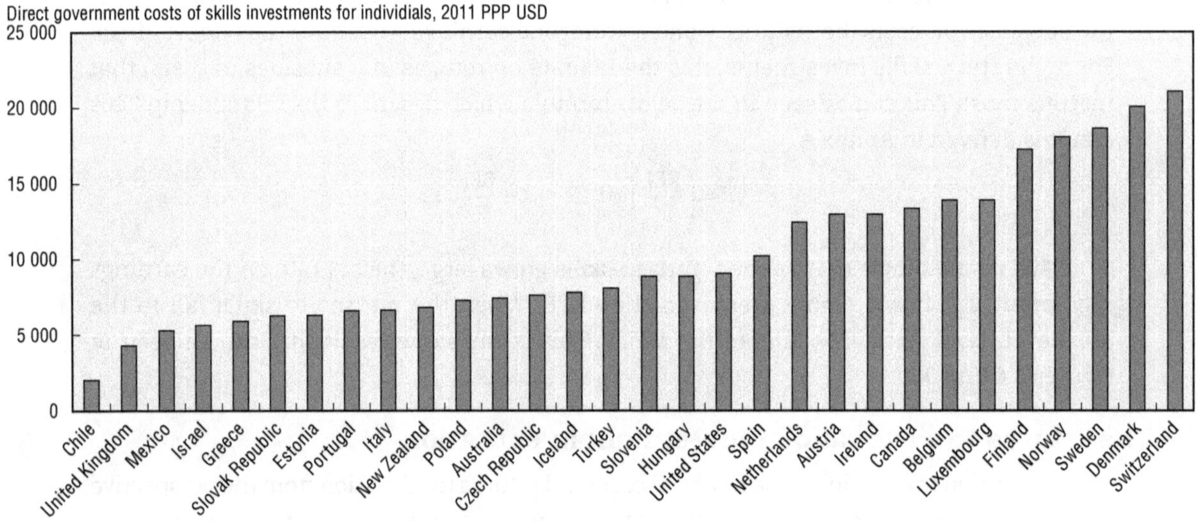

Source: (OECD, 2014) Education at a Glance 2014. Data are expressed in 2011 PPP USD.

StatLink http://dx.doi.org/10.1787/888933446290

In terms of returns, the model considers only returns to government in the form of increased tax revenue from the higher wages that workers earn after education. In doing so, it abstracts from the many other positive benefits that increased education will bring to the government, such as increased indirect taxation when the extra income earned is spent, reduced spending on employment and social benefits due to a more productive population, higher growth, lower probability of unemployment, and potentially greater social cohesion. The true returns to governments from education are likely to be considerably higher than those estimated in the model.

Average returns to cost ratio

A very simplified formula of the ARCR can be expressed as follows:

$$ARCR = \frac{Increased\ Taxes\ after\ Education}{Lost\ Taxes + Direct\ Educational\ Spending + Grant\ Spending + Loan\ Costs}.$$

In the model, this formula is appropriately time-discounted. A more technical expression of the ARCR can be found in Annex A of this study.

This formula is, like the METR, AETR and BEI, incorporated into the *Taxing Wages* models to calculate future tax revenue based on earnings assumptions. As with the AETR, labour market estimates of the lifetime tertiary education premium are used to estimate the increased tax revenues from upskilling for the government.

From a technical perspective, the ARCR functions as a 'Tobin's q' in economic investment theory. Values of the ARCR below one suggest that the returns to education (in tax revenue alone) are insufficient to recoup the costs of education for the government. Values of the ARCR above one suggest that the returns to education in the form of tax revenue more than cover the government's costs.

This in turn has implications for government spending on education, and for the government's taxation of the returns to skills. In investment theory, a Tobin's q above one suggests that the investment should be continued. In similar terms, ARCRs that far surpass one suggest that governments could increase tax revenue by increasing skills investments. By contrast, very low ARCR values could suggest that the returns to government in income tax revenue do not cover its costs from investments in upskilling at current spending levels.

It is important to realise that the ARCR does not provide information about the overall ratio of costs and benefits of education for society. It merely does so for the government. For example, it is possible for the ARCR to be far below one for the government, but for the skills investment to be profitable from an overall social perspective. It could simply be that the tax rate is too low for the government to recoup its spending on education; meaning that returns to a skills investment for the student are very high. Similarly, a high ARCR could mean that the government is spending little on education; that a large fraction of education spending is being financed privately by students, but the returns are being taxed away by the government.

Essentially, then, the ARCR is a measure not of the total ratio of costs to returns of education, but of the way these costs and returns are being shared between the government and the student. Low ARCRs suggest that the government is receiving a lower share of the returns to education than it is bearing in costs. This may not mean that education is not profitable or worthwhile overall, but simply that large shares of the returns are being captured by the student. Higher ARCRs suggest that the government is receiving a higher share of the returns to skills investments than it is bearing in costs. In such cases, the financial incentives to invest in education on the part of the student may be lower than they should be. This is illustrated in a very simple way in Table 3.2.

The results also suggest that raising the employment rate provides significant returns to the government by increasing the returns to its skills investment. For existing members of the labour force the formula suggests that unemployment can be very costly for governments who pay a large fraction of the costs of skills investments; a high unemployment rate means that sunk costs of skills investment are not being recouped by the government in the form of tax revenue.

Table 3.2. **Components of the MRCR and ARCR**

	High Taxes on Earnings Increments	Low Taxes on Earnings Increments
Low Government Spending/Low Taxes on Lost Earnings	High ARCR – Government receives a higher share of the returns than its share of the costs	ARCR near 1 – low share of the returns, but a low share of costs as well
High Government Spending/High Taxes on Lost Earnings	ARCR near 1 – high share of the returns, but a high share of the costs as well	Low ARCR – Government receives a smaller share of the returns than its share of the costs

It is important to note that many simplifying assumptions are made in the model. As mentioned, the model does not account for a wide variety of the financial and social benefits to education. These other benefits may occur in terms of tax revenue from taxes other than income tax, reducing social and other expenditure, and other social benefits. In addition, the model is static in its approach; the tax system is assumed to remain the same over years to come, as are the responses of wages to increased skills. Present taxes and present tertiary education premiums proxy for taxes and tertiary education premiums in years to come. As such, it is likely that the model underestimates the returns to education for both the student and government. The returns to skills are likely to rise steadily over the years to come, and comprise much more than just income tax revenue. The ARCR indicator is more useful as a guide of the relative position of countries with respect to how the costs and returns to education are distributed between governments and students, as opposed to an overall measure of the benefits of skills investment itself.

Marginal returns to cost ratio

Sections 3.4 and 3.5 discussed two tax rates on individual's investment in skills, the METR and the AETR. As discussed, the AETR measures the effect of the tax system on the financial incentives to invest in skills for a student earning the average return to skills in the labour market. By contrast, the METR on skills measures the effect of the tax system on the financial incentives to invest in skills for a student earning a breakeven return on a skills investment.

In addition to the Average Returns to Cost Ratio, the model allows for the calculation of a Marginal Returns to Cost Ratio. As outlined, the ARCR measures the ratio of returns to costs from the government's perspective where a student earns an average amount of returns on their skills investment. This means that from the government's perspective, returns in the form of tax revenue will be average as well. By contrast, the MRCR measures the ratio of returns to costs for the government when the student earns just a breakeven return. This indicator measures the incentives of the government to educate a student who will just break even on a skills investment. As with the ARCR, values of the MRCR above one suggest that the government will more than recoup their costs from skills investments.

As will be discussed in Chapter 4, breakeven earnings levels in the OECD are usually well below the average tertiary education premium: students more than recoup the costs of their education. This means that a hypothetical "breakeven" student will earn much less in this analysis than the average student. This in turn means that the tax revenue the government receives from a breakeven student will usually be significantly lower than that of the average student. This is true regardless of the other components of the ARCR and MRCR.

This in turn means that MRCRs are usually much lower than ARCRs in OECD countries. This is illustrated for a sample case in Figure 3.9. It can be seen here that ARCRs are larger than one for most countries at most income levels. However for most countries and for most income levels – though not all – MRCRs are not above one. This illustrates that for the government, the returns from educating a student who is just breaking even on a skills investment are lower than the returns to educating an average student.

Figure 3.9. **Comparing average and marginal returns to costs ratios**

Tax rate by income level as % of average wage

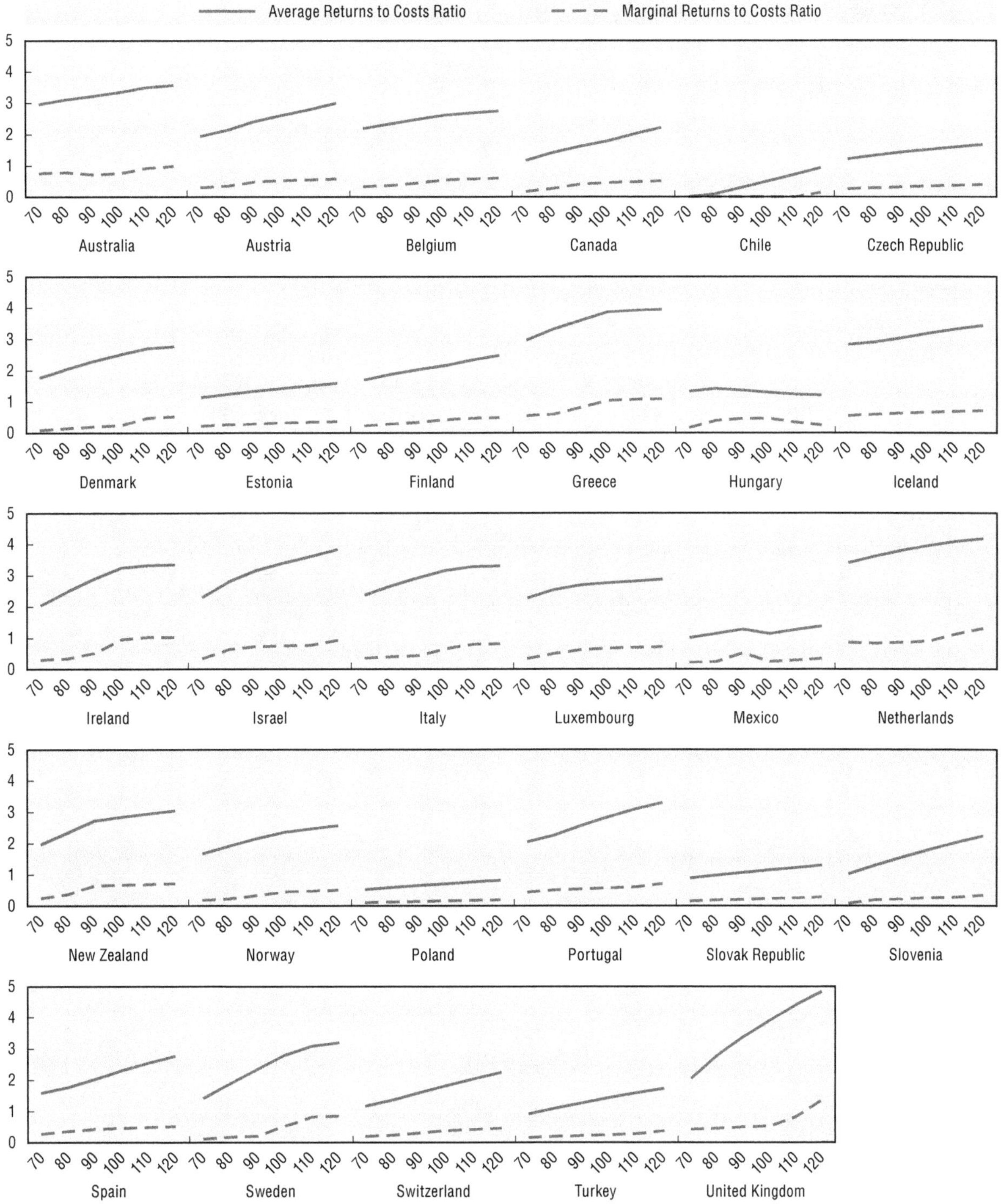

Note: Data are for a 27-year-old single taxpayer with no children, who undertakes a 1 year course of non-job-related education, earning 25% of the average wage during schooling. This figure shows results that incorporate tax deductions and tax credits for direct costs, tax exemptions for scholarship income, and reduced taxes on student wage income. Tax incentives in the personal income tax system are incorporated, but not the social security contribution system. They do not incorporate STEs that subsidise parental spending on education or that subsidise firm spending on education. It is assumed that the skills investment is financed wholly with savings: students do not incur any debt to make a skills investment.

StatLink http://dx.doi.org/10.1787/888933446303

Notes

1. Data for direct costs of education in Luxembourg are not available in Education at a Glance; data for Belgium are used as a proxy.
2. Data on scholarship and grant income in Luxembourg are not available in Education at a Glance; data for Belgium are used as a proxy. More details are provided in Box 3.1.
3. In the presence of capital taxes, the capital tax inserts a further wedge between what the student can earn on a risk-free investment and the rate at which he can borrow. This is because capital taxes must be paid on the nominal return on any investment opportunity. In this case, instead of $r-r^*$, the difference would be $(1-T_c)(r+\pi)-r^*+\pi$.
4. This is true in a setting without uncertainty, as is the case in the framework presented here.
5. The mechanics of the METR and BEI are discussed in detail in Brys and Torres (2013).

References

Brys, B. and C. Torres (2013), "Effective Personal Tax Rates on Marginal Skills Investments in OECD Countries: A New Methodology", *OECD Taxation Working Papers*, No. 16, *http://dx.doi.org/10.1787/5k425747xbr6-en.*

Klemm, A. (2008) "Effective Average Tax Rates for Permanent Investment", IMF Working Paper, No WP/08/56

OECD (2014), *Education at a Glance 2014: OECD Indicators*, OECD Publishing, Paris, *https://doi.org/10.1787/eag-2013-en.*

OECD (2016), *Taxing Wages 2016*, OECD Publishing, Paris, *http://dx.doi.org/10.1787/tax_wages-2016-en.*

Chapter 4

Tax and skills statistics: Effective tax rates and returns to costs ratios

This chapter presents the main results for the indicators surrounding the financial incentives to invest in skills discussed in this tax policy study. The key indicators are the Breakeven Earnings Increment (BEI), the Marginal Effective Tax Rate on Skills (METR), the Average Effective Tax Rate on Skills (AETR), the Marginal Returns to Costs Ratio for Governments (MRCR), and the Average Returns to Costs Ratio for Governments (ARCR). The chapter presents results for four stylised education, scenarios: a 17-year-old student undertaking a four-year degree, a 27 year-old undertaking a one-year degree, a 32-year old undertaking a short course of job-related training, and a 50-year old undertaking a one-year degree. The chapter also examines the impact of the form of financing of education on indicator outcomes, as well as the way the results vary by gender.

The statistical data for Israel are supplied by and under the responsibility of the relevant Israeli authorities. The use of such data by the OECD is without prejudice to the status of the Golan Heights, East Jerusalem and Israeli settlements in the West Bank under the terms of international law.

4.1 Introduction

This chapter presents the main results for the indicators surrounding the financial incentives to invest in skills discussed in this tax policy study. The key indicators are the Breakeven Earnings Increment (BEI), the Marginal Effective Tax Rate on Skills (METR), the Average Effective Tax Rate on Skills (AETR), the Marginal Returns to Costs Ratio for Governments (MRCR), and the Average Returns to Costs Ratio for Governments (ARCR). The methodology outlined in Chapter 3 is flexible; it allows for these indicators to be developed using a wide variety of assumptions about the length, nature, and cost of a given skills investment. It also allows for considerable variation with respect to the student; the income, family status, age, lost earnings, and future earnings potential of a student can all be varied. Finally, the model allows for flexibility with respect to the extent of education subsidies available; the government can pay for more or less of the direct costs of education, and it can subsidise the student with scholarship income, by writing down loan principals, by allowing students to borrow at reduced interest rates, and by using skills tax expenditures (STEs) to offset educational costs.

In this chapter results are presented for four stylised "types" of person engaged in upskilling, though the chapter also shows how these results vary by income, age, and taxes considered. The stylised cases are:

- **Tertiary Education:** A 17-year-old student, single and childless, who could earn 70% of the average wage in the labour market, but instead undertakes a four-year basic undergraduate degree. During this time, the student earns 25% of the Average Wage in part-time work. This is discussed in Sections 4.2 and 4.3.
- **Graduate Education:** A 27-year-old worker, single and childless, who could earn the Average Wage in the labour market, but instead undertakes a one-year graduate degree. During education the student earns 25% of their previous wage in part-time work. This is discussed in Section 4.4.
- **Job-Related In-Work Training:** A 32-year-old worker, single and childless, who earns 100% of the Average Wage, and undertakes a short course of job-related training. During education the worker's earnings fall to 95% of their previous wage, though they earn their previous wage for the rest of the year. This is discussed in Section 4.5.
- **Life-long Learning:** A 50-year-old worker, single and childless, who could earn 100% of the Average Wage, but instead undertakes a one-year retraining program unrelated to their current job. During education the worker earns 25% of their previous wage in part-time work. This is discussed in Section 4.6.

For university students, the manner in which education is financed is allowed to vary. In some countries, tertiary is financed primarily by governments, while in some countries the student finances most of their tertiary education. A student can finance their education with retained earnings, debt, or a combination of the two. This is discussed in Section 4.3.

In addition, Section 4.7 examines the way in which differing expected wages for men and women in the labour market in OECD countries can affect incentives to invest in skills for individual men and women. The discussion will also examine how the gender wage gap affects expected returns for governments.

The results in this study incorporate personal income taxes (PIT) only, not social security contributions (SSCs). This means that in countries where SSCs form a large part of the labour tax wedge, the results presented in this study may differ from those that would result from incorporating both PIT and SSCs. SSCs may raise the tax rate on foregone earnings, increasing the extent to which the tax system subsidises skills investment and reducing the tax burden on skills, while at the same time raising the tax rate on earnings increments, thus raising the tax burden on skills. Thus adding SSCs to the analysis may raise or reduce the overall burden on skills investments.

The results in some countries may be particularly sensitive to the inclusion of SSCs due to the fact that in some instances there are ceilings above which an extra dollar of income may not be liable for future SSCs. This may mean that SSCs may be a component of the tax rate on foregone earnings, but not of the tax rate on the earnings increment. In these cases, accounting for SSCs may reduce the tax burden on skills substantially.

In other cases however, the SSC burden may rise with income; SSC schedules may be progressive. In these cases, accounting for SSCs will raise the tax rate on the earnings increment by more than the tax rate on foregone earnings is reduced. In these cases, the overall tax rate on skills may be higher where SSCs are taken into account.

It is also important to account for the ways in which the SSC system interacts with the PIT system. In many countries, SSCs are deductible from the PIT base. In this study the results presented factor in the impact of these deductions from the PIT system. Thus while SSCs are not taken into account in the results presented here, the study does account for their impact on the PIT system. This approach follows that taken in *Taxing Wages* (OECD, 2016).

Finally, it is important to account for certain skills tax expenditures that may be provided through the SSC system. For example, in certain cases student income may be subject to a reduced SSC burden relative to other forms of income. These kinds of skills tax expenditures through the SSC system are discussed further in Chapter 5.

4.2 Tertiary education

The tertiary education case examines a 17-year old person undertaking a four-year course of study. Tertiary education students receive an average level of government scholarship income and pay an average amount of direct costs.[1] Their earnings during education are set at 25% of the Average Wage in any given country: that is, students are assumed to earn some part-time employment income, but at a comparatively low level.

Importantly, it is assumed that the student receives no financial support from parents towards their education costs, nor do the parents receive subsidies through the tax system for supporting their child through university. This strong assumption is made on tractability grounds. Aside from government support, the student is assumed to be independent from their parents when it comes to financing the course of study.

As discussed in Chapter 3, a variety of assumptions about how the students finance their education are examined. In this section it is assumed that students finance their education with savings. In Section 4.3, it is assumed that the student finances their education with a student loan. The amounts borrowed by the student as well as the interest rate at which they can borrow are both varied in the analysis.

Government support in OECD countries for tertiary education is usually significant; per-annum scholarship spending per student is on average USD 1 606 among the countries examined in this study.[2] In many OECD countries the student's scholarship or grant income is tax-free, which is a subsidy for tertiary education through the tax system. Direct costs of tertiary education are usually not tax deductible. In addition in some countries (notably Belgium and the Slovak Republic) students' wage income is taxed at a lower rate than standard wage income.

It is important to note that the model is unrepresentative of tertiary education in many ways. Many students receive significant support from their parents; this support is often subsidised through the tax system many countries also allow tax deductibility of the costs of supporting a child; the model does not capture these provisions. This means that it is likely that the METRs in the model are higher than their true value.

The BEI is highest for a 17-year-old completing a four-year degree than it is for any other case examined in detail in this study. This is largely due to the long duration of tertiary education for students. Foregone earnings are larger in the case of a four-year degree than in other shorter cases examined. Figure 4.1 shows that the BEI expressed as a percentage of the previous wage in this case ranges from 4.5% (Denmark) to 23.3% (Chile), with an un-weighted average among the countries in the sample of 15%.

In spite of these comparatively high costs; tertiary education pays for itself in the model. Though the BEI in the model is highest for tertiary education compared to other forms of education; the extra earnings needed to break even on a typical tertiary education are below the levels of earnings available for university students in the labour market. These values range from 20% (Denmark) to 137% (Chile); with an un-weighted average among the countries in the sample of 45%. Figure 4.2 shows the size of the gaps between the BEI (at the bottom) and the labour market premium for tertiary education (at the top).

Figure 4.1. **Breakeven earnings increments for tertiary education (% of wage before education)**

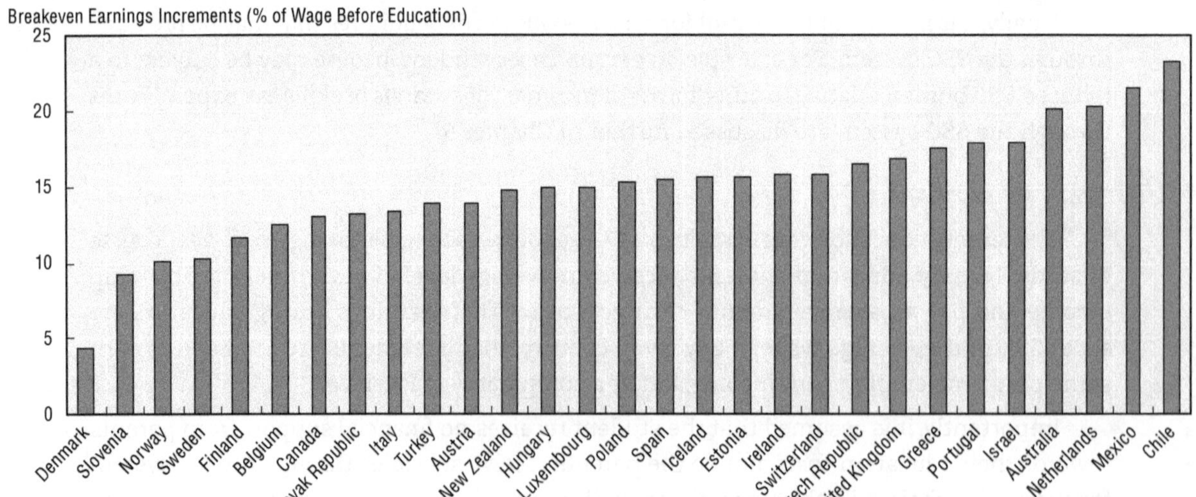

Note: Data are for a 17-year-old single taxpayer with no children, who undertakes a four-year course of non-job-related education, earning 25% of the average wage during schooling. This figure shows results that incorporate tax deductions and tax credits for direct costs, tax exemptions for scholarship income, and reduced taxes on student wage income. Tax incentives in the personal income tax system are incorporated, but not the social security contribution system. They do not incorporate skills tax expenditures that subsidise parental spending on education or that subsidise firm spending on education. It is assumed that the skills investment is financed wholly with savings: students do not incur any debt to make a skills investment.

StatLink http://dx.doi.org/10.1787/888933446312

Figure 4.2. **Comparing the breakeven tertiary earnings increment to the tertiary labour market premium**

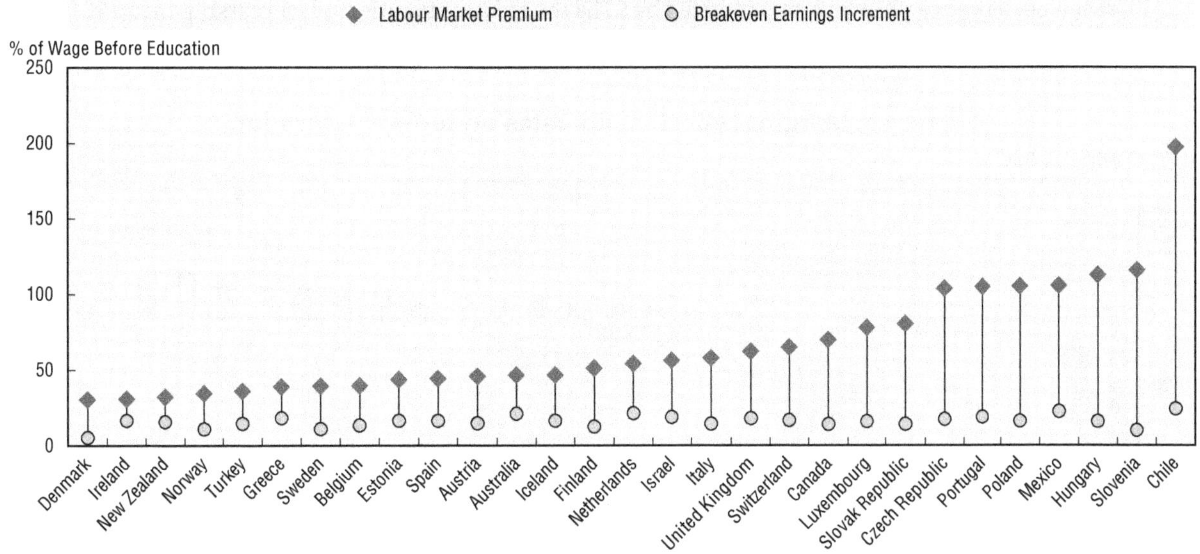

Note: Data are for a 17-year-old single taxpayer with no children, who undertakes a four-year course of non-job-related education, earning 25% of the average wage during schooling. This figure shows results that incorporate tax deductions and tax credits for direct costs, tax exemptions for scholarship income, and reduced taxes on student wage income. Tax incentives in the personal income tax system are incorporated, but not the social security contribution system. They do not incorporate skills tax expenditures that subsidise parental spending on education or that subsidise firm spending on education. It is assumed that the skills investment is financed wholly with savings: students do not incur any debt to make a skills investment. Labour market data are based on the tertiary education premium earned by 15-64-year-olds.

StatLink http://dx.doi.org/10.1787/888933446329

For some countries such as Slovenia and Chile, there are significant rewards to tertiary education in the labour market; the gap between what is necessary to break even on a skills investment and what is available on average is very large. This points to the possibility of skills shortages in these countries. It also raises questions about the performance of education markets in these countries; if skills investments are so lucrative and (as indicated by lower BEIs compared to available returns) so affordable, why are more students not undertaking them?

By contrast, many other countries – some that are known to have very high levels of third-level education in their labour forces – have relatively small gaps between available earnings and breakeven earnings. This suggests that these educational investments may not be profitable for some students given the current mixture of education costs, scholarship and grant levels, and tax rates.

Overall, skills investments for marginal tertiary education students are taxed comparatively lightly. Figure 4.3 shows that for 17-year old tertiary education students whose outside employment opportunities are at 70% of the Average Wage, METRs range from -56% (Denmark) to 34.5% (Netherlands), with an average value in the sample of 2.9%. This means that, in the Danish case for example, that the tax system reduces the BEI by 56%, compared to what it would be in a world without taxes. These negative METRs mean that the tax system is increasing individuals' incentives to invest in skills, compared to what these incentives would be if no taxes were levied.

There are several reasons for these low METRs. First, the model assumes that the unskilled worker would earn a low wage, which lowers the cost of studying and, as it results in a relatively low BEI, means their extra earnings are modestly affected by the tax system.

In some countries – notably Denmark – the amount of scholarship income is such that the student's foregone earnings are almost entirely nullified by extra scholarship income received. Moreover, BEIs are also reduced by STEs that reduce taxation of scholarship income and student wage income.

Figure 4.3. **Marginal effective tax rates on tertiary education**

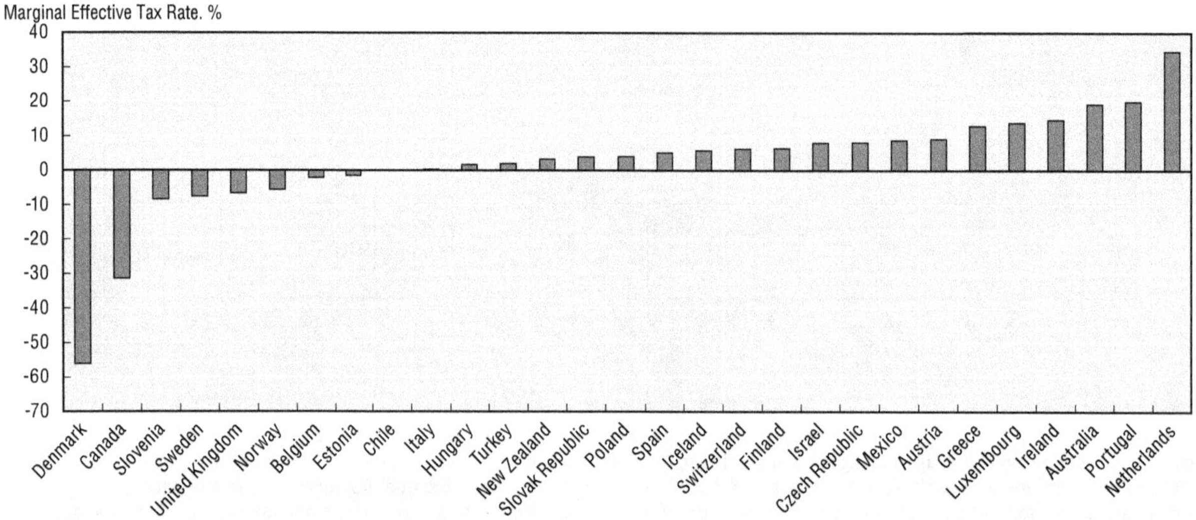

Note: Data are for a 17-year-old single taxpayer with no children, who undertakes a four-year course of non-job-related education, earning 25% of the average wage during schooling. This figure shows results that incorporate tax deductions and tax credits for direct costs, tax exemptions for scholarship income, and reduced taxes on student wage income. Tax incentives in the personal income tax system are incorporated, but not the social security contribution system. They do not incorporate STEs that subsidise parental spending on education or that subsidise firm spending on education. It is assumed that the skills investment is financed wholly with savings: students do not incur any debt to make a skills investment.

StatLink http://dx.doi.org/10.1787/888933446333

AETRs are higher than METRs as can be seen in Figure 4.4. Higher-than-breakeven earnings after education push taxpayers into higher brackets, decreasing their incentives to invest in skills. The AETRs are based on the assumption that students' earnings after university increase by the average lifetime tertiary labour market premium. Under this assumption, these AETRs range from 2.1% (Chile) to 37.9% (Netherlands) with an un-weighted average of the countries in the sample of 19.8%. Note that AETRs tend to rise towards the statutory top PIT rates in a given country as the returns to skills investments rise. This is partly why the Netherlands has the highest AETR on tertiary education in the model; it has comparatively high PIT rates commencing at relatively low levels of income, and so has relatively high PIT progressivity. This is in contrast to Chile which has one of the lowest statutory PIT rates in the sample of countries, and so has one of the lowest AETRs.

These tax rates yield significant returns to the government in the form of tax revenue. Figure 4.5 shows the ARCR of government investment in education. Recall from Section 3.7 that ARCRs measure the ratio of government returns to education (extra tax revenue) to the costs of education (lost tax revenue, direct costs, and scholarship or grant income given to a student and value of skills tax expenditures). It should be noted that only the returns to education in the form of extra income taxes are considered; the model does not incorporate estimates of the broader returns to education such as higher employment, faster growth, or increased productivity. The estimates of the returns to education are almost certainly lower in the model than the true estimates, as only income taxes are considered.

Figure 4.4. **Average effective tax rates on tertiary education**

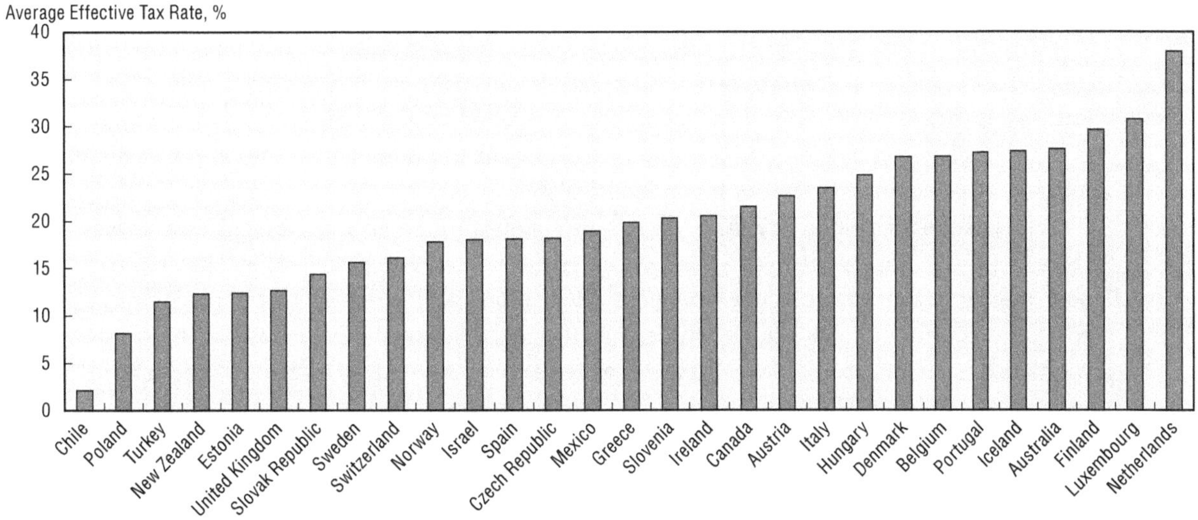

Note: Data are for a 17-year-old single taxpayer with no children, who undertakes a four-year course of non-job-related education, earning 25% of the average wage during schooling. This figure shows results that incorporate tax deductions and tax credits for direct costs, tax exemptions for scholarship income, and reduced taxes on student wage income. Tax incentives in the personal income tax system are incorporated, but not the social security contribution system. They do not incorporate STEs that subsidise parental spending on education or that subsidise firm spending on education. It is assumed that the skills investment is financed wholly with savings: students do not incur any debt to make a skills investment.

StatLink http://dx.doi.org/10.1787/888933446344

Figure 4.5. **Average returns to costs ratio of government investment in tertiary education**

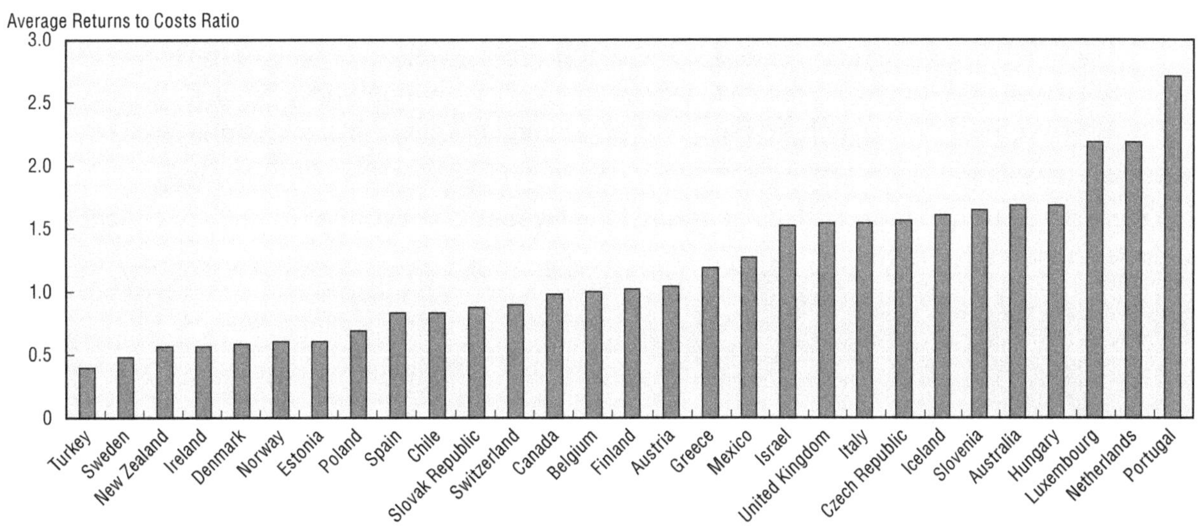

Note: Data are for a 17-year-old single taxpayer with no children, who undertakes a four-year course of non-job-related education, earning 25% of the average wage during schooling. This figure shows results that incorporate tax deductions and tax credits for direct costs, tax exemptions for scholarship income, and reduced taxes on student wage income. Tax incentives in the personal income tax system are incorporated, but not the social security contribution system. They do not incorporate STEs that subsidise parental spending on education or that subsidise firm spending on education. It is assumed that the skills investment is financed wholly with savings: students do not incur any debt to make a skills investment. Due to data limitations, results for Mexico are omitted. Labour market data are based on the tertiary education premium earned by 15-64-year-olds.

StatLink http://dx.doi.org/10.1787/888933446357

Based on the existing labour market, tax and expenditure data, the ARCR is on average larger than 1 in the OECD. This could suggest that extra investment in education would yield positive returns for governments in the OECD in terms of income tax revenue. The average value of the ARCR in the sample is 1.2, where an ARCR of 1 would be the level at which the present value of the stream of returns was equal to that of the costs.

For some countries, such as the Netherlands and Portugal, the returns to education are more than double the costs. This is driven by comparatively low spending, both on scholarships and directly to universities in these countries, coupled with a comparatively high labour market premium for tertiary education. The results also suggest that for some countries the share of the costs borne by the government in education is comparatively high. For countries such as Ireland and New Zealand, a larger fraction of the costs of education are borne by governments than is recouped in costs.

In contrast to the results for ARCRs, MRCRs are significantly lower for most OECD countries. This is due to the gap between the BEI and the tertiary education premium available in the labour market, as shown in Figure 4.2. In the ARCR case, the student earns the premium in the labour market. For the MRCR, the student is assumed to earn just the break-even earnings level, which is substantially lower than the average wage earned by a tertiary graduate in most countries. These values can be considered to be the government's returns to educating a student who just breaks even on a skills investment. As is the case with the ARCR, the returns are probably underestimated, as the analysis in this study only incorporates returns in the form of higher income taxes, and so does not include a broader set of financial or social returns.

As is shown in Figure 4.6, MRCRs are usually below one in OECD countries. The highest value is in the Netherlands at 0.85, while the lowest is Chile with a MRCR of 0. This reflects the high PIT thresholds in Chile; taxpayers who are just breaking even on a skills investment will not pass the threshold to begin to pay PIT in Chile, so the government's returns on a skills investment will be zero. The mean value across the countries modelled is 0.198. This low value suggests that while skills investments more than make up their costs from the government's perspective on average, for marginal students income tax revenues do not cover the governments costs in income tax revenue; these costs may however be recouped in terms of lower social spending, higher revenues from other tax categories, and lower unemployment. However the results nonetheless suggest the government's share of income taxes received from marginal students are lower than its share of the costs of skills investments.

Figure 4.6. **Marginal returns to costs ratio of government investment in tertiary education**

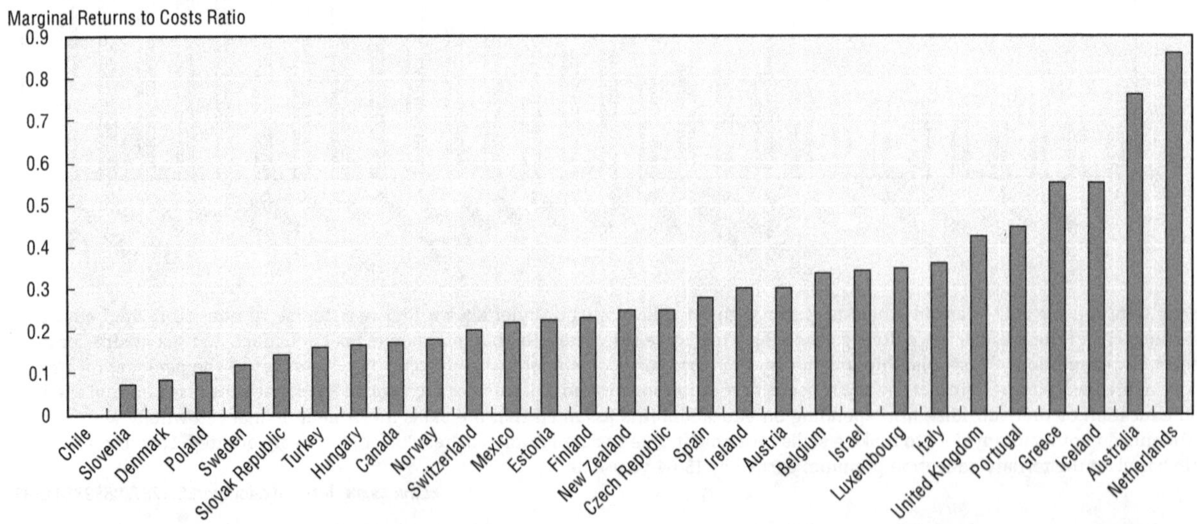

Note: Data are for a 17-year-old single taxpayer with no children, who undertakes a four-year course of non-job-related education, earning 25% of the average wage during schooling. This figure shows results that incorporate tax deductions and tax credits for direct costs, tax exemptions for scholarship income, and reduced taxes on student wage income. Tax incentives in the personal income tax system are incorporated, but not the social security contribution system. They do not incorporate STEs that subsidise parental spending on education or that subsidise firm spending on education. It is assumed that the skills investment is financed wholly with savings: students do not incur any debt to make a skills investment.

StatLink http://dx.doi.org/10.1787/888933446362

Figure 4.7. **Average effective tax rates on skills, marginal effective tax rates on skills and breakeven earnings increments varied by income before education: tertiary education student**

Tax rate by income level as % of average wage

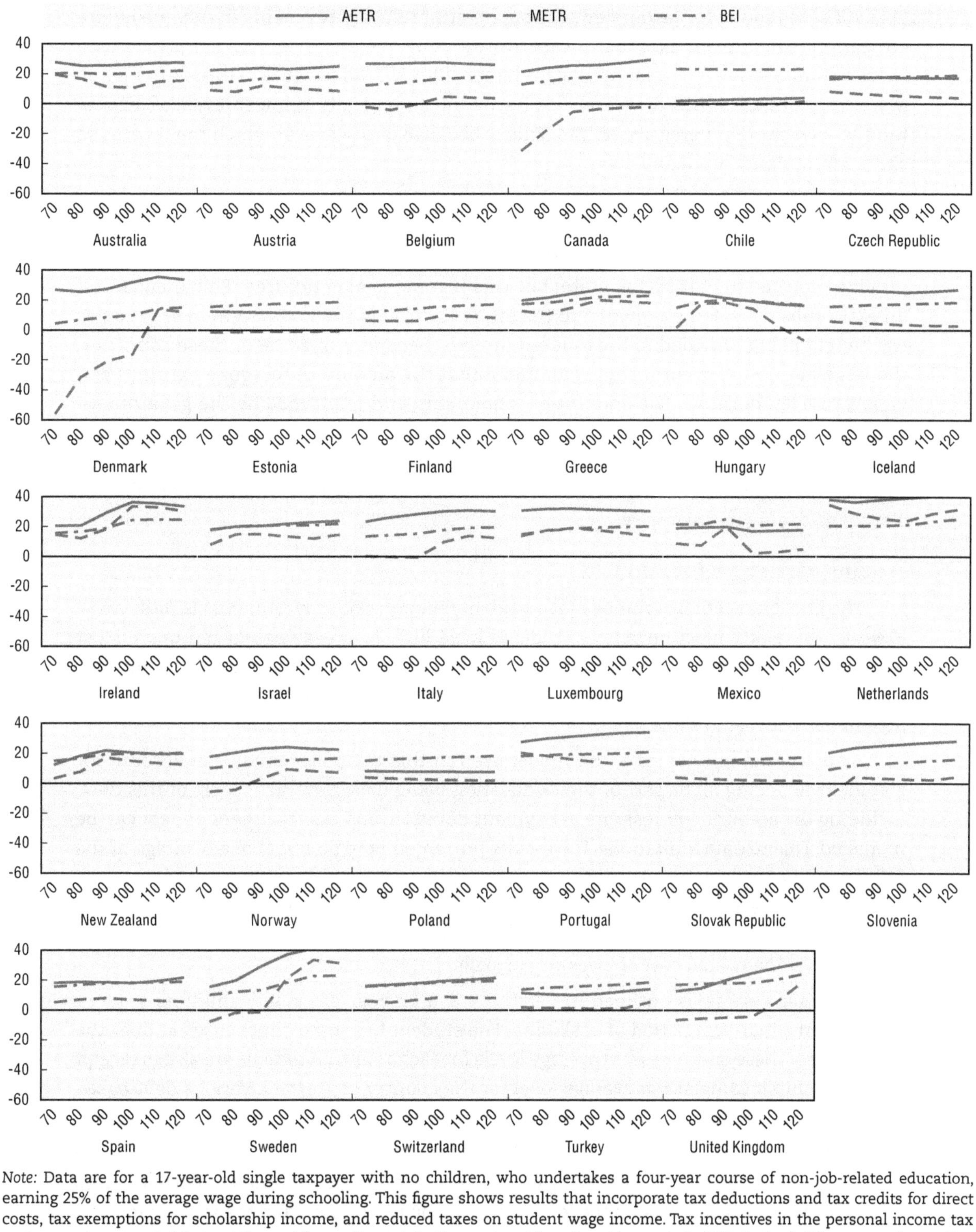

Note: Data are for a 17-year-old single taxpayer with no children, who undertakes a four-year course of non-job-related education, earning 25% of the average wage during schooling. This figure shows results that incorporate tax deductions and tax credits for direct costs, tax exemptions for scholarship income, and reduced taxes on student wage income. Tax incentives in the personal income tax system are incorporated, but not the social security contribution system. They do not incorporate STEs that subsidise parental spending on education or that subsidise firm spending on education. It is assumed that the skills investment is financed wholly with savings: students do not incur any debt to make a skills investment.

StatLink http://dx.doi.org/10.1787/888933446379

Figure 4.7 shows results when the assumption that students earn 70% of the average wage in the absence of upskilling is relaxed. In this figure, the income the student forgoes is allowed to vary, allowing the calculation of METRs and AETRs at various income levels. These results for tertiary education are either flat or increasing in income before education, though this is not the case for all countries, most notably Hungary. The results from Section 3.6 hold; AETRs are larger than METRs because returns are higher. Moreover, countries with progressive PIT schedules especially at lower levels of income tend to have more progressive AETRs. This is because of the rate at which the returns to skills investments are taxed away.

Denmark and Sweden have sharply negative METRs at very low income levels; this is due to the provision of comparatively large amounts of tax-free scholarship and grant income in these countries. In these examples, not only is a significant amount of income provided to the student by the state; but this income is also tax-free. This means that an extra subsidy is being provided to the student through the tax system in addition to the benefit being provided to the student directly. Secondly, in some of these countries, the large amount of grant income can mean that the amount of foregone earnings can be low or even negative; the amount of scholarship and grant income the government provides is as much or even exceeds what a low-income student could earn in the labour market. In such cases the incentives to invest in skills become high indeed. This may lead to problems regarding tertiary completion in these countries as it becomes profitable for a student to stay in university.

4.3 Financing tertiary education

The previous section assumes that a student finances skills investments using savings. However, in reality most university students have little or no savings to call upon. Most students finance their education through their parents or through student debt. This section examines how the costs of this financing can affect students' and workers' financial incentives to invest in skills.

As discussed in Chapter 3, the model used in this tax policy study can account for a student financing all or part of their education using debt. Several aspects of this debt, including the amount, interest rate, repayment duration, and tax treatment of debt can be modelled. Due to data limitations, the results presented here do not take advantage of the full flexibility available in the model. Data on average rates of interest on student loans are not available, nor are data on average loan amounts. Hypothetical interest rates and loan amounts are used instead. These still offer suggestive results as to the importance of financing for the overall cost of investing in skills.

The base case is as outlined in Section 4.2: a 17-year old single childless student engaging in a four-year period of upskilling. The student has some direct costs, as does the government. These costs are set at average levels for each country. Students are also in receipt of scholarship income at the average level for the country concerned. Various debt-based provisions are incorporated concerning the treatment of student debt in OECD countries, such as the deductibility of interest payments and income contingent repayments of debt.

Throughout this section, borrowing levels and interest rates are varied uniformly across countries. More detailed data on the level of borrowing per student and the average interest rate pertaining to student loans are not available. A second reason as to why borrowing levels are varied uniformly is to increase comparability across countries. In spite of this, it should be noted that the results presented here, though they incorporate statutory provisions in individual countries concerning the tax treatment of student debt and the structure of repayments, are not representative of any particular country in terms of average debt levels or interest rates.

Figure 4.8 shows how these financing costs impact the overall costs of skills investments. In this figure it is assumed that the student can borrow at a nominal interest rate of 6%, which in the model corresponds to a real rate of 4%. Having to borrow to finance the cost of education raises the BEI substantially; the student must earn more to pay interest on student debt in addition to whatever other costs they must earn to break even on their skills investment.

The black squares show the BEIs with no borrowing; these are the same BEIs as outlined in Figures 4.1 and 4.2. The blue triangles show BEIs when the student borrows just the direct costs of a skills investment. These costs are taken from *Education at Glance* (OECD, 2014): details are given in Box 3.1 in Chapter 3. These costs are roughly analogous to the student borrowing tuition fees to finance their education. BEIs rise most in these circumstances where private direct costs are high for students. This means that countries such as Chile have large gaps between black squares (BEIs with no borrowing) and blue triangles (BEIs where direct costs are borrowed). By contrast, in countries where direct costs for the individual student are modest, the amount of borrowing is modest too. In these cases the BEI does not rise much as the amount of debt incurred is low.

The circles in Figure 4.8 show the BEIs when students borrow not just these direct costs of their education, but rather the entirety of the costs: they borrow their after-tax foregone earnings as well. This can be thought of as analogous to a situation in which a student borrows not just to pay tuition fees but also to maintain their standard of living at a level that they would have had if they had worked instead of entering the workforce. The circles are substantially higher than the black squares in Figure 4.8, sometimes double in size. These BEIs can rise to up to 33% (Chile).

Figure 4.8. **Breakeven earnings increments for a tertiary education student at a 6% nominal interest rate**

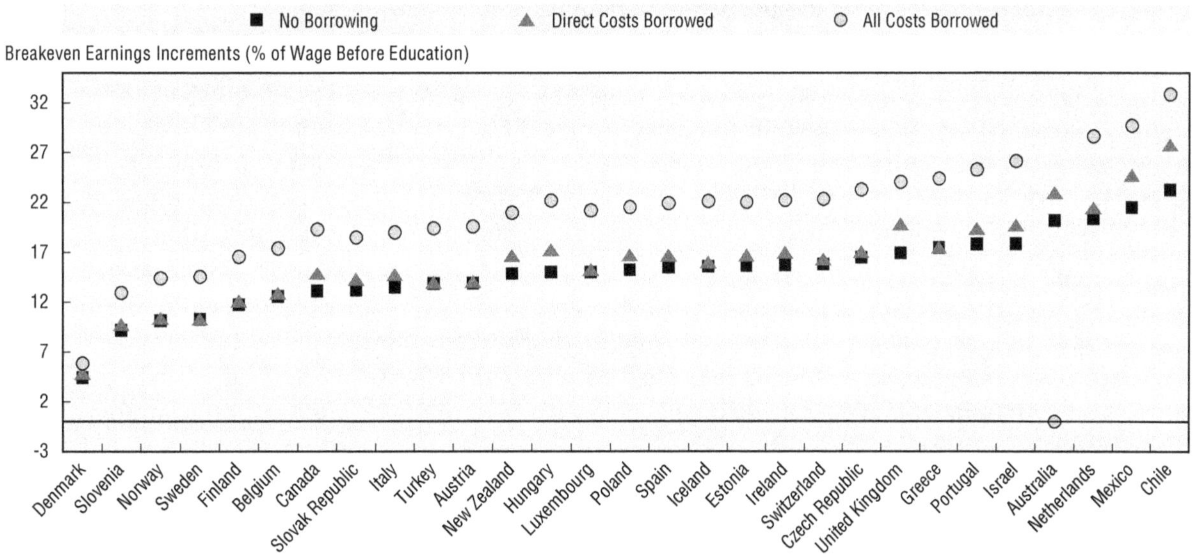

Note: Data are for a 17-year-old single taxpayer with no children, who undertakes a four-year course of non-job-related education, earning 25% of the average wage during schooling. This figure shows results that incorporate tax deductions and tax credits for direct costs, tax exemptions for scholarship income, and reduced taxes on student wage income. Tax incentives in the personal income tax system are incorporated, but not the social security contribution system. They do not incorporate STEs that subsidise parental spending on education or that subsidise firm spending on education. This figure does not incorporate interest deductibility of student loans in Finland.

StatLink http://dx.doi.org/10.1787/888933446387

An exception to this pattern is the circle for Australia, which illustrates the effect of the Australian income contingent loan scheme.[3] In the Australian case, students do not repay any part of their loan unless their earnings pass a certain threshold. In this modelling, a marginal student who earns 70% of the average wage in Australia will not pass the threshold to begin repaying their loans, and will so not need to pay back their loans. This is because an amount that is 70% of the average wage plus the BEI does not add up to enough to pass the threshold for repayment. This means that the costs of a skills investment is essentially zero, though these costs will rise if they move up the income distribution. It is important to note that in the case where Australian students borrow a lower fraction of the total cost of their education, they may still benefit as their loan principal will be written down, but as their borrowing will be low, they will not benefit as much they would if they had borrowed all of their costs. It should be noted that this modelling pertains to 2011; average wages, thresholds and other features of the policy may have changed in Australia.

These results illustrate several points. First, student debt, when the interest rate is sufficiently high, can act as a significant barrier to upskilling, in some cases nearly doubling the required earnings level at which a student can breakeven. Without knowing details on interest rates that students face in OECD countries it is not possible to determine the exact size of this barrier, however it is worth noting that the BEIs in this model are very sensitive to the amount borrowed.

A second point worth noting is that the impact of borrowing on the BEI is much larger when lost earnings are borrowed than when just direct costs are borrowed. This highlights the importance of the mix of education costs in determining the financial barriers to investing in skills. Some students receive support in kind for day-to-day living expenses from parents. This means that they do not have to borrow to finance their living expenses during periods of upskilling. In such cases the barriers to educational investment in terms of the returns that must be earned post-education are reduced substantially. The results highlight that the implications of these in-kind benefits should not be underestimated.

Figure 4.9 shows the impact of differing levels of borrowing on BEIs for university students. The difference in this figure compared to Figure 4.8 is the real interest rate faced by students. Many countries, such as Australia and the United Kingdom offer students low-interest rate loans. This example examines these kinds of provisions. In the results shown in Figure 4.9 the student can borrow at a 0% real interest rate. The results are instructive; where a student can borrow cheaply the BEIs falls by a significant margin. Again the difference is apparent with varying borrowing levels. Where direct costs for students are large, reduced interest rates even on direct costs alone reduce BEIs substantially. However, for most countries, having students borrow just the direct costs of their education at a reduced rate does not affect their costs of education to a large extent. It nonetheless does lower the BEI below the level of the BEI for a skills investment financed with savings.

Where the full costs of education are borrowed, Figure 4.9 shows that BEIs can fall dramatically. It is important to realise the impact of reduced borrowing rates on BEIs in the model. In the model developed in this study, a key component of the BEI is the opportunity cost of the funds directed towards a skills investment.[4] Students who choose to spend savings on a skills investment must not only recoup back those savings, but they must also recoup whatever those savings would have earned had they been invested in some other non-skills investment. In the model used in this study, it is assumed that had the funds used for a skills investment been invested elsewhere, they would yield a 3% real return per year. This 3% is used to calculate the opportunity cost component of the BEI in these results.

Figure 4.9. **Breakeven earnings increments for a tertiary education student and a 0% nominal rate of interest**

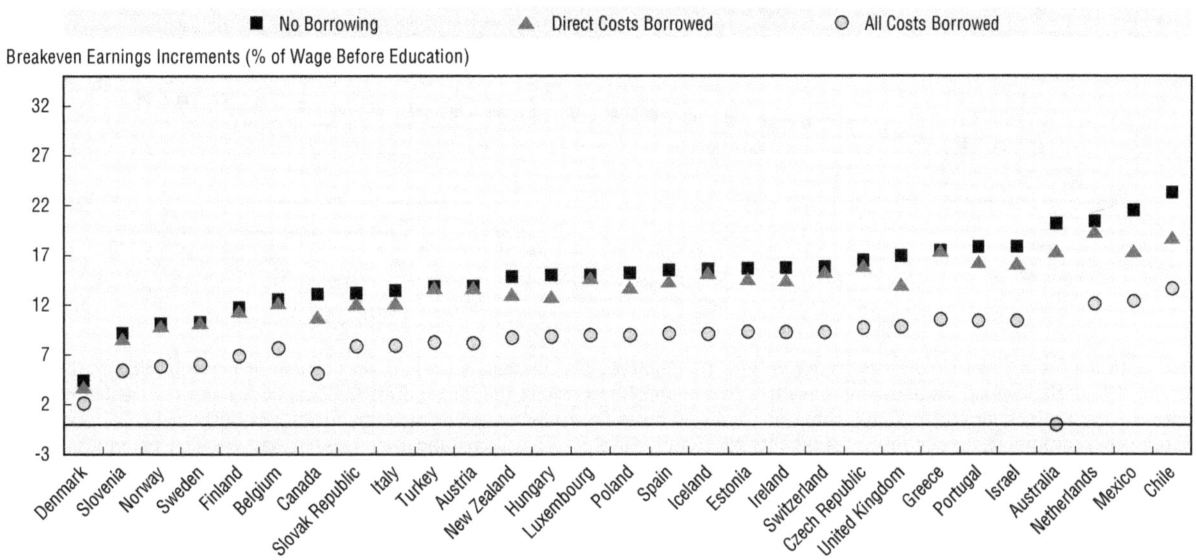

Note: Data are for a 17-year-old single taxpayer with no children, who undertakes a four-year course of non-job-related education, earning 25% of the average wage during schooling. This figure shows results that incorporate tax deductions and tax credits for direct costs, tax exemptions for scholarship income, and reduced taxes on student wage income. Tax incentives in the personal income tax system are incorporated, but not the social security contribution system. They do not incorporate STEs that subsidise parental spending on education or that subsidise firm spending on education. This figure does not incorporate interest deductibility of student loans in Finland.

StatLink http://dx.doi.org/10.1787/888933446396

The ability to borrow the costs of a skills investment changes these incentives substantially. Where a student can borrow at a real rate of interest that is below the real rate of return that they might earn an alternative investment, the BEI is reduced substantially. Due to the fact that the student can borrow at a rate lower than the rate of return on a risk-free bond, the availability of education finance acts as an extra subsidy for the student. Even where a student has sufficient savings to finance a skills investment, the student may have an incentive to borrow to finance the investment, and invest their savings to earn the opportunity return. The financial gain made will reduce the cost of the investment substantially. In these scenarios, indeed, a large gap between the after-tax opportunity return at the interest rate on student debt means that higher levels of borrowing reduce the BEI steadily: if an investment yields returns at a higher rate than the interest rate through which they are financed, more borrowing is preferable. These results emphasise the impacts of financing costs on the overall financial incentives to invest in skills. Figure 4.10 highlights these effects showing that as borrowing costs rise, the BEIs rise commensurately.

Figure 4.10. **Breakeven earnings increments for a tertiary education student at various levels of student debt**

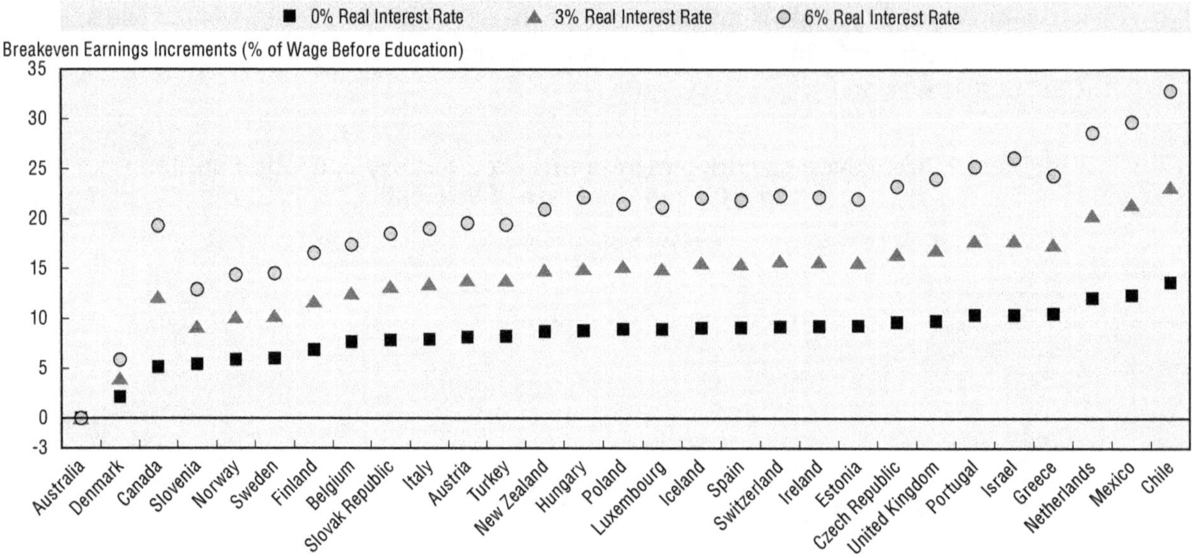

Note: Data are for a 17-year-old single taxpayer with no children, who undertakes a four-year course of non-job-related education, earning 25% of the average wage during schooling. This figure shows results that incorporate tax deductions and tax credits for direct costs, tax exemptions for scholarship income, and reduced taxes on student wage income. Tax incentives in the personal income tax system are incorporated, but not the social security contribution system. They do not incorporate STEs that subsidise parental spending on education or that subsidise firm spending on education. This figure does not incorporate interest deductibility of student loans in Finland.

StatLink http://dx.doi.org/10.1787/888933446406

4.4 Graduate education

The graduate education model examines a 27-year old person undertaking a one-year course of study. As with the case of a university student, they are in receipt of an average level of government scholarship income and pay an average amount of direct costs.[5]

The calculations assume that a graduate student earns 25% of the wage they earned before commencing a one-year course of study. This is instead of earning 25% of the average wage, which was assumed in the case of the tertiary education results. This is a proxy for the idea that while a university student's skills in the labour market will be lower, a graduate student may have developed some skills so that their earnings throughout their period of additional studies are likely to be a function of their earnings before they began their graduate education. In these examples, as in Section 4.2, it is assumed that education is financed with savings, not with debt.

BEIs are lower in the model for graduate education than for tertiary education. This is largely because graduate education is shorter and so less costly for students. Direct costs are assumed to be the same on a per-year basis for graduate and undergraduate education. Undergraduate education is, however, assumed to be four years long while graduate education is only one year long, so the costs are commensurately higher. Figure 4.11 shows that BEIs range from 2.5% (Denmark) to 6.3% (Greece) with an un-weighted average in the sample of 4.7% (see Figure 4.11). Variation in these figures is driven in part by the amount of education spending in a given country and in part by the reduced taxation that comes with reduced earnings.

Figure 4.11. **Breakeven earnings increments for graduate education (% of wage before education)**

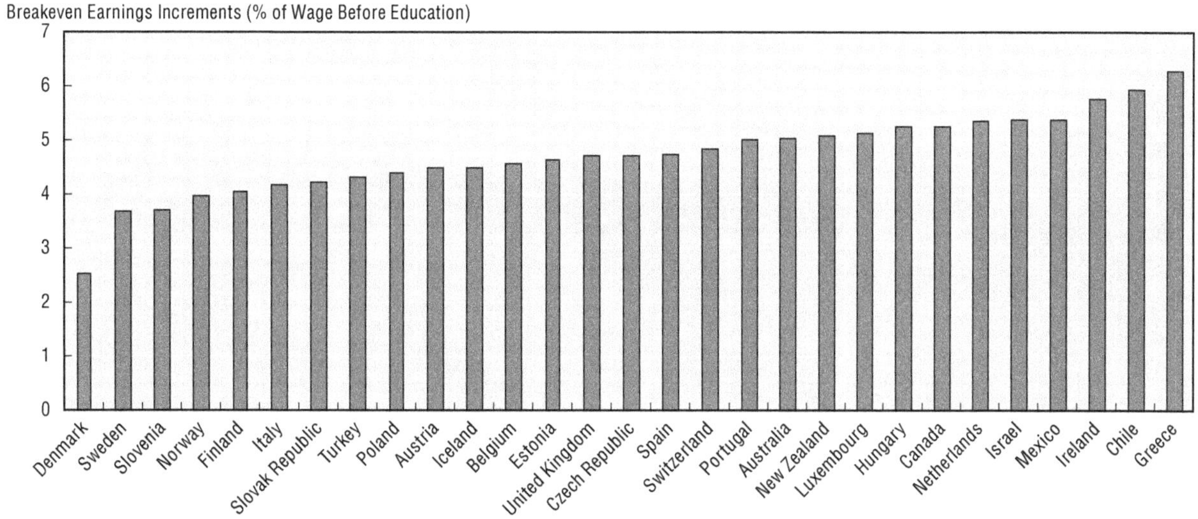

Note: Data are for a 27-year-old single taxpayer with no children, who undertakes a one-year course of non-job-related education, earning 25% of their wage before education during education. This figure shows results that incorporate tax deductions and tax credits for direct costs, tax exemptions for scholarship income, and reduced taxes on student wage income. Tax incentives in the personal income tax system and the social security contribution system are incorporated. The results do not incorporate STEs that subsidise parental spending on education or that subsidise firm spending on education. It is assumed that the skills investment is financed wholly with savings: students do not incur any debt to make a skills investment.

StatLink http://dx.doi.org/10.1787/888933446417

Despite these lower BEIs, METRs are often – though not always – higher in the model for graduate education than they are for tertiary education. They range from -16.2% (Denmark) to 27.7% (Ireland), with an un-weighted average of 7.6% (see Figure 4.12). These higher METRs result in large part from the impact of the tax rate on foregone earnings. The typical graduate student is assumed to earn the Average Wage if they do not enter education, whereas the typical university student is assumed to earn only 70% of the Average Wage. Tax progressivity means that the returns to skills investments are taxed away at a higher rate for the graduate student than they are for the typical university student, at least initially. Many of these METRs depend on the marginal tax rates on earned income over the middle of the income distribution; where these marginal rates are steepest, METRs are higher.

To calculate the AETR, a 5% increase in earnings from graduate education is assumed compared with those without graduate education.[6] As is the case throughout, AETRs are usually higher than the METRs, as the assumed returns to skills investments are higher than the breakeven level. This means that they are taxed away at a higher rate by a progressive tax system. Figure 4.13 shows that the AETRs range from 0.0% (Chile) to 42.2% (Ireland) with an average in the sample of countries of 24.6%. As is discussed in Chapter 3 of this study, the higher returns to average skills investments over marginal skills investments means that AETRs are often closer to the tax rate on the extra earnings that come after education. Thus, those countries that have high and progressive taxes are more likely to have a higher average tax burden on skills.

Figure 4.12. **Marginal effective tax rates on graduate education**

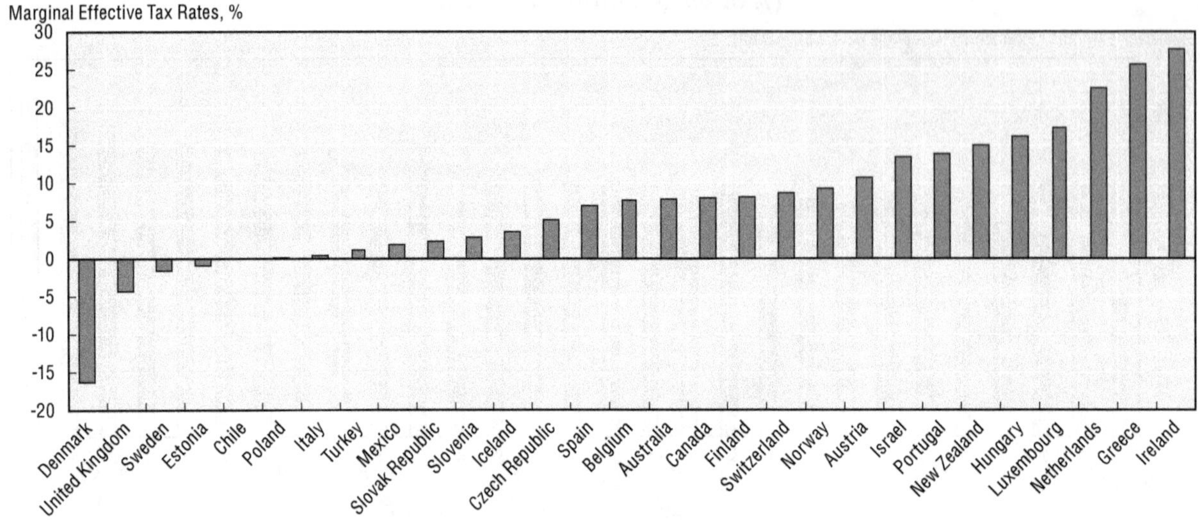

Note: Data are for a 27-year-old single taxpayer with no children, who undertakes a one-year course of non-job-related education, earning 25% of their wage before education during education. This figure shows results that incorporate tax deductions and tax credits for direct costs, tax exemptions for scholarship income, and reduced taxes on student wage income. Tax incentives in the personal income tax system and the social security contribution system are incorporated. The results do not incorporate STEs that subsidise parental spending on education or that subsidise firm spending on education. It is assumed that the skills investment is financed wholly with savings: students do not incur any debt to make a skills investment.

StatLink http://dx.doi.org/10.1787/888933446429

Figure 4.13. **Average effective tax rates on graduate education**

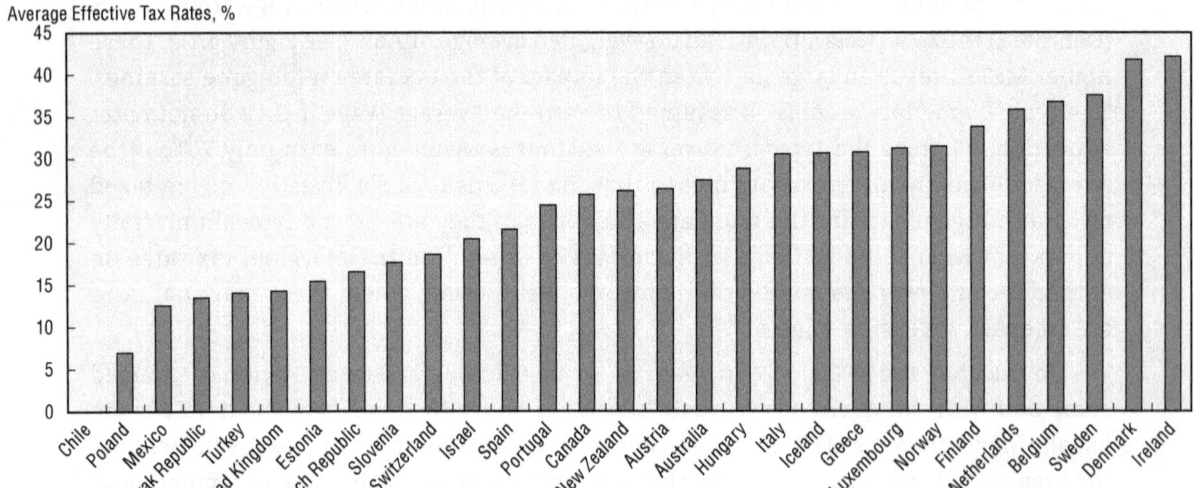

Note: Data are for a 27-year-old single taxpayer with no children, who undertakes a one-year course of non-job-related education, earning 25% of their wage before education during education. This figure shows results that incorporate tax deductions and tax credits for direct costs, tax exemptions for scholarship income, and reduced taxes on student wage income. Tax incentives in the personal income tax system and the social security contribution system are incorporated. The results do not incorporate STEs that subsidise parental spending on education or that subsidise firm spending on education. It is assumed that the skills investment is financed wholly with savings: students do not incur any debt to make a skills investment.

StatLink http://dx.doi.org/10.1787/888933446431

Figure 4.14. **Average effective tax rates on skills, marginal effective tax rates on skills and breakeven earnings increments varied by income before education: graduate student**

Tax rate by income level as % of average wage

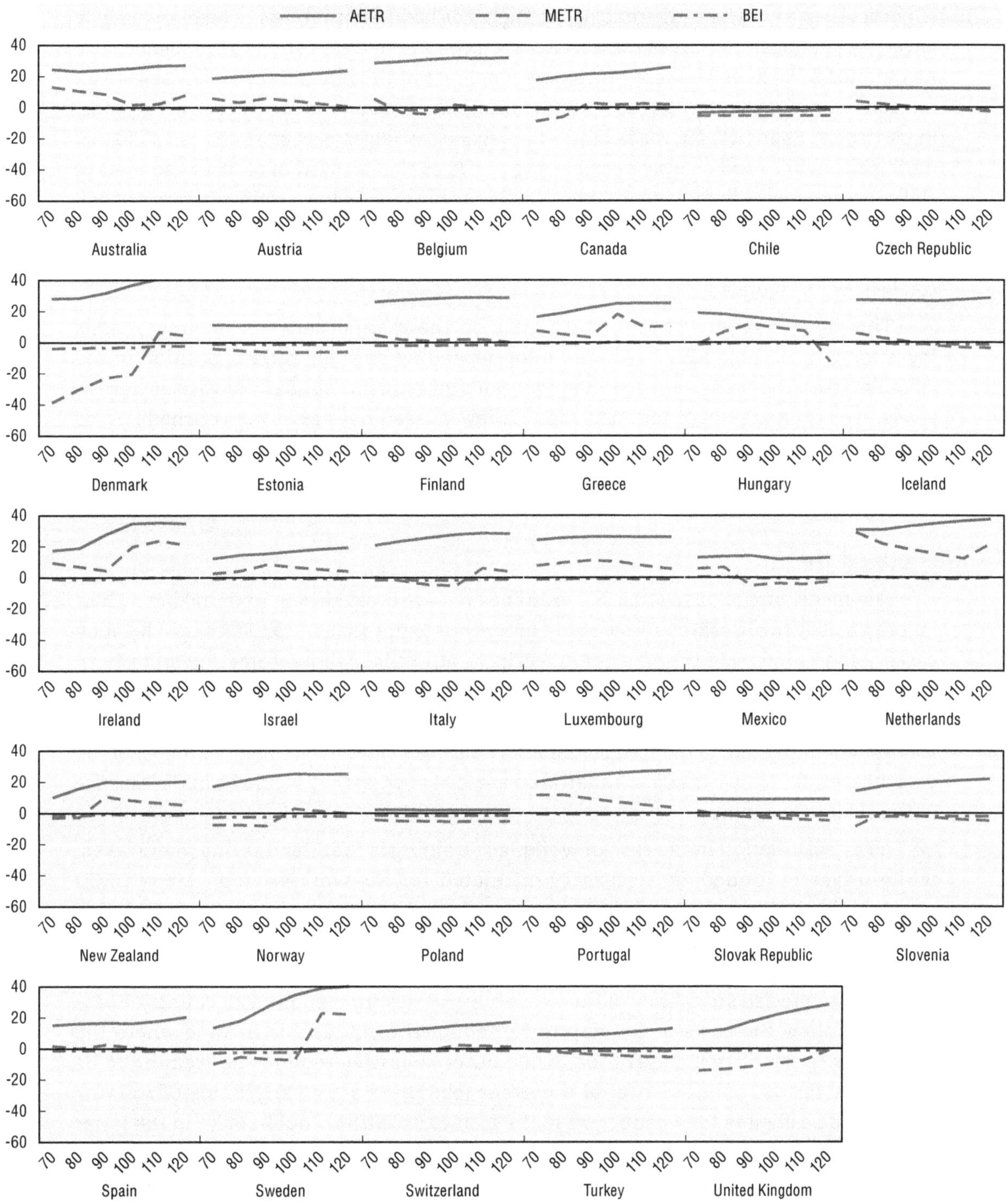

Note: Data are for a 27-year-old single taxpayer with no children, who undertakes a one-year course of non-job-related education, earning 25% of their wage before education during education. This figure shows results that incorporate tax deductions and tax credits for direct costs, tax exemptions for scholarship income, and reduced taxes on student wage income. Tax incentives in the personal income tax system and the social security contribution system are incorporated. The results do not incorporate STEs that subsidise parental spending on education or that subsidise firm spending on education. It is assumed that the skills investment is financed wholly with savings: students do not incur any debt to make a skills investment.

StatLink http://dx.doi.org/10.1787/888933446446

Figure 4.14 shows how the BEI, METR, and AETR vary with income. AETRs are usually rising in income before education. This is due to tax progressivity; being at a higher income level before education means that any extra earnings are taxed away at a higher rate. This is particularly true where the returns are high. For breakeven returns, which are usually lower, the relationship between the tax rate and income before education varies significantly. As outlined in Section 3.6 these METRs are a product of the interaction of the tax rate on foregone earnings with the tax rate on the earnings increment (this can be seen in Figure 3.6 in particular). Sharp rises in the tax rate on foregone earnings - because taxes fall suddenly during education - will sharply decrease the METR, as the tax system reduces the costs of skills investments. Similarly, sharp increases in the tax rate on the earnings increment will cause sharp rises in the METR, as extra earnings cause taxpayers to shift to higher brackets. These interactions cause the non-linear METR schedules over income before education that can be seen in Figure 4.14.

This figure suggests that for taxpayers on the margin between making a skills investment or not, the METR can vary a lot depending on their current position in the labour market. The tax system does not treat skills investments similarly at various income levels. This is an argument for ensuring that fewer steep rises exist in tax schedules, as these can exacerbate the METR on skills at certain points in the tax schedule. A shift to fewer brackets and away from large tax increases over narrow bands could be broadly friendly to investments in skills.

4.5 Job-related training

The model of workplace training examines a 32-year old person undertaking a short (approximately two-week) course of study. In contrast to the graduate and tertiary education cases, it is assumed that they are not in receipt of any scholarship income, but still pay an average amount of direct costs (usually tuition fees).[7] As with the graduate education case, it is assumed that earnings during education are a function of earnings before education. It is assumed that due to reduced labour effort during a skills investment, earnings in the year where a skills investment is undertaken are 95 % of what they would be in the absence of the skills investment.

A key assumption in the case of workplace training is that the training undertaken, while privately funded, is "necessary or related for the workers' job". Many OECD countries have STEs in their tax systems that offer tax deductions or credits for training where this training is job-related.[8] These STEs are often not available for education in general – they are not, for example, available for tertiary education or for normal graduate studies. The precise stringency of the availability varies from country to country. Some countries allow the costs of training to be deducted from taxable income where the training is "related" to a current job, while other countries require the training to be 'necessary for the maintenance' of a current job. There are clearly kinds of training that would be eligible for a deduction in the former case that would not be in the latter case. The model does not consider these nuances in detail; rather it simply makes a distinction between two broad categories: "job-related" training, which is modelled as eligible for all of these deductions and credits, and non-job-related training, which is modelled as ineligible.

As with tertiary and graduate education, a variety of simplifying assumptions are made. Just as tertiary education is significantly subsidised by parents in the OECD, so job-related training is likely to be heavily, if not wholly, subsidised by firms. The model does not, however, cover the effective tax rate on human capital investment by firms, as this would require a broader discussion of the effective tax rate on corporate income, which is beyond the scope of this study. This means that despite being job-related, the model assumes that the training is financed by the individual. As before, it is assumed that training is financed with savings, not with debt.

METRs on job-related training are usually, though not always, lower than those on graduate education, and often roughly similar in size to those on tertiary education. There are several drivers of this. First, the length of the education period considered here is the shortest of any of the kinds of education considered in this study. This means that the costs are the lowest of those modelled, directly and in terms of lost earnings. A result of this is that BEIs are similarly low. In this case, BEIs range from 1.16% (Iceland) to 1.7% (Chile), with an un-weighted average of 1.3%. These results are shown in Figure 4.15. This means that the amount that earnings need to rise tends to be comparatively small; reducing the impact of tax progressivity on the METRs.

Figure 4.15. **Breakeven earnings increments for job-related education (% of wage before education)**

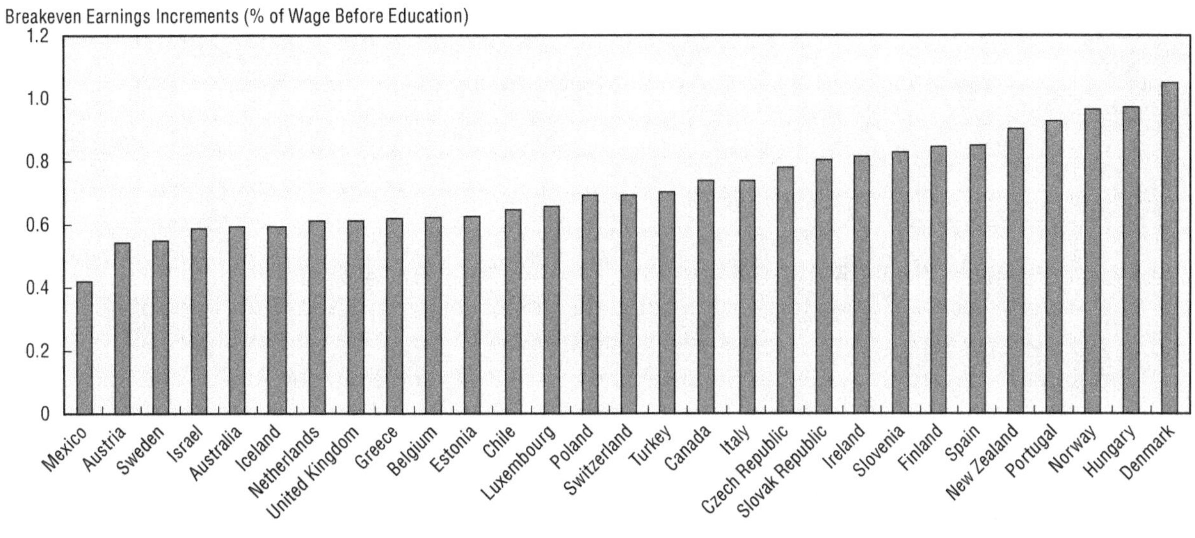

Note: Data are for a 32-year-old single taxpayer with no children, who undertakes a short course of job-related education, earning 95% of the average wage over the year while they study. This figure shows results that incorporate tax deductions and tax credits for direct costs, tax exemptions for scholarship income, and reduced taxes on student wage income. Tax incentives in the personal income tax system are incorporated, but not the social security contribution system. They do not incorporate STEs that subsidise parental spending on education or that subsidise firm spending on education. It is assumed that the skills investment is financed wholly with savings: students do not incur any debt to make a skills investment.

StatLink http://dx.doi.org/10.1787/888933446455

A second reason why METRs are low in this case is the impact of the tax deductions and exemptions discussed above. These offset many of the direct costs of education, and are usually not available in the two cases – graduate education and tertiary education – that have been discussed previously. While some STEs did exist in those cases – some countries do offer tax credits for the costs of tertiary education, and scholarship income is usually tax exempt – job-related training is usually in receipt of the largest amount of STEs. This means that METRs are comparatively modest, ranging from -15.1% (Mexico) to 10.6% (Norway), with an average in the sample of 1.8%. For most countries, however, the METR is between -1% and 5%. These results are shown in Figure 4.16. The efficiency of these tax expenditures is discussed further in Chapter 5.

Figure 4.16. **Marginal effective tax rates for job-related education**

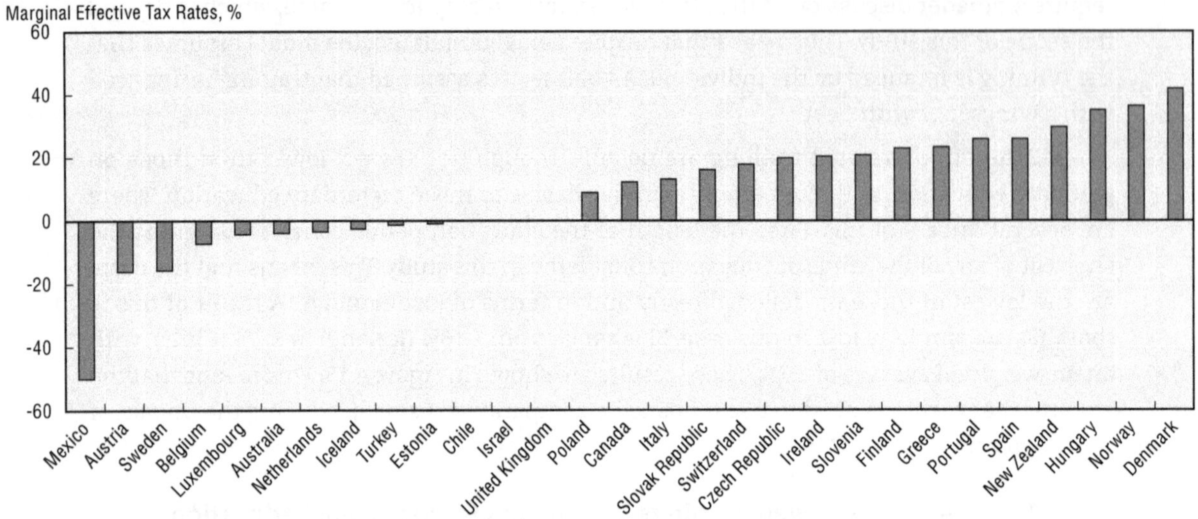

Note: Data are for a 32-year-old single taxpayer with no children, who undertakes a short course of job-related education, earning 95% of the average wage over the year while they study. This figure shows results that incorporate tax deductions and tax credits for direct costs, tax exemptions for scholarship income, and reduced taxes on student wage income. Tax incentives in the personal income tax system are incorporated, but not the social security contribution system. They do not incorporate STEs that subsidise parental spending on education or that subsidise firm spending on education. It is assumed that the skills investment is financed wholly with savings: students do not incur any debt to make a skills investment.

StatLink http://dx.doi.org/10.1787/888933446460

4.6 Lifelong learning

The model of a worker reskilling in later life examines a 50-year old person undertaking a one-year course of study. It is assumed that the worker can earn 25% of previous earnings, and that they are in receipt of some scholarship income. In contrast to the case of workplace training, it is assumed that the course is not "job-related" and so is not eligible for most tax deductions for skills expenditures. In doing so, the results highlight the fact that it can potentially be more costly to finance training that may involve changing careers than training that facilitates advances within careers. In this way, the tax system may place a hidden burden on labour market mobility and flexibility, though this will vary from country to country.

BEIs are among the highest in this example of any of the stylised cases considered, ranging from 4.2% in Denmark to 13.3% in Greece, with an average in the sample of 8.7% (see Figure 4.17). These values are higher than the value for a similar one-year course of education for 27 year-old, as examined in Section 3.2. This is because older workers have fewer years in which to recoup the cost of education. This means that the per-year amount by which earnings must increase is much higher. This is intuitive; workers who plan to retire soon may not benefit from leaving the labour market for a year to raise their earnings; after all, they may only be working for a few more years. This draws attention to the fact that it may be very difficult, and financially very costly, for the government to provide sufficient financial incentives for older workers to invest in skills, even when those workers face deterioration or obsolescence of their existing skills. It can become costly on a per-year basis for them to make such investments.

Figure 4.17. **Breakeven earnings increments for lifelong learning (% of wage before education)**

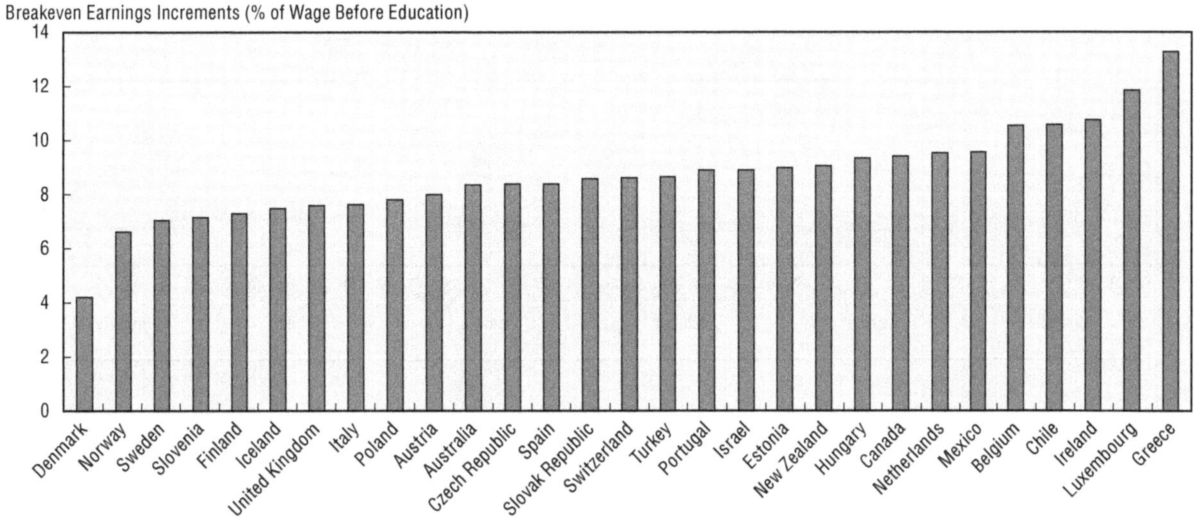

Note: Data are for a 50-year-old single taxpayer with no children, who undertakes a one-year course of non-job-related education, earning 25% of the average wage during schooling. This figure shows results that incorporate tax deductions and tax credits for direct costs, tax exemptions for scholarship income, and reduced taxes on student wage income. Tax incentives in the personal income tax system are incorporated, but not the social security contribution system. They do not incorporate STEs that subsidise parental spending on education or that subsidise firm spending on education. It is assumed that the skills investment is financed wholly with savings: students do not incur any debt to make a skills investment.

StatLink http://dx.doi.org/10.1787/888933446472

Figure 4.18 shows this pattern in further detail. It shows the BEI by income for three different ages of worker under similar circumstances: one year of non-job related education earning 25% of the previous wage. Ages are varied from 32 to 40 to 50 years old. The figure shows that the BEI rises steadily with age. This highlights the financial barriers that older workers have in pursuing educational opportunities.

There are of course key implications arising from these results in relation to the activation of older workers. Workers who have better skills and commensurately higher capacity to earn are more likely to remain in the labour market. Increasing the skills of older workers may provide a several-fold return to government; higher tax revenue while a worker continues to work, but also an expansion of the expected time that the worker remains a productive member of the labour force. This may provide a financial rationale for increased incentives to upskill workers early enough during their careers when returns will allow the investments to break even.

However, this logic works both ways; in this model, the more years that are left in the labour market, the more years a skills investment has to break even. This means that BEIs fall with the number of years left to retirement. A clear way to increase the incentives that workers have to upskill is to increase the number of years they expect to stay in the labour force by raising the retirement age.

Overall, the tax burden on skills investment of older workers is lower than that for similar younger workers. Figure 4.19 shows that average rates range from 0% (Chile) to 39% (Ireland) with an average value in the sample of 21%. Figure 4.20 shows that these rates are slightly lower for older workers than for younger workers.

Figure 4.18. **Breakeven earnings increments by age and income (% of wage before education)**

Breakeven earnings increment by income level as % of average wage

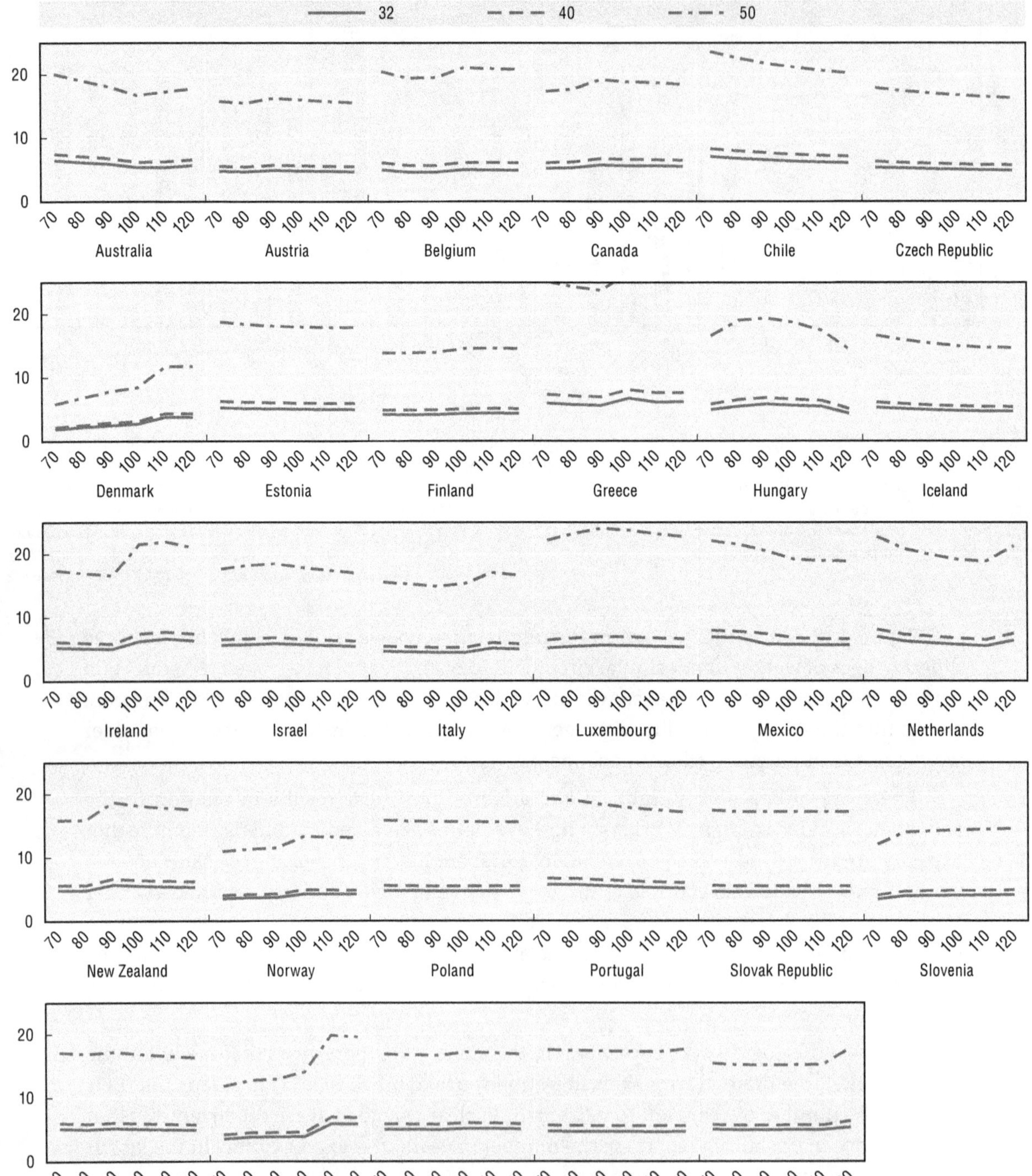

Note: Data are for a single taxpayer with no children, who undertakes a one-year course of non-job-related education, earning 25% of the average wage during schooling. This figure shows results that incorporate tax deductions and tax credits for direct costs, tax exemptions for scholarship income, and reduced taxes on student wage income. Tax incentives in the personal income tax system are incorporated, but not the social security contribution system. They do not incorporate STEs that subsidise parental spending on education or that subsidise firm spending on education. It is assumed that the skills investment is financed wholly with savings: students do not incur any debt to make a skills investment.

StatLink http://dx.doi.org/10.1787/888933446486

Figure 4.19. **Average effective tax rates on lifelong learning**

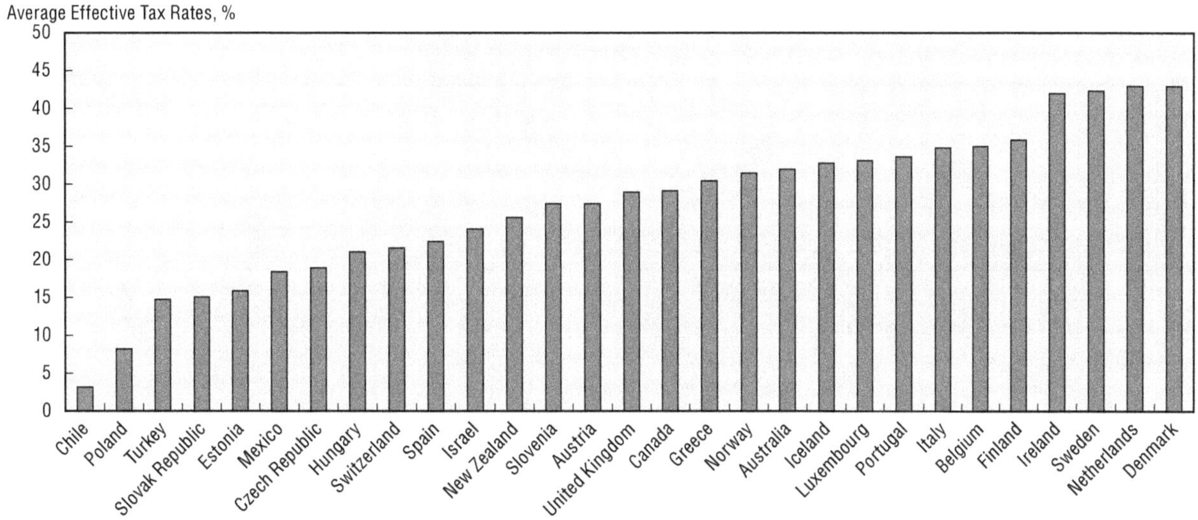

Note: Data are for a 50-year-old single taxpayer with no children, who undertakes a one-year course of non-job-related education, earning 25% of the average wage during schooling. This figure shows results that incorporate tax deductions and tax credits for direct costs, tax exemptions for scholarship income, and reduced taxes on student wage income. Tax incentives in the personal income tax system are incorporated, but not the social security contribution system. They do not incorporate STEs that subsidise parental spending on education or that subsidise firm spending on education. It is assumed that the skills investment is financed wholly with savings: students do not incur any debt to make a skills investment.

StatLink http://dx.doi.org/10.1787/888933446496

This seems counterintuitive: Figure 4.18 has shown that BEIs are higher where workers are older; however AETRs fall as workers age. The reason for this is in the discussion of the equation behind the AETR in Section 3.5. The AETR is the difference between the value of a skills investment with and without taxes, expressed as a fraction of the discounted value of the EI. The definition is restated below:

$$AETR = \frac{\textit{Skills Investment Value (Without Taxes)} - \textit{Skills Investment Value (With Taxes)}}{\textit{NPV of the Earnings Increment (with Taxes)}}$$

The returns to skills investments fall with age; this is because a worker has fewer years left in the labour market to earn any higher wages. This means the total difference in the returns with and without taxes also falls, even though it may not fall on a per-year basis. This means that the overall AETR falls with age.

Figure 4.20. **Average effective tax rates by age and income**

Tax rate by income level as % of average wage

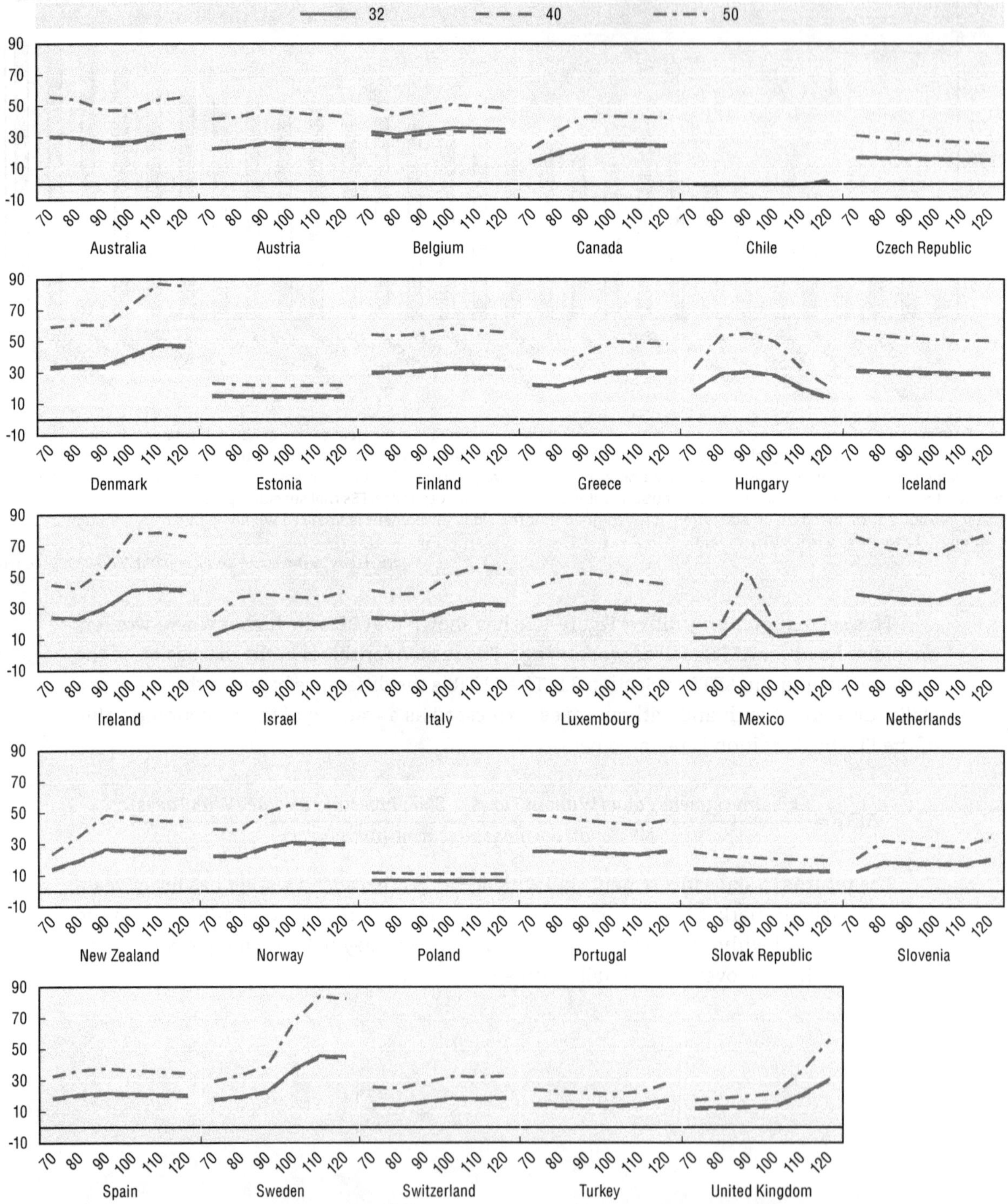

Note: Data are for single taxpayer with no children, who undertakes a one-year course of non-job-related education, earning 25% of the average wage during schooling. This figure shows results that incorporate tax deductions and tax credits for direct costs, tax exemptions for scholarship income, and reduced taxes on student wage income. Tax incentives in the personal income tax system are incorporated, but not the social security contribution system. They do not incorporate STEs that subsidise parental spending on education or that subsidise firm spending on education. It is assumed that the skills investment is financed wholly with savings: students do not incur any debt to make a skills investment.

StatLink http://dx.doi.org/10.1787/888933446503

4.7 Gender differentials

The returns to education differ widely for men and women. An important question in designing skills policies is whether the financial incentives to upskill are as strong for women as they are for men. Moreover, differing returns in the labour market to skills investments raises the question as to whether skills policies are properly calibrated.

The returns to skills investments may vary for women and men for various reasons. Female labour market participation is usually lower in OECD countries than that of men. Women may foresee that, in the period after a skills investment, they may be less likely to stay in the labour market over the remainder of their working-age life. This reduces their returns to skills investments, and may make some skills investments less worthwhile from a financial perspective. Some investments may make sense if an individual were to assume full labour market participation until retirement, but not if an individual foresees extended periods of labour market absence, or lack of labour market activity at all. In such cases, skills investments may not make financial sense.

These issues may be compounded where gaps exist in the returns to skills investments across genders. Figure 4.21 shows the size of the tertiary education earnings premium disaggregated by gender for the countries examined in this study. In most countries, going to university is more financially rewarding for men than it is for women. This is not the case for all countries: for Spain, Switzerland, and the United Kingdom the pattern is reversed as evidenced below.

Figure 4.21. **Earnings increment by gender**

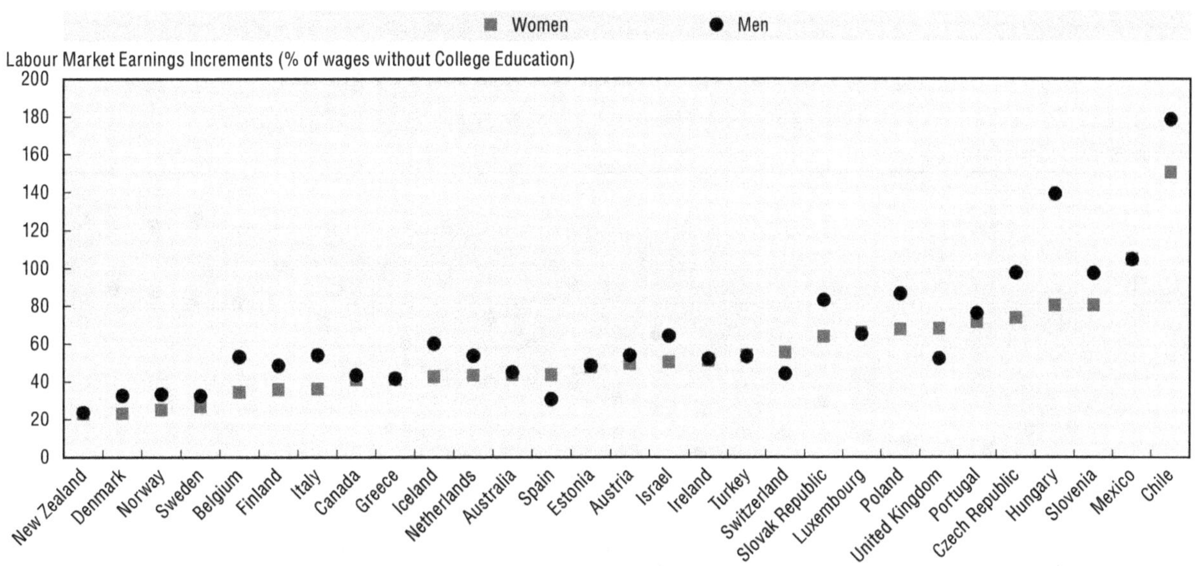

Note: Data are for 2011 where available.

Source: Data based on OECD Education at a Glance (2014), and author's calculations.

StatLink http://dx.doi.org/10.1787/888933446513

Reduced earnings for women may mean that a tertiary skills investment decision may not be optimal from the perspective of the student. Financial returns to skills investments may not exist for a given student; the breakeven earnings level may not be available for women when they invest in skills. Though these data are of course presented for average cases – as are the hypothetical BEIs in previous sections – they do point to a potential issue:

the gaps in wages and in labour market participation lead to different incentives to invest in human capital across gender.

There is evidence to suggest that even though the returns to skills investments may differ across gender, these differences may not be affecting enrolment rates too much. Recent OECD research (OECD, 2014) has demonstrated that enrolment rates at third level are usually higher among women than among men in OECD countries. This may be because the generation of women currently in third-level education may expect to see their wage rates and participation rates rise to parity with those of men over their working lives.

From the government's perspective, Figure 4.22 shows ARCRs for men and women. The calculations of the returns to government are based on the earnings data in Figure 4.21. In general, the government's returns from educating men are higher than its returns from educating women. This is due to higher expected wages for men than for women which means expected higher tax returns for the government, raising the ARCR. In the model, both genders cost the same amount to upskill. This means that those countries with the highest gaps in the ARCR are those countries that combine high or very progressive tax rates (so the government captures a substantial amount of the returns to skills investments) with comparatively high gaps in the tertiary education premium across gender (so that the returns to skills investments vary widely by gender). These gaps in the ARCR are highest for Hungary, Italy, Israel, and the Netherlands. By contrast, where the tertiary education premium is higher for women than for men, the gap in the ARCR by gender runs in the opposite direction; the returns to educating women are higher on average from the government's perspective. This is the case for Spain, Switzerland, and the United Kingdom.

Figure 4.22. **Average returns to costs ratio by gender**

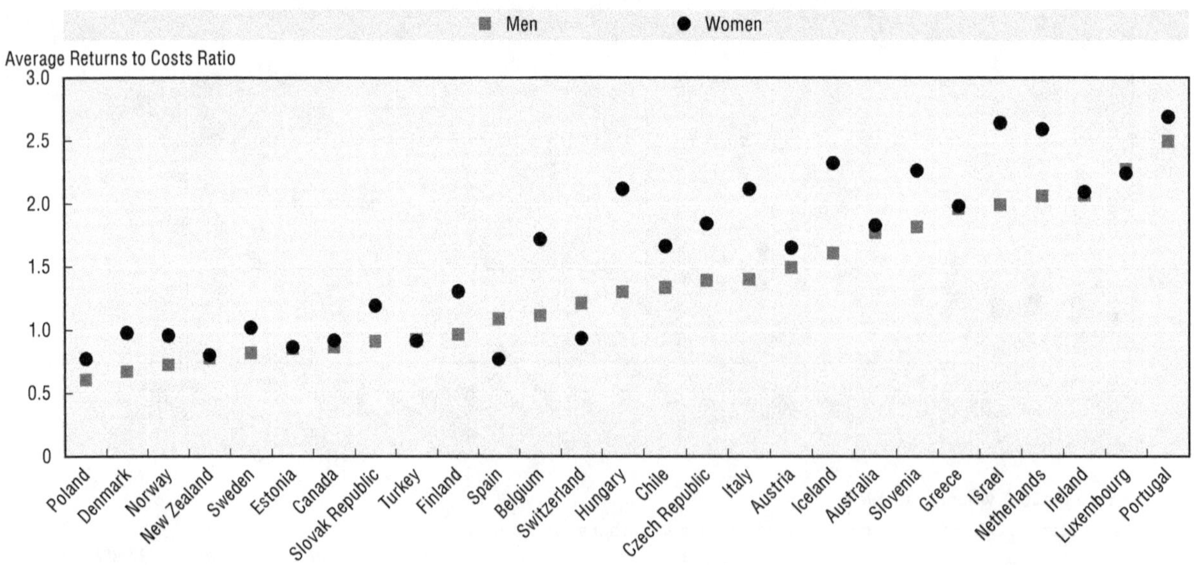

Note: Data are for a 17-year-old single taxpayer with no children, who undertakes a four-year course of non-job-related education, earning 25% of the average wage during schooling. This figure shows results that incorporate tax deductions and tax credits for direct costs, tax exemptions for scholarship income, and reduced taxes on student wage income. Tax incentives in the personal income tax system are incorporated, but not the social security contribution system. They do not incorporate STEs that subsidise parental spending on education or that subsidise firm spending on education. It is assumed that the skills investment is financed wholly with savings: students do not incur any debt to make a skills investment. Labour market data are based on the tertiary education premium earned by 15-64-year-olds.

StatLink http://dx.doi.org/10.1787/888933446524

These results present important challenges and opportunities for governments. The analysis suggests that for some governments the returns to education for women may be low due to the wage gap. Though this analysis does not account for gaps in labour market participation, accounting for these differences would likely increase the gap between the genders with respect to the returns to skills investments from the government's perspective. This means that reducing the wage gap by raising female labour market participation and raising female wage rates could see the government recoup a greater degree of its spending on skills investments for women.

Notes

1. These costs are discussed in Chapter 3.
2. Throughout, the results refer to 2011 USD.
3. This would also be the case in selected other countries with income contingent loan schemes that have not been modelled in this study. For example, this would also be the case in Canada for students with Canada Student Loans through the Repayment Assistance Plan, and other provincial/ territorial government loans through their respective repayment assistance plans.
4. This is discussed further in Section 3.3.
5. Note that the estimations of the costs of graduate education are the same as those for tertiary education. This is due to data limitations. These costs are discussed more in Chapter 3.
6. This is due to data limitations. There are good data on the premium earned in the labour market by tertiary-educated workers over non-tertiary-educated workers, but the data on the premium earned by graduate-educated workers over tertiary-educated workers is less comprehensive. A broad assumption of a 5% per annum return on the skills investment is made, while recognising that this misses a lot of between-country variation.
7. Note that the estimations of the direct costs of in-work training are the same as those for tertiary education. As with graduate education, this is due to data limitations.
8. See Chapters 2 and 5, and Annex B, for more details on STEs.

References

OECD (2014), *Education at a Glance 2014: OECD Indicators*, OECD Publishing, Paris, *https://doi.org/10.1787/eag-2013-en*.

OECD (2016), *Taxing Wages 2016*, OECD Publishing, Paris, *http://dx.doi.org/10.1787/tax_wages-2016-en*.

Chapter 5

Tax and non-tax financial incentives to support skills investments

This chapter analyses the costs and impact of specific tax expenditures aimed at encouraging skills investment. The chapter discusses tax expenditures targeted at tertiary education and lifelong earnings separately. The impacts on skills development are discussed, as well as the equity implications of the tax expenditures. Tax and non-tax approaches to encouraging skills investment are compared and analysed. The chapter concludes with a discussion of optimal policy mixes from a skills perspective.

The statistical data for Israel are supplied by and under the responsibility of the relevant Israeli authorities. The use of such data by the OECD is without prejudice to the status of the Golan Heights, East Jerusalem and Israeli settlements in the West Bank under the terms of international law.

5.1 Introduction

The support provided by the tax system to improve individuals' financial incentives to invest in skills varies widely. Chapter 4 of this study has provided estimates of the overall impact of the tax system on different kinds of skills investment decisions. The incentives to invest in skills depend on the overall personal income tax (PIT) system, but also on specific skills tax expenditures (STEs) countries have in their tax systems.[1] Some countries allow students to deduct the private costs of education from their taxable income or credit this expenditure against their tax liability; some countries exempt scholarship income from taxation; some countries exempt student income from social security contributions. Since all of these measures are designed to increase investment in skills, assessing their impact and comparing their impact to those of other skills policies is crucial in assessing the overall impact of the tax system on skills.

This chapter approaches these issues in several ways. It analyses the value of these financial incentives to different kinds of students at various income levels and for different kinds of skills investment scenarios. It also assesses the distributional impact of STEs, discusses students' responses to these incentives and presents estimates of the effects of these expenditures, by drawing upon analysis from the economic literature. The analysis in the chapter makes several key points.

- The value of STEs in the countries modelled is modest. Though dependent on the costs of skills investment and other assumptions, the results suggest that for university students, scholarship income and direct government support are much larger channels through which governments financially support skills investments.
- STEs are progressive. This means that the estimated value of these STEs is larger for those on lower incomes in most countries. STEs are more progressive for university students than they are for workers job-related training. This is particularly the case where the STEs are reduced social security contributions (SSCs) on student income.
- Direct support for university students in the form of direct grants and scholarships is more progressive than STEs, in part because direct support does not depend on an individual's taxable income, which is often the case for STEs.
- While the model notes that STEs can benefit those students on low incomes more than students on higher incomes, empirical research has suggested that the impact of these STEs on student outcomes such as enrolment and time-to-completion is modest or even zero.
- In order to be effective, STEs must be very carefully designed. Existing STE policies are often designed in ways that make it difficult for students to access them, in ways that do not encourage completion of courses of study in a timely manner, and in ways that do not encourage the completion of the kinds of education that might be most effective in raising wages and employment prospects.

- The impact of STEs on financial incentives to invest in skills is higher for those skills investments that yield low returns than for those skills investments that yield high returns. For high-return skills investments, the way the returns to skills are taxed away (i.e. tax progressivity) has a much larger impact than the way the costs of skills are offset (including STEs). For low-return skills investments, the support the financial system provides by reducing the costs of skills investments has a larger impact than the way these returns are taxed away.
- As policy levers to encourage investments in skills, STEs may be less effective in comparison to direct spending on educational institutions or direct support to students in the form of scholarships and grants.
- Existing skills tax expenditures are often only available where training pertains to a workers' current employment, and may not facilitate workers who need or want to change careers. These tax provisions may therefore reduce labour market flexibility and exacerbate skills mismatch.

These key points lead to important conclusions that clarify choices for policy makers when it comes to tax and skills. A uniquely "best" set of tax and skills policies does not exist. The ways in which tax and skills policies and indeed financial support for skills in general should be designed depends on the goals of the policy maker with respect to skills outcomes in a given country. As discussed in Chapter 4, the tax system apportions the costs and returns of skills investments between the student, firm and government. Where governments want a very progressive income tax system, a large amount of government support for skills investment will be required to maintain and expand the level of human capital in the economy. Where the tax burden on human capital is low, government support for skills investments can be more modest without excessively impacting students' and individuals' incentives to invest in skills – provided adequate support is provided to credit-constrained and otherwise disadvantaged students.

Other considerations must also be borne in mind when considering the impact of the tax system on skills. Tax expenditures are often more complex for governments to administer and for taxpayers to understand than direct spending on skills investment. Many tax expenditures are only of value to those students who earn taxable income. This means that they may be a costly way of investing in human capital for governments, and may have low take-up rates, especially among those with low incomes and low skills. Tax expenditures may not be as effective an approach to supporting skills investments as direct spending. Tax expenditures may also involve significant deadweight losses, providing subsidies to skills investments that would occur even in the absence of government support (though this may be true of direct spending on skills as well). To raise the overall level of skills in the economy, a combination of reduced labour income taxation and increased government support for those on low incomes or those who are credit constrained may be appropriate.

The chapter proceeds as follows. Section 5.2 reviews the size and impact of STEs. Section 5.3 reviews other non-tax approaches to improving students' financial incentives to invest in tertiary education, such as loans, scholarships and grants, and reducing tuition fees by providing more government support to educational institutions. Section 5.4 considers tax and non-tax issues targeted at lifelong learning and worker training. Section 5.5 concludes with an overall consideration of the role of the tax system in education finance and the system of incentives surrounding skills investment.

5.2 Tax incentives for tertiary education

This section analyses STEs for tertiary education. As has been outlined in Chapter 1, the returns to tertiary education are significant (OECD, 2015a). In most OECD countries, the government provides significant direct support for tertiary education (see Chapter 3, Section 3.1). By contrast, the support provided to tertiary education through the tax system is more modest. STEs supporting tertiary education come in several different forms, including:

- Exemption of scholarship income from personal income taxes or employee and employer SSCs,
- Exemption of student earnings from personal income taxes or employee and employer SSCs,
- Deductibility of tuition costs and other educational expenses from the personal income tax base,
- Tax credits by which skills expenditure can be credited against tax liability,
- Deductibility of interest on student loans from the personal income tax base,
- Income contingent loans.

This section will outline the approximate size of the value of these STEs for the stylised tertiary student outlined in Section 4.2, and will then discuss the impact of these expenditures on educational outcomes and income distribution. The section will conclude with a discussion of design considerations with regard to tax expenditures for tertiary education.

Size of tax incentives for tertiary education

This section provides estimates of the value of STEs in the sample of countries for tertiary education on a per-person basis. In assessing the value of these expenditures, the 'skills spending' that happens through the tax system can be assessed for stylised cases. This allows spending on skills that happens through the tax system to be compared with spending on skills that is provided directly, for example through direct grants to universities or students.

Assessing the overall value of STEs is challenging. These STEs may vary in value depending on the income of the taxpayer, the kind of education undertaken, the amount of tuition fees, the amount of scholarship income and other factors. Moreover, different STEs may exist in the same system, and may interact with each other. For example, student income may be exempt from social contributions, but increased student income may reduce eligibility for a tax-free scholarship. The model outlined in Chapter 3 of this study allows all STEs to be analysed together, to arrive at a general estimate of the value of these STEs for a stylised student.

In terms of the model as outlined in Chapter 3 of this study, the key parameter that will be analysed is the difference between the tax rates applied to earnings during education with and without STEs. This can also be expressed as:

$$\left(T_{E_d} - T^*_{E_d}\right)E_d,$$

where T_{E_d} is the rate of tax paid on in-education earnings E_d without STEs, and T^*_{Ed} is the rate paid on these earnings with STEs. Estimations of the value of STEs depend on a variety of factors and assumptions of the model, which are also discussed in Chapter 3 and in more technical detail in Annex A. For example, where scholarship income is tax exempt, those receiving larger amounts of scholarship income will receive a larger tax expenditure. In the model, an estimate of an average amount of scholarship income for each student in each country is taken, and the estimate of the size of the tax benefit stemming from the exemption of scholarship income depends on this assumption.

These estimates also depend on the income and family circumstances of the taxpayer. The results presented here are for single taxpayers without children. In addition, the model does not account for parental spending on education and for tax support for that spending.[2] This is due to the challenges of accounting for the mix of spending between parents and children, the nature of that spending (whether parental spending on children's education is an investment or consumption form of spending) and the apportionment of returns. These considerations all make it difficult to fully account for parental spending on education in the model.[3]

Figures 5.1 and 5.2 show an estimation of the size of STEs in the personal income tax system based on the stylised university education scenario outlined in Chapter 4. The university education case examines a 17-year old person undertaking a four-year course of study. University students receive an average level of government scholarship income and pay an average amount of direct costs.[4] Their earnings during education are set at 25% of the Average Wage in any given country – that is, students are assumed to earn some part-time employment income, but at a comparatively low level. Figure 5.1 shows the value of STEs in PPP 2011 US dollars. Figure 5.2 shows the value of STEs as a share of the average wage in a given country.

Figure 5.1. **Value of skills tax expenditures for tertiary students, in 2011 PPP USD, incorporating personal income tax only**

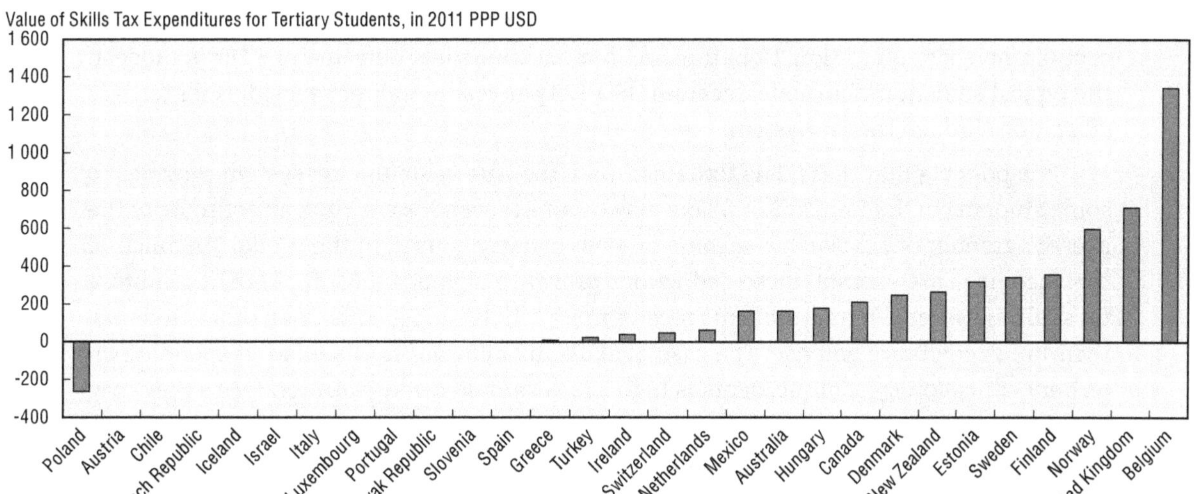

Note: Data are for a 17-year-old single taxpayer with no children, who undertakes a four year course of non-job-related education, earning 25% of the average wage during schooling. This figure shows results that incorporate tax deductions and tax credits for direct costs, tax exemptions for scholarship income, and reduced taxes on student wage income. Tax incentives in the personal income tax system are incorporated, but not the social security contribution system. The results do not incorporate STEs that subsidise parental spending on education or that subsidise firm spending on education. It is assumed that the skills investment is financed wholly with savings: students do not incur any debt to make a skills investment.

StatLink http://dx.doi.org/10.1787/888933446537

Figure 5.2. **Value of skills tax expenditures for tertiary students as a percentage of the average wage, incorporating personal income tax only**

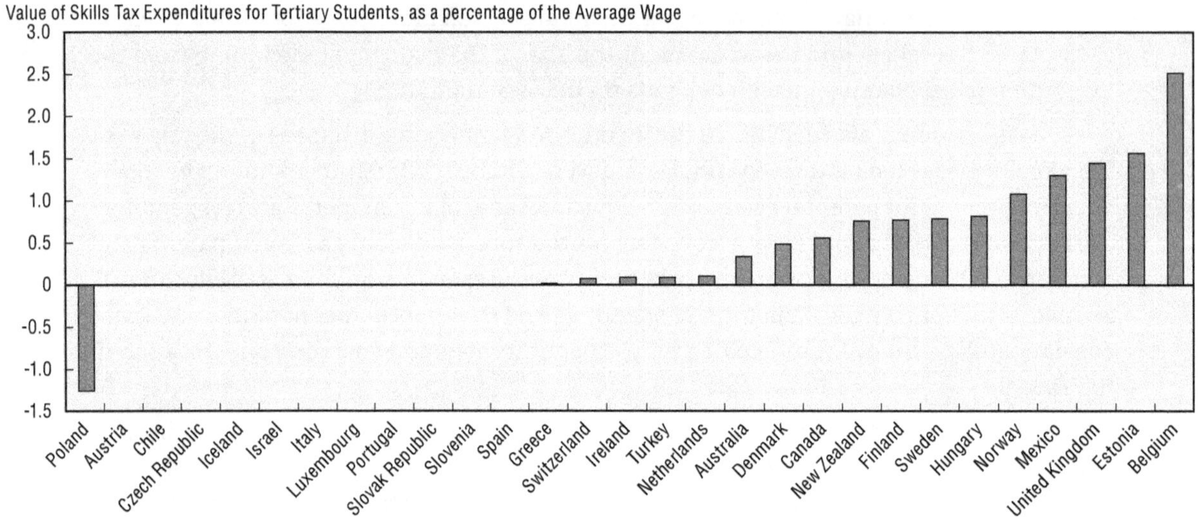

Note: Data are for a 17-year-old single taxpayer with no children, who undertakes a four-year course of non-job-related education, earning 25% of the average wage during schooling. This figure shows results that incorporate tax deductions and tax credits for direct costs, tax exemptions for scholarship income, and reduced taxes on student wage income. Tax incentives in the personal income tax system are incorporated, but not the social security contribution system. The results do not incorporate STEs that subsidise parental spending on education or that subsidise firm spending on education. It is assumed that the skills investment is financed wholly with savings: students do not incur any debt to make a skills investment.

StatLink http://dx.doi.org/10.1787/888933446543

The value of STEs as outlined in Figure 5.1 is comparatively small. Significant subsidies are provided through the tax system in Belgium, in Norway, and in the United Kingdom. These results are mainly driven by tax deductibility of scholarship income. In these three countries scholarship income is both tax deductible and large compared to the estimated cost of university education. Nonetheless, in most countries the value of STEs is modest: the typical student in the model receives USD 128 per year in indirect subsidies for tertiary education through the tax system.

It is possible that these data underestimate the true value the tax system provides to some students in the form of STEs. This may occur in several ways. First, an estimate of the average amount of scholarship income in each country is used in the model. As much of this income is tax-exempt, these deductions provide a significant form of tax expenditure for skills. However if certain students receive more scholarship income than other students, their tax expenditure will rise. The case of skills tax allowances is similar. If spending on tertiary education by some students is high – for example through tuition fees – they may benefit further from tax deductions for these skills investments than they do in the model.

It is notable that for several countries the estimated value of STEs at tertiary level is zero. For Iceland no such STEs are currently provided to students. For certain other countries such as Chile, Italy and Israel, STEs are available, but student income is assumed too low in the model for the STEs to be of benefit – students are already assumed to have little or no tax liability. This will be discussed further below.

It is notable that for Poland the estimates reported are negative. This can be explained by noting the results in the figure pertain to STEs in the personal income system only. This graph omits tax expenditures that may benefit students through SSCs. This conforms to the approach taken in Chapter 4, where only personal taxes are considered. A key method by which Poland and other countries support skills investments at the tertiary level is through reduced SSCs for students. However, as personal income tax in these countries is levied on income net of SSCs, reducing these contributions means that taxable income net of these contributions rises, and so PIT liability also rises. This results in the negative effect, when only PIT is accounted for in the graph.

Figure 5.3 reports the value of STEs incorporating SSCs. The graph shows that STEs that come in the form of SSC reductions (as is the case in Poland) are significant in size compared to STEs that come in other forms. For some countries it alters the value of STEs. Incorporating these provisions, the typical student in the model receives USD 860 per year in STEs for tertiary education through the tax system, a substantial increase from the USD 128 discussed above. Countries like Poland, with negative support for skills in the PIT system and countries such as Slovenia and the Slovak Republic who do not provide support for skills through the PIT and SSC systems are shown to have significant support when tax exemptions for SSCs on student income are taken into account. These results are dependent on the amount of student income being earned. Many of the STEs being provided through the SSC system are reductions on student wage income, meaning that those with higher wages will see the value of their STEs rise.

Figure 5.3. **Value of skills tax expenditures for tertiary students incorporating employee and employer social security contributions, in 2011 PPP USD**

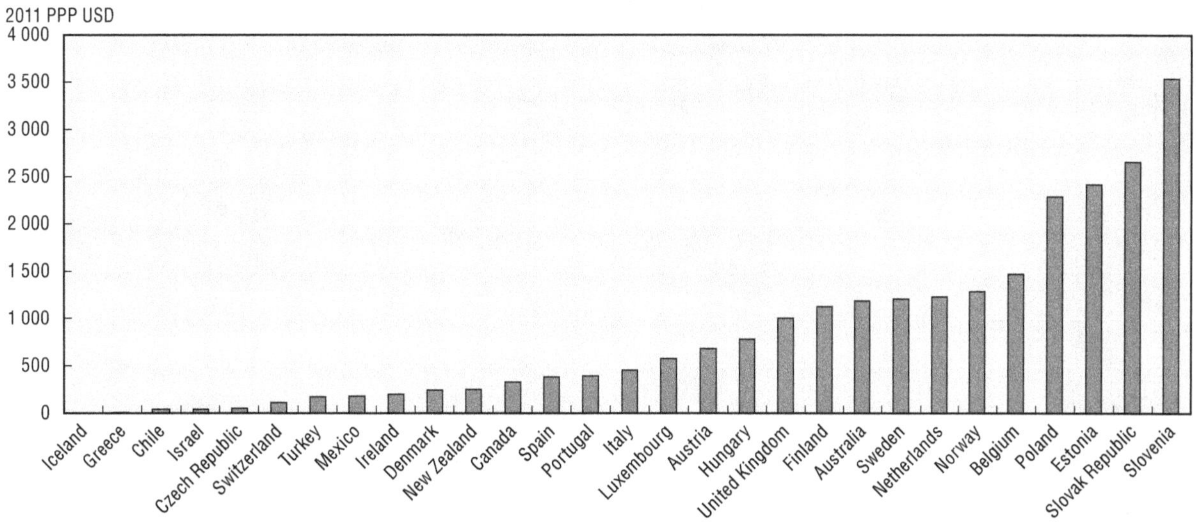

Note: Data are for a 17-year-old single taxpayer with no children, who undertakes a four-year course of non-job-related education, earning 25% of the average wage during schooling. This figure shows results that incorporate tax deductions and tax credits for direct costs, tax exemptions for scholarship income, and reduced taxes on student wage income. Tax incentives in the personal income tax system and with regard to employee and employer social security contributions are incorporated. The results do not incorporate STEs that subsidise parental spending on education or that subsidise firm spending on education. It is assumed that the skills investment is financed wholly with savings: students do not incur any debt to make a skills investment.

StatLink http://dx.doi.org/10.1787/888933446553

The model shows overall that the value of STEs remains modest for tertiary education, especially compared to direct support for tertiary education provided by governments. This section has also noted that there are reasons to believe that this support is heterogeneous across the population in the group of countries analysed. The value of STEs is often conditional on tuition fees, scholarship income, and wage income for students. In addition, significant support is provided in the form of reduced SSCs on student income. As students on low incomes or from low-income households are more likely to receive scholarship income, and work during their years of tertiary education, it is likely that those students from low-income households receive more benefit from the tax system than is estimated in the model.

Impact of tax incentives for tertiary education

This section assesses the impact of STEs on financial incentives to invest in skills. Specifically, this section considers the extent to which the presence or absence of these STEs impact the Breakeven Earnings Increment (BEI), the overall indicator of incentives to invest in skills in the model. It also assesses the extent to which the presence or absence of STEs affects the overall indicators of the impact of the tax system on financial incentives to invest in skills, the Marginal Effective Tax Rate on Skills (METR) and the Average Effective Tax Rate on Skills (AETR).

Figure 5.4 shows the BEI for the typical stylised tertiary education student. With STEs, the data are the same as those presented in Chapter 4. Also shown are values of the BEI in the absence of STEs. In most OECD countries the BEI is higher in a world without STEs than in a world with STEs. This suggests that in the OECD countries considered, STEs reduce the amount of earnings needed to break even on a skills investment over time for a hypothetical student. This is only for a specific educational context (the 17-year old university student as discussed above) and for a specific set of assumptions about educational costs and scholarship income levels. As the value of STEs is closely associated with the values of these educational costs and scholarship income levels, these results reflect these assumptions.

Figure 5.4. **Breakeven earnings increments on skills with and without skills tax expenditures, incorporating personal income tax only**

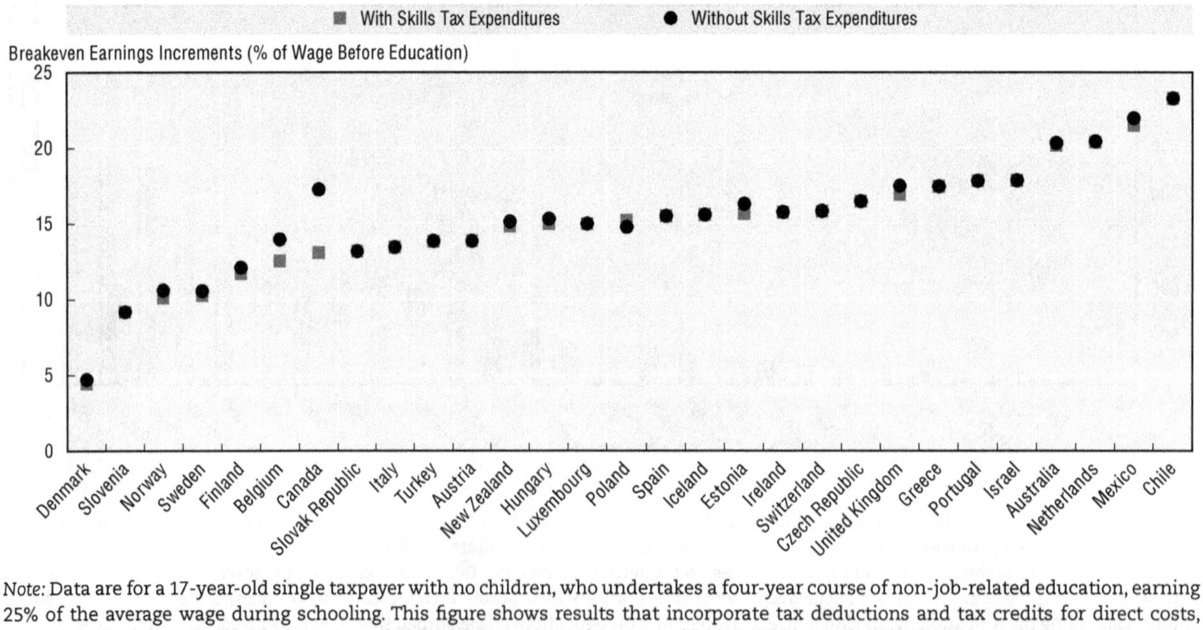

Note: Data are for a 17-year-old single taxpayer with no children, who undertakes a four-year course of non-job-related education, earning 25% of the average wage during schooling. This figure shows results that incorporate tax deductions and tax credits for direct costs, tax exemptions for scholarship income, and reduced taxes on student wage income. Tax incentives in the personal income tax system but not the social security contribution system are incorporated. The results do not incorporate STEs that subsidise parental spending on education or that subsidise firm spending on education. It is assumed that the skills investment is financed wholly with savings: students do not incur any debt to make a skills investment.

StatLink http://dx.doi.org/10.1787/888933446568

Figures 5.5 and 5.6 analyse the changes in the METR and AETR when STEs are not taken into account. While Figure 5.4 showed the impact of STEs on overall incentives to invest in education or not, Figures 5.5 and 5.6 show whether METRs and AETRs are impacted by STEs. The extent to which METRs and AETRs are impacts by STEs measures whether the impact of the tax system on financial incentives to invest in skills occurs mainly through the impact of STEs or it occurs through other tax factors such as the taxation of returns to education.

Figure 5.5. **Marginal effective tax rates on skills with and without skills tax expenditures, incorporating personal income tax only**

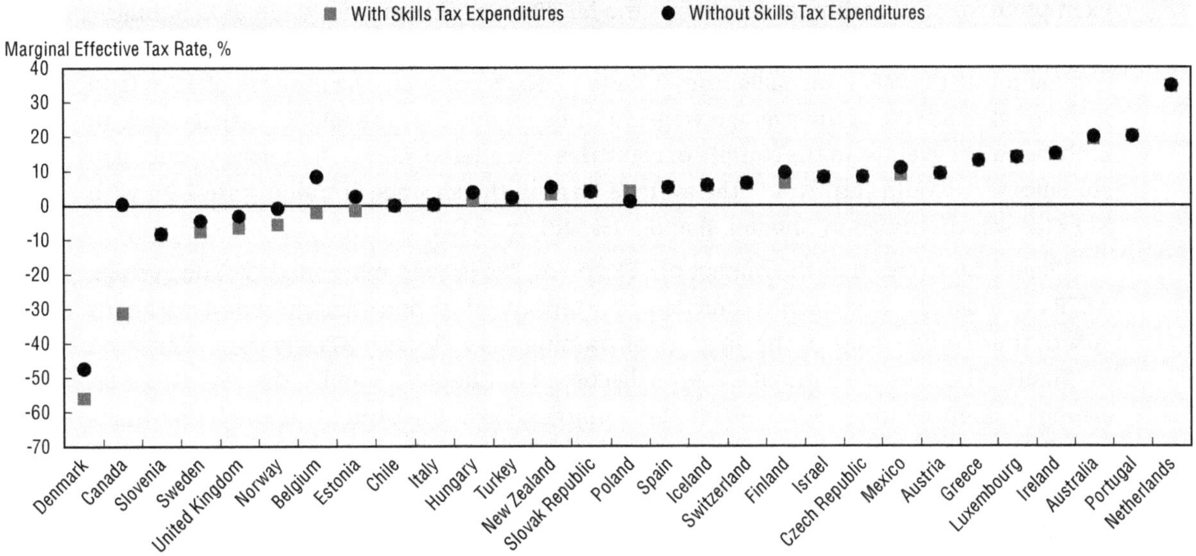

Note: Data are for a 17-year-old single taxpayer with no children, who undertakes a four-year course of non-job-related education, earning 25% of the average wage during schooling. This figure shows results that incorporate tax deductions and tax credits for direct costs, tax exemptions for scholarship income, and reduced taxes on student wage income. Tax incentives in the personal income tax system but not the social security contribution system are incorporated. The results do not incorporate STEs that subsidise parental spending on education or that subsidise firm spending on education. It is assumed that the skills investment is financed wholly with savings: students do not incur any debt to make a skills investment.

StatLink http://dx.doi.org/10.1787/888933446578

Figure 5.6. **Average effective tax rates on skills with and without skills tax expenditures, incorporating personal income tax only**

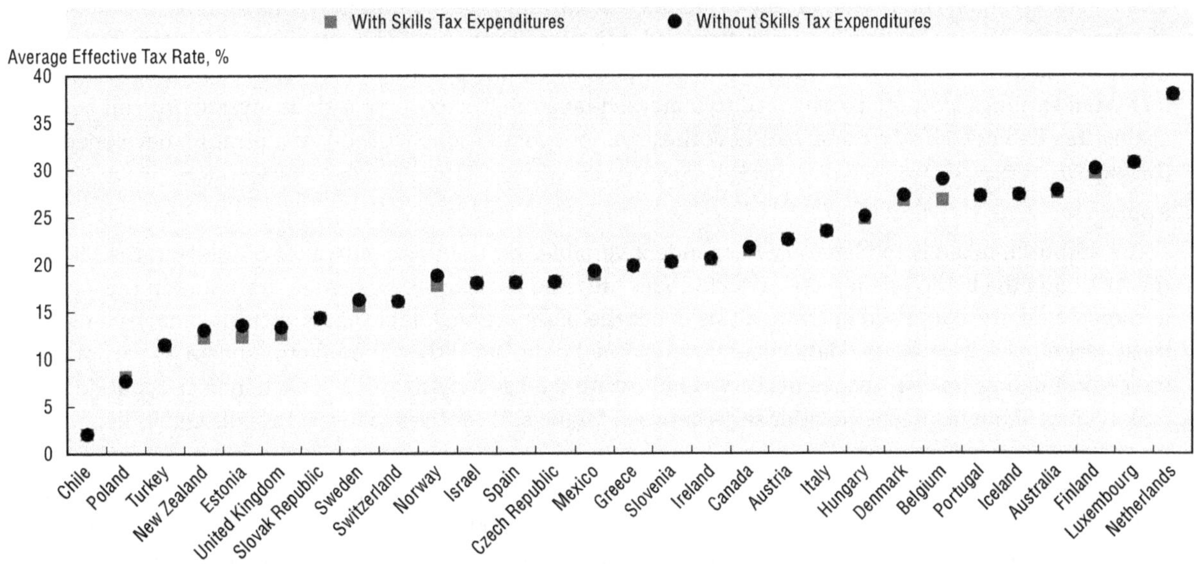

Note: Data are for a 17-year-old single taxpayer with no children, who undertakes a four-year course of non-job-related education, earning 25% of the average wage during schooling. This figure shows results that incorporate tax deductions and tax credits for direct costs, tax exemptions for scholarship income, and reduced taxes on student wage income. Tax incentives in the personal income tax system but not the social security contribution system are incorporated. The results do not incorporate STEs that subsidise parental spending on education or that subsidise firm spending on education. It is assumed that the skills investment is financed wholly with savings: students do not incur any debt to make a skills investment.

StatLink http://dx.doi.org/10.1787/888933446585

Figure 5.5 shows that the STEs do reduce the METR on skills for most of the countries considered, although modestly in most countries. For example, removing Norway's tax exemption for scholarship income raises the METR on skills from -5.6% to -.85%. Similarly removing Belgium's tax deduction for student income and tax exemption for scholarship income raises the METR on skills from 3.2% to 8.3%. By contrast, the absence of STEs (and income taxes at 70% of the average wage) in Chile means that the METR on skills is 0% in both cases. On average in the sample of countries considered, METRs for tertiary education students who would earn 70% of the average wage in the absence of training are 2.9% with STEs (as was discussed in Chapter 4) and 5.1% without STEs.

Figure 5.6 shows that the impact of STEs on AETRs is even more modest. The average AETR in the sample of countries considered for tertiary education students who would earn 70% of the average wage in the absence of training is 19.1% with STEs (as was discussed in Chapter 4) and 20.5% without STEs. As discussed in Chapters 3 and 4, the tax rate on an average skill investment is larger than on a marginal skill investment, as the larger-than-marginal return on an average skill investment is usually taxed away by progressive taxation.

A regression analysis of the STEs on these three key dependent variables suggests that the impact of STEs on incentives to invest in skills is indeed modest (see Box 5.1). However, this does not mean that the tax system overall has no impact on incentives to invest in skills. Specifically, the extent to which the tax system offsets foregone earnings, or taxes away the returns to skills was shown to have a larger impact on the overall financial incentives to invest in skills (as measured by the BEI) than STEs.

Box 5.1. **The Drivers of the Tax and Skills Statistics**

This box examines the drivers of the key indicators of the tax and skills system outlined in Chapter 4, the METR on Skills, the AETR on Skills, and the BEI on Skills. As discussed in Chapters 3 and 4, incentives to invest in skills depend on a wide variety of factors; lost earnings, the potential returns to skills, the amount of scholarship income available, tuition fees and non-pecuniary costs. The tax system impacts financial incentives to invest in skills in a variety of ways; reduced earnings during study lead to reduced taxation; increased earnings after study may lead to increased taxation; the costs of a skills investment can be set against tax liability. This box analyses how these various factors impact the key indicators developed in this study.

Approach

The approach taken is to regress key dependent variables on the three outcomes of interest: the METR, the AETR and the BEI. While regression techniques are used to analyse the results presented in this study in more detail, the data used in the analysis is not the observational data that is typically analysed using these techniques. Because the data is not observational data, but rather manufactured data as part of the indicator-building process, the results serve to illustrate the key moving parts of each indicator, but do not make claims about the deeper relationships between financial incentives to invest in skills and individuals' responses to these incentives.

The key variables used are the tax rate on foregone earnings (TFE) and the tax rate on the earnings increment that individuals earn after education (TEI). A variable for STEs is also included (STE). This variable is expressed as the difference between the take-home income of a student who works while studying with and without STEs (normalised to thousands of 2011 PPP USD for all countries). Student income before education is also included to measure the opportunity costs of education (INCb). The number of years of education is also included (Years). A sample regression equation is presented below:

$$Y_{ij} = \beta_0 + \beta_1 T\_FE_{ij} + \beta_2 T\_EI_{ij} + \beta_3 STE_{ij} + \beta_4 INCb_{ij} + \beta_5 Years_{ij} \varepsilon_{ij}$$

Box 5.1. **The Drivers of the Tax and Skills Statistics** *(cont.)*

Each *i* is a particular person or education scenario, and each *j* is a country. The variable T_FE_{ij} is the tax rate on foregone earnings for person *i* in country *j*. The variable T_EI_{ij} is the tax rate on an earnings increment for person *i* in country *j*. STE_{ij} is the value of STEs accruing to person *i* in country *j*. The β coefficients measure the impact of a given explanatory variable on the outcome variable Y_{ij}. Country fixed effects are included throughout.

Results

Column 1 shows the impact of various aspects of the tax system on the BEI. As discussed in Chapters 3 and 4, this shows the extent to which gross earnings must rise after a skills investment is made in order to break even on that skills investment. The coefficient on the TFE variable shows that higher taxes on foregone earnings decrease the costs of investing in skills and so reduce the earnings increment needed for a worker's investment to break even. For example, Column 1 shows that when the taxes on foregone earnings increase by one percentage point (such as from 18% to 19%), the BEI decreases by 0.19 percentage points.

This is a key means by which the tax system impacts on financial incentives to invest in skills. When workers engage in skills investments, their incomes fall. This is less the case when taxes are present than when they are not; the tax system offsets this cost component of skills. These indirect costs of skills investments including the impact of the tax system on foregone earnings seldom feature in the literature on ways to incentivise skills investments. This analysis shows that the BEI of a skills investment is quite sensitive to personal income taxes which reduce foregone earnings during periods of investment.

Converse results are obtained for the effects of the TEI on the BEI. The regression in Column 1 shows that the TEI has a comparatively higher, but negative impact on the incentives to invest in skills: an increase in TEI increases the BEI. The impact of STEs is also noticeable – a USD 1 000 increase in the extent to which the tax system offsets the direct costs of skills is associated with a reduction in the BEI by .5%.

Table 5.1. **Regression results**

Dependent Variable	(1)	(2)	(3)
	BEI	METR	AETR
Taxes on Foregone Earnings (FE)	-0.192***	-1.357***	0.017
	-0.006	-0.02	-0.012
Taxes on the Earnings Increment (EI)	0.227***	1.500***	0.461***
	-0.006	-0.018	-0.011
Skills Tax Expenditures	-0.519***	-6.572***	-1.310***
	-0.092	-0.296	-0.176
Income Before Education	0.366***	1.401***	1.887***
	-0.064	-0.206	-0.123
Years of Education	3.807***	-0.418***	-2.133***
	-0.024	-0.079	-0.047
Sample Size	11 880	11 880	11 880
Adjusted R-Squared	0.743	0.426	0.508

Note: Data incorporate tax deductions and tax credits for direct costs, tax exemptions for scholarship income, and reduced taxes on student wage income. The results do not incorporate STEs that subsidise parental spending on education or that subsidise firm spending on education. Stars indicate for the statistical significance of the coefficients. *** means that the variable is significant at the 1% level, ** at the 5% level and * at the 10% level.

The logic behind the key levers in the tax system in Column 1 is clear. The tax system impacts financial incentives to invest in skills in two important ways: it offsets costs both through tax expenditures and through reducing foregone earnings and it reduces the returns through the taxation of higher post-education earnings. These findings are further illustrated in Column 2, which shows similar results for the three key tax variables on the METR. Higher TFEs mean lower BEIs and METRs, higher TEIs mean higher BEIs and METRs. More generous STEs raise incentives to invest in skills for marginal students.

Box 5.1. **The Drivers of the Tax and Skills Statistics** *(cont.)*

These similar coefficients highlight that the BEI and the METR are closely linked – the BEI measures financial incentives to invest in skills for a marginal student, the METR measures the extent to which the tax system affects these incentives. Figure 5.7 confirms the intuition regarding the overall impact of the tax system. This figure shows a positive correlation between the METR and the BEI. Each data point in the graph is a country-observation; multiple observations per country are different age and income levels in each country. The METR presented in the graph includes not only both tax rates on foregone earnings and on the earnings increment but also specific STEs. There is a strong positive correlation between the two variables. Higher taxes, as evidenced by the METR, impact the individual's incentives to invest in skills.

Figure 5.7. **Correlations between the breakeven earnings increment and marginal effective tax rate on skills**

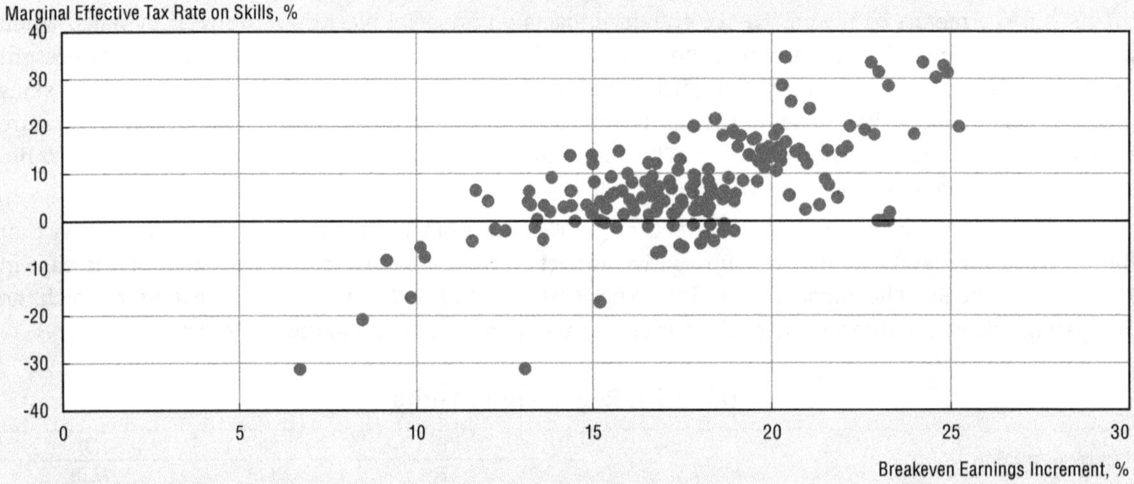

Note: This figure shows results that incorporate tax deductions and tax credits for direct costs, tax exemptions for scholarship income, and reduced taxes on student wage income. The results do not incorporate STEs that that subsidise parental spending on education or that subsidise firm spending on education.

The relationship between the METR, the TFE and the TEI is further illustrated in Figure 5.8. The horizontal and vertical axes show the TFE and TEI respectively. The strong positive correlation between the TFE and the TEI can be seen in the figure: on average, when TFEs are high, TEIs will be high as well. Figure 5.8 shows that the PIT systems of the countries included in the study are progressive on average as TEIs are typically higher than the corresponding TFEs. This progressivity effect results in higher METRs. In fact METRs are increasing in the difference between the TEI and the TFE. METRs are lower in cases where TFEs are more similar to TEIs, such as in the case of a proportional tax system.

The relationship between these two constituent taxes and the METR can be seen by examining the colours in Figure 5.8. Darker colours represent higher METRs. METRs are darker in the top left of the figure where tax rates on the earnings increment are high, and tax rates on foregone earnings are low. These are two ways in which the tax system can incentivise investment in skills: by reducing the costs and increasing their returns.

Column 3 of Table 5.1 shows the same variables regressed on the AETR. In this case, the effects of the TEI are the same as in the marginal case however the effect of foregone earnings is not statistically significantly different from zero. This means that for the average student, the extent to which the tax system reduces the costs of skills through reduced taxation of foregone earnings is not a significant driver of the overall impact of the tax system on incentives to invest in skills. The way the tax system taxes away the returns to skills is an important driver, but the extent to which it reduces the costs of skills is not.

Box 5.1. **The Drivers of the Tax and Skills Statistics** *(cont.)*

Figure 5.8. **Cross-country correlations between tax rates on foregone earnings, tax rates on breakeven earnings increments, and the marginal effective tax rates on skills**

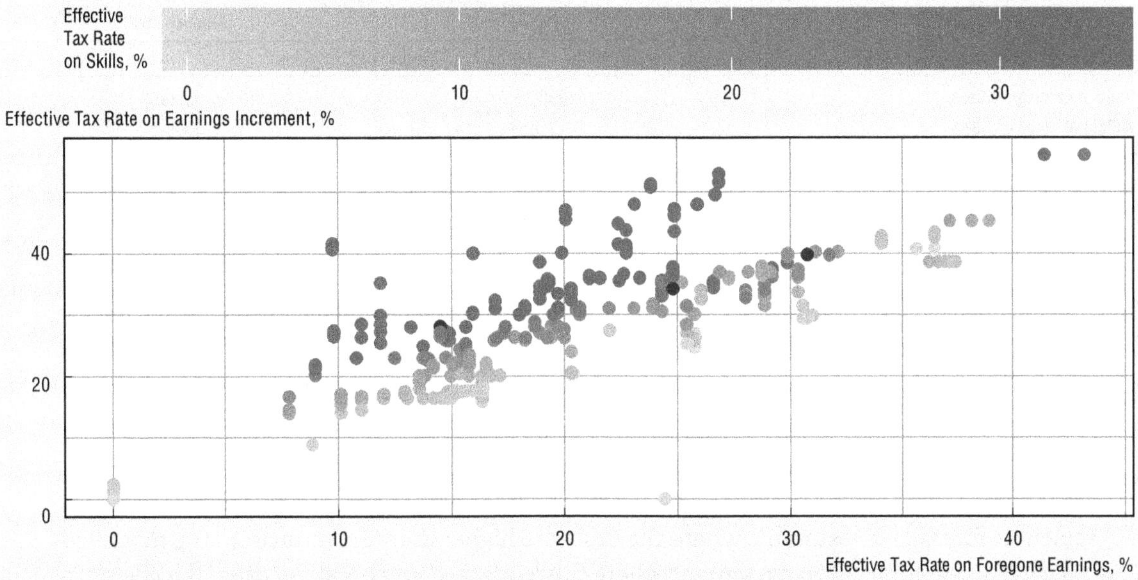

Note: This figure shows results that incorporate tax deductions and tax credits for direct costs, tax exemptions for scholarship income, and reduced taxes on student wage income. The results do not incorporate STEs that that subsidise parental spending on education or that subsidise firm spending on education.

These results can be understood by considering the components of the METR and AETR. A marginal student is just breaking even on a skills investment; therefore their costs are high compared to their returns. An average student, by contrast, receives much higher returns than costs. The comparative weight of costs and returns is mirrored in the impacts of the tax system – the returns are higher in the average case, the tax rate on these returns has a greater weight in the AETR. By contrast, the TFE matters more for the marginal student, where the ratio of returns to costs for the student is lower. For the average student with fairly high returns to skills, the impact of the tax system on incentives to invest in skills through taxing foregone earnings is overshadowed by the impact through taxing away returns. The different effects are summarised in Table 5.2.

These results highlight key differences between average and marginal students in terms of how the tax system affects their decision to invest in skills. For marginal students, the returns to skills are modest compared to the costs. Therefore the tax treatment of the costs matters more for the overall METR than the tax treatment of returns for these students. By contrast, for a student earning a greater-than-marginal return, the tax treatment of costs may not matter as much as the tax treatment of returns in determining the tax systems overall impact on that student's decision to invest in skills.

This in turn has important implications for how the tax system can be designed to encourage skills investment. For the average student, a tertiary skills investment yields a significant return (Heckman and Jacobs, 2010). To encourage students to make these investments, or to attract and retain new students into a country to make these investments, reducing the tax rate on the return to skills is an important policy lever – which may mean reducing the level or progressivity of the income tax system.

However, for low-return skills investments, lowering the tax rate on the return to skills may have little impact. Low-return skills investments may include skills investments in declining sectors of the economy, or skills investments by students who have low aptitude in a given area or low innate skills. To encourage these kinds of skills investments, reducing the progressivity of the labour income tax system may have little impact on skills investments. Action on the costs side of skills investment is what is required.

Box 5.1. **The Drivers of the Tax and Skills Statistics** *(cont.)*

Table 5.2. **Effects of income on the AETRs and METRs on average in the tax systems of 30 OECD countries**

	Average Student	Marginal Student
	Impact of Tax System	
Ratio of Earnings to Costs	Higher	Lower
Weight of Taxes on Costs	Lower	Higher
Weight of Taxes on Returns	Higher	Lower
Impact of TEI	Strong	Strong
Impact of TFE	Weaker	Strong

Regression analysis in Box 5.1 also suggests that STEs also had very little impact on the AETR. Average skills investments are usually profitable: the returns are much larger than the costs. This means that the fact that the tax system taxes away the returns to skills matters much more overall than the impact of the tax system on the costs of skills investments.

STEs are more impactful for marginal and low-return skills investments. The impact of the tax system on the costs of STEs is a much larger part of the overall skills investment calculus for skills investments where the costs are higher than the returns. In the modelled cases of a marginal skills investment where the student is just breaking even, the costs are the same as the returns. In these cases, the impact of STEs on the overall skills investment calculus is more significant.

Empirical analyses of impact of tax incentives for tertiary education

The above analysis has sought to quantify the overall size of STEs in the sample of countries considered, as well as to assess their impact on the key indicators developed in this study. The overall impact of STEs is modest for a typical student, though it may be larger for students in receipt of larger amounts of scholarship income, with larger amounts of tuition expenses, or with larger amounts of student earned income. This section provides some evidence of the impact of STEs on the tertiary enrolment and completion outcomes for students.

The country that uses the tax system to encourage skills investment most is the United States. Details of the STEs in the United States are discussed in more detail in Annex D of this study. Turner (2011) finds the introduction of tax-based student aid increases full-time enrolment in the first two years of tertiary education. However, recent empirical studies suggest that expansion of the key tax credits for education expenses used in the United States – the expansion of the American Opportunity Tax Credit over its predecessor, the Hope Tax Credit has no statistically significant effect on the tertiary enrolment decisions of students. Bulman and Hoxby (2015) find, using two separate identification strategies including regression kink and simulated instruments, that the credit does not increase enrolment. This is not to say that the credit provides no financial benefit to certain students who receive them. Rather, the results suggest that near the phase-out portion of the schedule that the reduction in credit amount does not impact enrolment, and also that the expansion of the credits does not induce students to enroll. Similar effects are found in other research for the tax deduction for post-secondary education (Hoxby and Bulman, 2015). Though only based on one country with comparatively high tuition fees, these results suggest that two key kinds of STEs used in the OECD – tax credits for education expenses and tax deductions for education expenses – may be limited in their impacts on student outcomes.

In a further US study based on the enactment of the tax credit programs in 1998, and from the increase in the value of the Lifetime Learning Tax Credit and introduction of the Tuition Deduction between the 1999-2000 and 2003-04 school years, Turner (2012) finds that for a subset of four-year institutions, that the schools reduced aid to students in response to the tax subsidies. By examining tertiary tuition prices, he finds that much of the increases in financial resources provided to students through the tax cut were captured by tertiary institutions by decreases in school grant aid. It may be that these extra resources increased the quality of education available to those students who did attend university, but this is difficult to demonstrate. These results suggest crowding out of student aid provided by tertiary institutions in the United States: credits targeted at reducing student costs may in fact be a form of subsidy to educational institutions through the tax system. Though this research raises questions as to the efficacy of tax credits as a means to raise skills investments, it is possible that tuition fee responsiveness will be lower in non-US OECD countries, which have more heavily regulated tertiary sectors. This means that other countries may have more success in using these kinds of credits to reduce the costs for students.

Some modest effects for tax credits are found by other authors. Guzman (2013) finds that in the US tax credits for education caused more students to attend private for-profit colleges, which may suggest that the credits allow students to attend more expensive for-profit schools, though effects at the intensive margin may not exist. In a subsample of 30 and 40 year-olds, LaLumia (2012), finds that while the Lifetime Learning Tax Credit had no statistically significant effect on average, eligibility for an education tax subsidy was associated with an increase in the probability of tertiary attendance among "men whose 1998 educational attainment falls short of early-life educational expectations". This conclusion supports the OECD data analysis presented above. While STEs targeted at average students may not have significant impacts as a means of increasing skills investments, STEs may have an impact among students with low potential returns to skills investments. Positive impacts of STEs on enrolment are also found by Bednar and Gicheva (2013), but with respect to graduate education instead of tertiary education.

The evidence on reducing taxes on student labour income also suggests that this policy lever may not be ideal for governments. Reduced social contributions on student wage income are a significant source of government support for students. However, there is also need for caution – increasing the amount of student part-time work may reduce credit constraints for students from low-income families, but may negatively impact educational outcomes for these students. Using data from a Swedish reform, Avdic and Gartell (2015) find that when financial aid policies changed to give students an incentive to work longer hours, some students worked more. This in turn negatively impacted the amount of time required to complete a degree for some students. While reducing the tax burden on student work may provide students with increased resources with which to invest in education, it may do so while depleting their ability to study and complete their degrees.

There are different reasons why STEs may be of limited use in encouraging skills investments at tertiary level. Cameron and Heckman (1999) argue that a wider variety of factors are behind the decision not to attend university in addition to financial factors. For low-income families, the non-pecuniary costs of attending a tertiary institution (lack of motivation, lack of success in secondary education, lack of family role models, lack of information) may constitute an additional burden to tertiary attendance. This means that attempting to increase tertiary enrolment by using STEs without addressing other obstacles may prove ineffective. Similar conclusions are discussed in Cunha et al. (2006) and in Heckman and Jacobs (2010). They find that the overall education decision comes with both pecuniary costs (tuition fees, lost earnings) and non-pecuniary costs (study effort, lost leisure time). In such situations where pecuniary costs are heavily subsidised, they may crowd out non-pecuniary costs such as study effort. In such situations, they argue "high subsidies on education may then go hand in hand with long study durations, high drop-out rates and low student performance" (Heckman and Jacobs, 2010).

The evidence suggests that the existing STEs are of limited effectiveness in increasing the amount of skills investments at tertiary level. In addition, these policies may have unintended consequences such as increased tuition fees by universities in response to tax credits, or reduced student effort or longer student working hours which can increase time-to-completion of degrees. Dynarski et. al. (2015) point to many design flaws with the system of STEs in the United States, which limit their effectiveness.

Distributional impact of tax incentives for tertiary education

A key component in the discussion of tax and skills policy is the distributional impacts of STEs. As discussed in Chapter 1 of this study, skills policies are a key inclusive growth policy measure. Increasing the human capital for those whose existing levels are low has many beneficial effects; it raises wages, productivity and labour market attachment. By decreasing wage inequality, it reduces the need to implement distortionary taxes and pay benefits to reduce disposable income disparities. Assessing tax and skills policies from the perspective of those with low skills and low incomes is crucial for assessing these policies' effectiveness.

The distributional aspects of tax and skills policies have two related but distinct dimensions. Tax and skills policies can be addressed towards those with low incomes but for whom skills investments will be very profitable; those with low incomes but strong innate skills. Skills investments yielding high returns are very beneficial from the perspective of addressing income inequality. But another distributional margin is also important: that between low-return skills investments and high-return skills investments. Box 5.1 has described how STEs have larger effects on a marginal skills investment than on an average skills investment. Policies that reduce skills costs may benefit low-return skills investments more than policies that reduce the taxation of those returns.

These policies – that may benefit a marginal skills investment more than an average skills investment – may also yield positive distributional outcomes. In providing benefits to skills investments with low returns, policies targeted at reducing skills costs are beneficial in that they may provide larger benefits to those with low innate skills, who may receive lower benefits from further skills investments than those with higher skills. In providing benefits to those making these investments, these policies may simply offer a form of insurance against the unlucky: those who have made a skills investment yielding positive expected net returns to investment but negative actual returns. This means that these policies are a potential targeted measure towards those whose lifetime income is expected to be low.

Figure 5.9 assesses STEs in the sample of countries by income before a skills investment. It shows the impact of removing all STEs including SSCs on the BEI – the same data as Figure 5.4 – but varies the results over the income distribution. It shows, in part, whether these STEs raise financial incentives to invest in skills more for those on lower incomes or those on higher incomes. In other words, analysing BEIs with and without STEs over the income level is the same as analysing whether these STEs are progressive with respect to income before education.

Figure 5.9. **Breakeven earnings increments on skills with and without skills tax expenditures, incorporating employee and employer social security contributions**

Tax rate by income level as % of average wage

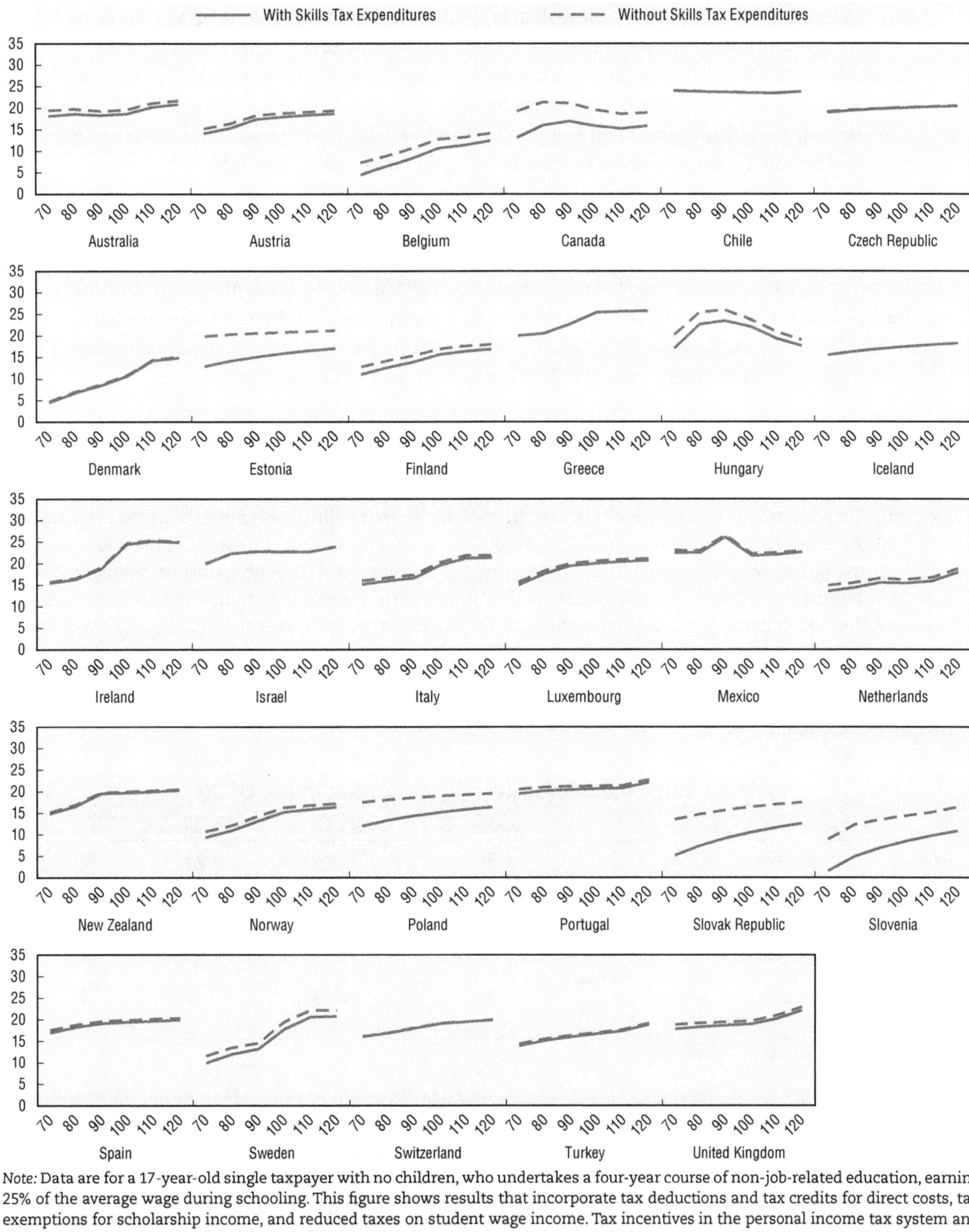

Note: Data are for a 17-year-old single taxpayer with no children, who undertakes a four-year course of non-job-related education, earning 25% of the average wage during schooling. This figure shows results that incorporate tax deductions and tax credits for direct costs, tax exemptions for scholarship income, and reduced taxes on student wage income. Tax incentives in the personal income tax system and with regard to employee and employer social security contributions are incorporated. The results do not incorporate STEs that subsidise parental spending on education or that subsidise firm spending on education. It is assumed that the skills investment is financed wholly with savings: students do not incur any debt to make a skills investment.

StatLink http://dx.doi.org/10.1787/888933446597

Figure 5.9 shows that in the OECD these STEs are usually progressive; though not always. For some countries, STEs are modest in size (for example, in Greece, Turkey, and Switzerland). In these countries, their impact is not particularly large for university students, either at the higher or lower end of the income distribution. However, in other countries, STEs exist that provide proportionally larger reductions in the necessary breakeven returns to skills to those on low incomes than to those on higher incomes. These BEI gaps are likely a result of provisions that exempt some student wage income from taxes or SSCs (e.g. Belgium). There are also some countries for which the proportional reduction in the BEI remains broadly constant across the income levels considered (e.g. for Norway and Sweden).

A key factor in the degree of progressivity of STEs is that many of them come in the form of allowances or credits, so that resources spent on skills investments can be claimed against taxable income or tax payable. However this means that the credits provide value when a taxpayer is making a skills investment and has some taxable income. Students with no taxable income will in general receive less benefit from tax allowances and credits than other students, unless the credit is fully refundable. This may make STEs in the form of deductions and credits less progressive than other forms of STEs. This is discussed further in Box 5.2.

Box 5.2. **Carry-forwards of Tax Credits in the OECD**

Six countries in the sample considered in this study provide tax credits for tertiary education. A drawback of tax credits for education is that they may not benefit students from low-income families, who may not have sufficient tax liabilities to benefit fully from the credit. This is also the case with respect to tax allowances. Details of the credits as they existed in 2011 are provided in Table 5.3. Different countries deal with this issue in different ways. Some countries (such as the United States) make the credit partially refundable, to ensure that low-income households benefit from the credit. Other countries such as Canada allow the value of the credit to be transferred to other members of the household, though this may not be effective if other household members also have low incomes. Finally, some countries including Canada and Israel allow a student to carry forward the value of the credit to future years. A full carry forward of STEs is further analysed by Stantcheva (2015).

Table 5.3. **Tax credits for university education in the OECD**

	Amount (for single households)	Minimum Value	Maximum Value	Refundable	Carry Forward
Canada	15% of eligible expenses	None	None	No	Yes
Israel	ILS 2 508	NA (fixed amount)	NA (fixed amount)	No	Yes
Ireland	20% of eligible expenses	EUR 2 000[1]	EUR 7 000	No	No
Italy	19% of eligible expenses	None	None	No	No
Portugal	30% of eligible expenses	None	EUR 475	No	No
United States	100% of first USD 2 000 of expenses less related scholarships and 25% of next USD 2 000 of expenses less related scholarships.	None	USD 2 500	Yes	No

1. In Ireland, this value was EUR 3 000 in 2016.

Canada's Tuition Tax Credit provided a 15% non-refundable tax credit of the costs of tuition in 2011 (the year estimated in the model underlying this study). There was no limit on the amount of tuition that could be claimed, but claims must have been higher than CAD 100. In addition, the credit could be carried forward against future tax liability for students who do not exhaust the value of the credit in the first year, or transferred to a supporting individual. In addition to the AOTC (American Opportunity Tax Credit) presented in Table 5.3, the United States has the Lifetime Learning Tax Credit that is not refundable. The AOTC also phases out at USD 80 000 (see Annex D).

Box 5.2. **Carry-forwards of Tax Credits in the OECD** *(cont.)*

Figure 5.10 shows the value of the refundability of the tax credit for students compared to a no-refundability scenario at various income levels, for various costs of education. Students at low income levels gain more by being able to carry forward the value of the credit. Students with higher fees benefit more still. This shows that making tax credits refundable specifically benefits those with low resources during education and higher costs of education.

Figure 5.10. **Extra value accruing due to tax credit carry-forward, by annual cost of education**

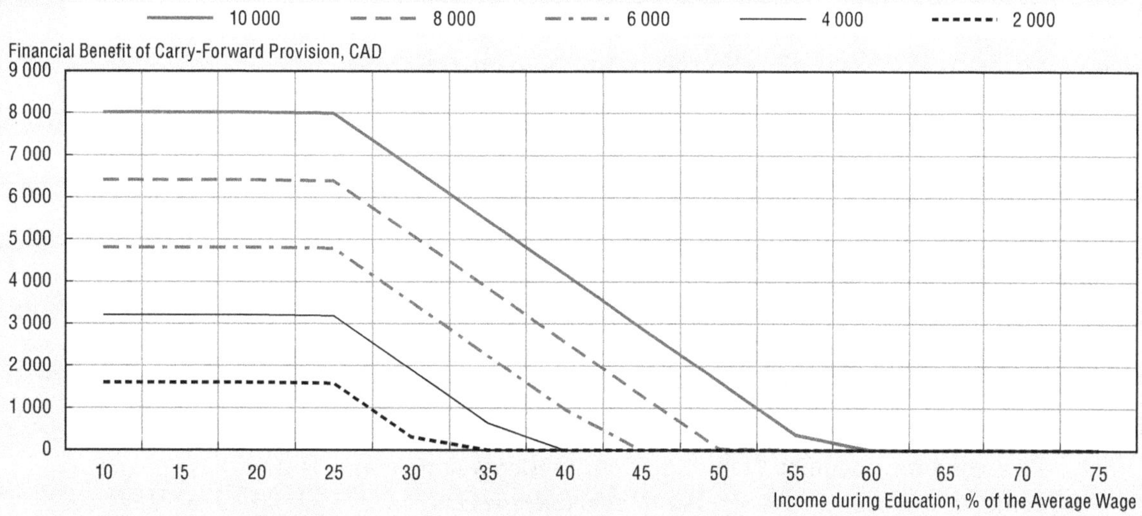

Note: This figure shows results that incorporate tax deductions and tax credits for direct costs, tax exemptions for scholarship income, and reduced taxes on student wage income. The results do not incorporate STEs that subsidise parental spending on education or that subsidise firm spending on education.

The richest academic studies assessing the distributional impact of STEs are based on the US experience (Bulman and Hoxby, 2015; Hoxby, 1998; Turner, 2012). The US tax credits are partially refundable, and also phase-out at higher income levels (see Annex D for further details). Bulman & Hoxby argue convincingly that the tax credits for education provide greatest benefits for middle classes, but do so inefficiently. Poorer households tend not to have sufficient tax liability to benefit from the credits, or are in receipt of direct grants to support skills investments. Higher income households tend to pass the phase-out period of the credit, and so receive little benefit. In the United States these tax benefits are focused on those at the middle of the income distribution.

One approach to increase the value of tax allowances or credits as a form of STEs has been to allow the value of these credits or allowances to be carried forward to future years. Stantcheva (2015) argues that a system of tax deductions with full carry-forward can ensure that those on low incomes or whose skill investments yield low returns benefit from STEs as much as higher income individuals or those whose skills investments yield high returns, providing similar benefits to a system of income-contingent loans. A partial carry-forward system has been implemented in Canada; the Canadian credit can be transferred (up to a dollar limit) to a supporting individual such as a parent, and/or carried forward for use in subsequent years (see Box 5.2). While this approach may not provide the full benefits of a credit to low-income households in net present value terms, it improves the equity of such credits relative to a non-refundable credit without a carry-forward provision.

Design considerations of tax incentives for tertiary education

The above discussion has highlighted potential issues with STEs as a means of increasing the level of skills investments. These instruments may be biased against individuals with low skills and households with low incomes. There is mixed evidence about the extent to which STEs achieve their goals when it comes to tertiary education. Nonetheless, these tools remain an important part of the policy mix in many OECD countries. With this in mind, this section discusses several key recommendations that should be considered when tax policy makers are designing STEs for tertiary education so that their impact can be maximised.

The literature in the area of tertiary-based STEs has highlighted that the complexity of STEs can reduce their effectiveness. OECD countries provide scholarships, grants, student loans, tax deductions and tax credits to students and parents, as well as tax or SSC reductions for student work. Many STEs interact with each other; in some countries it is not possible to benefit from some provisions with some others. Eligibility criteria for loans, deductions, credits and student grants can be designed in an uncoordinated way. Interactions between different aspects of the tax and student support system must be designed in a holistic way, especially where these provisions are administered and designed by different ministries or agencies. Where eligibility for one program removes eligibility for another, the effective marginal rates of support can be very far from policy makers' original intentions.

A second consideration stemming from overlapping programs is that these programs are complex and difficult to understand for taxpayers. This can lead taxpayers to make poor choices as to which programs are best for them. This complexity has been argued to be a key component as to why some of these policy measures are not effective (Davis, 2002; Dynarski and Scott-Clayton, 2015). In one US-based study, one in four taxpayers were found to mis-claim credits or deductions or not to choose the method of support that would be most beneficial for them (Turner, 2011). This study also found that low-income taxpayers are also more likely to mis-claim tax support for skills investments. Simplicity of tax and other forms of support is a key means of both ensuring the effectiveness and the equity of this form of support.

A third issue that can be important in designing the tax benefits for skills is that many low-income families may be credit constrained with respect to human capital investments (Carneiro and Heckman, 2002). Grants, scholarships, and tax benefits may provide an important means of reducing these constraints. However, for many households, the costs of human capital investments are incurred up-front, while the tax benefits can only be realised later in the tax year. For some families, this may nullify the usefulness of STEs (Dynarski and Scott-Clayton, 2015). This is another reason why direct support in the form of grants made available to individuals and families when skills investments are made may be a superior policy tool when compared to STEs which are available later in the tax year.

5.3 Non-tax financial incentives for tertiary education

Section 5.2 of this chapter discussed the ways in which the STEs can impact incentives to invest in skills for tertiary education. This section focuses on non-tax provisions that can provide financial incentives for students to invest in skills, such as reduced tuition fees, scholarships, grants and subsidised loans. The model developed in this study also accounts for the wide variety of non-tax financial measures provided to support educational investments by governments. This section considers the impact of these provisions from an efficiency and equity perspective. Data on this support has been taken from the OECD's *Education at a Glance* publication (OECD, 2014). Details of the assumptions made around these forms of support are provided in Chapter 3 of this study.

Size of non-tax financial incentives for tertiary education

Figure 5.11 shows the overall components of government spending on skills investments, incorporating three key aspects of government spending: direct spending on tertiary institutions, scholarship spending, and STEs. Data are expressed in 2011 PPP USD, and the graph uses the measure of STEs based on both personal income taxes and SSCs. Direct spending is larger than the two other categories combined (an estimated USD 10 227 per student per year), while spending via scholarship income is USD 1 492 per student per year. Spending through the tax system is estimated to be USD 860 per student per year when SSC-based STEs are incorporated. In every country, direct spending is larger than estimated scholarship income (though this may vary per student) in some countries the amount of support offered through the tax system is greater than the amount of scholarship income (Estonia, Iceland, Poland, Slovak Republic, Slovenia and Spain). These results depend on the amount of scholarship income received, and the amount of student income modelled. Nonetheless, non-tax support is far larger than tax support for tertiary education.

Figure 5.11. **Components of government expenditures on skills, in 2011 PPP USD, incorporating employee and employer social security contributions**

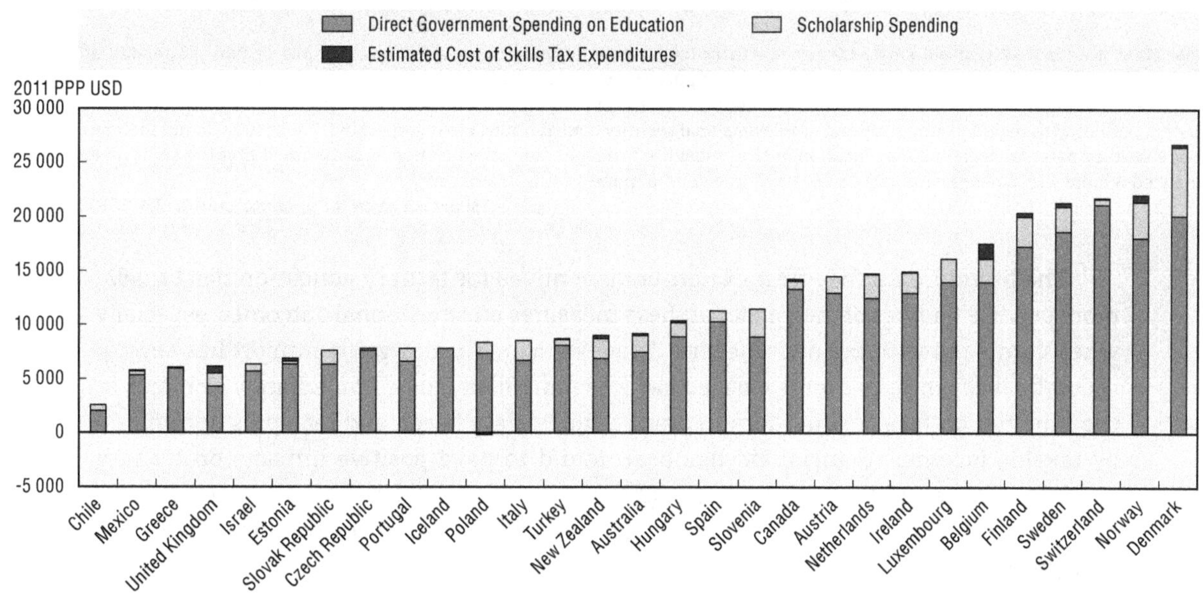

Note: Data are for a 17-year-old single taxpayer with no children, who undertakes a four-year course of non-job-related education, earning 25% of the average wage during schooling. This figure shows results that incorporate tax deductions and tax credits for direct costs, tax exemptions for scholarship income, and reduced taxes on student wage income. Tax incentives in the personal income tax system and with regard to employee and employer social security contributions are incorporated. The results do not incorporate STEs that subsidise parental spending on education or that subsidise firm spending on education. It is assumed that the skills investment is financed wholly with savings: students do not incur any debt to make a skills investment.

StatLink http://dx.doi.org/10.1787/888933446600

Figure 5.12 shows the impact of the withdrawal of scholarship income on BEIs in the countries included in the study. As in Section 5.2, the data used incorporates the impact of SSCs in the analysis. The increase in BEIs is substantial in almost every country. BEIs are estimated to be 15% on average with scholarship and grant income considered, and 19% with the level of all scholarship and grant income set to zero. Removing scholarship and grant support raises the estimated BEI by 22.6%.

Figure 5.12. **Breakeven earnings increments with and without scholarship income, incorporating personal income tax only**

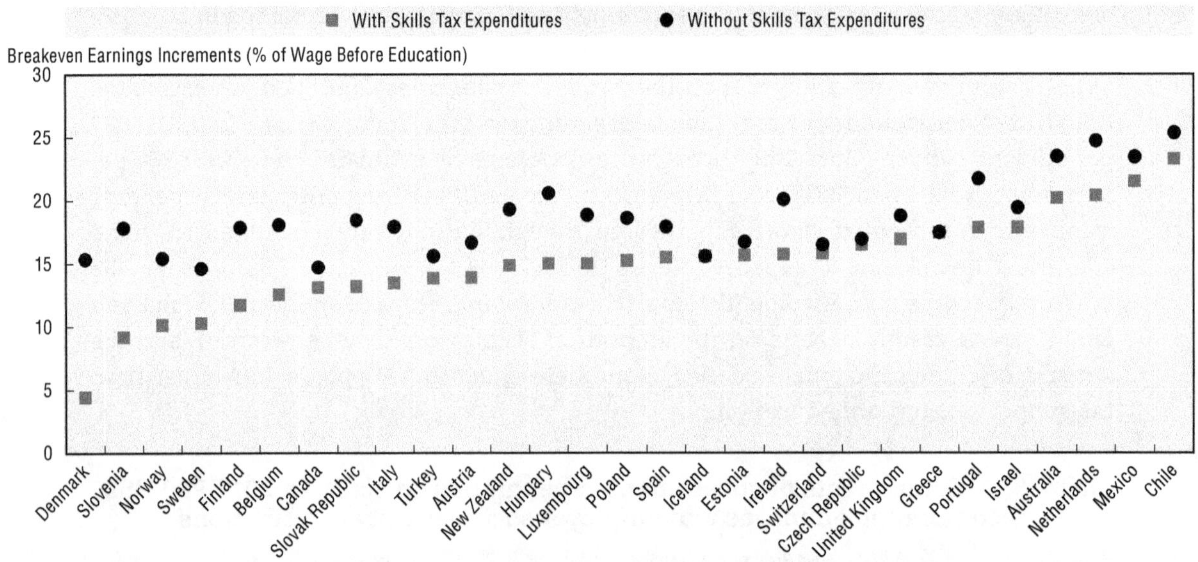

Note: Data are for a 17-year-old single taxpayer with no children, who undertakes a four-year course of non-job-related education, earning 25% of the average wage during schooling. This figure shows results that incorporate tax deductions and tax credits for direct costs, tax exemptions for scholarship income, and reduced taxes on student wage income. Tax incentives in the personal income tax system but not with regard to employee and employer social security contributions are incorporated. The results do not incorporate STEs that subsidise parental spending on education or that subsidise firm spending on education. It is assumed that the skills investment is financed wholly with savings: students do not incur any debt to make a skills investment.

StatLink http://dx.doi.org/10.1787/888933446618

The literature on the effect of non-tax incentives for tertiary education has broadly more positive findings of the impact of these measures on educational outcomes, especially when compared with tax policy levers. Direct scholarship and grant support has several theoretical advantages over tax-based aid; it is more likely to be immediately available at the time tuition fees are due, administrative barriers are fewer, and receipt is not limited by taxable income. Financial aid has been found to have positive impacts on tertiary enrolment in the United States (see Kane (2006) for a review), and in Germany (Baumgartner and Steiner, 2004). Denning (2016) finds that financial aid improves time-to-completion of degrees.

A large number of studies also suggest that higher tuition fees can negatively impact college enrolment in a variety of countries (Dynarski, 2005; Kroth, 2015). Studies have also found positive relationships between tuition fees and time-to-completion of degrees (Bruckmeier et al., 2013). It is not clear how the impact of tuition fees and scholarship income differs, or how the extent of the impact of tuition fees is dependent on the amount of scholarship income or vice versa. Nonetheless the literature does suggest that non-tax financial incentives may be more impactful than tax-based incentives.

Distributional impact of non-tax financial incentives for tertiary education

Figure 5.13 shows the impact of scholarship income on the BEI at various points in the income distribution, by showing BEIs with and without scholarship income in the model. The figure shows that in almost every country, removing scholarship income would increase the BEI, often substantially. It is instructive to compare Figure 5.13 to Figure 5.9, which shows similar results, but removing STEs instead of scholarship income. The impact of removing scholarships and grants is worse for BEIs on average than removing all STEs. This suggests that scholarships and grants are at present a larger form of government support for skills than STEs. Setting all grants and scholarships to zero would increase BEIs for all students in most countries in the OECD, but BEIs would increase more for low-income students based on this model. This suggests that, due to the features mentioned above, scholarship and grant income is progressive in OECD countries, and more so than STEs.

This conclusion is borne out by the literature on the impact of scholarships, grants and financial aid in OECD countries. This literature has long concluded that higher tuition levels reduce enrolment (Leslie and Brinkman, 1987). Kane (2006) reviews substantial evidence that demonstrates that there are greater responses to the tuition fee differences amongst lower-income households, with a USD 1 000 reduction in the private costs of education having an estimated impact that is twice as large for a household from the lowest income quartile compared to a household from the highest income quartile. The literature varies on whether these differences across incomes are due to the increased likelihood of credit constraints amongst lower households or other factors. In either case, the evidence suggests that spending through tuition reductions or increases in scholarship and grant spending currently has positive distributional and efficiency consequences; direct spending in the form of fee reductions or scholarship and grant provision is more effective at raising enrolment and completion rates compared to tax-based subsidies, it is also better targeted towards those on lower incomes, and finally it is more likely to raise the enrolment rates of those on lower incomes compared to STEs, which are often less beneficial to those on lower incomes due to a lack of taxable income or to the administrative burden of applying for STEs.

Debt-based support for tertiary education

While reducing tuition fees and increasing scholarship and grant support is important, students in OECD countries still bear significant private costs of education in the current policy environment. Figure 5.14 outlines the up-front cost components of a skills investment for the stylised 17-year old student.[5] Data are presented in 2011 PPP USD, exclusive of SSCs. This data is similar to the BEI, with the exception that the BEI also accounts for extra taxes a student must earn after education as their earnings rise. The data in Figure 5.14 focuses solely on the net costs of education in terms of net fees and government sponsorship, as well as net lost earnings. The returns to skills are not examined.

The figure demonstrates that foregone earnings are the largest cost component for all OECD countries, usually substantially so. While direct private costs borne by students such as tuition fees can be large, in every case they are smaller than foregone earnings. Similarly, foregone taxes are, in the majority of OECD countries, the most significant means by which the government offsets the costs of skills investments. Foregone taxes are larger than both STEs and scholarships and grants for students.

Figure 5.13. **Breakeven earnings increments with and without scholarship income, incorporating personal income tax only**

Breakeven earnings increment by income level as % of average wage

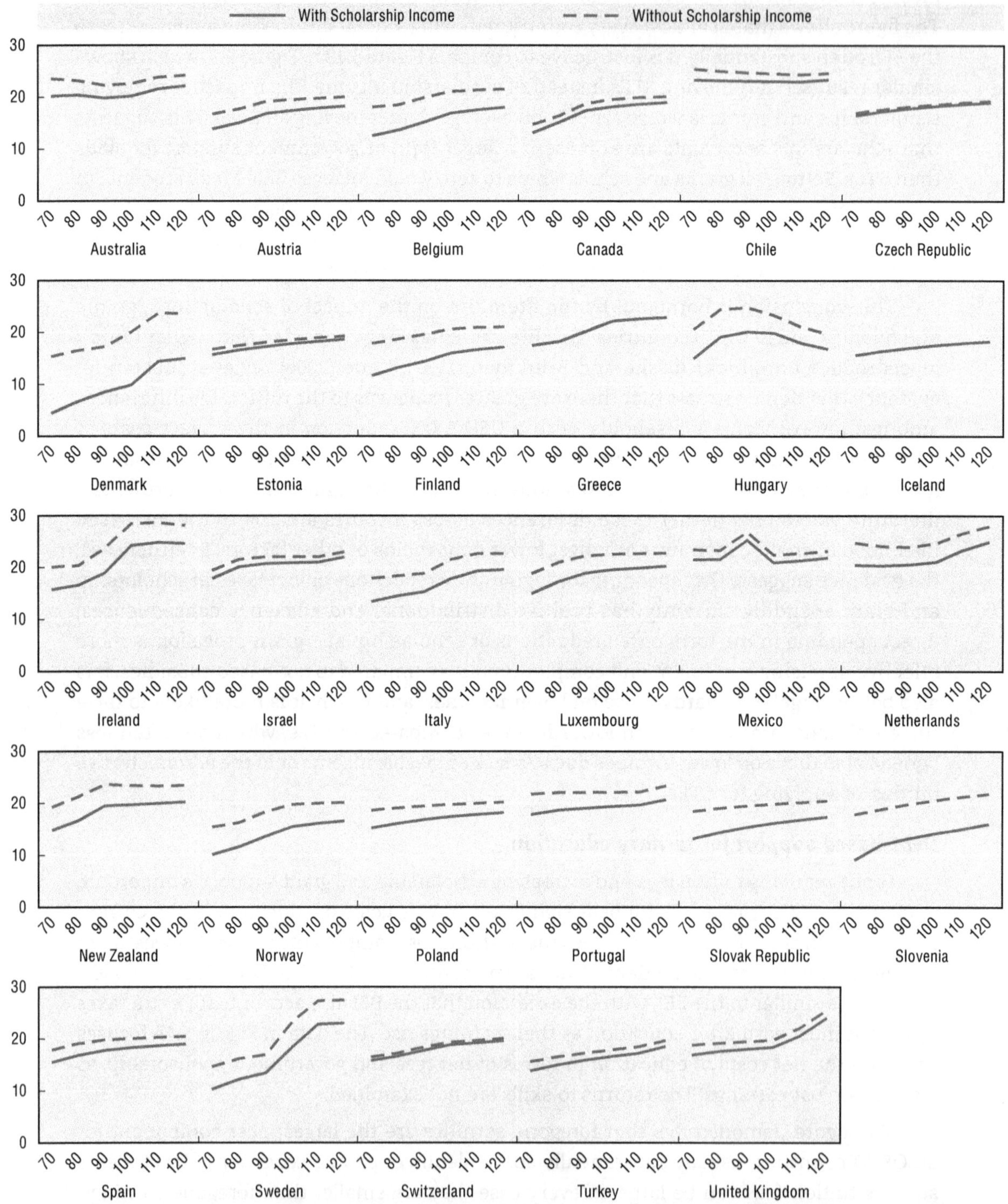

Note: Data are for a 17-year-old single taxpayer with no children, who undertakes a four-year course of non-job-related education, earning 25% of the average wage during schooling. This figure shows results that incorporate tax deductions and tax credits for direct costs, tax exemptions for scholarship income, and reduced taxes on student wage income. Tax incentives in the personal income tax system but not with regard to employee and employer social security contributions are incorporated. The results do not incorporate STEs that subsidise parental spending on education or that subsidise firm spending on education. It is assumed that the skills investment is financed wholly with savings: students do not incur any debt to make a skills investment.

StatLink http://dx.doi.org/10.1787/888933446623

Figure 5.14. **One-period cost components of skills investments for students, excluding taxes on earnings increments, incorporating employee and employer social security contributions**

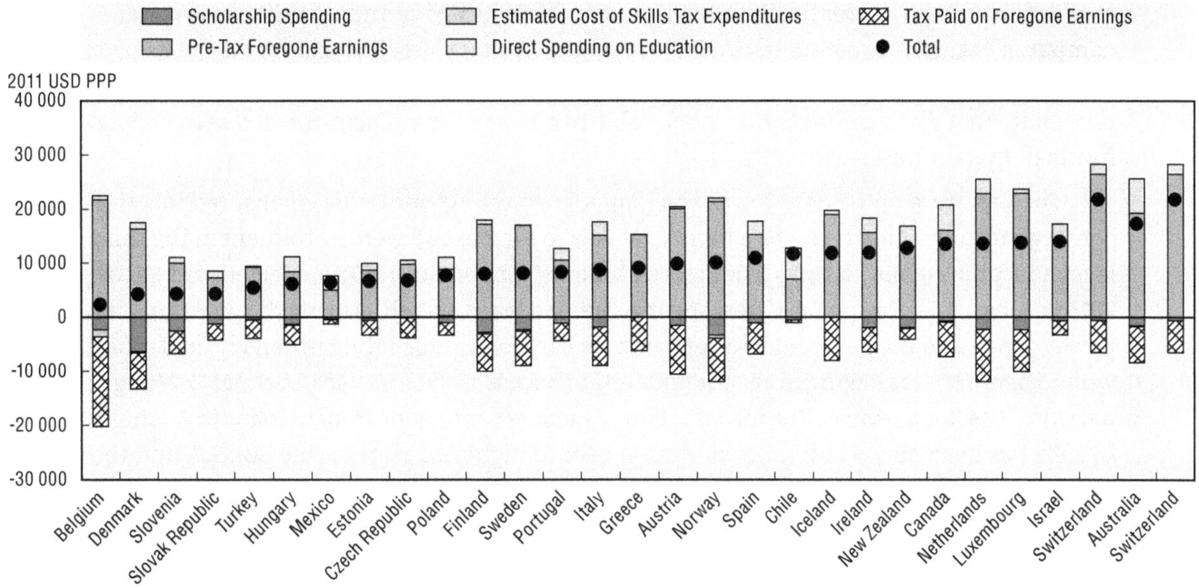

Note: Data are for a 17-year-old single taxpayer with no children, who undertakes a four-year course of non-job-related education, earning 25% of the average wage during schooling. This figure shows results that incorporate tax deductions for direct costs, tax exemptions for scholarship income, and reduced taxes on student wage income. Tax incentives in the personal income tax system and with regard to employee and employer social security contributions are incorporated. The results do not incorporate STEs that subsidise parental spending on education or that subsidise firm spending on education. It is assumed that the skills investment is financed wholly with savings: students do not incur any debt to make a skills investment.

StatLink http://dx.doi.org/10.1787/888933446638

The data suggests that even in the presence of the current set of government policies to support tertiary skills investments in OECD countries, the private costs are still significant. As has been shown in Section 4.2 of the study, however, the returns to skills are larger than the costs for a typical student in OECD countries; skills investments are profitable, both from the student's and the government's perspective. This raises the question as to why skills investments that yield positive returns are not undertaken.

A key explanation as to why skills markets may fail leaving worthwhile skills investments not undertaken is credit constraints on the part of students. Unlike physical capital, human capital or future labour supply cannot be offered as collateral on a loan to fund an investment (Cameron and Heckman, 1999). This means that loans may not be provided to profitable skills investments as recipients would rationally choose not to repay. This breakdown in private markets for skills investments is a key motivation for government intervention in the human capital market. In the presence of credit constraints there may be underinvestment in human capital, concentrated on those with low incomes. There is evidence that nearly 10% of the US population underinvests in human capital due to credit constraints (Carneiro and Heckman, 2002; Lochner and Monge-Naranjo, 2002). There is also evidence that these credit constraints persist throughout life (Popov, 2014).

To address these issues, a significant component of government education support also comes in the form of subsidised or guaranteed student loans. Chapter 4, Section 4.3 of this study has outlined how assuming that students finance their investments through debt instead of through savings can have significant effects on the affordability of education depending on the interest rate available to students. Increased or reduced interest on student loans can dramatically alter the attractiveness of human capital investments compared to other investments. While the model in this study has examined the impact of debt-financing and equity financing of skills investments, it has not considered the possibility that some students may not be able to access debt financing at all due to various forms of market failure.

The literature on student loans has long argued that government-sponsored income-contingent student loans can be a beneficial way to increase student enrolment in the third level education while sharing risk across students (Chapman, 1997; Findeisen and Sachs, 2014; Jacobs, 2002). Having the government guarantee loans as well as using the government's power to tax as a means to ensure repayments can both reduce the burden on the lender, while ensuring that low-income students retain access to finance (see Lochner & Monge-naranjo (2014) for a review). The introduction of income contingent student loans in Australia in 1989 has been successful in expanding access to higher education (see Box 5.3, and the discussion in Chapman (1997)).

Income contingent loans can be an attractive policy option because the income-contingent nature of the loan means that redistribution occurs from those whose skills investments yield high returns (who repay their loans) to those whose skill investments do not yield high returns (who may repay only in part or not at all). The discussion in Chapter 4 shows that while on average, a skills investment will pay for itself, many students make skills investments that may just break even or may not breakeven at all. This can be the case even if the investment did have positive expected returns. Loans that feature income contingent repayment offer insurance for the student against these risks.

The discussion in Box 5.1 of this chapter has highlighted that the progressivity of tax and skills policies need to be considered along two dimensions. Tax and skills policies can redistribute between high and low income students making skills investments. These policies can also redistribute between those whose skills investments yield high and low returns. In other words the tax system can redistribute across the income distribution ex ante of skills investments, or ex post. Income contingent loans do both. By ensuring access to education finance amongst the credit constrained, they redistribute ex ante. This is because low-income students are most likely to be credit constrained ex ante. In addition, by making repayment of the loans conditional on earnings after a skills investment, they redistribute ex post – those skills investments yielding low returns are taxed at lower rates.

A system of loans instead of graduate taxes can reduce potential adverse selection issues that may result from graduate taxes. Graduate taxes are similar to student loans in that the returns to student income are spread between students and governments through means other than through taxes. However unlike income-contingent loans where the returns to education after costs have been repaid accrue to students, graduate taxes see the returns shared between government and students even after costs have been repaid. With graduate taxes, students making high-value education investments may choose to invest elsewhere or move in response to taxes, relative to a system of loans where high returns will accrue to students (after loans have been repaid (Dynarski, 2015).

Finally, loans can facilitate higher tuition fees, potentially ensuring that the government receives an acceptable rate of return on profitable skills investments without reducing access for those students who are credit-constrained, risk- or debt-averse, or making risky

Box 5.3. **The Australian system of income-contingent loans**

Income-contingent loans are available to Australian students enrolling in eligible university courses. Repayments are connected to a graduate's ability to pay, not the amount of the loan, or its age. If a graduate loses their job or takes time out from work, no repayments are required where their income is below the repayment threshold. The repayment schedule for 2016-2017 is provided in Table 5.4.

Table 5.4. **Repayment schedules for HELP loans, 2016-2017**

Repayment income	% of Loan to be Repaid
Below AUD 47 196	0
AUD 47 196 - 52 572	4.00%
AUD 52 572.- 57 947	4.50%
AUD 57948 - 60 993	5.00%
AUD 60994 - 65 563	5.50%
AUD 65654 - 71 006	6.00%
AUD 71 007 - 74 743	6.50%
AUD 74 744 - 82 253	7.00%
AUD 82 254 - 87 649	7.50%
AUD 87 650 and above	8.00%

Figure 5.15 shows the impact of Australia's Income Contingent Loan Scheme for students by mapping the BEI for various marginal students. These results are presented based on the case of the stylised university student borrowing at a 3% real interest rate (Sections 4.2-4.3 provide further details of the assumptions behind this case). The results clearly show that the income-contingent loan scheme substantially reduces the necessary BEI for low-income marginal students relative to the scenario where education is financed wholly with a students retained earnings.

Figure 5.15. **Australian system of income contingent loans**

BEIs under various loan scenarios, as a percentage of the average wage

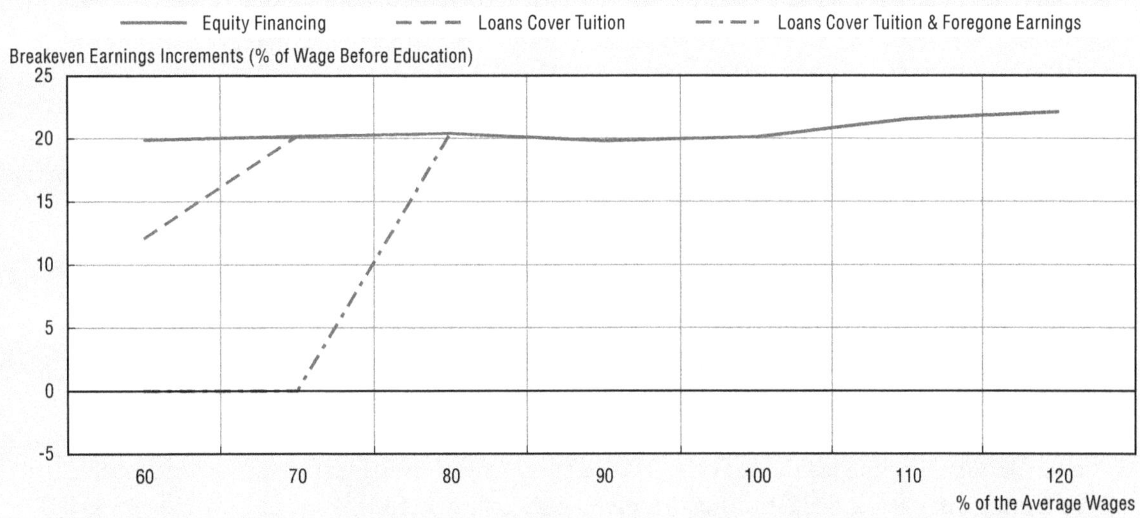

Data are for a 17-year-old single taxpayer with no children, who undertakes a four-year course of non-job-related education, earning 25% of the average wage during schooling. This figure shows results that incorporate tax deductions and tax credits for direct costs, tax exemptions for scholarship income, and reduced taxes on student wage income. The results do not incorporate STEs that subsidise parental spending on education or that subsidise firm spending on education.

investments. By raising tuition fees, and at the same time expanding access to income contingent loans, the governments returns to education can be maintained, access for low-income students can be maintained, and risky-yet-worthwhile investment can be maintained (Blöndal et al., 2002).

5.4 Tax Incentives for mid-career training

Importance of lifelong learning has been long acknowledged by policy makers. Due to rapid technological change, globalisation, and increased longevity, increasing numbers of older workers face challenges in keeping their skills up-to-date in the face of changing work practices. This means that maintaining human capital levels throughout workers' careers is an important part of skills policy.

Maintaining and increasing human capital can be challenging, particularly for older workers. Employers may be less likely to train workers who may soon leave the labour market; workers' propensity to undertake new training declines with age; research suggests that workers' ability to learn new skills also declines with age (OECD, 2013). For many, making significant skills investments in later life requires time out of the labour market. This often means very high levels of foregone earnings for older workers, dis-incentivising lifelong learning. These comparatively higher costs of training older workers have led some scholars to argue that investments in human capital are best focused on younger workers (Heckman and Jacobs, 2010). However addressing challenges such as increased market inequality, stagnant wages, and demographic challenges will require improved human capital of older workers as well as younger workers, and so providing effective training for older workers remains a significant policy objective (McCall et al., 2016).

This section provides an assessment of the existing policies, particularly STEs, designed to encourage worker training. Based on the model detailed in Chapters 3 and 4 of this study, the section first outlines the value of these provisions for the hypothetical example of job-related mid-career training discussed in Chapter 4. These provisions are then discussed from the perspective of their effectiveness in encouraging skills investment, as well as from a distributional perspective. The section will discuss non-tax approaches to encouraging lifelong learning, and will end by briefly discussing some issues policy makers may need to consider when designing STEs for worker training.

Size of tax incentives for mid-career training

Figure 5.16 shows the value of STEs for the in-work training example outlined in Chapter 4, expressed as a percentage of the costs of training. This example is for a worker at the average wage who undertakes a short period of job-related training. In this instance, incentives through the SSC system are not incorporated. Eleven of the countries modelled have no STEs for mid-career training, and so the value of STEs is zero in the model. The remainder of the countries modelled have STEs, mainly in the form of tax deductions in the personal income tax system. The model for in-work training assumes that this training is "job-related" in the sense that the training is necessary for a workers' job and thus becomes a tax deductible expense in many OECD countries. As will be discussed below, many OECD countries offer a tax deduction for training costs only where this training is related to a worker's current employment.

Figure 5.16. **Value of skills tax expenditures for mid-career training, as a percentage of the direct costs of training, incorporating personal income tax only**

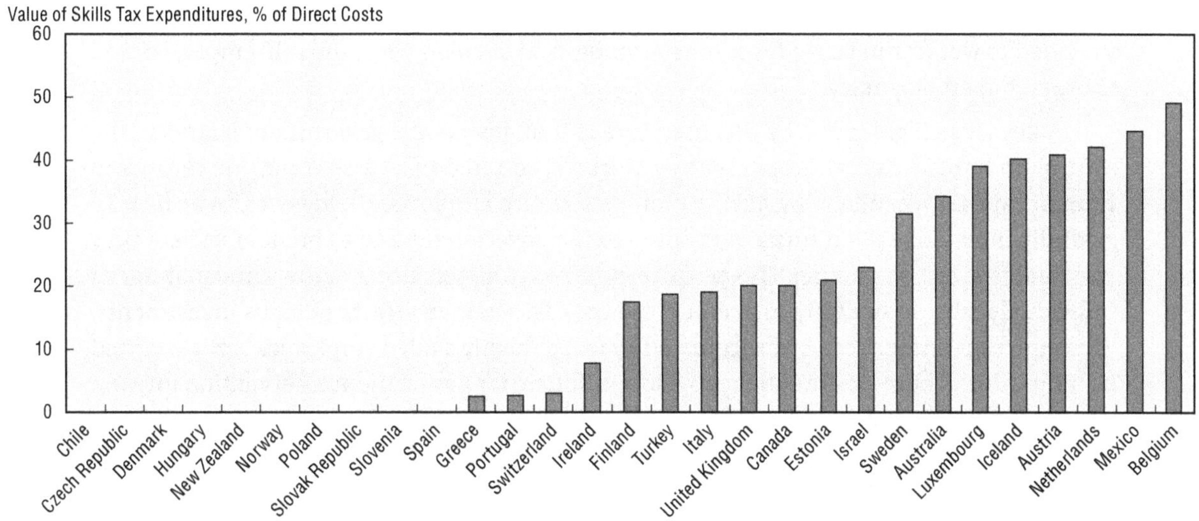

Note: Data are for a 32-year-old single taxpayer with no children, who undertakes a short course of job-related education, earning 95% of the average wage during schooling. This figure shows results that incorporate tax deductions and tax credits for direct costs, tax exemptions for scholarship income, and reduced taxes on student wage income. Tax incentives in the personal income tax system, but not the social security contribution system are incorporated. The results do not incorporate STEs that subsidise parental spending on education or that subsidise firm spending on education. It is assumed that the skills investment is financed wholly with savings: students do not incur any debt to make a skills investment.

StatLink http://dx.doi.org/10.1787/888933446648

Across the modelled countries, the average value of the costs of training that are offset through STEs for a worker at the average wage is 15.3% of the costs of training. Amongst the countries that do have STEs for worker training, the average value is 24.7% of the costs of training. Because the STEs for worker training tend to come in the form of tax allowances, the value of these tax allowances depends on the marginal rate of income tax in the country concerned. So countries such as Belgium with high tax rates on the average worker also see comparatively more valuable STEs in the model.

Many of the countries that have large STEs to encourage college education do not have similarly large STEs aimed at worker training. This is in part due to that fact that 28 of the 30 countries examined in this study have tax exemptions for scholarship income. It is assumed that those workers undertaking a period of in-work training do not receive any scholarship income, and so do not receive any tax benefit through STEs that come in the form of tax exemptions for scholarships. This reduces the size of STEs measured in several countries, notably Finland and Norway where scholarship income is tax-exempt and comparatively generous.

In addition to the support provided by the tax system to training through the personal income tax system as modelled in this study, significant support is also provided through the corporate income tax system. Details of the support provided to firms through the corporate income tax are outlined in Torres (2012). These provisions are not modelled in this study, but a study by (Bassanini et. al., 2007) suggested that three-quarters of all worker training was provided by employers in the EU. The costs of this firm-provided training are usually deductible from corporate taxable income. STEs in the personal and corporate income tax system should be designed in a coherent way. In the absence of STEs for job-related training in the personal income tax system, the tax system will induce businesses to pay for the job-related training for workers. Workers will request that their training be paid for by employers, as this will be deductible from the corporate income tax base. Moreover, these payments will not be included as a fringe benefit from the taxable personal income of the worker. Such a system will however add a distortion between the levels of tax support provided to workers in larger firms versus workers in smaller firms, the self-employed, and those not in employment.

A key issue highlighted by this literature is that, just as the government shares in the returns to human capital investment by workers, so too do firms share in the returns to human capital investment, by having more productive employees.[6] However, as firms may not fully internalise the returns to training to the government and to broader society they may under-invest in training. This positive externality affects firms in the same manner as individuals who do not fully internalise the broader positive effects of skills investments. This under-investment can be exacerbated by fear of highly skilled employees being poached by other firms. These externalities provide a rationale for government intervention into the market for worker training.

Impact of tax incentives for mid-career training

Though STEs for mid-career training exist in many OECD countries, the evidence on their effectiveness in terms of encouraging worker training is limited.[7] There are several reasons for this comparative lack of evidence. A large part of mid-career training is provided by employers, who may select high-performance employees into training programmes: this means that the causal effect of training (as opposed to simply being a high-performance employee) cannot be identified. Similar problems exist with studies examining training financed by individuals: talented individuals may be more likely to self-select into training, so comparing wages across individuals who do and do not invest in training will pick up effects that are partially driven by training, and partially by talent. In addition, on-the-job learning is difficult to measure, and many employers do not keep records of the amount of training their staff receive. These effects make it difficult to examine the returns to work-related training; and the impact and value-for-money of tax subsidies in this area.

Despite these difficulties, some studies evaluating the impact of STEs for mid-career training on training participation do exist. An early study by Holzer et. al. (1993) based on a grant program for firms in the United States, found that the receipt of training grants was associated with a significant, though "one-off", increase in training hours. Another recent study used a regression discontinuity approach based on a Dutch provision that granted a training deduction for workers over 40 years of age. This study found an increase in training rates for workers over 40, however, this was driven by workers postponing training, not by an increase in training overall (Leuven and Oosterbeek, 2004). A further study by the same authors using kinks in the income tax schedule to identify the impacts of tax incentives on training participation found positive effects: a 10% increase in the tax deductibility increases the training rate by between 10% and 25%. (Leuven and Oosterbeek, 2006). A study based on Italian data also found positive effects of tax incentives on training participation (Brunello et al., 2012). So the evidence suggests that STEs for training do have an impact – in contrast to those at third level. However, more research is needed in this area to properly assess the size of the impact of different provisions, and to assess how the impact varies across countries, demographics, and kinds of training.

The existing evidence on the financial returns to worker training is also mixed. Observational studies tend to find positive impacts of worker training on productivity and on wages. For example, Brunello (2004), using survey data for Italian large enterprises finds that a 10 percent increase in the average number of hours of training per head increase productivity in his sample by 1.32 percent. Brunello et. al. (2012) find that one additional week of training increases monthly after-tax earnings by 1.4 percent.

By contrast, more recent studies involving random assignment or instrumental variables find smaller effects on wages or no effects at all. For example, Görlitz and Tamm (2016) find no effect of a randomly assigned voucher for training on wages and employment, though those who are trained are assigned more cognitive tasks. Overall, the literature suggests that while training may have an impact, it is comparatively small and dependent both on the kind of training, whether it is related to current work, and whether is supplied by the employer. The returns to training also vary across the population and between countries. There is some evidence that training low-skilled workers may yield higher returns than higher-skilled workers (Fouarge et. al. 2013; Schwerdt et. al. 2012). For older workers, one study found that training did not improve wages, but did improve employability (Brunello, 2007).

Distributional impact of tax incentives for mid-career training

A key concern when evaluating worker training is assessing the distributional impact of policies that affect training. This is in part due to the fact that worker training is often cited as a key policy to improve distributional outcomes in OECD countries (OECD, 2015b). Figure 5.18 shows the value of STEs for mid-career training as a percentage of the direct costs of training across the OECD as derived from the model used in this study. The absence of tax deductions for training as seen in Figure 5.16 is also clearly visible for the countries that do not have STEs for worker training. Also apparent is the increasing benefits of existing STEs for workers on higher incomes. Most STEs for worker training come in the form of tax deductions for the private costs of training. As with tax deductions for university training, these provisions may not benefit low-income taxpayers to the same extent as higher-income taxpayers, due to low-income taxpayers' lack of tax liability. Unemployed or non-participating workers may benefit from active labour market programmes but these programmes may not be useful for those who are working but at low incomes (McCall et al., 2016). In addition, as discussed in Section 5.2 tax deductions for worker training also do not address liquidity constraints for low-income taxpayers stemming from the fact that the costs of training may accrue during the tax year, but the benefits of the tax deduction do not accrue until the end of the tax year.

On the corporate side, most mid-career training is financed by firms and not by workers themselves. However, this firm training may not be optimal from a social perspective. The literature suggests that those with low skills are less likely to be trained by their employers (Hansson, 2008). There is also evidence that women and older workers are also less likely to receive employer training: women are more likely to self-finance their worker training (Bassanini, et. al. 2007). So firm-sponsored training may have unintended distributional consequences.

Figure 5.18 compares the value of training for the stylised worker training example outlined in Chapter 4 of this study. The results for "job-related" training are the same as those in Figure 5.16 - incentives through the social contribution system are not incorporated. However, in this figure the results for job-related training are compared to those for non-job-related training. Many countries that allow training to be tax-deductible where it is job-related do not allow deductibility where the training is not job-related (including Australia, Austria, Belgium, Finland, Iceland, Israel, Mexico, and the United Kingdom). The average value of STEs for non-job-related training is 6.9%, compared to 15.3% for job-related training.

Figure 5.17. **Value of skills tax expenditures for mid-career training, as a percentage of direct costs of education across income levels, incorporating personal income tax only**

Tax rate by income level as % of average wage

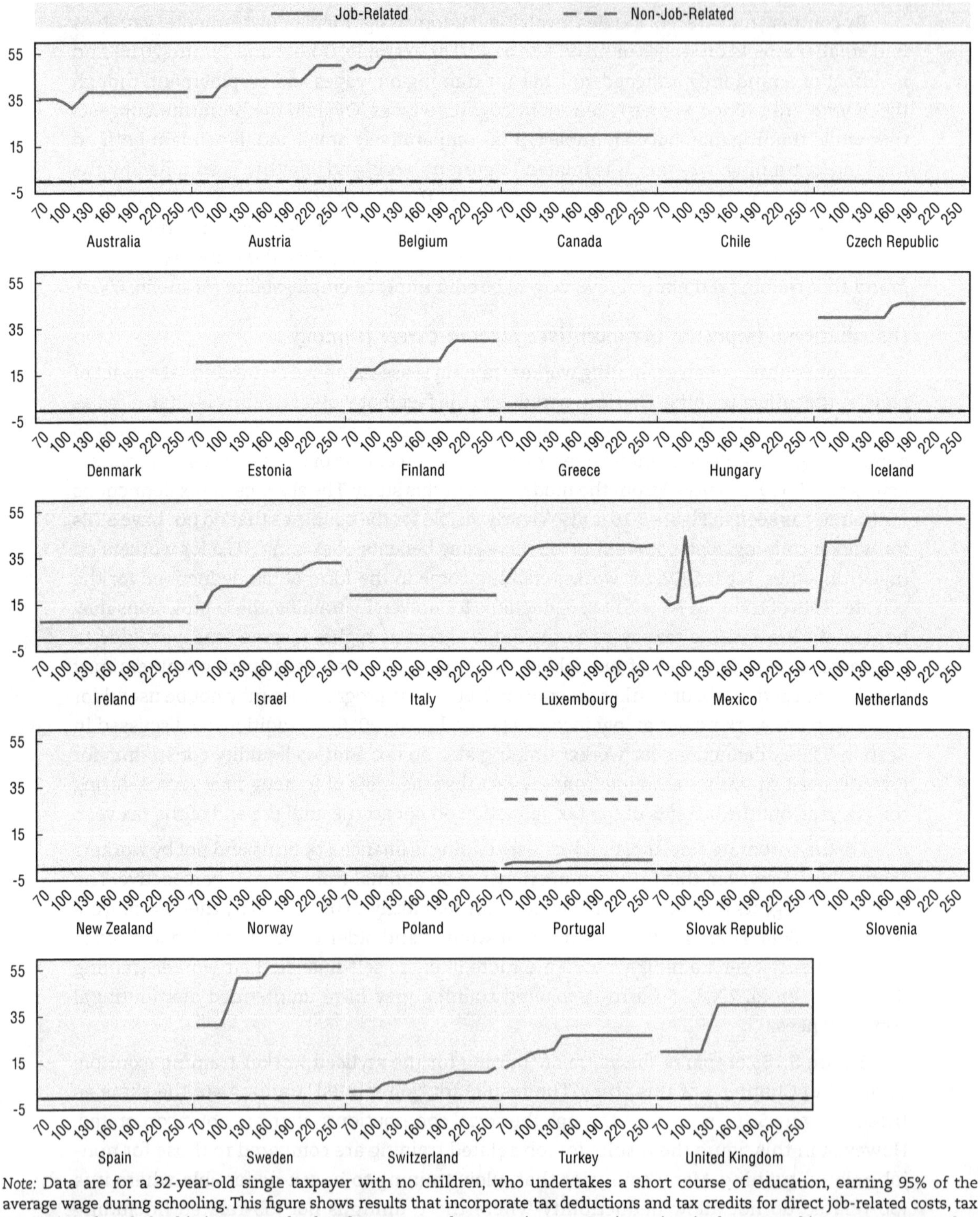

Note: Data are for a 32-year-old single taxpayer with no children, who undertakes a short course of education, earning 95% of the average wage during schooling. This figure shows results that incorporate tax deductions and tax credits for direct job-related costs, tax exemptions for scholarship income, and reduced taxes on student wage income. Tax incentives in the personal income tax system, but not the social security contribution system are incorporated. It is assumed that the skills investment is financed wholly with savings: students do not incur any debt to make a skills investment.

StatLink http://dx.doi.org/10.1787/888933446651

Figure 5.18. **Value of skills tax expenditures for job-related training versus non-job-related training, incorporating personal income tax only**

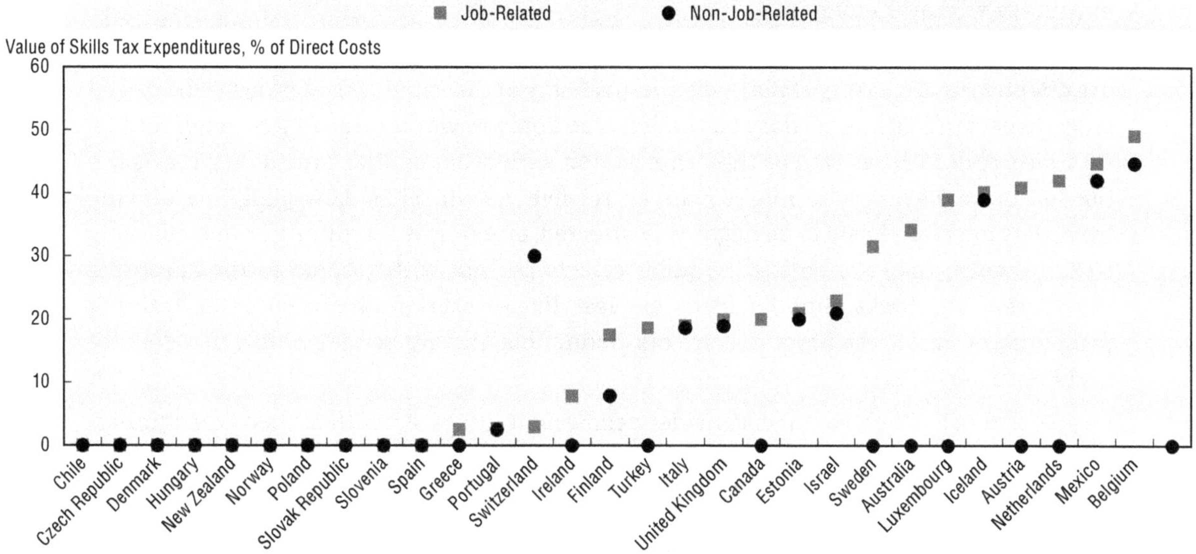

Note: Data are for a 32-year-old single taxpayer with no children, who undertakes a short course of education, earning 95% of the average wage during schooling. This figure shows results that incorporate tax deductions and tax credits for direct costs, tax exemptions for scholarship income, and reduced taxes on student wage income. Tax incentives in the personal income tax system, but not the social security contribution system are incorporated. It is assumed that the skills investment is financed wholly with savings: students do not incur any debt to make a skills investment.

StatLink http://dx.doi.org/10.1787/888933446667

Restrictions of training eligible for tax deductions to "job-related" training can also potentially be problematic from a distributional perspective. Many OECD countries that have tax deductions for training require that the training be related to a worker's current employment. This is designed to prevent inefficient subsidisation of skills spending that is consumption. However, these measures may also mean that workers in secure employment or in a fixed career may receive more benefits than workers who need to train to move careers, or who are in casual employment.

Finally, a key concern about financing worker training through tax deductibility in the personal and corporate income tax system is that these provisions may not encourage training participation in the SME sector (Müller and Behringer, 2012; Stone et al., 2008). The evidence shows that SMEs are less likely to invest in training than larger firms (Bassanini et al., 2007). This may be because SMEs are often less profitable than larger firms; they may also have cash-flow issues that means that even training that is eligible for tax deductions is deemed unfeasible. This means that employees of SMEs may receive an inefficiently low level of training compared to their counterparts in larger firms. As SMEs are a key source of job growth and innovation, low human capital levels can be very problematic for longer-term productivity.

Design considerations of tax incentives for mid-career training

The existing STEs in the personal income tax system do seem to play a role in encouraging workers to invest in skills. There are concerns about the distributional consequences of these measures. Both the economic literature and the model developed in this study suggest that STEs may provide larger benefits to men, to those on higher incomes, to those in secure jobs, to those working for larger firms, and to those with higher skills. By contrast, women, older workers, those with lower incomes, those in insecure employment, those working for SMEs, and those with lower skills may not receive the same benefits from STEs designed to encourage worker training.

In implementing STEs, design considerations are important in ensuring that STEs are effective in increasing skills investments. Many of the same considerations discussed with respect to STEs for tertiary education also apply to worker training throughout life. Complexity of STEs, as well as their interaction with other similar provisions, raises the burden on taxpayers who might want to receive certain STEs. Low-skill, low-income taxpayers are more likely to be negatively affected, either by not claiming or mis-claiming STEs to which they are entitled. Similar effects pertain with respect to the corporate tax system and SMEs. Smaller firms are less likely to take part in complex training programs, even if these programs are tax-deductible and are beneficial to a firm (Müller and Behringer, 2012).

Design of STEs should also consider deadweight losses. As with all tax expenditures, a key concern is the additionality of the effect of the tax expenditure: how much extra training STEs actually generate (OECD, 2010a). Poorly-designed tax expenditures may result in deadweight losses of up to 60% (European Centre for the Development of Vocational Training, 2009). Thresholds, for example, can lead to unintended effects. One study of a Dutch scheme gave an extra tax deduction to older workers (workers above 40), which had the effect of causing workers in their late 30s to postpone training in order to avail themselves of the tax incentive later. The overall effect of the measure on training was found to be minimal (Leuven and Oosterbeek, 2004).

Non-tax incentives for mid-career training

In addition to providing tax incentives for training, governments across the OECD use a wide variety of non-tax policy approaches to encourage worker training and lifelong learning. A detailed discussion of these policies is beyond the scope of this study, but these policies include active labour market programmes targeted towards the unemployed, vouchers to workers to choose their own training, and employment funds financed by firms that provide training. Detailed discussion of these policies is available elsewhere for Europe (European Centre for the Development of Vocational Training, 2009; European Commission, 2015) and more broadly (Bassanini et al., 2007; McCall et al., 2016).

Vouchers have been argued to be less administratively costly than STEs at the personal level (Messer and Wolter, 2009; Müller and Behringer, 2012). However, many of the distributional biases that occur with respect to STEs also obtain with respect to vouchers: those low-skilled workers most likely to benefit from them are also least likely to use them (Schwerdt et al., 2012). Deadweight losses also arise with respect to vouchers: increased government provision of vouchers may crowd out firm spending on skills, in part because firms do not fully internalise the benefits of investing in their workers (their workers may not remain with the firm) (European Centre for the Development of Vocational Training, 2009).

Another non-tax policy approach to worker training is communal training funds. These are funds that can be organised at the local, sectoral, or national level. Employers pay mandatory fees into these funds – either as a share of sales, payrolls, or profits – and then have access to the training programmes provided by these funds. Stone & Braidford (2008) argue that these funds may be more effective in encouraging worker training than tax deductions for training as firms, once having paid into a fund, will be more likely to use it. Moreover, as payments into these funds are usually compulsory, SMEs are also more likely to use them, addressing the issue of reduced SME participation in worker training (Stone et al., 2008). A potential issue with sectoral level funds is that firms – and their employees – in small or low-growth sectors in an economy may lose out through having access to a smaller fund compared to larger or high-growth areas of the economy. Similar effects could arise between wealthier regions and poorer regions if funds are set up on a regional basis. Maintaining a multiplicity of funds can result in political economy challenges if different funds are in states of varying levels of financial security.

5.5 Tax, skills and education finance

How does the tax system impact skills investments?

The preceding sections have discussed the effects of tax expenditures designed to encourage skills investments. The model developed in this study illustrates several key issues concerning STEs:

- In most OECD countries STEs are modest in size, though they can be larger when social contributions are taken into account.
- As a result, their impact on the overall financial incentive to invest in skills is also modest, particularly at tertiary level.
- In the hypothetical cases outlined, STEs benefit workers on higher incomes more than workers on lower incomes.
- In spite of this, STEs are a larger factor in the skills investment decisions of those making low-return skills investments than those who may see higher returns from their skills investments. This is because the costs of skills investments are a larger component of the overall financial decision to invest in skills than the returns for marginal students, so the way the tax system impacts those costs has a large impact on the overall effects of the tax system.

These arguments are supported by the findings from the academic literature. Though this literature is limited in many ways, some key conclusions are as follows:

- Tax expenditures have limited effects on students' decisions to enrol in tertiary education.
- Tax expenditures for mid-career training do encourage training, but can come with significant deadweight losses.
- Those on low incomes are less likely to benefit from themselves of STEs, both for college education and for worker training. STEs for training are often poorly designed: credits accrue to students at the wrong time of the tax year and provisions are overly complex. Training provided by employers can disadvantage certain workers due to employer bias.
- The literature is broadly supportive of non-tax approaches to providing support for skills investments in the form of tertiary education, including scholarships, reduced tuition, and income-contingent loans. These approaches may be more beneficial for low-income students.
- Support to students through income-contingent loans has been found to be particularly effective, in terms of ensuring access to education for low-income students, sharing the financial burden between government and students, distributing the risk of human capital investments, and balancing equity and efficiency considerations.

The largest impact of the tax system on skills investments does not come through STEs but through the broader income tax system. The regression analysis discussed in Box 5.1 has highlighted the impact of the tax system on financial incentives to invest in skills, which goes far beyond the impacts of STEs. The strong relationship between the METR on skills and the BEI is shown in Figure 5.7. This impact occurs in two ways: through the way the tax system reduces foregone earnings, and through the way that the returns to skills investments are taxed away.

The tax rate on foregone earnings is a key driver of financial incentives for skills investment for marginal students who just break even on a skills investment. For these students the costs of skills are large relative to the returns. The ways in which the government reduces these costs is therefore crucial to financial incentives to invest in skills or not. Figure 5.14 shows that foregone earnings are a large component of total educational costs; the extent to which the tax system reduces these earnings is also large. For the typical college student in the model, foregone taxes are larger than direct government support to tertiary educational institutions in 24 of the 29 countries modelled. This highlights the impact of the tax schedule on education decisions for students.

The way the tax system taxes the returns to skills is just as important as the impact of the tax system on foregone earnings, but mainly for students earning higher returns. The higher the return on a skills investment, the greater the extent to which high and progressive taxes will act as a disincentive. These taxes may also reduce incentives to participate in the labour market, further reducing the incentives to invest in skills. The literature on the impact of tax progressivity on skills investment is quite limited, especially in comparison to the literature on STEs (Cameron and Heckman, 1999). Nonetheless, Figure 5.19 shows a suggestive relationship in this area: those countries with higher levels of tax progressivity also have higher levels of public expenditure on education as a percentage of GDP. This could suggest that those countries that reduce the incentives to invest in skills through the tax system may compensate for this by reducing the costs of skills for students through increased government support: policies are aligned, albeit imperfectly, with the recommendations in this study.

Figure 5.19. **Tax progressivity and education spending**

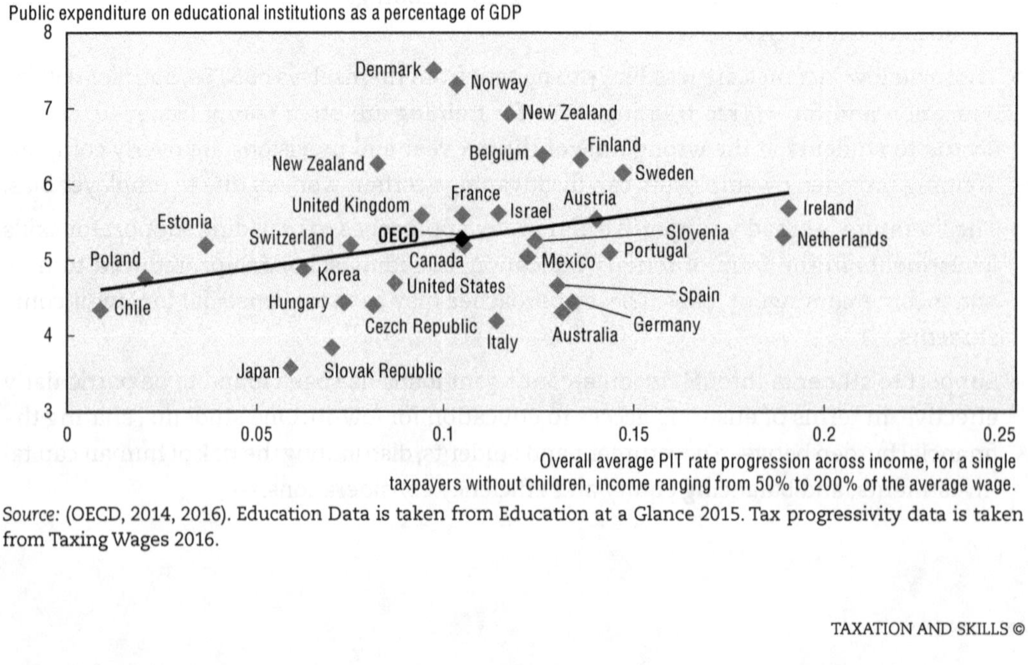

Source: (OECD, 2014, 2016). Education Data is taken from Education at a Glance 2015. Tax progressivity data is taken from Taxing Wages 2016.

Policy mixes for skills: taxes, spending, and debt support

Many academic studies have highlighted the potential problems that high and progressive taxes can have on incentives to invest in skills. Tax progressivity can raise the tax rate on the earnings increment thus raising tax rates on skills. However, tax progressivity can also raise the tax rate on foregone earnings, thus reducing tax rates on skills. The impact of progressivity on skills investments may thus be smaller than has been argued previously. For each individual skills investment, this impact will depend on where in the tax schedule a potential student currently sits: local progressivity matters.

Holding other factors constant, the negative impact of tax progressivity on incentives to invest in skills will be strongest when the gap between the tax rate on the earnings increment on skills and the tax rate on foregone earnings is large. This typically occurs when the returns to skills are highest. This means that while tax progressivity can negatively impact skills investments, it does so at its highest rate for those skills investments that are most profitable: those skills investments that are most likely to be undertaken even in the presence of taxes. Therefore, incentives to invest in skills could be thus increased by reducing income taxes, and these effects would be strongest for high-return skills investments.

The discussion in this chapter has also highlighted the importance of direct spending as a means to improve incentives to invest in skills, particularly for those who are credit constrained. Reducing income taxes and increasing spending are imperfect substitutes from a skills perspective: reduced income taxes may provide larger incentives for high-return skills investments compared to low-return skills investments. Reduced income taxes may also not assist affect credit-constrained students to the same extent as additional education spending.

Additional education spending or reduced income taxation may be complemented by income-contingent loans for students. Income contingent loans address credit constraints that may be present for positive-return skills investments. In addition, they may also provide a way to increase skills investments without placing a severe burden against short-term fiscally constrained governments. A further benefit of income contingent loans is that they can potentially provide a level of insurance for risky investments: the risk of skills investments are shared not just between governments and students, but across the population of students. Those human capital investments that yield high returns subsidise those skills investments that yield low returns. Complementing the loans with government support for education can further allow the costs and returns to be shared between the government and students (Gottardi et al., 2014; Krueger and Ludwig, 2013).

Skills investments are crucial for productivity, for growth, for wages, employment and for well-being in OECD economies (see Heckman & Jacobs, 2010, and Chapter 1 of this study). While government spending on skills is substantial, continued high returns to skills investments, as well as the high returns to costs ratios developed in this study, suggest that further government support for skills investments can yield positive returns for many countries. These findings echo on the returns to education elsewhere in the literature (de la Fuente and Jimeno, 2008). Though this study has focused on skills investments from college to later in life, the literature suggests that by far the highest returns to further skills spending come early in life, particularly through increased spending on early childhood education (Bulman and Hoxby, 2015; Cameron and Heckman, 1999).[8]

A key insight of this study has been that the tax system apportions both the returns and costs of skills between the government and the individual. Where governments have both high income taxes and low levels of skills spending, the incentives for individuals to invest in skills will be low compared to those countries that have low income taxes and high levels of skills spending. In these latter cases, countries' incentives to invest in skills will be high.

There is significant heterogeneity both within and between countries in terms of the distribution of returns and costs between governments and students. For some countries, the current policy mix of below-average education spending and an above-average labour income tax and social security contribution burden suggests that more needs to be done to incentivise skills investments. This is particularly the case where high labour market premiums for tertiary education suggest a lack of highly-educated workers in the workforce. In such countries, the policy mix is discouraging education: extra education spending could result in governments recouping the cost of their investment in higher income tax revenues, with further returns accruing from other forms of social and economic benefits. The Average Returns to Costs Ratio (ARCR) indicator suggests that altering the tax and spending mix to increase incentives to invest in education could be particularly beneficial and even self-financing, in Hungary, Slovenia and Portugal. These countries have both high ARCRs and high college premiums; suggesting that skills investments will yield positive returns for governments.

However, it is not the case that more government educational spending is always optimal. For other countries such as Norway and Denmark, the current policy mix features a high level of education spending, often combined with very low college premiums due to high levels of education in the population. In some countries the analysis suggests that while on average skills investments provide positive returns for governments, the costs of low-return skills investments may not be recouped in their entirety, at least through income tax.[9] There are two potential reasons for this. The first is that extensive government funding of education could be resulting in poor educational choices by students: students who may be better off working may be choosing to invest in skills that will not yield sufficiently high returns. Students may also choose to make skills investments that do not have high financial returns but have high non-pecuniary benefits (e.g. students may prefer certain subjects because they enjoy them). High or poorly-designed educational subsidies may distort student choices in ways that lower the returns to education.

A second reason why ARCRs may be low is that the returns to education may be high, but may be captured by students and not by government. Where the costs of education are heavily subsidised by governments relative to the extent to which the returns are taxed away, then the educational decision may be very profitable for students, at a cost to the government, and thus, to the taxpayer. Whether governments want to allow these private returns to accrue to students or not is a normative policy decision, but in such instances it may be possible to reduce, or better target education expenditures without negatively affecting investment in human capital in an economy.

The optimal mix of tax and spending policies with regard to skills will depend on a variety of factors. This study has sought to highlight the ways in which loans, spending, and taxes can be complements and substitutes for governments seeking to both finance skills investments themselves, and provide incentives for individuals to finance their own skills investments. Different countries may successfully choose different policy mixes. Countries that prefer high or progressive income taxes may need to provide extra education financing to students. Countries that have high levels of private education or high tuition fees may want to provide direct support or income contingent loans to students. Countries wishing to raise the overall level of skills investment in their workforce may want to reduce the AETR on skills by reducing income taxes. Countries that want to increase the skills of low-skilled, marginalised or disadvantaged groups may want to focus on the METR on skills; they could lower the METR by providing extra income support through scholarships and grants to certain students. Countries where credit constraints or risk-aversion is reducing skills investment may want to implement an income-contingent loan program. Different policy objectives will require different policy levers.

The issues addressed in this tax policy study only begin to address the policy questions concerning the impact of the tax system on skills investment. While this study has calculated measures of the impact of the tax system on financial incentives to invest in skills, the overall incentive to invest in skills, and the returns to government from skills investments, more needs to be done. Detailed work on how the returns to skills investments varies by field of study, by type of education, and by demographic would inform policy analysis on government spending in these areas. While the literature on the responses of tertiary education decisions to financial incentives is growing, further research is needed to separate out the effects of financial incentives, credit constraints, and variation in the value of education on skills investment decisions, especially for those on lower incomes. For lifelong learning, there remains a lack of detailed evidence of both the impact of training on wages and other economic outcomes and of the impact of financial incentives on training participation. Finally, this study has not considered in detail the impact of migration on skills policies. In a globalised world, countries with high skills spending and high taxes may attract more foreign students, but lose workers after education. The extent to which education and work decisions across borders are impacted by financial incentives will be increasingly important for policy makers as economies become increasingly more integrated. These issues are left for future research.

Notes

1. Tax expenditures are defined as 'Tax reliefs in the form of exemptions from tax, reductions of the tax liability (deductions and credits) or tax rates that are lower than the standard rate'. They can be seen as "equivalent to public expenditure implemented through the tax system" (OECD, 2010b).
2. For example, Portugal allows employers to provide education vouchers for children, tax-free. Such subsidies are not modelled in this version of the analysis.
3. To estimate the value of STEs in the hands of parents it would be necessary to estimate a value of parental transfers to students for education, and then assess the joint impact of the overall impact of STEs and the rest of the tax system on parent and student income, and on parental transfers to dependents. The value of STEs would likely depend on both the income of the student and the parent. The impact of these factors on the student skills investment decision would then have to be assessed. This process would be further complicated if the skills investment decision was made at the household level (i.e. by the student and parent jointly) as the returns and costs in both scenarios would need to be hypothetically divided between student and parent.
4. These costs are discussed further in Chapter 3.
5. These estimates do not incorporate the costs of increased taxes on necessary future income. Nor do they incorporate the opportunity return on alternative investments.
6. The model presented in this study would be extended to examine the ratio of returns to costs for firms, governments and individuals, but this would require a fully specified corporate income tax model, which is left for future research.
7. Existing evidence is reviewed in Bassanini et. al. (2007) and McCall et. al. (2016).

8. An analysis tax support for this kind of skills investment is left for further research.
9. The broader social returns may still outweigh the costs, but these broader social returns are not calculated in this study.

References

Avdic, D. and M. Gartell (2015), "Working while studying? Student aid design and socioeconomic achievement disparities in higher education", *Labour Economics*, Vol. 33, pp. 26–40.

Bassanini, A., A. Booth, G. Brunello, M. De Paola, and E. Leuven (2007), "Workplace Training in Europe", in Brunello, G., Garibaldi, P., Wasmer, E. (Eds.), *Education and Training in Europe*, Oxford University Press, Oxford.

Baumgartner, H.J. and V. Steiner (2004), "Student Aid, Repayment Obligations and Enrolment into Higher Education in Germany: Evidence from a Natural Experiment", *DIW Discussion Paper*, No. 444.

Bednar, S. and D. Gicheva (2013), "Tax Benefits for Graduate Education: Incentives for whom?", *Economics of Education Review*, Vol. 36, pp. 181–197.

Blöndal, S., S. Field, and N. Girouard (2002), "Investment in human capital through upper-secondary and tertiary education", *OECD Economic Studies*, Vol. 2002/1, *http://dx.doi.org/10.1787/eco_studies-v2002-art3-en*.

Bruckmeier, K., G.-B. Fischer, and B.U. Wigger (2013), "Does Distance Matter? Tuition Fees and Enrollment of First-Year Students at German Public Universities", *CESIFO Working Paper*, No. 4258.

Brunello, G. (2007), "The effects of training on employment, wages and productivity: a European perspective", *Thematic Review Seminar of the European Employment Strategy*, *http://www.voced.edu.au/content/ngv%3A28646*.

Brunello, G., S.L. Comi, and D. Sonedda (2012), "Training subsidies and the wage returns to continuing vocational training: Evidence from Italian regions", *Labour Economics*, Vol. 19, pp. 361–372.

Bulman, G.B. and C.M. Hoxby (2015), "The Returns to the Federal Tax Credits for Higher Education", *NBER Working Paper*, No. 20833.

Cameron, S. V. and J.J. Heckman (1999), "Can Tuition Policy Combat Rising Wage Inequality", in Kosters, M.H. (Ed.), *Financing College Tuition: Government Policies and Educational Priorities*, The AEI Press, Washington, D.C.

Carneiro, P. and J.J. Heckman (2002), "The Evidence on Credit Constraints in Post-Secondary schooling", *The Economic Journal*, Vol. 112, pp. 989–1018.

Chapman, B. (1997), "Conceptional Issues and the Australian Experience with income-contingent charges for higher education", *The Economic Journal*, Vol. 107 No. 442, pp. 738–751.

Cunha, F., J.J. Heckman, L. Lochner, and D. V. Masterov (2006), "Interpreting the Evidence on Life Cycle Skill Formation", in Hanushek, E.A. and Welch, F. (Eds.), *Handbook of the Economics of Education*, Elsevier, *https://doi.org/10.1016/S1574-0692(06)01012-9*.

Davis, A.J. (2002), "Choice Complexity in Tax Benefits for Higher Education", *National Tax Journal*, Vol. 55 No. 3, pp. 509–538.

Denning, J.T. (2016), "Born Under a Lucky Star: Financial Aid, College Completion, Labor Supply, and Credit Constraints", *Unpublished Working Paper*, *https://aefpweb.org/sites/default/files/webform/41/BornUnderALuckyStar.pdf*.

Dynarski, S. (2005), "Building the Stock of College-Educated Labor", *NBER Working Paper*, No. 11604.

Dynarski, S. (2015), "An Economist's Perspective on Student Loans in the United States", *CESifo Working Paper*, No. 5579.

Dynarski, S. and J. Scott-Clayton (2015), "Tax Benefits for Education: History and Prospects for Reform", *https://doi.org/10.1017/CBO9781107415324.004*.

European Centre for the Development of Vocational Training (2009), *Using Tax Incentives to Promote Education and Training*, *https://www.cedefop.europa.eu/files/5180_en.pdf*.

European Commission (2015), *An in-Depth Analysis of Adult Learning Policies and Their Effectiveness in Europe*, *https://doi.org/10.2767/076649*.

Findeisen, S. and D. Sachs (2014), "Education Policies and Taxation without Commitment", *University of Mannheim Department of Economics Working Paper Series*, No. 14–16.

Fouarge, D., T. Schils, and A. de Grip, (2013), "Why do low-educated workers invest less in further training?", *Applied Economics*, Vol. 45 No. 18, pp. 2587–2601.

Görlitz, K. and M. Tamm (2016), "The returns to voucher-financed training on wages, employment and job tasks", *Economics of Education Review*, Vol. 52, pp. 51–62.

Gottardi, P., A. Kajii, and T. Nakajima (2014), "Optimal Taxation and Debt with Uninsurable Risks to Human Capital Accumulation", *Federal Reserve Bank of Atlanta Working Paper Series*, No. 2014–24.

Guzman, T. (2013), "To Choose or Not to Choose: Federal Income Tax Credits and Deductions and College Choice Decisions", *Indiana University School of Public and Environmental Affairs Research Paper*, No. 2013-01-01.

Hansson, B. (2008), "Job-Related Training and Benefits for Individuals: A Review of Evidence and Explanations", *OECD Education Working Papers*, No. 19.

Heckman, J.J. and B. Jacobs (2010), "Policies to Create and Destroy Human Capital in Europe", *NBER Working Paper*, No. 15742.

Holzer, H.J., R.N. Block, M. Cheatham, and J.H. Knott (1993), "Are Training Subsidies for Firms Effective? The Michigan Experience", *Industrial and Labor Relations Review*, Vol. 46 No. 4, pp. 625–636.

Hoxby, C.M. (1998), "Tax Incentives for Higher Education", in Poterba, J.M. (Ed.), *Tax Policy and the Economy*, Vol. 12, MIT Press, Cambridge, MA, pp. 49–82.

Hoxby, C.M. and G.B. Bulman (2015), "The Effects of the Tax Deduction for Postsecondary Tuition: Implications for Structuring Tax-Based Aid", *Economics of Education Review*, Vol. 51, pp. 23–60.

Jacobs, B. (2002), "An investigation of education finance reform - graduate taxes and income contingent loans in the Netherlands", *CPB Discussion Paper*, No. 9.

Kane, T.J. (2006), "Public Intervention in Post-Secondary Education", in Hanushek, E.A. and Welch, F. (Eds.), *Handbook of the Economics of Education*, Vol. 2, Elsevier, *https://doi.org/10.1016/S1574-0692(06)02023-X*.

Kroth, A.J. (2015), "The Effects of the Introduction of Tuition on College Enrollment in Germany: Results from a Natural Experiment With Special Reference to Students from Low Parental Education Backgrounds", University of Michigan, *https://deepblue.lib.umich.edu/handle/2027.42/111597*.

Krueger, D. and A. Ludwig (2013), "Optimal Progressive Labor Income Taxation and Education Subsidies When Education Decisions and Intergenerational Transfers are Endogenous", *American Economic Review: Papers & Proceedings*, Vol. 103 No. 3, pp. 496–501.

de la Fuente, A. and J.F. Jimeno (2008), "The Private and Fiscal Returns to Schooling and the Effect of Public Policies on Private Incentives to Invest in Education: a General Framework and Some Results for the EU", *Barcelona Graduate School of Economics Working Paper*, No. 342, *http://www.barcelonagse.eu/research/working-papers/private-and-fiscal-returns-schooling-and-effect-public-policies-private*.

LaLumia, S. (2012), "Tax Preferences for Higher Education and Adult College Enrollment", *National Tax Journal*, Vol. 65 No. 1, pp. 59–90.

Leslie, L.L. and P.T. Brinkman (1987), "Student Price Response in Higher Education: The Student Demand", *The Journal of Higher Education Studies*, Vol. 58 No. 2, pp. 181–204.

Leuven, E. and H. Oosterbeek (2004), "Evaluating the Effect of Tax Deductions on Training", *Journal of Labor Economics*, Vol. 22 No. 2, pp. 461–488.

Leuven, E. and H. Oosterbeek (2006), "The responsiveness of training participation to tax deductability", *Unpublished Working Paper*.

Lochner, L. and A. Monge-Naranjo (2014), "Student Loans and Repayment: Theory , Evidence and Policy", in Hanushek, E.A., Machin, S.J. and Woessmann, L. (Eds.), *Handbook of the Economics of Education*, 1st ed., Vol. 5, Elsevier B.V., pp. 397–498.

Lochner, L. and A. Monge-Naranjo (2002), "Human Capital Formation with Endogenous Credit Constraints", *NBER Working Paper*, No. 8815.

McCall, B., J. Smith, and C. Wunsch (2016), "Government-Sponsored Vocational Education for Adults", *Handbook of the Economics of Education*, Elsevier B.V., Vol. 5, pp. 479–652.

Messer, D. and S.C. Wolter (2009), "Money Matters – Evidence from a Large-Scale Randomized Field Experiment with Vouchers for Adult Training", *CESifo Working Paper*, No. 2548.

Müller, N. and F. Behringer (2012), "Subsidies and Levies as Policy Instruments to Encourage Employer-Provided Training", *OECD Education Working Papers*, No. 80, OECD Publishing, Paris, *http://dx.doi.org/10.1787/5k97b083v1vb-en*.

OECD (2010a), "Tax Policy Reform and Economic Growth", *OECD Tax Policy Studies*, No. 20, OECD Publishing, Paris, *http://dx.doi.org/10.1787/9789264091085-en*.

OECD (2010b), "Choosing a Broad Base – Low Rate Approach to Taxation", *OECD Tax Policy Studies*, No. 19, OECD Publishing, Paris, *http://dx.doi.org/10.1787/9789264091320-en*.

OECD (2013), *OECD Skills Outlook 2013 - First Results from the Survey of Adult Skills*, OECD Publishing, Paris, *https://doi.org/10.1787/9789264204256-en*.

OECD (2014), *Education at a Glance 2014: OECD Indicators*, OECD Publishing, Paris, *https://doi.org/10.1787/eag-2013-en*.

OECD (2015a), *Education at a Glance 2015: OECD Indicators*, OECD Publishing, Paris, *http://dx.doi.org/10.1787/eag-2015-en*.

OECD (2015b), *In It Together: Why Less Inequality Benefits All, OECD Publishing*, OECD Publishing, Paris, *https://doi.org/10.1787/9789264235120-en*.

OECD (2016), *Taxing Wages 2016*, OECD Publishing, Paris, *http://dx.doi.org/10.1787/tax_wages-2016-en*.

Popov, A. (2014), "Credit constraints and investment in human capital: Training evidence from transition economies", *Journal of Financial Intermediation*, Vol. 23, pp. 76–100.

Schwerdt, G., D. Messer, L. Woessmann, and S.C. Wolter (2012), "The impact of an adult education voucher program: Evidence from a randomized field experiment", *Journal of Public Economics*, Vol. 96 No 7-8, *https://doi.org/10.1016/j.jpubeco.2012.03.001*.

Stantcheva, S. (2015), "Optimal Taxation and Human Capital Policies over the Life Cycle", *NBER Working Paper*, No. 21207.

Stone, I., P. Braidford, and SSDA (2008), *Engaging Small Employers in Continuing Training: An International Review of Policies and Initiatives*, Sector Skills Development Agency, *http://dera.ioe.ac.uk/9571/1/report_30_3.pdf*.

Torres, C. (2012), "Taxes and Investment in Skills", *OECD Taxation Working Papers*, No. 13, OECD Publishing, Paris, *http://dx.doi.org/10.1787/5k92sn0qv5mp-en*.

Turner, N. (2011), "Why Don't Taxpayers Maximize their Tax-Based Student Aid? Salience and Inertia in Program Selection", *The B.E. Journal of Economic Analysis & Policy*, Vol. 11 No. 1.

Turner, N. (2012), "Who benefits from student aid? The economic incidence of tax-based federal student aid", *Economics of Education Review*, Vol. 31, pp. 463– 481.

ANNEX A

Technical approach to calculating tax and skills indicators

A.1 Introduction

This annex outlines an approach to estimating the financial incentives for individuals and governments to invest in individuals' skills, and the effect of the tax system on these incentives. Specifically, the annex derives Marginal Effective Tax Rates (METRs) and Average Effective Tax Rates (AETRs) on Human Capital Investment, as well as Marginal Returns to Costs Ratios (MRCRs) and Average Returns to Costs Ratios (ARCRs) of Government Investment in Human Capital. The annex also explains how these measures relate to each other, and outlines the effect of government taxes and spending on incentives to invest in skills.

The annex revises and significantly extends the Effective Tax Rates on Skills Methodology outlined in Brys and Torres (2013). This annex clarifies some of their notation and incorporates more explicitly the tax treatment of scholarship income into their definition of the METR. The approach in this study relaxes their assumption that students finance their education using savings by allowing the student to borrow some fraction of the cost of their education. Their calculation of the METR and the Breakeven Earnings Increment (BEI) is extended by also calculating an AETR, for cases where an individual may earn economic rents on a skills investment. In addition to examining the financial returns to education from an individual's perspective, the returns for governments are also examined. A Returns to Costs Ratio (RCR) of Government Investment in Education (a Tobin's q of the government investment decision) is also calculated. This figure provides a summary statistic of the government's financial incentives (in terms of tax revenue) to invest in the education of students. This is calculated for two cases; where an individual breaks even on a skills investment (the "marginal" case), and where an individual earns economic rents (the "average" case). Combining the RCR with the BEI for the individual highlights how the personal income tax (PIT) system apportions the returns and costs of skills investments between the government and the individual.

The formulae throughout this annex are designed to explicate the interaction with the OECD's Taxing Wages models (OECD, 2014). Throughout, certain formulae are exactly the equations modelled in the calculations. These formulae are Equation 16 for the AETR, Equation 21 for breakeven income after education, Equation 22 for the BEI, Equation 28 for the METR, Equation 44 for the ARCR, and Equation 48 for the MRCR.

The approach for the individual taken is as follows.[1] Section A.2 begins by outlining the key benefits of education – the extra earnings earned in the labour market – and how they are impacted by the tax system. The key individual costs of education are outlined:

lost earnings, direct costs of education, and the offsetting benefits of scholarship income. The way in which the tax system can interact with these different factors is outlined. These costs and benefits, appropriately discounted, together form the NPV of the Educational Investment.[2] This NPV is calculated with and without taxes; this is then used to calculate the AETR on Skills.

The focus then turns to calculating the BEI, which is the value of the earnings increment necessary to just breakeven on an educational investment (i.e. when the NPV of the investment is equal to zero). This is referred to as the BEI. This value is calculated with and without taxes; the difference forms the core of the METR. The relationship between the AETR and the METR is calculated, noting that as the amount of extra earnings from a skills investment converges towards the BEI, the AETR converges towards the METR. Conversely, as the earnings from a skills investment grow larger and move away from the BEI the AETR moves away from the METR and converges towards the marginal effective tax rate on the earnings increment. This result is analogous to the results in Devereux and Griffith (1998) for physical capital, where the AETR converges to the statutory corporate income tax rate.

Section A.3 moves to the perspective of the government.[3] As discussed, two RCRs are calculated; a "Tobin's q" of the government's investment in skills. This is simply the NPV of the returns to education for the government over the replacement cost of the educational investment for the government. Two RCRs are calculated, an ARCR, where the earnings increment obtained by the individual is held fixed; and a MRCR, where the earnings increment is set to the BEI.

The consideration of the returns to the government is narrow; it is limited to returns in the form of tax revenue from higher wages. There is no accounting for the higher tax revenue that may result from the skills investment in the form of higher economic growth, increased productivity or increased employment. Nor is there any accounting for non-tax benefits such as reduced spending on unemployment, greater well-being among the population and so on. This means that an ARCR value of less than one in the model does not mean that educational investments do not pay for themselves at all; it merely reflects that they do not pay for themselves solely in the form of recouped tax revenue from higher wages.

Section A.4 expands the analysis by relaxing the assumption that students finance their education with retained earnings. In this section, students are assumed to borrow some fraction of the cost of their investments in skills. It is assumed this borrowing occurs in the form of an interest-only bond. Interest is paid in each year of the duration of the loan, and the principal is repaid in the final year of the loan. The interest rate of the loan as well as its length is allowed to vary. The tax treatment of interest on the loan is considered, as well as the possibility that some fraction of the principal can be written off by the government.

In this section, the definitions of the key statistics, the BEI, METR, AETR, ARCR and MRCR are defined to account for the possibility of financing skills investments from debt as well as savings. It is assumed in the consideration of the returns to government that the government is the creditor of the student. Hence, reduced interest rates for the student constitute a cost for the government, as are parts of the loan principal that are written off. Finally, tax deductibility or exemptions of interest on the student loan are also a cost from the perspective of the government.

A.2 Private costs and benefits of education and their relationship to the tax system: deriving the AETR, BEI, and METR

The benefits of a skills investment

The first consideration is the returns to education. It is important to note that a key difference between human and physical capital is the fact that human capital cannot be sold by its owner at the end of use; when a worker retires or stops working; their skills cannot be readily sold to another worker for use. This key difference means that for a worker's remaining years in the labour force, the skills investment will yield a return, but upon retirement these returns fall to zero.[4] This also means that in order to break even on a skills investment, a worker must recoup the cost of the investment over the years of its use. In contrast, this cost need not be recouped for a physical asset which may be sold. This is discussed further in Box 1.

This per period return is defined as TR_W (Total Returns to the Worker). It can be written as:

$$TR_W = g(\cdot)_{t \le 1/\lambda} = (1-T_a)I_a - (1-T_b)I_b \qquad (1)$$

Where $g(\cdot)$ are the returns dependent on the period, t is the time period, and $1/\lambda$ is the expected holding period of the investment, which in the model is the number of years to retirement. Equation 1 can be simplified as:

$$TR_W = g(\cdot)_{t \le 1/\lambda} = (1-T_{EI})EI \qquad (2)$$

Where:

$$EI = I_a - I_b \text{ and } T_{EI} = \frac{T_{I_a} I_a - T_{I_b} I_b}{I_a - I_b} \qquad (3)$$

In this formulation, the following variables are defined:

- EI = before-tax annual **Earnings Increment** during the holding period, which is the amount by which before-tax income after making the investment exceeds baseline earnings. This is written as per-period income in the periods *after* education (I_a) less per-period income *before* education (I_b). It is the extent to which education increases pre-tax wages.
- T_{EI} = **Marginal Effective Tax Rate on the Earnings Increment**, where the 'margin' is the earnings increment.[5] It is the rate at which the increase in earnings after education is taxed away. As with per-period income, the per-period tax rates faced before and after education are written as T_{Ib} and T_{Ia} respectively.

EI is the amount by which earnings after making the investment exceed baseline earnings. With progressive PIT systems, tax rates increase as incomes increase. Increasing amounts of tax will have to be paid when the earnings increment rise. This means that the tax rate T_{EI} is one of the key ways in which the tax system can affect the incentives to invest in skills.

The costs of a skills investment

The undiscounted cost for the individual of an investment in skills is written as:

$$TC_W = (1-T_{I_b})I_b - (1-T_{E_d})E_d + (1-\theta)DC_W - (1-\varphi)SG \qquad (4)$$

Where:

I_b Before-tax annual **baseline income** before acquiring/ in the absence of additional skills.

E_d Before-tax annual earnings **during** the period of skills acquisition. The term earnings is used to distinguish between earnings from wages and income from scholarships and grants, as the tax treatment of this income may be different (see below).

DC_W Private direct costs for the worker.

SG Scholarship or grant income for the worker.

T_{I_b} Average effective tax rate on I_b.

T_{Ed} Average effective tax rate on E_d, excluding deductions and tax credits for the costs of education.

θ Value of the tax benefit applied to DC_W, as a share of DC_W.

φ Effective tax rate on scholarship and grant income.

Equation 4 can be simplified as:

$$TC_W = (1 - T_{FE})FE + (1 - \theta)DC_W - (1 - \varphi)SG \qquad (5)$$

Where: $FE = I_b - E_d$ and $T_{FE} = \dfrac{T_{I_b}I_b - T_{E_d}E_d}{I_b - E_d}$. In this formulation:

- FE is the before-tax annual **Foregone Earnings** during the period of skills acquisition. There is a distinction between earnings and income in each period to allow for the separate treatment of other forms of income such as scholarship and grant income. During education (in "d" periods) $I_d = E_d + SG$; income is equal to wage earnings and scholarship or grant income.
- T_{FE} is the marginal effective tax rate on FE, also written as the extent to which the tax system increases or offsets the costs of education. It is also the change in the taxes paid, as a share of the change in earnings. As with T_{EI}, T_{FE} will be a core element of the AETR and METR.

Many countries provide tax relief for the costs of education. Many countries also subsidise education through reduced tax rates on scholarship or grant income. Like tax rates on labour earnings, these policy measures are characterised by a variety of deductions, exemptions, thresholds, rates and so on. The aggregate value of these skills tax expenditures (STEs) is encapsulated by the terms θ and φ.

The term θ refers to the fraction of the private direct costs of education (DC_W) that can be offset against a worker's tax bill. For example, for countries with a refundable tax credit for educational expenses, the model defines $\theta = 1$, the private costs of education are wholly offset by (non-wasteable) reductions in tax liability. By contrast, where no tax relief exists, the model defines $\theta = 0$, and the full amount DC_W is borne by the worker.

The term φ refers to the tax paid on scholarship income. For countries where scholarship income is completely exempt from taxation, the model has $\varphi = 0$, and so the full amount of any scholarship or grant is deducted from the costs of education. In this case the amount of tax paid on total income during education will be $T_{I_d} I_d = T_{E_d} E_d$. Where scholarship or grant income is taxed as ordinary earnings, the model taxes scholarship or grant income and earned income are taxed at the same rate, $T_{I_d} I_d = T_{I_d} (E_d + SG)$.

The values of θ and φ may be a function of DC_W, SG, and E_d; for example, deductibility may decline as DC_W increases beyond a certain threshold. Furthermore, in the absence of transferability, refundability or full loss offset, θ begins to decline as DC_W exceeds E_d (or more precisely, *taxable* E_d before the deduction for education and training costs). It is assumed here that the deductibility of costs is non-transferable. However, if the deductibility of direct costs could be transferred to a higher income taxpayer (e.g. the student's parent(s)), θ may also depend on the income of the transferee.

These interactions will vary across countries, indeed often education costs are deductible only net of scholarship income; conversely, in some countries scholarship income is taxable to the extent that it exceeds the direct costs of education. The term χ is used to define the *overall* extent to which these STEs alter the tax liability of the worker. Specifically, the term χ is defined as follows, noting by the brackets $\chi(DC_W, SG)$ that it is a function of DC_W and SG:

$$\chi(DC_W, SG) = \frac{\theta DC_W - \varphi SG}{DC_W - SG} = \frac{\left(T_{E_d} - T^*_{E_d}\right)E_d}{DC_W - SG} \gtrless 0 \tag{6}$$

Where $T^*_{E_d}$ is the average effective tax rate on taxable income corresponding to the earnings level E_d taking into account any tax provisions for the costs of education, as well as the taxation of scholarship income. The tax rate T_{E_d} does not take these provisions into account. Equation 6 therefore writes the effective tax gain χ as the total value of any STEs as a share of the direct costs of education less scholarship income.

When a tax allowance or tax credit for investment in skills is provided, Equations 4 and 5 can be rewritten as:

$$TC_W = (1 - T_b)I_b - (1 - T^*_{E_d})E_d + DC_W - SG = (1 - T^*_{FE})FE + DC_W - SG \tag{7}$$

Where T_{FE}^* is the marginal effective tax rate on *FE*, where the tax on earnings during education E_d ($T^*_{E_d}$) takes into account any deduction for the costs of education. This means that $T^*_{FE} = \frac{T_b I_b - T^*_{E_d}E_d}{I_b - E_d}$. This formulation of the costs of education simplifies the exposition substantially.

$T^*_{FE} = \frac{T_b I_b - T^*_{E_d}E_d}{I_b - E_d}$ is the tax rate on foregone earnings **inclusive** of STEs such as deductions for skills costs, and exemptions for scholarship income and the like. That is, $T^*_d E_d = T_d E_d - \theta DC_W + \varphi SG$; $T^*_d E_d$ is equal to $T_d E_d$, the normal tax rate on earnings during education, less any allowances or credits based on direct costs, θDC_W, and including any tax paid on scholarship income φSG.

Defining the private net present value of a skills investment

Defining the private net present value with taxes

The NPV of an investment in skills, evaluated in period *m*, is given by:

$$V = -\int_{n=0}^{m} TC_W e^{(\rho-\pi)n} dn + \int_{n=m}^{\infty} \lambda e^{-\lambda(n-m)} \left[\int_{t=m}^{n} TR_W e^{-(\rho-\pi)(t-m)} dt + 0\, e^{-(\rho-\pi)(n-m)} \right] dn \tag{8}$$

Box A1. **Brys and Torres (2013)**

The nomenclature used in this study differs in some respects to that used in Brys and Torres (2013) on which it is based. Here differences are outlined for readers wishing to link this annex with their study. There are several differences.

First, Brys and Torres explicitly break down income earned after education into the part that is the true "return" to the student, and the part that is required to repay the initial costs of the skills investment. In the physical capital literature this original outlay to pay for an asset does not need to be recouped in each period after the investment, as it is recouped when the asset is sold. As a skills asset cannot be sold (one cannot costlessly transfer skills to another person when one is finished with them), it must be recouped explicitly. This means that only the fraction of earnings *after* enough has been earned to repay the initial skills outlay really constitutes the "return" to the skills investment in the strict sense of the physical capital literature. This is the after-cost return that Brys and Torres define as $income_a$; the real "return" on a skills investment. Brys and Torres define the annual after tax net cash flow as a result of a skills investment as:

$$g(\cdot)_{t\leq 1/\lambda} = (1-T_a)\left[income_a + \lambda\ (income_b - income_d + DC_W)\right] - (1-T_b)income_b$$

In this way, Brys and Torres separate the amount needed to recoup the initial pre-tax cost of the educational investment ($income_b$ + $income_d$ + DC_W) from the rest of the returns to the investment, $income_a$. In their formulation, λ is the reciprocal of the number of years left in the labour force after the student has completed the educational investment. In other words, λ is the fraction of the initial cost of the educational investment that must be repaid in each period, so that, in expectation, by the end of the remaining years in the labour force the entirety of the initial cost of the educational investment will have been repaid.

This formulation highlights a difference between the human capital and physical capital literature. In the physical capital literature, the initial cost of an investment can be recouped when the investment is sold at the end of the period of use. If this were possible for skills, the term λ ($income_b + income_d + DC_W$) would be equal to zero. In the physical capital literature the term $income_a$ is the entire breakeven return to an investment. In the skills case, in order to break even, λ ($income_b + income_d + DC_W$) must be earned as well.

In the formulation in this study, the definition of the term income after education (I_a) as used by Brys and Torres differs to that term income after education. The formulation in this study is equivalent to Brys-Torres in the following way:

$$I_a = income_a + \lambda\ (income_b - income_d + DC_W)$$

This term for income after education encompasses the 'return on investment' as defined by the physical capital literature, *and* the amount necessary to recoup costs, as defined by Brys and Torres.

Second, Brys and Torres do not explicitly model interactions that may take place between the tax exemptions for scholarship income and tax deductions for the direct costs of upskilling. They explicitly model a tax allowance for skills costs, but do not account for other STEs. Specifically, Equation 5 in this study, a statement of the upfront costs reads:

$$TC_W = (1-T_{FE})FE + (1-\theta)DC_W - (1-\varphi)SG$$

The costs of education include:

- After-tax foregone earnings, $(1 - T_{FE})FE$
- Plus the private costs of education DC_W
- Which may be reduced by any STEs. The value of these STEs, expressed as a fraction of DC_W, is written θ
- The costs of education are offset by scholarship income SG. This scholarship income is sometimes taxed at the same rate as earned income I_d but is often subject to a special rate φ.

The equivalent equation in Brys and Torres is equation 2, which reads:

$$f(\cdot) = (1-T_b)income_b - (1-T_d)income_d + (1-\theta\gamma)DC_W$$

Box A1. **Brys and Torres (2013)** *(cont.)*

It is important to note that there is no explicit accounting for scholarship income and the tax treatment it may receive. It is considered part of $income_d$ and the effects of scholarship income are incorporated into T_d. This amendment to their approach allows the calculation of the parameter χ (defined in Equation 6 below), which is an overall summary parameter that captures the value of the taxpayer of STEs related to scholarship income, direct costs and so on. This allows the analysis of all these factors together.

Where TC_W and TR_W are as defined above, and

- r is the real interest rate,
- π is the inflation rate,
- T_c is the average tax rate on capital income,
- $\rho = (1 - T_c)(r + \pi)$, is the nominal after-tax return on an alternative capital investment,
- m is the length of the period of education,
- n is the expected number of years left until retirement,
- λ is the inverse of the number of years left until retirement, or the fraction of the cost of the investment that must be paid back in each year to be paid off by retirement, 1/(n-m).

It is assumed that $r > 0$, $\pi > 0$ and $T_c<1$, so that $\rho>0$.

As discussed, the first term of Equation 8 indicates the cost of the investment, TC_W, which is assumed to begin taking place in period 0 and takes m units of time. The second term (the double integral) is the *expected present value*[6] of the return on the skills investment, where TR_W is the net annual cash flow generated by the investment. The term $0.e^{-(\rho - \pi)(n - m)}$ indicates that the human capital asset cannot be sold when the skills acquired are no longer used (e.g. when the worker retires), implying that its value eventually drops to zero.

The probability that the investment will yield a return in period n is assumed to decrease exponentially as n increases, as implied by the integral of the term $\lambda e^{-\lambda(n - m)}$. The inverse of λ, $1/\lambda$, is the expected holding period of the investment, which is assumed to be positive. The holding period is assumed to be the period of time over which skills are used in the labour force; it decreases if the retirement age increases.

The net annual cash flow generated by the investment, TR_W, is discounted at the rate ρ and increases at the rate π for a net growth rate of $-(\rho - \pi)$, where ρ is the nominal discount rate applicable to a human capital investment and π is the rate of inflation (assuming that wages increase with inflation).[7] It is assumed that the investment can begin to yield a return in period m and that the cash flow stream begins to be discounted in period m. To adjust for the lag in discounting the stream of benefits, the costs incurred during the first period are grossed-up by the real discount rate, $\rho-\pi$, which is assumed to be positive. These discounting assumptions imply that the present in the net *present* value calculation is assumed to be period m rather than period 0 as in traditional investment models.

Solving this equation yields, after some manipulations, Equations 9, 10, and 11:

$$V = -TC_W\left(\frac{e^{(\rho-\pi)m} - 1}{\rho - \pi}\right) + \frac{TR_W\lambda}{(\rho - \pi)}\left[\int_{n=m}^{\infty} e^{-(\lambda+\rho-\pi)(n-m)}\,dn - \int_{n=m}^{\infty} e^{-\lambda(n-m)}dn\right] \Rightarrow \tag{9}$$

$$V = -TC_W \left(\frac{e^{(\rho-\pi)m} - 1}{\rho - \pi} \right) - \frac{TR_W \lambda}{(\rho - \pi)} \left[\frac{1}{\lambda + \rho - \pi} - \frac{1}{\lambda} \right] \Rightarrow \quad (10)$$

$$V = -\frac{1}{Z} TC_W + \frac{TR_W}{\lambda + \rho - \pi} \quad (11)$$

Where $Z = \frac{\rho - \pi}{e^{(\rho-\pi)m} - 1}$, is the gross-up of the current costs to the period in which the skills investment begins. Henceforth, a notational convenience is used, so that:

- The gross-up factor of the costs of investment in education as $\delta_{TC}^{T} = \frac{1}{Z} = \frac{e^{(\rho-\pi)m} - 1}{\rho - \pi}$
- The discount factor of the returns to investment in education as $\delta_{TR}^{T} = \frac{1}{\lambda + \rho - \pi}$

The superscript T is used to denote that these discount factors incorporate the effects of taxes on capital income (δ_{TC}^{NT} and δ_{TR}^{NT} will later be used to denote the discount factors without taxes on capital income). From Equation 11, the NPV of a skills investment becomes:

$$V_T = -\delta_{TC}^{T}\left[\left(1 - T_{FE}^{*}\right)FE + DC_W - SG\right] + \delta_{TR}^{T}\left[\left(1 - T_{EI}\right)EI\right] \quad (12)$$

Defining the private net present value without taxes

To find the overall effect of the tax system on a skills investment, it is necessary to estimate the difference between the NPV of a skills investment with and without the tax system. Equation 12 above gives the NPV in the case with taxes, it remains to consider the NPV without taxes.

In the no tax case, each tax rate is simply set to zero. This includes the tax rate on income before education, during education, and after education, the tax rate on capital, as well as any deductions, or exemptions for direct costs and scholarship income. This means that:

$$T_{I_b} = T_{E_d} = T_a = \varphi = \theta = 0 \quad (13)$$

There are several implications to this:

- Given the previous formulae for the effective tax rates on foregone earnings and the effective tax rate on the earnings increment, $T_{FE} = \frac{T_b I_b - T_{E_d} E_d}{I_b - E_d}$ and $T_{EI} = \frac{T_a I_a - T_b I_b}{I_a - I_b}$, it follows that $T_{FE} = T_{EI} = 0$.
- Moreover, $T_c = 0$ implies that the nominal after-tax return on an alternative capital investment, $\rho = (1 - T_c)(r + \pi)$, now becomes simply $\rho = r + \pi$.
- This in turn implies that the discount factors, $\delta_{TC}^{T} = \frac{1}{Z} = \frac{e^{(\rho-\pi)m} - 1}{\rho - \pi}$ and $\delta_{TR}^{T} = \frac{1}{\lambda + \rho - \pi}$, change also. δ_{TC}^{NT} and δ_{TR}^{NT} are defined as the discount factors in the no-tax case (that is, where $\rho = r + \pi$). This means that $\delta_{TC}^{NT} = \frac{e^{(r)m} - 1}{r}$, and $\delta_{TR}^{NT} = \frac{1}{\lambda + r}$.

Substituting in these various values into V_T, a value for V_{NT} is obtained as follows:

$$V_{NT} = -\delta_{TC}^{NT}\left[FE + DC_W - SG\right] + \delta_{TR}^{NT} EI \quad (14)$$

This equation is analogous to Equation 12 above.

The average effective tax rate on skills investments

Following both Devereux and Griffith (2003) and Klemm (2008), the AETR is defined as simply the difference between the NPV of the skills investment with and without taxes, expressed as a share of the after tax cash-flow from the investment.

$$AETR = \frac{(V_{NT} - V_T)}{\delta_{TR}^{NT} EI} = \frac{(V_{NT} - V_T)}{\frac{EI}{\lambda + r}} \tag{15}$$

Substituting in the values for V_T and V_{NT} from Equations 12 and 14 above, a more complete definition can be obtained.

$$\begin{aligned} AETR = \frac{1}{\delta_{TR}^{NT} EI} \Big[& -\delta_{TC}^{NT} [FE + DC_W - SG] + \delta_{TR}^{NT} EI \\ & + \delta_{TC}^{T} \big[(1 - T_{FE}) FE + (1-\theta) DC_W - (1-\varphi) SG\big] - \delta_{TR}^{T} \big[(1 - T_{EI}) EI\big] \Big] \end{aligned} \tag{16}$$

This is the expression that is used in the *Taxing Wages* modelling. In the absence of capital taxes, $T_c = 0$, $\delta_{TC}^{NT} = \delta_{TC}^{T}$ and $\delta_{TR}^{NT} = \delta_{TR}^{T}$, the expression simplifies considerably to become:

$$AETR = -\frac{1}{\delta_{TR}^{NT} EI} \Big[\delta_{TC}^{NT} \big[T_{FE} FE + \chi (DC_W - SG) \big] - \delta_{TR}^{NT} \big[T_{EI} EI \big] \Big] \tag{17}$$

Which simplifies further to become:

$$AETR = T_{EI} - \frac{\delta_{TC}^{NT}}{\delta_{TR}^{NT}} \frac{\big[T_{FE} FE + \chi (DC_W - SG) \big]}{EI} \tag{18}$$

This equation makes it clear that in the model the tax system interacts with the financial incentives to invest in skills in three key ways, expressed here as three key tax rates, T_{EI}, T_{FE}, and χ. First, the tax system taxes away the returns to skills in the form of the earnings increment (T_{EI}). Second, it reduces the cost of skills by reducing the cost of foregone earnings (T_{FE}). Third, the tax system offsets, or may offset, the cost of education through tax deductions or credits for the direct cost of education, or through tax exemptions for scholarship income (χ).

Breakeven earnings increment on skills investments

The AETR defines the effect of the tax system on a skills investment for any investment in skills, for any level of earnings that result from the investment. However, it can also be useful to define the effect of the tax system on a *marginal* skills investment; one where the worker is *just indifferent* between making the investment and not making it. In other words, the marginal worker faces the same net financial return to making the investment and not making it. In order to calculate the METR on skills the approach is to define what it means to be just indifferent between making a skills investment and not. Subsequently, the level of earnings at which a worker is indifferent between investing in skills and not investing is calculated. The METR is then simply a function of how this earnings level changes in the presence or absence of taxes.

The alternative to making a skills investment consists of earning the baseline earnings (I_b) and a return from investing the cost of education in an alternative capital investment (whose original cost can be fully recovered at the time of the asset's disposition). An investment in skills is defined as *marginal* when a prospective student is indifferent between making this investment and the alternative. In other words, a marginal skills investment is one where the NPV of the skills investment is zero, where $\hat{V} = 0$, with the "hat" denoting the breakeven level of V. This is essentially saying that the costs of the skills investment are just covered by the returns.

$$\hat{V} = -\delta_{TC}^{T} TC_W + \delta_{TR}^{T} TR_W = 0 \Rightarrow \frac{\delta_{TC}^{T}}{\delta_{TR}^{T}} TC_W = TR_W \quad (19)$$

All of the expressions follow from the AETR case. Substituting the expressions of TC_W and for TR_W, another expression for $\hat{V}$ can be obtained.

$$\frac{\delta_{TC}^{T}}{\delta_{TR}^{T}}\left[\left(1-T_{FE}^{*}\right)FE + DC_W - SG\right] = \left(1-T_a\right)\hat{I}_a - \left(1-T_b\right)I_b \quad (20)$$

Where, solving for I_a, the result is:

$$\hat{I}_a = \frac{\left(\frac{d_{TC}^{T}}{d_{TR}^{T}}\left[\left(1-T_{FE}^{*}\right)FE + DC_W - SG\right] + \left(1-T_b\right)I_b\right)}{\left(1-T_a\right)} \quad (21)$$

Again, the pre-tax annual earnings increment defined such that V = 0 (the earnings increment required for a skills investment to break even) is the BEI. The BEI is referred to as the difference between the breakeven earnings level, and the previous income I_b.

$$BEI = \hat{I}_a - I_b \quad (22)$$

Equation 20 can be re-expressed in a similar way by substituting the now-familiar $(1-T_{EI})BEI$ formulation for $(1-T_a)\hat{I}_a - (1-T_b)I_b$.

$$\frac{\delta_{TC}^{T}}{\delta_{TR}^{T}}\left[\left(1-T_{FE}^{*}\right)FE + DC_W - SG\right] = \left(1-T_{EI}\right)BEI \quad (23)$$

Where, as before:

$$BEI = \hat{I}_a - I_b \text{ and } T_{EI} = \frac{T_a\hat{I}_a - T_b I_b}{\hat{I}_a - I_b} \quad (24)$$

BEI (in the presence of taxes) is defined as:

$$BEI = \frac{\delta_{TC}^{T}}{\delta_{TR}^{T}} \frac{\left[\left(1-T_{FE}^{*}\right)FE + DC_W - SG\right]}{\left(1-T_{EI}\right)} \quad (25)$$

To find the METR, it is necessary to find a similar breakeven income level $\hat{I}_a$ and BEI in the absence of tax. As with the AETR case, the no-tax case involves setting each tax rate to zero. This means that $T_{I_b} = T_{E_d} = T_a = \varphi = \theta = 0$, as mentioned before. To repeat, the implications of this are that:

- Given that $T_{FE} = \frac{T_b I_b - T_{E_d} E_d}{I_b - E_d}$ and $T_{EI} = \frac{T_a I_a - T_b I_b}{I_a - I_b}$, it follows that $T_{FE} = T_{EI} = 0$.
- $T_c = 0$ implies that the nominal after-tax return on an alternative capital investment, $\rho = (1-T_c)(r+\pi)$, now becomes simply $\rho = r + \pi$.
- This in turn implies that the discount factors, $\delta_{TC}^{T} = \frac{1}{Z} = \frac{e^{(\rho-\pi)m}-1}{\rho-\pi}$ and $\delta_{TR}^{T} = \frac{1}{\lambda+\rho-\pi}$, change also. δ_{TC}^{NT} and δ_{TR}^{NT} are defined as the discount factors in the no-tax case, where $\rho = r + \pi$. This means that, $\delta_{TC}^{NT} = \frac{e^{(r)m}-1}{r}$, and $\delta_{TR}^{NT} = \frac{1}{\lambda + r}$.

$\widehat{I_a^{NT}}$ can be expressed as:

$$\widehat{I_a^{NT}} = \frac{\delta_{TC}^{NT}}{\delta_{TR}^{NT}}\left[FE + DC_W - SG\right] + I_b \tag{26}$$

The no-tax BEI can similarly be expressed as:

$$BEI_{NT} = \frac{\delta_{TC}^{NT}}{\delta_{TR}^{NT}}\left[FE + DC_W - SG\right] \tag{27}$$

The marginal effective tax rate on skills investments

The METR on skills is the difference between the Earnings Increment needed to make the investment in the presence and absence of taxes expressed as a share of the minimum earnings increment required to make the investment in the presence of taxes. Essentially it answers the question: for a *marginal* skills investor, what fraction of the required return is attributable to tax? This equation is expressed concisely below:

$$METR = \frac{BEI_T - BEI_{NT}}{BEI_T} \tag{28}$$

Substituting in the expressions for BEI_T and BEI_{NT} from Equations 25 and 27 the definition of the METR in Equation 28 can be written as:

$$METR = \frac{\left[\left(1 - T_{FE}^{*}\right)FE + DC_W - SG\right] - \frac{\delta_{TC}^{NT}}{\delta_{TC}^{T}}\frac{\delta_{TR}^{T}}{\delta_{TR}^{NT}}\left(1 - T_{EI}\right)\left[FE + DC_W - SG\right]}{\left(1 - T_{FE}^{*}\right)FE + DC_W - SG} \tag{29}$$

If it is assumed that $T_c = 0$, then this expression simplifies to:

$$METR = \frac{-T_{FE}^{*}FE + T_{EI}\left[\left(FE + DC_W - SG\right)\right]}{\left(1 - T_{FE}^{*}\right)FE + DC_W - SG} \tag{30}$$

Which, by adding and subtracting $T_{EI}T_{FE}^{*}FE$ to the numerator, becomes:

$$METR = T_{EI} - \frac{T_{FE}^{*}FE(1 - T_{EI})}{\left[\left(1 - T_{FE}^{*}\right)FE + DC_W - SG\right]} \tag{31}$$

Like Equation 18, this equation demonstrates that the METR is a function of differing tax effects: the tax rate on the earnings increment, as well as the tax rate on the costs of education, incorporating both the tax rate on foregone earnings, as well as the tax rate on the costs of education χ, both of which are incorporated into the rate T_{FE}^{*}.

Upper and lower bounds of the average effective tax rate

In a result similar to those found in the literature on the tax treatment of physical capital, it can be seen that the AETR is a weighted average of the METR and the statutory tax rate on human capital. The AETR on skills is equal to the METR when the earnings increment falls such that it is just equal to the amount needed to breakeven. Where the earnings increment from the skills investment is higher, the average tax rate is a mix between this marginal rate and the top tax rate on skills. In this case, the latter tax rate is the tax rate on the earnings increment. This can be expressed in Equation 32:

$$AETR = \left(\frac{BEI}{EI}\right)METR + \left(1 - \frac{BEI}{EI}\right)T_{EI} \tag{32}$$

Box A2. **Interpreting the Breakeven Earnings Increment**

The intuition behind the BEI can further be explored by substituting the terms δ^{T}_{TC} for $\frac{1}{Z}$ and δ^{T}_{TR} for $\frac{1}{\lambda+\rho-\pi}$, which yields the expression below:

$$BEI = \frac{1}{Z}(\lambda+\rho-\pi)\frac{\left[\left(1-T^{*}_{FE}\right)FE+DC_{W}-SG\right]}{\left(1-T_{EI}\right)}$$

This highlights the key components of the BEI:

- The foregone return on the after-tax cost of investment borne by the student: $(\rho-\pi)\left[\left(1-T^{*}_{FE}\right)FE+DC_{W}-SG\right]$
- An amount to gradually recover the after-tax cost of the investment over the holding period $\lambda\left[\left(1-T^{*}_{FE}\right)FE+DC_{W}-SG\right]$
- Enough to pay for any extra taxes incurred by these extra earnings, $(1-T_{EI})$.

This intuition is highlighted in the figure below, which shows the fall in earnings and the direct costs of education during an educational period, followed by the extra earnings needed to breakeven on the skills investment. The three key components of the BEI highlighted above: the tax wedge, the opportunity cost of capital and the recovery of the costs of a skills investment are highlighted. This graph is based on Norwegian data.

Figure A.1. **Interpreting the BEI: sample path of skills costs and returns**

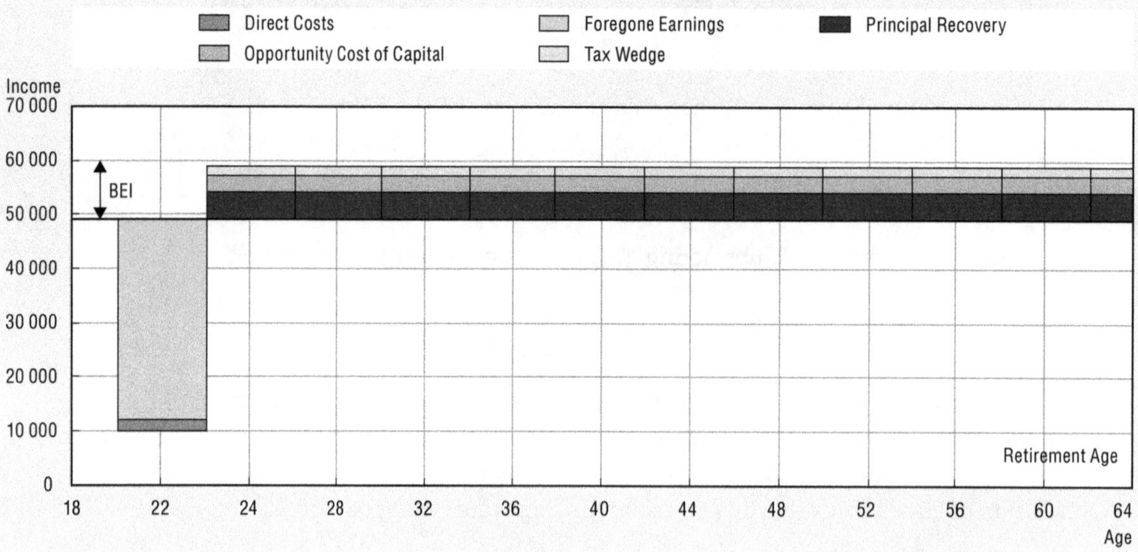

In other words, when a project just breaks even (when $BEI = EI$); there are no economic rents earned. In this instance, the average tax rate on the project is just the marginal rate; the investment is on a knife-edge between taking place and not, there is no infra-marginal return. This is shown in Equation 32; as $EI \rightarrow BEI$, the ratio $\frac{BEI}{EI} \rightarrow 1$. The second term in the equation disappears, and $AETR \rightarrow METR$.

Similarly, as the earnings increment grows large, the inframarginal return grows large as well. In this case the statutory tax rate becomes a larger share of the AETR. To see this simply note that as $EI \rightarrow \infty$, the ratio $\frac{BEI}{EI} \rightarrow 0$. This will see the first term in the Equation 32 tend to 0, and $AETR \rightarrow T_{EI}$.

To demonstrate the veracity of Equation 32, recall the definitions of METR, BEI and AETR. These are taken from Equations 31, 25, and 18, respectively.

$$METR = T_{EI} - \frac{T^{*}_{FE}FE(1-T_{EI})}{\left[(1-T^{*}_{FE})FE + DC_{W} - SG\right]} \quad (33)$$

$$BEI = \frac{\delta^{T}_{TC}}{\delta^{T}_{TR}} \frac{\left[(1-T^{*}_{FE})FE + DC_{W} - SG\right]}{(1-T_{EI})} \quad (34)$$

$$AETR = T_{EI} - \frac{\delta^{T}_{TC}}{\delta^{T}_{TR}} \frac{\left[T_{FE}FE + \chi(DC_{W} - SG)\right]}{EI} \quad (35)$$

Substituting Equation 33 into Equation 32 above, the following result is obtained:

$$AETR = \left(\frac{BEI}{EI}\right)T_{EI} - \left(\frac{BEI}{EI}\right)\frac{T^{*}_{FE}FE(1-T_{EI})}{\left[(1-T^{*}_{FE})FE + DC_{W} - SG\right]} + T_{EI} - \left(\frac{BEI}{EI}\right)T_{EI} \quad (36)$$

Cancelling the first and last terms and adding in the definition of the BEI from Equation 34 above yields:

$$AETR = T_{EI} - \frac{\delta^{T}_{TC}}{\delta^{T}_{TR}} \frac{\left[(1-T^{*}_{FE})FE + DC_{W} - SG\right]}{(1-T_{EI})EI} \frac{T^{*}_{FE}FE(1-T_{EI})}{\left[(1-T^{*}_{FE})FE + DC_{W} - SG\right]} \quad (37)$$

Simplifying, and noting that $T^{*}_{FE}FE = T_{FE}FE + \chi(DC_{W} - SG)$, yields Equation 35 above, demonstrating the result.

A.3 Public costs and benefits and the relationship to the tax system: deriving the ARCR and MRCR

The discussion so far has considered the costs and benefits, and the effect of the tax system on them, from the perspective of the worker or individual. Throughout, the other party to the educational investment has been the government.[8] The second key set of indicators in this study examines the costs and benefits of skills investments from the perspective of the government. It is important to note that unlike in the individual case, no optimisation is assumed; there is no breakeven action on the part of the government. This section describes a 'Tobin's q' for the investment in human capital from the perspective of the government; a ratio of the NPV of the earnings streams from education to the NPV of the costs of education. Two of these indicators are presented. The first is for a pre-specified level of student earnings after-education. This is the ARCR for the government. The second RCR assumes that the earnings stream for the individual worker is such that the individual just breaks even. This indicator calculates the RCR for the government for this *marginal student*; this is the MRCR. These two indicators are analogous to the AETR and METR developed previously.

The key insight from these RCR indicators, as discussed in the main text, is that the tax system helps to divide the costs and benefits of the educational investment between the government and the individual worker. On the cost side, it does so partially; the tax rate on foregone earnings and the tax breaks given for scholarship income and direct costs perform this function. However, the ratio of individual direct spending to government direct spending matters too. On the benefits side, however, the tax system performs the entirety of the division of benefits between the government and the individual worker. This insight has been discussed in the main text, and will be outlined mathematically below.

The approach is as follows: first the overall costs of upskilling are modelled: lost earnings, direct spending by students, direct spending by the government. The benefits of the educational investment are then examined. The model then discusses how these benefits are apportioned, and calculates the costs and benefits for the government. Having done this, the model calculates the ARCR and the MRCR. The difference between these two indicators is simply that the ARCR calculates the government's RCR for the *average* individual making an educational investment; the average student is assumed to receive a more-than-breakeven return to the investment. The MRCR calculates the RCR for the *marginal* individual, who just breaks even on the investment. In other words, the MRCR is simply the ARCR where the $EI = BEI$. Throughout this section, the assumption that $T_c = 0$ is maintained for simplicity.

The total cost of upskilling

The total cost of upskilling is defined as follows:

$$TC = I_b - E_d + DC_W + DC_G \tag{38}$$

Where I_b, E_d, and DC_W are as before, and DC_G is the direct costs of education borne by the government. Note that an assumption of this approach is that all scholarship and grant income is supplied by the government; this scholarship income is not a "cost" of education per se, but rather a transfer from the government to the individual worker; this means that it nets out of Equation 38.

The fraction of TC borne by the government (TC_G) is $TC - TC_W$, where TC_W are the costs borne by the worker. Substituting the expression of TC_W from Equation 4, yields:

$$TC_G = T_{I_b} I_b - T_{E_d} E_d + \theta DC_W + (1 - \varphi) SG + DC_G \tag{39}$$

This can be divided into several parts:

- The lost tax revenue from the worker's reduced earnings, $T_{I_b} I_b - T_{E_d} E_d$,
- The revenue losses result from the tax treatment of direct costs θDC_W,
- The lost scholarship income SG (offset by any tax received on this scholarship income φSG).
- Plus the direct government spending on education, DC_G.

Similarly, the total per period returns to upskilling are simply characterised by the earnings increment:

$$TR = EI = I_a - I_b \tag{40}$$

as defined in Equation 3. Recall that the fraction of TR borne by the government, TR_G is $TR - TR_W$, where TR_W are the part of the return received by the worker. Substituting the expression for TR_W from Equation 2 yields $TR_G = T_{EI} EI$. Here, $T_{EI} = \frac{T_a I_a - T_b I_b}{I_a - I_b}$ as before.

This means that the tax system apportions the returns between the student and the government; more progressive taxes will mean a higher T_{EI}, which will mean a higher share of returns from upskilling for the government.

The average returns to costs ratio of government spending

A Tobin's q – a returns to costs ratio for a government investment in skills – can be defined. This is the ratio of the present value of the returns to the skills investment to the replacement cost of the skills investment. As with the second term in Equation 8, the NPV for the individual worker, the government's present value of the returns to an educational investment can be defined as:

$$V = \int_{n=m}^{\infty} \lambda e^{-\lambda(n-m)} \left[\int_{t=m}^{n} TR_G e^{-(r)(t-m)} dt + 0 \cdot e^{-(r)(n-m)} \right] dn \tag{41}$$

Whereas in Section A.2, the $0 \cdot e^{-(\rho-\pi)(n-1)}$ is a representation of the fact that the value of the investment falls to zero when a person retires. The ARCR can be defined as:

$$ARCR_G = \frac{\int_{n=m}^{\infty} \lambda e^{-\lambda(n-m)} \left[\int_{t=m}^{n} T_{EI} EI\, e^{-(\rho-\pi)(t-m)} dt \right] dn}{\delta_{TC}^{NT} TC_G} \tag{42}$$

Solving the integrals gives:

$$ARCR_G = \frac{\delta_{TR}^{NT}}{\delta_{TC}^{NT}} \frac{T_{EI} EI}{TC_G} \tag{43}$$

It is important to note that in Equation 43 with respect to the government, "no tax" discount factors are used, δ_{TR}^{NT} and δ_{TC}^{NT}. This is due to the assumption that capital taxation raises no wedge between the returns to skills and an alternative capital investment for the government; the government would not pay capital taxes to itself on an alternative capital investment. Note, however, that there is no accounting for lost capital taxes for the government when an individual invests in skills instead of investing in an alternative capital investment. The overall formula for $ARCR_G$ will be:

$$ARCR_G = \frac{\delta_{TR}^{NT}}{\delta_{TC}^{NT}} \frac{T_{EI} EI}{\left[T_{FE} FE + \chi(DC_W - SG) + DC_G + SG \right]} \tag{44}$$

Equation 44 is exactly the formula used in the Taxing Wages models. This formula is essentially a ratio of returns to costs; where it is greater than one; the discounted stream of benefits are larger than grossed-up costs; in such situations, investing in skills is profitable for the government from a tax revenue perspective. Where it is less than one, the discounted stream of returns to the government is less than the grossed-up costs. In such situations, the educational investment does not pay for itself in the form of tax revenue.

The marginal returns to costs ratio of government spending

The previous section takes the term EI as exogenous, however, under the assumption that the individual worker continues to invest in education up to the point where the returns fall to the breakeven level, the RCR for the government differs. In this case, the expected return from the investment is simply the breakeven earnings level. This is in contrast to the ARCR in Equation 44, where the earnings level is not specified.

Note the equation for the BEI derived previously (in Equation 25), stated below.

$$BEI = \frac{\delta_{TC}^{T}}{\delta_{TR}^{T}} \frac{\left[(1 - T_{FE}^{*}) FE + DC_W - SG \right]}{(1 - T_{EI})} = \frac{\delta_{TC}^{T}}{\delta_{TR}^{T}} \frac{\left[(1 - T_{FE}) FE - \chi(DC_w - SG) + DC_W - SG \right]}{(1 - T_{EI})} \tag{45}$$

The MRCR is derived by substituting the BEI for the EI into Equation 44. This yields an expression for the MRCR as follows:

$$MRCR_G = \frac{\delta_{TR}^{NT}}{\delta_{TC}^{NT}} \frac{\delta_{TC}^{T}}{\delta_{TR}^{T}} \frac{\left[(1 - T_{FE}) FE - \chi(DC_w - SG) + DC_W - SG \right]}{\left[T_{FE} FE + \chi(DC_w - SG) + DC_G + SG \right]} \frac{T_{EI}}{(1 - T_{EI})} \tag{46}$$

Multiplying by $\frac{EI}{EI}$ yields:

$$MRCR_G = \frac{\frac{\delta_{TR}^{NT}}{\delta_{TR}^{T}} \frac{T_{EI}EI}{(1-T_{EI})EI}}{\frac{\delta_{TC}^{NT}}{\delta_{TC}^{T}} \frac{\left[T_{FE}FE + \chi(DC_W - SG) + DC_G + SG\right]}{\left[(1-T_{FE})FE - \chi(DC_W - SG) + DC_W - SG\right]}} \qquad (47)$$

While this expression seems complicated, it can be simplified greatly by noting that

- $TR_G = T_{EI}EI$
- $TR_W = (1-T_{EI})EI$
- $TC_G = \left[T_{FE}FE + \chi(DC_W - SG) + DC_G + SG\right]$
- $TC_W = \left[(1-T_{FE})FE - \chi(DC_W - SG) + DC_W - SG\right]$

Simplifying, $MRCR_G$ becomes:

$$MRCR_G = \frac{\frac{\delta_{TR}^{NT}}{\delta_{TR}^{T}} \frac{TR_G}{TR_W}}{\frac{\delta_{TC}^{NT}}{\delta_{TC}^{T}} \frac{TC_G}{TC_W}} \qquad (48)$$

To explain this, note that:

- $\delta_{TR}^{NT}TR_G$ is the government's discounted returns to the skills investment,
- $\delta_{TR}^{T}TR_W$ is the worker's discounted returns to the skills investment,
- $\delta_{TC}^{NT}TC_G$ is the government's discounted costs for the skills investment,
- $\delta_{TC}^{T}TC_W$ is the worker's discounted returns to the skills investment.

The 'Tobin's q', the governments' MRCR, is a ratio of ratios; it is a ratio of the ratio of discounted government and individual benefits to the ratio of discounted government and individual costs.

The ARCR (as defined in Equation 44) is a ratio of discounted benefits to discounted costs. Where this ratio is greater than one, the government is recouping the entirety of its benefits, in NPV terms, in later tax revenue. The MRCR functions in a similar way. The difference is rather that the breakeven response of the individual is built into the MRCR in a way that is not the case for the ARCR. The MRCR presumes that the amount invested by the individual worker is such that they break even. But this rate itself is a function of the division of costs and benefits for the government.

What matters for the government, in terms of the return on its investment, is not the ratio of its costs to its returns, but rather whether the ratio of its costs to the costs of the individual are higher or lower than the ratio of its returns to the individuals. Put another way, if the government receives a higher share of the returns than the share of the costs it bears, then the MRCR is greater than 1. If it receives a lower share of the returns than the share of the costs it bears, then the MRCR is less than one.

A.4 Including student debt and its effects on public and private costs and benefits of education

This section extends the analysis in Sections A.2 and A.3 to allow for the possibility that students finance part or all of the costs of their education by borrowing from the government. The section repeats the discussion and finds the same key equations for the

AETRs, BEI, METR, ARCR and MRCR, but also incorporates several key terms that account for the impact of financing costs or subsidies that reduce the costs of skills financing, such as through reduced interest rates on student loans, loan write-offs, and the tax treatment of student debt. The debt is constructed as a bond for ease of exposition, though the underlying principles remain the same as if the debt was constructed as a standard bank loan.

Several key areas of flexibility are including in the modelling.

- The **percentage of total costs borrowed** is allowed to vary.
- The **length of the loan period** is allowed to vary.
- The **rate at which the student borrows** can also vary. It can be set equal to the risk-free real return on a capital investment r, or it can be a rate lower or higher than the risk free rate. In the case, for example, of a government subsidy in the form of a reduced-interest loan, the rate may be lower than the risk-free rate. Where the rate it is higher, it can be conceived to represent a premium for student debt, potentially due to higher riskiness of student debt.
- The **interest on student debt can be deductible** from the student's taxable income after they finish their schooling. The rate of this tax deduction can vary (it can be deducted at the marginal after-education tax rate, but limits can also be placed on the deductibility. Note that tax deductibility of repayments of the principal of the debt is not accounted for; only the interest is treated as being tax-deductible.
- A fraction of the student debt can also be written off by the government, meaning that this part of the principal does not need to be repaid at the end of the loan period. The model does not account for the tax treatment of debt-write offs.

The approach proceeds analogously to the approaches in Section A.2. Throughout, equations from these latter two sections are re-defined incorporating loan provisions. The first section defines the adjusted costs of education incorporating student debt. The next section incorporates these revised costs and returns into the calculation of the AETR. The next section incorporates the same adjusted costs and returns into the calculation of the BEI. The next section incorporates this revised BEI into the calculation of the METR. The final two sections calculate revised versions of the ARCR and MRCR respectively.

Defining costs of education

The modelling proceeds as follows. The costs of education, involving lost post-tax earnings $(1-T_{I_b})I_b-(1-T_{Ed})E_d$, direct costs DC_W, scholarship income SG, and STEs (θ and φ), are all retained. It is then assumed that the student borrows α % of the cost of upskilling.

$$\alpha TC_W=\alpha\left[(1-T_{I_b})I_b-(1-T_{Ed})E_d+(1-\theta)DC_W-(1-\varphi)SG\right] \tag{49}$$

It is important to note that $(1-\alpha)TC_W$ remains to be paid by the student from their existing savings, as in Section A.2. Note that it could be assumed that the student only borrows the fixed costs of education that they bear $(1-\theta)DC_W$. In this case the definition of α would be $\alpha=\frac{(1-\theta)DC_W}{TC_W}$.

However, the student could also borrow the full costs of the education, inclusive of any lost earnings. In this case the value of α would be 1.

Interest on the loan is set at a nominal rate of $\left(r^{*}+\pi\right)$, so the real rate of interest is r_l. It is assumed, for ease of exposition, that interest starts to be paid when the student starts using the skills, so interest is not paid while the student continues in education. As mentioned, the real interest rate on the student loans can be set to equal to the risk-free real return on capital investments r, or r_l can be set to be equal to some other value.The nominal amount of interest paid on the loan is assumed to be tax deductible at rate T_l. Generally, it will be assumed that $T_l = T_a$, though the modelling can also account for situations in which the size of the deductibility might be capped, and thus where $T_l < T_a$.

The principal is paid back at the end of the expected holding period of the loan. This expected holding period is defined as β years. In such cases as where the holding period of the loan is the student's expected future years in the labour market, then $\beta = \lambda$. Further, it is important to note that the principal amount that is repaid is not indexed for inflation – only the nominal value of the loan taken out is repaid.

A portion of the nominal value of the loan is forgiven $(1-\varepsilon)\%$; $\varepsilon\%$ is repaid. It is assumed that this increase in wealth coming from loan forgiveness is not taxed.

By incorporating all these factors together, an expression for the NPV of the Costs of Education is obtained.

$$NPVC = -\left[\int_{n=0}^{m} TC_W e^{(\rho-\pi)n} dn\right] \cdot \left[(1-\alpha)+\alpha\left(\int_{n=m}^{\infty} \beta e^{-\beta(n-m)}\left[\int_{t=m}^{n}(1-T_l)(r^{*}+\pi)e^{-(\rho)(t-m)}dt+\varepsilon\cdot e^{-(\rho)(n-m)}\right]dn\right)\right] \quad (50)$$

Rearranging yields the following equation:

$$NPVC = -\left[\int_{n=0}^{m} TC_W e^{(\rho-\pi)n} dn\right] \cdot \left[(1-\alpha)+\alpha\left(\int_{n=m}^{\infty} \beta e^{-\beta(n-m)}\left[-\frac{(1-T_l)(r^{*}+\pi)}{\rho}\left(e^{-(\rho)(n-m)}-1\right)+\varepsilon\cdot e^{-(\rho)(n-m)}\right]dn\right)\right] \quad (51)$$

This can be seen as analogous to the first term in Equation 8 in Section A.2 of this Annex, except that the expression for total costs is weighted by the extent to which borrowing these costs increases or decreases the costs in NPV terms. A term, F^T can then be defined as the overall extent to which the treatment of student debt reduces or increases the costs of education to the student. This means that the true cost to the student is reduced or increased by $(1-F^T)$ times the fraction of the total nominal costs of upskilling - as defined in Equation 4 of this Annex - borrowed by the student. This weight is defined as:

$$1-F^T = \left(\int_{n=m}^{\infty} \beta e^{-\beta(n-m)}\left[-\frac{(1-T_l)(r^{*}+\pi)}{\rho}\left[e^{-(\rho)(n-m)}-1\right]+\varepsilon e^{-(\rho)(n-m)}\right]dn\right) \quad (52)$$

A series of rearrangements and simplifications yields a simplified expression for F^T:

$$\Rightarrow 1-F^T = \left(\beta\left(\varepsilon-\frac{(1-T_l)(r^{*}+\pi)}{\rho}\right)\int_{n=m}^{\infty} e^{-(\beta+\rho)(n-m)}\,dn+\left[\frac{\beta(1-T_l)(r^{*}+\pi)}{\rho}\right]\int_{n=m}^{\infty} e^{-\beta(n-m)}\,dn\right)$$

$$\Rightarrow 1-F^{T} = -\frac{\beta}{(\beta+\rho)}\left(\varepsilon-\frac{(1-T_{l})(r^{*}+\pi)}{\rho}\right)\left(e^{-(\beta+\rho)(n-m)}\Big|_{n=m}^{\infty}\right)-\frac{\beta\dfrac{(1-T_{l})(r^{*}+\pi)}{\rho}}{\beta}\left(e^{-\beta(n-m)}\Big|_{n=m}^{\infty}\right)$$

$$\Rightarrow 1-F^{T} = \frac{\beta}{(\beta+\rho)}\left(\varepsilon-\frac{(1-T_{l})(r^{*}+\pi)}{\rho}\right)+\frac{(1-T_{l})(r^{*}+\pi)}{\rho}$$

$$\Rightarrow F^{T} = \frac{\left[\beta(1-\varepsilon)\right]+\left[\rho-(1-T_{l})(r^{*}+\pi)\right]}{\beta+\rho} \tag{53}$$

The definition of Total Costs of Education incorporating financing costs for the individual is as follows:

$$TFC = -TC_{W}\left(\frac{e^{(\rho-\pi)m}-1}{\rho-\pi}\right)\cdot\left[(1-\alpha)+\alpha(1-F^{T})\right] \tag{54}$$

As mentioned, this is an expression analogous to the first term in Equation 8 above. Following from this, Equation 8, incorporating student debt, can be redefined as follows:

$$V = TFC+\int_{n=m}^{\infty}\lambda e^{-\lambda(n-m)}\left[\int_{t=m}^{n}TR_{W}e^{-(\rho-\pi)(t-m)}dt+0\,e^{-(\rho-\pi)(n-m)}\right]dn \tag{55}$$

This can be rewritten as:

$$V = -\frac{1}{Z}TC_{W}\left[(1-\alpha)+\alpha(1-F^{T})\right]+\frac{TR_{W}}{\lambda+\rho-\pi}$$

$$\Rightarrow V = -\frac{1}{Z}\left[(1-T_{FE}^{*})FE+DC_{W}-SG\right](1-\alpha F^{T})+\frac{(1-T_{EI})EI}{\lambda+\rho-\pi} \tag{56}$$

Defining the average effective tax rate on skills

Recall from Section A.2 that $\delta_{TC}^{T} = \frac{1}{Z} = \frac{e^{(\rho-\pi)m}-1}{\rho-\pi}$ and that $\delta_{TR}^{T} = \frac{1}{\lambda+\rho-\pi}$. Given this, V can also be expressed concisely as:

$$V = -\delta_{TC}^{T}\left[(1-T_{FE}^{*})FE+DC_{W}-SG\right](1-\alpha F^{T})+\delta_{TR}^{T}(1-T_{EI})EI \tag{57}$$

This equation is analogous to Equation 12 in Section A.2 of this Annex. In the no-tax case, as discussed, all taxes are set to zero. This means that $T_{I_b} = T_{E_d} = T_a = \varphi = \theta = 0$. In accounting for student loans, this also means that $T_l = 0$. This in turn means that V_{NT} becomes:

$$V_{NT} = -\delta_{TC}^{NT}\left[FE+DC_{W}-SG\right](1-\alpha F^{NT})+\delta_{TR}^{NT}EI \tag{58}$$

Where $\delta_{TC}^{NT} = \frac{e^{(r)m}-1}{r}$, $\delta_{TR}^{NT} = \frac{1}{\lambda+r}$, and $F^{NT} = \frac{\beta(1-\varepsilon)+(r-r^{*})}{\beta+r+\pi}$. Hence, in the no-tax case, the effects of the introduction of student loans on the overall NPV of upskilling are confined to two factors. The first is the difference in the real interest rate that the student pays and the real interest rate the student has to pay to the government on its student debt. The second is the value of any loan write-off provided.

Building on this definition of the NPV of education, the AETR definition from Section A.2 is simply restated as the difference between the NPV of education with and without taxes, as a share of the discounted increase in earnings after education.

$$\text{AETR} = \frac{(V_{NT} - V_T)}{\delta_{TR}^{NT} EI} = \frac{(V_{NT} - V_T)}{\frac{EI}{\lambda + r}} \tag{59}$$

In this context, the AETR incorporating student debt is defined as:

$$\begin{aligned} \text{AETR} = \left[\frac{\lambda + r}{EI}\right] & \left(-\delta_{TC}^{NT}[FE + DC_W - SG](1 - \alpha F^{NT}) + \delta_{TR}^{NT} EI\right) \\ & + \delta_{TC}^{T}\left[(1 - T_{FE}^{*})FE + DC_W - SG\right](1 - \alpha F^{T}) - \delta_{TR}^{T}(1 - T_{EI})EI) \end{aligned} \tag{60}$$

Defining the breakeven earnings increment

Setting V= 0 in Equation 57 yields a definition for the BEI:

$$\text{BEI} = \frac{\delta_{TC}^{T}}{\delta_{TR}^{T}} \frac{\left[(1 - T_{FE}^{*})FE + DC_W - SG\right](1 - \alpha F^{T})}{(1 - T_{EI})} \tag{61}$$

Which is analogous to Equation 25. $\widehat{I}_a$, the necessary amount of pre-tax income needed to be earned to break even on a skills investment can be defined similarly as in Equation 21 as:

$$\widehat{I}_a = \frac{\frac{\delta_{TC}^{T}}{\delta_{TR}^{T}}\left[(1 - T_{FE}^{*})FE + DC_W - SG\right](1 - \alpha F^{T}) + (1 - T_b)I_b}{(1 - T_a)} \tag{62}$$

Disaggregating F^T yields:

$$\begin{aligned} \widehat{I}_a = & \frac{(1 - T_b)I_b}{(1 - T_a)} + \left(\frac{1}{(1 - T_a)}\frac{\delta_{TC}^{T}}{\delta_{TR}^{T}}\right)\left[(1 - T_{FE}^{*})FE + DC_W - SG\right] \\ & - \alpha\left(\frac{1}{(1 - T_a)}\frac{\delta_{TC}^{T}}{\delta_{TR}^{T}}\right)\left[(1 - T_{FE}^{*})FE + DC_W - SG\right]\left[\frac{[\beta(1 - \varepsilon)]}{\beta + \rho}\right] \\ & - \alpha\left(\frac{1}{(1 - T_a)}\frac{\delta_{TC}^{T}}{\delta_{TR}^{T}}\right)\left[(1 - T_{FE}^{*})FE + DC_W - SG\right]\left[\frac{\rho - (r^{*} + \pi)}{\beta + \rho}\right] \\ & - \alpha\left(\frac{1}{(1 - T_a)}\frac{\delta_{TC}^{T}}{\delta_{TR}^{T}}\right)\left[(1 - T_{FE}^{*})FE + DC_W - SG\right]\left[T_l\left(\frac{r^{*} + \pi}{\beta + \rho}\right)\right] \end{aligned} \tag{63}$$

Note that the first two terms in the above Equation 63 are the same as in Equation 21. They imply that breakeven income after education must be equal to income before education, plus enough to pay back the discounted costs of education, plus any additional taxes that may result due to higher earnings after education. The three last terms – new to this equation – are the three ways in which student debt impacts breakeven income. The first term accounts for potential gains from loan write-offs ε. The size of this write off is multiplied by the post-tax discounted value of borrowing.

The second term is the value of any special interest rate provisions provided to a student. This interest differential is defined as $\rho - (r^{*} + \pi)$. Note that where capital taxes are zero it can be defined as $r - r^{*}$, the difference between the risk-free interest rate and the rate at which the student borrows. Note further that if the student borrows at the rate r, this second-last term falls to zero.

The third term is the value of any interest deductibility or any other student debt tax interest relief. Note that $T_l = \frac{T_a^{+}\widehat{I}_a - T_a\widehat{I}_a}{Interest}$ and $Interest = \frac{\left[(1 - T_{FE}^{*})FE + DC_W - SG\right]}{Z}\alpha(r^{*} + \pi)$. The marginal rate of interest deductibility T_l is the difference between tax paid in the presence of interest relief $T_a^+\hat{I}_a$ and tax paid without this relief $T_a\hat{I}_a$. This is analogous to the definition of χ in Equation 6.

Defining the marginal effective tax rate on skills

Recalling the definition of the METR from Equation 28, $METR = \frac{BEI_T - BEI_{NT}}{BEI_T}$. Recalling also the definition of V_{NT} from Equation 58.

$$V_{NT} = -\delta_{TC}^{NT}\left[FE + DC_W - SG\right](1 - \alpha F^{NT}) + \delta_{TR}^{NT} EI$$

Whereas previously $\delta_{TC}^{NT} = \frac{e^{(r)m} - 1}{r}$, $\delta_{TR}^{NT} = \frac{1}{\lambda + r}$, and $F^{NT} = \frac{\beta(1-\varepsilon) + (r - r^*)}{\beta + r + \pi}$. This means that the definition of BEI_{NT} (analogous to Equation 27) is as follows:

$$BEI_{NT} = \frac{\delta_{TC}^{NT}}{\delta_{TR}^{NT}}\left[FE + DC_W - SG\right]\left(1 - \alpha F^{NT}\right) \tag{64}$$

Putting this equation together with the definition of the BEI in Equation 61 and the definition of the METR from Equation 28 yields the overall required equation. Assuming $T_c = 0$, this can expressed as follows:

$$METR_{NT} = \frac{\dfrac{\left[\left(1 - T_{FE}^*\right)FE + DC_W - SG\right]\left(1 - \alpha F^T\right)}{\left(1 - T_{EI}\right)} - \left[FE + DC_W - SG\right]\left(1 - \alpha F^{NT}\right)}{\dfrac{\left[\left(1 - T_{FE}^*\right)FE + DC_W - SG\right]\left(1 - \alpha F^T\right)}{\left(1 - T_{EI}\right)}} \tag{65}$$

Defining the average returns to costs ratio for governments

Recall from Equation 38 the per-period total costs of education, including both the costs to the government and to the student, $TC = I_b - E_d + DC_W + DC_G$. Recalling the definition of TC_W incorporating student debt, $TC_W = \left[1 - \alpha F_W^T)\right]\left[\left(1 - T_{I_b}\right)I_b - \left(1 - T_{E_d}\right)E_d + (1-\theta)DC_W - (1-\varphi)SG\right]$. As in Equation 39, the difference in government costs are defined as the difference between total costs and the workers' costs $TC_G = TC - TC_W$. This assumes no private loan provision to students. It follows that:

$$TC_G = I_b - E_d + DC_W + DC_G - \left[\left(1 - T_{I_b}\right)I_b - \left(1 - T_{E_d}\right)E_d + (1-\theta)DC_W - (1-\varphi)SG\right]\cdot\left(1 - \alpha F^T\right) \tag{66}$$

This can be rearranged as follows:

$$TC_G = T_{I_b}I_b + T_{E_d}E_d + \theta DC_W + (1-\varphi)SG + DC_G + \alpha F^T\left[TC_W\right] \tag{67}$$

This is analogous to Equation 39 above, but where F^T is defined as in Equation 53. Note that the addition of $\alpha F^T\left[TC_W\right]$ to the equation raises costs for the government; subsidised student debt provision costs the government, and does so more where the size of student debt is larger. The definition of the ARCR in this case is just as in Equation 43 in Section 3.2 above: $ARCR_G = \frac{\delta_{TR}^{NT}}{\delta_{TC}^{NT}}\frac{T_{EI}EI}{TC_G}$, except where TC_G is defined as in Equation 67 above.

Defining the marginal returns to costs ratio

The approach to defining the MRCR in this case follows that in Section A.3; the BEI is substituted for the EI in the definition of the ARCR. Recalling the definition of the BEI:

$$BEI = \frac{\delta_{TC}^T}{\delta_{TR}^T}\frac{\left[\left(1 - T_{FE}^*\right)FE + DC_W - SG\right]\left(1 - \alpha F^T\right)}{\left(1 - T_{EI}\right)} \tag{68}$$

Where, $F^{T} = \frac{[\beta(1-\varepsilon)]+[\rho-(1-T_{l})(r^{*}+\pi)]}{\beta+\rho}$, $\delta_{TC}^{T} = \frac{1}{Z} = \frac{e^{(\rho-\pi)m}-1}{\rho-\pi}$, and $\delta_{TR}^{T} = \frac{1}{\lambda+\rho-\pi}$.

Noting from Section 3.3 that the definition of the MRCR is $MRCR_{G} = \frac{\delta_{TR}^{NT}}{\delta_{TC}^{NT}}\frac{T_{EI}BEI}{[TC_{G}]}$, substituting the BEI definition above yields the following expression:

$$MRCR_{G} = \frac{\delta_{TR}^{NT}\delta_{TC}^{T}}{\delta_{TC}^{NT}\delta_{TR}^{T}}\frac{\left[(1-T_{FE}^{*})FE+DC_{W}-SG\right](1-\alpha F^{T})}{[TC_{G}]}\frac{T_{EI}}{(1-T_{EI})} \tag{69}$$

Noting that as in Section A.3, $T_{c} = 0$ throughout, TC_{G} can be defined as as follows:

$$TC_{G} = [T_{FE}FE+\chi(DC_{W}-SG)+DC_{G}+SG]+\left[(1-T_{FE}^{*})FE+DC_{W}-SG\right]\alpha F^{T} \tag{70}$$

Hence, the MRCR can be defined as follows:

$$MRCR_{G} = \frac{\frac{\delta_{TR}^{NT}}{\delta_{TR}^{T}}}{\frac{\delta_{TC}^{NT}}{\delta_{TC}^{T}}}\frac{\frac{T_{EI}}{(1-T_{EI})}}{\frac{[T_{FE}FE+\chi(DC_{W}-SG)+DC_{G}+SG]+\left[(1-T_{FE}^{*})FE+DC_{W}-SG\right]\alpha F^{T}}{\left[(1-T_{FE}^{*})FE+DC_{W}-SG\right](1-\alpha F^{T})}} \tag{71}$$

Notes

1. Throughout, variables for the individual are denoted with a W subscript, for 'worker'. Variables for the government are denoted with a G subscript.
2. For computational simplicity, the 'Present' of the 'Net Present Value' of an educational investment is taken to be the *end* of the educational investment, not the beginning. This means that costs of education, when they take place over several years, are "grossed up' or 'reverse discounted'.
3. Throughout, the role of the firm is omitted from the analysis.
4. The discussion throughout abstracts from the returns to education that do not come in the form of increased expected earnings. For example, non-pecuniary benefits are omitted from the analysis, as are changes to employment probabilities.
5. T_{EI} is a marginal and not an average effective tax rate, although the margin *EI* can be quite large. Note that for each income level X > Y, the following relation holds (where T_X and T_Y represent the average effective tax rates on income X and Y respectively and T_{XY} is the marginal tax rate on the earnings increment X-Y): $T_X \cdot X = T_Y \cdot Y + T_{XY} \cdot (X-Y)$. In cases where only PITs are considered and depending on the statutory PIT brackets, the TEI is a weighted average of the marginal PIT rates over the EI interval (i.e. a 'weighted average' marginal PIT rate).
6. The probability that the investment yields a return TR_W in period 1, after which no further return is earned is λ; the probability that the investment earns a return TR_W in periods 1 and 2, after which no further return is earned equals $\lambda e^{-\lambda}$; which is slightly lower than λ; the probability that the investment earns a return TR_W in periods 1, 2, and 3, after which no further return is earned is even smaller ($\lambda e^{-2\lambda}$). The probability of earning a return in every period until *n* but not thereafter decreases as *n* increases. Note that the periodic return TR_W is assumed to be constant over time but is discounted after period 1. This setup implies that the investment will earn a return TR_W in period 1 with full certainty while the probability that the investment yields a return in the following periods decreases over time until *n* reaches infinity, when the probability that the investment earns a return is 0.
7. It would be possible to assume that wages also increase with productivity by adding a productivity growth term to ρ-π. It would also be possible to assume that wages increase by less than π, as if they were partly indexed, which could be incorporated as another extension of this work.
8. As is discussed in the main text, the role of firms or civil society in providing or financing education is ignored.

ANNEX B

Comparative Tables

This annex provides the country details that lie behind the comparative analysis. As outlined in the main text, the data provided are for 2011. The annex is structured in three sections. Section 1 provides comparative tables for each of the five main indicators presented in this Tax Policy Study. The indicators are the Breakeven Earnings Increment (BEI), the Marginal Effective Tax Rate on Skills (METR), the Average Effective Tax Rate on Skills (AETR), the Marginal Effective Tax Rate on Skills (METR), the Average Effective Tax Rate on Skills (AETR), the Marginal Returns to Costs Ratio, and the Average Returns to Costs Ratio. The calculations behind these variables are discussed in more detail in Chapter 3 and in Annex A of this study.

The statistical data for Israel are supplied by and under the responsibility of the relevant Israeli authorities. The use of such data by the OECD is without prejudice to the status of the Golan Heights, East Jerusalem and Israeli settlements in the West Bank under the terms of international law.

Table B.1. **Average Effective Tax Rate on Skills, as a % of the Earnings Increment**

		17 Years Old, Single No Children, 4 Years Education, No Borrowing, Scholarship Income	17 Years Old, Single No Children, 4 Years Education Borrows Direct Costs at 0%, Scholarship Income	17 Years Old, Single No Children, 4 Years Education Borrows Direct Costs and Lost Income at 0%, Scholarship Income	17 Years Old, Single No Children, 4 Years Education Borrows Direct Costs at 6%, Scholarship Income	17 Years Old, Single No Children, 4 Years Education Borrows Direct Costs and Lost Income at 6%, Scholarship Income	27 Years Old, Single No Children, 1 Year Education, No Borrowing, Scholarship Income	32 Years Old, Single No Children, Mid-Career Training, No Borrowing, No Scholarship Income	50 Years Old, Single No Children, 1 Year Education, No Borrowing, Scholarship Income
AUS	Australia	27.591	33.229	34.842	27.583	34.842	27.509	10.383	22.987
AUT	Austria	26.31	26.476	31.353	26.14	15.906	26.444	5.376	22.89
BEL	Belgium	36.287	36.698	42.865	35.865	24.674	36.694	12.514	25.173
CAN	Canada	22.85	24.892	28.835	19.769	7.619	25.719	17.032	21.731
CHL	Chile	0.0	4.545	7.051	-6.728	-16.953	0.0	0.0	0.0
CZE	Czech Republic	17.642	18.255	23.242	16.994	5.604	16.577	19.788	13.834
DNK	Denmark	40.527	41.398	44.555	39.398	32.782	41.794	41.674	34.695
EST	Estonia	16.128	17.375	22.662	14.744	3.029	15.473	7.171	10.854
FIN	Finland	33.603	33.993	38.666	33.196	23.875	33.747	24.715	28.937
GRC	Greece	27.547	27.564	33.219	27.531	15.894	30.797	24.254	24.941
HUN	Hungary	26.625	28.996	32.532	23.618	14.445	28.832	35.007	24.865
ISL	Iceland	32.201	32.644	39.347	31.744	18.63	30.727	13.987	25.511
IRL	Ireland	33.702	34.936	38.77	32.289	22.922	42.157	21.631	38.965
ISR	Israel	19.613	21.408	25.157	17.463	6.893	20.43	9.488	18.727
ITA	Italy	28.199	29.673	34.315	26.516	16.374	30.56	17.565	25.767
LUX	Luxembourg	30.95	31.212	35.809	30.68	21.009	31.26	9.065	25.056
MEX	Mexico	18.977	22.338	25.84	14.469	3.772	12.536	-11.745	9.579
NLD	Netherlands	39.836	40.67	44.557	38.92	29.436	35.838	13.538	32.176
NZL	New Zealand	23.178	25.136	28.614	20.764	11.635	26.166	29.534	23.182
NOR	Norway	28.573	28.854	33.607	28.284	18.859	31.465	36.442	27.799
POL	Poland	7.921	9.542	12.731	5.968	-3.109	6.925	8.707	5.43
PRT	Portugal	26.21	27.601	31.191	24.588	15.159	24.447	25.728	21.68
SVK	Slovak Republic	14.393	15.583	19.034	13.024	4.604	13.46	16.185	10.361
SVN	Slovenia	17.177	17.903	21.142	16.376	9.107	17.67	20.695	14.525
ESP	Spain	21.846	23.141	27.688	20.383	9.747	21.68	25.814	18.144
SWE	Sweden	29.528	29.548	34.412	29.508	19.947	37.512	2.946	33.817
CHE	Switzerland	17.272	17.841	22.649	16.671	5.587	18.633	18.141	16.239
TUR	Turkey	14.947	15.074	20.125	14.819	4.232	14.09	4.385	10.508
GBR	United Kingdom	14.873	18.236	22.735	10.517	-0.98	14.294	7.74	10.508

StatLink http://dx.doi.org/10.1787/888933446673

Table B.2. **Breakeven Earnings Increments on Skills Investments, % of previous earnings**

		17 Years Old, Single No Children, 4 Years Education, No Borrowing, Scholarship Income	17 Years Old, Single No Children, 4 Years Education Borrows Direct Costs at 0%, Scholarship Income	17 Years Old, Single No Children, 4 Years Education Borrows Direct Costs and Lost Income at 0%, Scholarship Income	17 Years Old, Single No Children, 4 Years Education Borrows Direct Costs at 6%, Scholarship Income	17 Years Old, Single No Children, 4 Years Education Borrows Direct Costs and Lost Income at 6%, Scholarship Income	27 Years Old, Single No Children, 1 Year Education, No Borrowing, Scholarship Income	32 Years Old, Single No Children, Mid-Career Training, No Borrowing, No Scholarship Income	50 Years Old, Single No Children, 1 Year Education, No Borrowing, Scholarship Income
AUS	Australia	20.177	17.383	0.0	22.97	0.0	5.023	0.594	9.108
AUT	Austria	13.868	13.72	8.147	14.016	19.588	4.497	0.542	8.963
BEL	Belgium	12.539	12.22	7.676	12.858	17.402	4.578	0.623	12.654
CAN	Canada	13.094	10.802	5.146	14.846	19.307	5.265	0.738	9.97
CHL	Chile	23.277	18.768	13.675	27.786	32.878	5.946	0.648	11.238
CZE	Czech Republic	16.485	15.936	9.685	17.035	23.285	4.718	0.781	8.525
DNK	Denmark	4.451	3.824	2.13	4.849	5.853	2.533	1.051	7.553
EST	Estonia	15.664	14.627	9.297	16.701	22.031	4.635	0.626	9.339
FIN	Finland	11.717	11.376	6.884	12.058	16.55	4.05	0.847	9.427
GRC	Greece	17.461	17.446	10.536	17.477	24.387	6.28	0.619	13.279
HUN	Hungary	14.992	12.804	8.808	17.241	22.183	5.251	0.973	11.281
ISL	Iceland	15.596	15.214	9.074	15.978	22.119	4.499	0.597	7.479
IRL	Ireland	15.735	14.495	9.244	16.976	22.226	5.762	0.815	12.734
ISR	Israel	17.859	16.142	10.391	19.716	26.139	5.366	0.587	9.407
ITA	Italy	13.457	12.191	7.906	14.723	19.008	4.184	0.738	9.321
LUX	Luxembourg	14.995	14.721	8.953	15.222	21.197	5.133	0.658	13.625
MEX	Mexico	21.498	17.422	12.384	24.707	29.745	5.381	0.42	10.233
NLD	Netherlands	20.39	19.338	12.112	21.443	28.669	5.359	0.612	10.914
NZL	New Zealand	14.844	13.036	8.721	16.653	20.967	5.094	0.904	10.746
NOR	Norway	10.139	9.923	5.899	10.355	14.379	3.988	0.965	8.434
POL	Poland	15.229	13.74	8.947	16.718	21.511	4.385	0.695	8.884
PRT	Portugal	17.833	16.308	10.387	19.357	25.278	5.01	0.927	10.159
SVK	Slovak Republic	13.185	12.119	7.868	14.25	18.502	4.217	0.805	10.542
SVN	Slovenia	9.18	8.616	5.449	9.744	12.911	3.698	0.83	9.821
ESP	Spain	15.509	14.346	9.112	16.672	21.916	4.729	0.849	9.23
SWE	Sweden	10.263	10.241	6.029	10.275	14.518	3.676	0.549	9.023
CHE	Switzerland	15.817	15.302	9.222	16.299	22.345	4.839	0.695	8.824
TUR	Turkey	13.828	13.724	8.238	13.932	19.418	4.324	0.704	9.313
GBR	United Kingdom	16.932	14.034	9.806	19.83	24.059	4.712	0.613	8.075

StatLink http://dx.doi.org/10.1787/888933446684

Table B.3. **Marginal Effective Tax Rate on Skills, % of Breakeven Earnings Increment**

		17 Years Old, Single No Children, 4 Years Education, No Borrowing, Scholarship Income	17 Years Old, Single No Children, 4 Years Education Borrows Direct Costs at 0%, Scholarship Income	17 Years Old, Single No Children, 4 Years Education Borrows Direct Costs and Lost Income at 0%, Scholarship Income	17 Years Old, Single No Children, 4 Years Education Borrows Direct Costs at 6%, Scholarship Income	17 Years Old, Single No Children, 4 Years Education Borrows Direct Costs and Lost Income at 6%, Scholarship Income	27 Years Old, Single No Children, 1 Year Education, No Borrowing, Scholarship Income	32 Years Old, Single No Children, Mid-Career Training, No Borrowing, No Scholarship Income	50 Years Old, Single No Children, 1 Year Education, No Borrowing, Scholarship Income
AUS	Australia	19.149	16.522	0.0	21.138	0.0	7.869	-4.038	8.537
AUT	Austria	9.142	8.957	9.142	9.324	9.142	10.707	-16.242	12.893
BEL	Belgium	-2.124	-3.244	-0.658	-1.059	-2.771	7.767	-7.306	13.5
CAN	Canada	-31.278	-43.902	-96.253	-26.873	-25.758	7.965	12.376	9.674
CHL	Chile	0.0	0.0	0.0	0.0	0.0	0.0	0.0	0.0
CZE	Czech Republic	8.174	7.763	8.174	8.558	8.174	5.165	19.7	5.399
DNK	Denmark	-56.042	-73.732	-89.716	-49.497	-68.298	-16.22	41.705	3.886
EST	Estonia	-1.468	-3.02	-1.468	-0.109	-1.468	-0.903	-0.725	-0.057
FIN	Finland	6.436	5.572	6.436	7.252	6.436	8.162	22.594	16.256
GRC	Greece	12.885	12.874	12.885	12.897	12.885	25.715	23.278	19.002
HUN	Hungary	1.667	-1.52	1.667	4.384	6.129	16.159	34.992	19.497
ISL	Iceland	5.771	4.946	5.771	6.556	5.771	3.597	-2.622	3.597
IRL	Ireland	14.67	13.615	14.67	15.571	14.67	27.718	20.41	33.81
ISR	Israel	8.091	7.462	8.091	9.256	10.945	13.42	0.0	13.915
ITA	Italy	0.267	-2.802	0.267	2.808	0.267	0.481	13.184	9.718
LUX	Luxembourg	13.825	13.445	12.918	13.928	14.862	17.325	-4.473	19.733
MEX	Mexico	8.773	3.848	6.958	9.041	6.867	1.817	-49.944	2.73
NLD	Netherlands	34.527	34.228	35.243	34.797	34.224	22.535	-3.294	24.734
NZL	New Zealand	3.292	1.321	3.292	4.835	3.292	14.95	29.484	17.31
NOR	Norway	-5.568	-6.299	-5.568	-4.867	-5.568	9.24	36.422	15.181
POL	Poland	3.993	3.467	3.993	4.425	3.993	0.086	8.647	1.156
PRT	Portugal	19.972	19.222	19.284	20.604	20.255	13.813	25.549	15.557
SVK	Slovak Republic	3.951	2.851	3.951	4.885	3.951	2.256	16.12	4.894
SVN	Slovenia	-8.282	-9.64	-8.282	-7.081	-8.282	2.843	20.626	7.779
ESP	Spain	5.151	3.747	5.151	6.36	5.192	7.012	25.742	8.719
SWE	Sweden	-7.586	-7.71	-7.602	-7.577	-7.433	-1.579	-15.725	14.316
CHE	Switzerland	6.249	5.795	5.53	6.481	6.264	8.69	17.544	8.823
TUR	Turkey	1.967	1.848	1.967	2.084	1.967	1.147	-1.208	2.302
GBR	United Kingdom	-6.55	-12.033	-6.55	-2.67	-6.55	-4.222	0.0	-3.511

StatLink http://dx.doi.org/10.1787/888933446696

Table B.4. **Average Returns to Costs Ratio of Government Investment in Education**

		17 Years Old, Single No Children, 4 Years Education, No Borrowing, Scholarship Income	17 Years Old, Single No Children, 4 Years Education Borrows Direct Costs at 0%, Scholarship Income	17 Years Old, Single No Children, 4 Years Education Borrows Direct Costs and Lost Income at 0%, Scholarship Income	17 Years Old, Single No Children, 4 Years Education Borrows Direct Costs at 6%, Scholarship Income	17 Years Old, Single No Children, 4 Years Education Borrows Direct Costs and Lost Income at 6%, Scholarship Income	27 Years Old, Single No Children, 1 Year Education, No Borrowing, Scholarship Income	32 Years Old, Single No Children, Mid-Career Training, No Borrowing, No Scholarship Income	50 Years Old, Single No Children, 1 Year Education, No Borrowing, Scholarship Income
AUS	Australia	1.68778	1.41643	0.70801	2.08773	0.70801	7.23612	14.02519	8.70542
AUT	Austria	1.03592	1.02664	0.76789	1.04537	1.59139	5.20919	7.16431	5.85762
BEL	Belgium	1.0051	0.99321	0.85004	1.01728	1.22935	4.84269	8.2971	4.20398
CAN	Canada	0.97892	0.88973	0.72645	1.06014	1.33072	6.53906	9.26291	7.35302
CHL	Chile	0.83398	0.43434	0.28182	10.43726	-0.86941	7.24507	8.5404	8.14692
CZE	Czech Republic	1.55766	1.50771	1.10463	1.61103	2.64062	7.51804	9.54375	8.45386
DNK	Denmark	0.58564	0.57539	0.54945	0.59233	0.60991	3.40016	6.26149	4.09056
EST	Estonia	0.6107	0.57734	0.45082	0.64815	0.94631	2.94334	3.98927	3.04228
FIN	Finland	1.02408	1.01156	0.8712	1.03691	1.24202	5.22973	7.93205	5.88072
GRC	Greece	1.19474	1.19309	0.7348	1.19639	3.1939	6.84543	11.25873	5.94258
HUN	Hungary	1.69286	1.54364	1.32953	1.87402	2.32945	6.73194	9.82068	7.5699
ISL	Iceland	1.60871	1.57494	1.17756	1.64397	2.53799	6.71351	12.90944	8.07668
IRL	Ireland	0.571	0.53667	0.42783	0.61003	0.85821	4.62929	6.61924	5.20552
ISR	Israel	1.51783	1.26176	0.80616	1.90431	12.95009	8.65954	11.69165	10.41786
ITA	Italy	1.54808	1.43432	1.14867	1.68143	2.37332	8.66049	17.98255	9.73852
LUX	Luxembourg	2.18367	2.15076	1.59601	2.2176	3.45632	10.09595	14.15512	8.7644
MEX	Mexico	1.27737	1.0927	0.89057	1.53714	2.25814	5.90647	6.774	6.6417
NLD	Netherlands	2.19745	2.06388	1.45604	2.34952	4.47724	9.92181	14.80145	11.15684
NZL	New Zealand	0.56434	0.49422	0.38122	0.65764	1.08604	4.07613	7.2746	4.58352
NOR	Norway	0.59788	0.592	0.50043	0.60387	0.74246	3.7374	6.20251	4.49628
POL	Poland	0.69446	0.63	0.48511	0.7736	1.22167	3.47731	4.31309	3.91016
PRT	Portugal	2.71825	2.46886	1.8202	3.02367	5.36546	14.81833	22.44828	16.66286
SVK	Slovak Republic	0.87991	0.83017	0.67738	0.93599	1.25521	4.37646	6.03244	4.30096
SVN	Slovenia	1.64313	1.59185	1.35448	1.69784	2.08815	10.50317	15.90975	10.85622
ESP	Spain	0.83315	0.77776	0.59862	0.89704	1.36982	4.18944	6.46095	4.71092
SWE	Sweden	0.48094	0.48064	0.40824	0.48124	0.58515	4.73061	6.13804	5.31946
CHE	Switzerland	0.90455	0.8772	0.64267	0.93365	1.52661	5.49978	6.7317	6.18436
TUR	Turkey	0.40358	0.40133	0.31022	0.40584	0.57732	2.12322	2.55467	2.11988
GBR	United Kingdom	1.53508	1.1891	0.89482	2.16502	5.39606	11.07618	30.29848	13.71686

StatLink http://dx.doi.org/10.1787/888933446702

Table B.5. **Marginal Returns to Costs Ratio of Government Investment in Education**

		17 Years Old, Single No Children, 4 Years Education, No Borrowing, Scholarship Income	17 Years Old, Single No Children, 4 Years Education Borrows Direct Costs at 0%, Scholarship Income	17 Years Old, Single No Children, 4 Years Education Borrows Direct Costs and Lost Income at 0%, Scholarship Income	17 Years Old, Single No Children, 4 Years Education Borrows Direct Costs at 6%, Scholarship Income	17 Years Old, Single No Children, 4 Years Education Borrows Direct Costs and Lost Income at 6%, Scholarship Income	27 Years Old, Single No Children, 1 Year Education, No Borrowing, Scholarship Income	32 Years Old, Single No Children, Mid-Career Training, No Borrowing, No Scholarship Income	50 Years Old, Single No Children, 1 Year Education, No Borrowing, Scholarship Income
AUS	Australia	0.76164	0.7419	0.0	0.82757	0.0	0.69252	0.15878	0.79739
AUT	Austria	0.30198	0.30251	0.38102	0.30151	0.32843	0.52286	0.08675	0.63019
BEL	Belgium	0.33395	0.3393	0.48429	0.32898	0.28809	0.57506	0.13411	0.73835
CAN	Canada	0.17081	0.17951	0.23852	0.16766	0.17918	0.4929	0.09456	0.54804
CHL	Chile	0.0	0.0	0.0	0.0	0.0	0.0	0.0	0.0
CZE	Czech Republic	0.25011	0.25043	0.3019	0.25034	0.30018	0.34548	0.07261	0.35485
DNK	Denmark	0.08736	0.09993	0.17128	0.08112	0.06919	0.2407	0.1839	0.48009
EST	Estonia	0.22378	0.22656	0.27832	0.22275	0.24655	0.31912	0.05846	0.34109
FIN	Finland	0.23198	0.23601	0.33591	0.22824	0.19918	0.40706	0.12188	0.60129
GRC	Greece	0.54984	0.54957	0.56045	0.55012	1.05248	1.26148	0.13196	1.0015
HUN	Hungary	0.16895	0.18038	0.22585	0.16609	0.20309	0.49481	0.13369	0.65905
ISL	Iceland	0.55048	0.55245	0.69255	0.54909	0.61238	0.66267	0.16912	0.66267
IRL	Ireland	0.30006	0.30616	0.38268	0.29714	0.31929	0.79781	0.10383	1.18163
ISR	Israel	0.34366	0.31606	0.31371	0.41337	2.5408	0.75599	0.11174	0.85624
ITA	Italy	0.35815	0.3663	0.45233	0.35555	0.38872	0.49302	0.18058	0.77205
LUX	Luxembourg	0.34677	0.34496	0.40394	0.34475	0.4106	0.67015	0.12256	0.86029
MEX	Mexico	0.21695	0.17618	0.22806	0.2122	0.239	0.24512	0.02195	0.27432
NLD	Netherlands	0.85662	0.85087	0.99221	0.8686	1.22176	0.8709	0.14839	1.101
NZL	New Zealand	0.24702	0.24634	0.28402	0.2566	0.33655	0.66824	0.21158	0.92687
NOR	Norway	0.1811	0.18322	0.26052	0.17909	0.15858	0.44524	0.17886	0.63166
POL	Poland	0.10151	0.10207	0.1207	0.10301	0.12642	0.14634	0.02875	0.18625
PRT	Portugal	0.44522	0.43985	0.49151	0.45827	0.63029	0.57373	0.16086	0.72954
SVK	Slovak Republic	0.14602	0.14988	0.18838	0.14371	0.14844	0.23045	0.06065	0.32667
SVN	Slovenia	0.07466	0.07706	0.10368	0.07268	0.06746	0.24966	0.0849	0.4151
ESP	Spain	0.27536	0.27789	0.33676	0.27579	0.32114	0.45724	0.12656	0.53539
SWE	Sweden	0.11818	0.11786	0.17063	0.11791	0.10247	0.23549	0.03927	0.48177
CHE	Switzerland	0.20378	0.20278	0.23547	0.20262	0.2437	0.38231	0.06418	0.39657
TUR	Turkey	0.15967	0.15999	0.20602	0.15937	0.16266	0.24568	0.04809	0.27602
GBR	United Kingdom	0.425	0.39719	0.42779	0.5118	1.05141	0.53419	0.19011	0.60023

StatLink http://dx.doi.org/10.1787/888933446718

ANNEX C

Country Tables

This annex provides country tables which detail the main results from Annex B as well as the variables that lie behind these results. As with Annex B results are given for a variety of different assumptions about age, income, student debt levels, and length of education. The results correspond to the different stylised education scenarios discussed in Chapter 4 of this study.

For each country, two tables are presented.[1] The first table for each country focuses on the education scenario of a 17-year college student engaging in a four-year period of education, corresponding to an undergraduate degree. In this table, differing assumptions surrounding the financing of the student's education are examined. In the second table for each country, it is assumed that all education spending is financed with retained earnings, but a variety of assumptions are examined regarding the students age and income, the length of the educational period, and whether the education is job-related or not.

In each table, the cost components of education are outlined, as discussed in Chapter 3 of this study and in Annex A. These costs include the direct costs of education less scholarship and grant income, as well as lost earnings. As discussed in Annex A and Chapter 3, these costs are offset by the tax system through the tax rate on foregone earnings, and the rate at which the tax system offsets direct costs. These two measures are also included. These components together comprise the total post-tax cost of education, which is what needs to be recouped in order to break even on a skills investment. Where a student borrows to finance the skills investment, the cost of this borrowing must also be recouped. A debt finance multiplier is included to account for the extent to which education finance increases or decreases the amount that needs to be recouped. This term corresponds to the F term in Annex A.

These costs must be recouped in the period after education after taxes. The tax rate on earnings after education is included in each table, as is the BEI in national currency units and as a percentage of earnings before education. The table then provides the five key measures outlined in this study, as are outlined in the cross-country tables in Annex B.

Australia

Table C.1. Comparing Financial Incentives for College Education with Different Financing Scenarios - Australia

Single, No Children, 17 Year-Old, Four Years of Education, 70% of the Average Wage					Currency: AUD
Scenario	No Borrowing	Direct Costs Borrowed, Low Interest Rate	All Costs Borrowed, Low Interest Rate	Direct Costs Borrowed, High Interest Rate	All Costs Borrowed, High Interest Rate
Non-Financing Education Costs					
Direct Costs of Education	9587	9587	9587	9587	9587
Pre-Tax Scholarship Income	2371	2371	2371	2371	2371
Income Before Education	48932	48932	48932	48932	48932
Income During Education	19847	19847	19847	19847	19847
Pre-Tax Foregone Earnings	29086	29086	29086	29086	29086
AETR Before Education (%)	16.8	16.8	16.8	16.8	16.8
AETR During Education (Exclusive of Tax Expenditures) (%)	5.6	5.6	5.6	5.6	5.6
Value of Education Tax Credits % of Direct Costs	3.3	3.3	3.3	3.3	3.3
AETR During Education (Inclusive of Tax Expenditures) (%)	4.4	4.4	4.4	4.4	4.4
METR on Foregone Earnings (%)	24.4	24.4	24.4	24.4	24.4
Total Annual Non-Financing Costs of Education (Direct Costs & Foregone Earnings)	28960	28960	28960	28960	28960
Education Financing Costs					
Fraction of Costs Borrowed	None	Direct Costs	All Costs	Direct Costs	All Costs
Total Amount Borrowed	0	9587	28960	9587	28960
Interest Rate (%)	NA	0.0	0.0	6.0	6.0
Annual Repayments	0	815	0	3260	0
Debt Finance Multiplier	1.00	0.58	0.00	1.42	0.00
Returns to Education					
Breakeven Earnings Level	58805	57438	48932	60172	48932
AETR After Education (%)	19.9	19.6	16.8	20.3	16.8
Breakeven Earnings Increment	9873	8506	0	11240	0
Breakeven Earnings Increment % of Previous Wage	20.2	17.4	0.0	23.0	0.0
METR Breakeven Earnings Increment (%)	35.5	35.5	0.0	35.5	0.0
Marginal Effective Tax Rate on Skills (%)	19.1	16.5	0.0	21.1	0.0
Average Effective Tax Rate on Skills (Assumed 15% Return, %)	30.7	33.2	34.8	27.6	34.8
Average Effective Tax Rate on Skills (Return based on Labour Market Premium, %)	27.6	32.0	34.8	22.1	34.8
Government Costs and Returns					
Government Educational Costs	20928	24937	49888	16918	49888
Marginal Returns to Costs Ratio	0.76	0.74	0.00	0.83	0.00
Average Returns to Costs Ratio (Return based on Labour Market Premium)	1.69	1.42	0.71	2.09	0.71

StatLink http://dx.doi.org/10.1787/888933446720

Table C.2. **Comparing Financial Incentives for Differing Savings-Financed Education Scenarios - Australia**

Single, No Children, Annual Data								**Currency: AUD**
Age	17	27	32	40	32	40	50	50
Income Before Education, %AW	70	100	100	100	100	100	100	100
Income During Education, %AW	25	25	25	25	95	95	25	25
Years of Education	4	1	1	1	0.05	0.05	1	1
Education is Job Related	No	No	No	No	Yes	Yes	No	Yes
Financial Costs of Up-Skilling								
Direct Costs of Education	9587	9587	9587	9587	6990	6990	9587	9587
Pre-Tax Scholarship Income	2371	2371	2371	2371	0	0	2371	0
Income Before Education	48932	69903	69903	69903	69903	69903	69903	69903
Income During Education	19847	19847	19847	19847	69728	69728	19847	17476
Pre-Tax Foregone Earnings	29086	50056	50056	50056	175	175	50056	52427
AETR Before Education (%)	16.8	22.3	22.3	22.3	22.3	22.3	22.3	22.3
AETR During Education (Exclusive of Tax Expenditures) (%)	5.6	5.6	5.6	5.6	22.3	22.3	5.6	5.0
Value of Education Tax Credits % of Direct Costs	3.3	3.3	3.3	3.3	34.2	34.2	3.3	9.2
AETR During Education (Inclusive of Tax Expenditures) (%)	4.4	4.4	4.4	4.4	18.8	18.8	4.4	0.0
METR on Foregone Earnings (%)	24.4	28.9	28.9	28.9	31.5	31.5	28.9	28.0
Total Costs of Education (Direct Costs & Foregone Earnings)	28960	42583	42583	42583	4718	4718	42583	46445
Financial Returns to Up-Skilling								
Breakeven Earnings Level	58805	73414	73652	74223	70318	70382	75740	76270
AETR After Education (%)	19.9	22.7	22.7	22.8	22.3	22.3	23.0	23.0
Breakeven Earnings Increment	9873	3511	3749	4320	415	479	5837	6367
Breakeven Earnings Increment % of Previous Wage	20.2	5.0	5.4	6.2	0.6	0.7	8.4	9.1
METR Breakeven Earnings Increment (%)	35.5	31.5	31.5	31.5	31.5	31.5	31.5	31.5
Marginal Effective Tax Rate on Skills (%)	19.1	7.9	7.9	7.9	-4.0	-4.0	7.9	8.5
Average Effective Tax Rate on Skills (Assumed 15% Return, %)	30.7	27.5	27.1	26.1	10.4	7.2	23.6	23.0
Government Costs and Returns								
Government Educational Costs	20928	28276	28276	28276	13663	13663	28276	26785
Marginal Returns to Costs Ratio	0.76	0.69	0.69	0.69	0.16	0.16	0.69	0.80
Average Returns to Costs Ratio (Assumed 15% Return)	2.96	2.93	2.74	2.38	0.27	0.23	1.76	1.86

StatLink http://dx.doi.org/10.1787/888933446736

Austria

Table C.3. **Comparing Financial Incentives for College Education with Different Financing Scenarios - Austria**

Single, No Children, 17 Year-Old, Four Years of Education, 70% of the Average Wage					Currency: EUR
Scenario	No Borrowing	Direct Costs Borrowed, Low Interest Rate	All Costs Borrowed, Low Interest Rate	Direct Costs Borrowed, High Interest Rate	All Costs Borrowed, High Interest Rate
Non-Financing Education Costs					
Direct Costs of Education	328	328	328	328	328
Pre-Tax Scholarship Income	1283	1283	1283	1283	1283
Income Before Education	27785	27785	27785	27785	27785
Income During Education	11207	11207	11207	11207	11207
Pre-Tax Foregone Earnings	16578	16578	16578	16578	16578
AETR Before Education (%)	10.2	10.2	10.2	10.2	10.2
AETR During Education (Exclusive of Tax Expenditures) (%)	-1.0	-1.0	-1.0	-1.0	-1.0
Value of Education Tax Credits % of Direct Costs	0.0	0.0	0.0	0.0	0.0
AETR During Education (Inclusive of Tax Expenditures) (%)	-1.0	-1.0	-1.0	-1.0	-1.0
METR on Foregone Earnings (%)	17.8	17.8	17.8	17.8	17.8
Total Annual Non-Financing Costs of Education (Direct Costs & Foregone Earnings)	12672	12672	12672	12672	12672
Education Financing Costs					
Fraction of Costs Borrowed	None	Direct Costs	All Costs	Direct Costs	All Costs
Total Amount Borrowed	0	328	12672	328	12672
Interest Rate (%)	NA	0.0	0.0	6.0	6.0
Annual Repayments	0	28	1077	112	4309
Debt Finance Multiplier	1.00	0.59	0.59	1.41	1.41
Returns to Education					
Breakeven Earnings Level	31638	31597	30049	31679	33227
AETR After Education (%)	12.2	12.2	11.4	12.2	12.9
Breakeven Earnings Increment	3853	3812	2264	3894	5443
Breakeven Earnings Increment % of Previous Wage	13.9	13.7	8.1	14.0	19.6
METR Breakeven Earnings Increment (%)	26.3	26.3	26.3	26.3	26.3
Marginal Effective Tax Rate on Skills (%)	9.1	9.0	9.1	9.3	9.1
Average Effective Tax Rate on Skills (Assumed 15% Return, %)	26.3	26.5	31.4	26.1	15.9
Average Effective Tax Rate on Skills (Return based on Labour Market Premium, %)	22.6	22.9	31.6	22.3	4.0
Government Costs and Returns					
Government Educational Costs	14976	15112	20204	14841	9749
Marginal Returns to Costs Ratio	0.30	0.30	0.38	0.30	0.33
Average Returns to Costs Ratio (Return based on Labour Market Premium)	1.04	1.03	0.77	1.05	1.59

StatLink http://dx.doi.org/10.1787/888933446746

Table C.4. **Comparing Financial Incentives for Differing Savings-Financed Education Scenarios - Austria**

Single, No Children, Annual Data								**Currency: EUR**
Age	17	27	32	40	32	40	50	50
Income Before Education, %AW	70	100	100	100	100	100	100	100
Income During Education, %AW	25	25	25	25	95	95	25	25
Years of Education	4	1	1	1	0.05	0.05	1	1
Education is Job Related	No	No	No	No	Yes	Yes	No	Yes
Financial Costs of Up-Skilling								
Direct Costs of Education	328	328	328	328	3926	3926	328	328
Pre-Tax Scholarship Income	1283	1283	1283	1283	0	0	1283	0
Income Before Education	27785	39693	39693	39693	39693	39693	39693	39693
Income During Education	11207	11207	11207	11207	39593	39593	11207	9923
Pre-Tax Foregone Earnings	16578	28486	28486	28486	99	99	28486	29769
AETR Before Education (%)	10.2	15.5	15.5	15.5	15.5	15.5	15.5	15.5
AETR During Education (Exclusive of Tax Expenditures) (%)	-1.0	-1.0	-1.0	-1.0	15.5	15.5	-1.0	-1.1
Value of Education Tax Credits % of Direct Costs	0.0	0.0	0.0	0.0	40.9	40.9	0.0	0.0
AETR During Education (Inclusive of Tax Expenditures) (%)	-1.0	-1.0	-1.0	-1.0	11.4	11.4	-1.0	-1.1
METR on Foregone Earnings (%)	17.8	22.0	22.0	22.0	31.0	31.0	22.0	21.0
Total Costs of Education (Direct Costs & Foregone Earnings)	12672	21271	21271	21271	2389	2389	21271	23838
Financial Returns to Up-Skilling								
Breakeven Earnings Level	31638	41477	41610	41936	39908	39945	42867	43250
AETR After Education (%)	12.2	16.2	16.2	16.3	15.6	15.6	16.6	16.8
Breakeven Earnings Increment	3853	1785	1917	2243	215	252	3175	3558
Breakeven Earnings Increment % of Previous Wage	13.9	4.5	4.8	5.7	0.5	0.6	8.0	9.0
METR Breakeven Earnings Increment (%)	26.3	31.0	31.0	31.0	31.0	31.0	31.0	31.0
Marginal Effective Tax Rate on Skills (%)	9.1	10.7	10.7	10.7	-16.2	-16.2	10.7	12.9
Average Effective Tax Rate on Skills (Assumed 15% Return, %)	26.3	26.4	26.1	25.3	5.4	1.0	22.9	22.9
Government Costs and Returns								
Government Educational Costs	14976	18285	18285	18285	12379	12379	18285	17002
Marginal Returns to Costs Ratio	0.30	0.52	0.52	0.52	0.09	0.09	0.52	0.63
Average Returns to Costs Ratio (Assumed 15% Return)	1.94	2.33	2.17	1.85	0.16	0.14	1.31	1.41

StatLink http://dx.doi.org/10.1787/888933446754

Belgium

Table C.5. **Comparing Financial Incentives for College Education with Different Financing Scenarios - Belgium**

Single, No Children, 17 Year-Old, Four Years of Education, 70% of the Average Wage					Currency: EUR
Scenario	No Borrowing	Direct Costs Borrowed, Low Interest Rate	All Costs Borrowed, Low Interest Rate	Direct Costs Borrowed, High Interest Rate	All Costs Borrowed, High Interest Rate
Non-Financing Education Costs					
Direct Costs of Education	630	630	630	630	630
Pre-Tax Scholarship Income	1898	1898	1898	1898	1898
Income Before Education	31245	31245	31245	31245	31245
Income During Education	13057	13057	13057	13057	13057
Pre-Tax Foregone Earnings	18188	18188	18188	18188	18188
AETR Before Education (%)	23.4	23.4	23.4	23.4	23.4
AETR During Education (Exclusive of Tax Expenditures) (%)	8.6	8.6	8.6	8.6	8.6
Value of Education Tax Credits % of Direct Costs	-88.4	-88.4	-88.4	-88.4	-88.4
AETR During Education (Inclusive of Tax Expenditures) (%)	0.0	0.0	0.0	0.0	0.0
METR on Foregone Earnings (%)	34.1	34.1	34.1	34.1	34.1
Total Annual Non-Financing Costs of Education (Direct Costs & Foregone Earnings)	9598	9598	9598	9598	9598
Education Financing Costs					
Fraction of Costs Borrowed	None	Direct Costs	All Costs	Direct Costs	All Costs
Total Amount Borrowed	0	630	9598	630	9598
Interest Rate (%)	NA	0.0	0.0	6.0	6.0
Annual Repayments	0	54	816	214	3263
Debt Finance Multiplier	1.00	0.60	0.60	1.40	1.40
Returns to Education					
Breakeven Earnings Level	35163	35063	33644	35263	36682
AETR After Education (%)	25.5	25.5	24.8	25.6	26.1
Breakeven Earnings Increment	3918	3818	2398	4018	5437
Breakeven Earnings Increment % of Previous Wage	12.5	12.2	7.7	12.9	17.4
METR Breakeven Earnings Increment (%)	42.1	42.1	42.9	42.0	41.7
Marginal Effective Tax Rate on Skills (%)	-2.1	-3.2	-0.7	-1.1	-2.8
Average Effective Tax Rate on Skills (Assumed 15% Return, %)	36.3	36.7	42.9	35.9	24.7
Average Effective Tax Rate on Skills (Return based on Labour Market Premium, %)	26.8	27.7	40.5	25.9	2.7
Government Costs and Returns					
Government Educational Costs	20870	21120	24677	20620	17063
Marginal Returns to Costs Ratio	0.33	0.34	0.48	0.33	0.29
Average Returns to Costs Ratio (Return based on Labour Market Premium)	1.01	0.99	0.85	1.02	1.23

StatLink http://dx.doi.org/10.1787/888933446768

Table C.6. **Comparing Financial Incentives for Differing Savings-Financed Education Scenarios - Belgium**

Single, No Children, Annual Data								Currency: EUR
Age	17	27	32	40	32	40	50	50
Income Before Education, %AW	70	100	100	100	100	100	100	100
Income During Education, %AW	25	25	25	25	95	95	25	25
Years of Education	4	1	1	1	0.05	0.05	1	1
Education is Job Related	No	No	No	No	Yes	Yes	No	Yes
Financial Costs of Up-Skilling								
Direct Costs of Education	630	630	630	630	4274	4274	630	630
Pre-Tax Scholarship Income	1898	1898	1898	1898	0	0	1898	0
Income Before Education	31245	44636	44636	44636	44636	44636	44636	44636
Income During Education	13057	13057	13057	13057	44524	44524	13057	11159
Pre-Tax Foregone Earnings	18188	31579	31579	31579	112	112	31579	33477
AETR Before Education (%)	23.4	28.8	28.8	28.8	28.8	28.8	28.8	28.8
AETR During Education (Exclusive of Tax Expenditures) (%)	8.6	8.6	8.6	8.6	28.8	28.8	8.6	4.8
Value of Education Tax Credits % of Direct Costs	-88.4	-45.8	-45.8	-45.8	49.1	49.1	-45.8	32.2
AETR During Education (Inclusive of Tax Expenditures) (%)	0.0	4.1	4.1	4.1	24.1	24.1	4.1	3.0
METR on Foregone Earnings (%)	34.1	37.2	37.2	37.2	45.3	45.3	37.2	36.8
Total Costs of Education (Direct Costs & Foregone Earnings)	9598	17982	17982	17982	2236	2236	17982	21576
Financial Returns to Up-Skilling								
Breakeven Earnings Level	35163	46679	46872	47393	44914	44979	49344	50284
AETR After Education (%)	25.5	29.5	29.6	29.8	28.9	29.0	30.4	30.7
Breakeven Earnings Increment	3918	2043	2236	2757	278	343	4708	5648
Breakeven Earnings Increment % of Previous Wage	12.5	4.6	5.0	6.2	0.6	0.8	10.5	12.7
METR Breakeven Earnings Increment (%)	42.1	45.3	45.3	45.3	45.3	45.3	45.3	45.3
Marginal Effective Tax Rate on Skills (%)	-2.1	7.8	7.8	7.8	-7.3	-7.3	7.8	13.5
Average Effective Tax Rate on Skills (Assumed 15% Return, %)	36.3	36.7	35.9	33.7	12.5	4.9	25.5	25.2
Government Costs and Returns								
Government Educational Costs	20870	25877	25877	25877	13799	13799	25877	24181
Marginal Returns to Costs Ratio	0.33	0.58	0.58	0.58	0.13	0.13	0.58	0.74
Average Returns to Costs Ratio (Assumed 15% Return)	2.19	2.51	2.30	1.86	0.22	0.17	1.09	1.17

StatLink http://dx.doi.org/10.1787/888933446777

Canada

Table C.7. Comparing Financial Incentives for College Education with Different Financing Scenarios - Canada

Single, No Children, 17 Year-Old, Four Years of Education, 70% of the Average Wage					Currency: CAD
Scenario	No Borrowing	Direct Costs Borrowed, Low Interest Rate	All Costs Borrowed, Low Interest Rate	Direct Costs Borrowed, High Interest Rate	All Costs Borrowed, High Interest Rate
Non-Financing Education Costs					
Direct Costs of Education	5667	5667	5667	5667	5667
Pre-Tax Scholarship Income	856	856	856	856	856
Income Before Education	31828	31828	31828	31828	31828
Income During Education	12224	12224	12224	12224	12224
Pre-Tax Foregone Earnings	19605	19605	19605	19605	19605
AETR Before Education (%)	12.4	12.4	12.4	12.4	12.4
AETR During Education (Exclusive of Tax Expenditures) (%)	-4.8	-4.8	-4.8	-4.8	-4.8
Value of Education Tax Credits % of Direct Costs	5.3	5.3	5.3	5.3	5.3
AETR During Education (Inclusive of Tax Expenditures) (%)	-6.9	-6.9	-6.9	-6.9	-6.9
METR on Foregone Earnings (%)	23.2	23.2	23.2	23.2	23.2
Total Annual Non-Financing Costs of Education (Direct Costs & Foregone Earnings)	19610	19610	19610	19610	19610
Education Financing Costs					
Fraction of Costs Borrowed	None	Direct Costs	All Costs	Direct Costs	All Costs
Total Amount Borrowed	0	5667	19610	5667	19610
Interest Rate (%)	NA	0.0	0.0	6.0	6.0
Annual Repayments	0	482	1667	1927	6667
Debt Finance Multiplier	1.00	0.53	0.53	1.36	1.36
Returns to Education					
Breakeven Earnings Level	35996	35266	33466	36553	37973
AETR After Education (%)	13.2	13.1	12.7	13.3	13.6
Breakeven Earnings Increment	4168	3438	1638	4725	6145
Breakeven Earnings Increment % of Previous Wage	13.1	10.8	5.1	14.8	19.3
METR Breakeven Earnings Increment (%)	18.7	18.7	18.7	18.7	19.4
Marginal Effective Tax Rate on Skills (%)	-31.3	-43.9	-96.3	-26.9	-25.8
Average Effective Tax Rate on Skills (Assumed 15% Return, %)	22.9	24.9	28.8	19.8	7.6
Average Effective Tax Rate on Skills (Return based on Labour Market Premium, %)	21.5	23.9	28.5	17.9	3.8
Government Costs and Returns					
Government Educational Costs	26408	29055	35586	24385	19426
Marginal Returns to Costs Ratio	0.17	0.18	0.24	0.17	0.18
Average Returns to Costs Ratio (Return based on Labour Market Premium)	0.98	0.89	0.73	1.06	1.33

StatLink http://dx.doi.org/10.1787/888933446781

Table C.8. **Comparing Financial Incentives for Differing Savings-Financed Education Scenarios - Canada**

Single, No Children, Annual Data								**Currency: CAD**
Age	17	27	32	40	32	40	50	50
Income Before Education, %AW	70	100	100	100	100	100	100	100
Income During Education, %AW	25	25	25	25	95	95	25	25
Years of Education	4	1	1	1	0.05	0.05	1	1
Education is Job Related	No	No	No	No	Yes	Yes	No	Yes
Financial Costs of Up-Skilling								
Direct Costs of Education	5667	5667	5667	5667	4616	4616	5667	5667
Pre-Tax Scholarship Income	856	856	856	856	0	0	856	0
Income Before Education	31828	45469	45469	45469	45469	45469	45469	45469
Income During Education	12224	12224	12224	12224	45355	45355	12224	11367
Pre-Tax Foregone Earnings	19605	33245	33245	33245	114	114	33245	34102
AETR Before Education (%)	12.4	15.8	15.8	15.8	15.3	15.3	15.8	15.8
AETR During Education (Exclusive of Tax Expenditures) (%)	-4.8	-4.8	-4.8	-4.8	15.2	15.2	-4.8	-7.4
Value of Education Tax Credits % of Direct Costs	5.3	5.3	5.3	5.3	20.1	20.1	5.3	0.1
AETR During Education (Inclusive of Tax Expenditures) (%)	-6.9	-6.9	-6.9	-6.9	13.2	13.2	-6.9	-7.4
METR on Foregone Earnings (%)	23.2	23.4	23.4	23.4	30.2	30.2	23.4	23.6
Total Costs of Education (Direct Costs & Foregone Earnings)	19610	30010	30010	30010	3770	3770	30010	31723
Financial Returns to Up-Skilling								
Breakeven Earnings Level	35996	47863	48040	48480	45805	45862	49747	50002
AETR After Education (%)	13.2	16.6	16.6	16.7	15.4	15.4	17.1	17.2
Breakeven Earnings Increment	4168	2394	2571	3011	336	393	4278	4533
Breakeven Earnings Increment % of Previous Wage	13.1	5.3	5.7	6.6	0.7	0.9	9.4	10.0
METR Breakeven Earnings Increment (%)	18.7	30.2	30.2	30.2	30.2	30.2	30.5	30.5
Marginal Effective Tax Rate on Skills (%)	-31.3	8.0	8.0	8.0	12.4	12.4	8.4	9.7
Average Effective Tax Rate on Skills (Assumed 15% Return, %)	22.9	25.7	25.3	24.4	17.0	14.8	21.7	21.7
Government Costs and Returns								
Government Educational Costs	26408	26289	26289	26289	17216	17216	26289	25439
Marginal Returns to Costs Ratio	0.17	0.49	0.49	0.49	0.09	0.09	0.50	0.55
Average Returns to Costs Ratio (Assumed 15% Return)	1.17	1.84	1.72	1.47	0.13	0.11	1.04	1.07

StatLink http://dx.doi.org/10.1787/888933446795

Chile

Table C.9. Comparing Financial Incentives for College Education with Different Financing Scenarios - Chile

Single, No Children, 17 Year-Old, Four Years of Education, 70% of the Average Wage					Currency: CLP
Scenario	No Borrowing	Direct Costs Borrowed, Low Interest Rate	All Costs Borrowed, Low Interest Rate	Direct Costs Borrowed, High Interest Rate	All Costs Borrowed, High Interest Rate
Non-Financing Education Costs					
Direct Costs of Education	1981921	1981921	1981921	1981921	1981921
Pre-Tax Scholarship Income	186736	186736	186736	186736	186736
Income Before Education	4062865	4062865	4062865	4062865	4062865
Income During Education	1637759	1637759	1637759	1637759	1637759
Pre-Tax Foregone Earnings	2425106	2425106	2425106	2425106	2425106
AETR Before Education (%)	0.0	0.0	0.0	0.0	0.0
AETR During Education (Exclusive of Tax Expenditures) (%)	0.0	0.0	0.0	0.0	0.0
Value of Education Tax Credits % of Direct Costs	0.0	0.0	0.0	0.0	0.0
AETR During Education (Inclusive of Tax Expenditures) (%)	0.0	0.0	0.0	0.0	0.0
METR on Foregone Earnings (%)	0.0	0.0	0.0	0.0	0.0
Total Annual Non-Financing Costs of Education (Direct Costs & Foregone Earnings)	4220290	4220290	4220290	4220290	4220290
Education Financing Costs					
Fraction of Costs Borrowed	None	Direct Costs	All Costs	Direct Costs	All Costs
Total Amount Borrowed	0	1981921	4220290	1981921	4220290
Interest Rate (%)	NA	0.0	0.0	6.0	6.0
Annual Repayments	0	168459	358716	673836	1434863
Debt Finance Multiplier	1.00	0.59	0.59	1.41	1.41
Returns to Education					
Breakeven Earnings Level	5008570	4825371	4618467	5191770	5398674
AETR After Education (%)	0.0	0.0	0.0	0.0	0.0
Breakeven Earnings Increment	945705	762506	555602	1128905	1335809
Breakeven Earnings Increment % of Previous Wage	23.3	18.8	13.7	27.8	32.9
METR Breakeven Earnings Increment (%)	0.0	0.0	0.0	0.0	0.0
Marginal Effective Tax Rate on Skills (%)	0.0	0.0	0.0	0.0	0.0
Average Effective Tax Rate on Skills (Assumed 15% Return, %)	0.0	4.5	7.1	-6.7	-17.0
Average Effective Tax Rate on Skills (Return based on Labour Market Premium, %)	2.1	3.9	5.0	-0.7	-4.8
Government Costs and Returns					
Government Educational Costs	888540	1706082	2629410	70998	-852330
Marginal Returns to Costs Ratio	0.00	0.00	0.00	0.00	0.00
Average Returns to Costs Ratio (Return based on Labour Market Premium)	0.83	0.43	0.28	10.44	-0.87

StatLink http://dx.doi.org/10.1787/888933446804

Table C.10. **Comparing Financial Incentives for Differing Savings-Financed Education Scenarios - Chile**

Single, No Children, Annual Data								**Currency: CLP**
Age	17	27	32	40	32	40	50	50
Income Before Education, %AW	70	100	100	100	100	100	100	100
Income During Education, %AW	25	25	25	25	95	95	25	25
Years of Education	4	1	1	1	0.05	0.05	1	1
Education is Job Related	No	No	No	No	Yes	Yes	No	Yes
Financial Costs of Up-Skilling								
Direct Costs of Education	1981921	1981921	1981921	1981921	590733	590733	1981921	1981921
Pre-Tax Scholarship Income	186736	186736	186736	186736	0	0	186736	0
Income Before Education	4062865	5804093	5804093	5804093	5804093	5804093	5804093	5804093
Income During Education	1637759	1637759	1637759	1637759	5789583	5789583	1637759	1451023
Pre-Tax Foregone Earnings	2425106	4166334	4166334	4166334	14510	14510	4166334	4353070
AETR Before Education (%)	0.0	0.0	0.0	0.0	0.0	0.0	0.0	0.0
AETR During Education (Exclusive of Tax Expenditures) (%)	0.0	0.0	0.0	0.0	0.0	0.0	0.0	0.0
Value of Education Tax Credits % of Direct Costs	0.0	0.0	0.0	0.0	0.0	0.0	0.0	0.0
AETR During Education (Inclusive of Tax Expenditures) (%)	0.0	0.0	0.0	0.0	0.0	0.0	0.0	0.0
METR on Foregone Earnings (%)	0.0	0.0	0.0	0.0	0.0	0.0	0.0	0.0
Total Costs of Education (Direct Costs & Foregone Earnings)	4220290	5961518	5961518	5961518	605243	605243	5961518	6334990
Financial Returns to Up-Skilling								
Breakeven Earnings Level	5008570	6149212	6174768	6237808	5841726	5848126	6417923	6456377
AETR After Education (%)	0.0	0.0	0.0	0.0	0.0	0.0	0.0	0.0
Breakeven Earnings Increment	945705	345119	370675	433715	37633	44033	613830	652284
Breakeven Earnings Increment % of Previous Wage	23.3	5.9	6.4	7.5	0.6	0.8	10.6	11.2
METR Breakeven Earnings Increment (%)	0.0	0.0	0.0	0.0	0.0	0.0	0.0	0.0
Marginal Effective Tax Rate on Skills (%)	0.0	0.0	0.0	0.0	0.0	0.0	0.0	0.0
Average Effective Tax Rate on Skills (Assumed 15% Return, %)	0.0	0.0	0.0	0.0	0.0	0.0	0.0	0.0
Government Costs and Returns								
Government Educational Costs	888540	888540	888540	888540	701804	701804	888540	701804
Marginal Returns to Costs Ratio	0.0	0.0	0.0	0.0	0.0	0.0	0.0	0.0
Average Returns to Costs Ratio (Assumed 15% Return)	0.0	0.0	0.0	0.0	0.0	0.0	0.0	0.0

StatLink http://dx.doi.org/10.1787/888933446814

Czech Republic

Table C.11. Comparing Financial Incentives for College Education with Different Financing Scenarios - Czech Republic

Single, No Children, 17 Year-Old, Four Years of Education, 70% of the Average Wage					Currency: CZK
Scenario	No Borrowing	Direct Costs Borrowed, Low Interest Rate	All Costs Borrowed, Low Interest Rate	Direct Costs Borrowed, High Interest Rate	All Costs Borrowed, High Interest Rate
Non-Financing Education Costs					
Direct Costs of Education	9814	9814	9814	9814	9814
Pre-Tax Scholarship Income	1530	1530	1530	1530	1530
Income Before Education	206691	206691	206691	206691	206691
Income During Education	75348	75348	75348	75348	75348
Pre-Tax Foregone Earnings	131343	131343	131343	131343	131343
AETR Before Education (%)	8.8	8.8	8.8	8.8	8.8
AETR During Education (Exclusive of Tax Expenditures) (%)	0.0	0.0	0.0	0.0	0.0
Value of Education Tax Credits % of Direct Costs	0.0	0.0	0.0	0.0	0.0
AETR During Education (Inclusive of Tax Expenditures) (%)	0.0	0.0	0.0	0.0	0.0
METR on Foregone Earnings (%)	13.8	13.8	13.8	13.8	13.8
Total Annual Non-Financing Costs of Education (Direct Costs & Foregone Earnings)	121493	121493	121493	121493	121493
Education Financing Costs					
Fraction of Costs Borrowed	None	Direct Costs	All Costs	Direct Costs	All Costs
Total Amount Borrowed	0	9814	121493	9814	121493
Interest Rate (%)	NA	0.0	0.0	6.0	6.0
Annual Repayments	0	834	10327	3337	41307
Debt Finance Multiplier	1.00	0.59	0.59	1.41	1.41
Returns to Education					
Breakeven Earnings Level	240765	239629	226709	241900	254820
AETR After Education (%)	10.4	10.3	9.8	10.4	10.9
Breakeven Earnings Increment	34074	32938	20018	35209	48129
Breakeven Earnings Increment % of Previous Wage	16.5	15.9	9.7	17.0	23.3
METR Breakeven Earnings Increment (%)	20.1	20.1	20.1	20.1	20.1
Marginal Effective Tax Rate on Skills (%)	8.2	7.8	8.2	8.6	8.2
Average Effective Tax Rate on Skills (Assumed 15% Return, %)	17.6	18.3	23.2	17.0	5.6
Average Effective Tax Rate on Skills (Return based on Labour Market Premium, %)	18.2	18.7	22.5	17.7	8.8
Government Costs and Returns					
Government Educational Costs	122199	126248	172315	118151	72084
Marginal Returns to Costs Ratio	0.25	0.25	0.30	0.25	0.30
Average Returns to Costs Ratio (Return based on Labour Market Premium)	1.56	1.51	1.10	1.61	2.64

StatLink http://dx.doi.org/10.1787/888933446823

Table C.12. **Comparing Financial Incentives for Differing Savings-Financed Education Scenarios - Czech Republic**

Single, No Children, Annual Data								**Currency: CZK**
Age	17	27	32	40	32	40	50	50
Income Before Education, %AW	70	100	100	100	100	100	100	100
Income During Education, %AW	25	25	25	25	95	95	25	25
Years of Education	4	1	1	1	0.05	0.05	1	1
Education is Job Related	No	No	No	No	Yes	Yes	No	Yes
Financial Costs of Up-Skilling								
Direct Costs of Education	9814	9814	9814	9814	29048	29048	9814	9814
Pre-Tax Scholarship Income	1530	1530	1530	1530	0	0	1530	0
Income Before Education	206691	295273	295273	295273	295273	295273	295273	295273
Income During Education	75348	75348	75348	75348	294535	294535	75348	73818
Pre-Tax Foregone Earnings	131343	219925	219925	219925	738	738	219925	221455
AETR Before Education (%)	8.8	12.2	12.2	12.2	12.1	12.1	12.2	12.2
AETR During Education (Exclusive of Tax Expenditures) (%)	0.0	0.0	0.0	0.0	12.1	12.1	0.0	0.0
Value of Education Tax Credits % of Direct Costs	0.0	0.0	0.0	0.0	0.0	0.0	0.0	0.0
AETR During Education (Inclusive of Tax Expenditures) (%)	0.0	0.0	0.0	0.0	12.1	12.1	0.0	0.0
METR on Foregone Earnings (%)	13.8	16.3	16.3	16.3	20.1	20.1	16.3	16.2
Total Costs of Education (Direct Costs & Foregone Earnings)	121493	192270	192270	192270	29638	29638	192270	195329
Financial Returns to Up-Skilling								
Breakeven Earnings Level	240765	309204	310235	312780	297579	297972	320050	320445
AETR After Education (%)	10.4	12.5	12.6	12.6	12.2	12.2	12.8	12.8
Breakeven Earnings Increment	34074	13931	14962	17507	2306	2699	24777	25172
Breakeven Earnings Increment % of Previous Wage	16.5	4.7	5.1	5.9	0.8	0.9	8.4	8.5
METR Breakeven Earnings Increment (%)	20.1	20.1	20.1	20.1	20.1	20.1	20.1	20.1
Marginal Effective Tax Rate on Skills (%)	8.2	5.2	5.2	5.2	19.7	19.7	5.2	5.4
Average Effective Tax Rate on Skills (Assumed 15% Return, %)	17.6	16.6	16.3	15.7	19.8	19.7	13.8	13.8
Government Costs and Returns								
Government Educational Costs	122199	140004	140004	140004	102684	102684	140004	138475
Marginal Returns to Costs Ratio	0.25	0.35	0.35	0.35	0.07	0.07	0.35	0.35
Average Returns to Costs Ratio (Assumed 15% Return)	1.21	1.46	1.36	1.17	0.09	0.08	0.82	0.83

StatLink http://dx.doi.org/10.1787/888933446830

Denmark

Table C.13. Comparing Financial Incentives for College Education with Different Financing Scenarios - Denmark

Single, No Children, 17 Year-Old, Four Years of Education, 70% of the Average Wage					Currency: DKK
Scenario	No Borrowing	Direct Costs Borrowed, Low Interest Rate	All Costs Borrowed, Low Interest Rate	Direct Costs Borrowed, High Interest Rate	All Costs Borrowed, High Interest Rate
Non-Financing Education Costs					
Direct Costs of Education	8917	8917	8917	8917	8917
Pre-Tax Scholarship Income	48682	48682	48682	48682	48682
Income Before Education	270520	270520	270520	270520	270520
Income During Education	145296	145296	145296	145296	145296
Pre-Tax Foregone Earnings	125223	125223	125223	125223	125223
AETR Before Education (%)	33.7	33.7	33.7	33.7	34.0
AETR During Education (Exclusive of Tax Expenditures) (%)	27.4	27.4	27.4	27.4	27.4
Value of Education Tax Credits % of Direct Costs	-4.7	-4.7	-4.7	-4.7	-4.7
AETR During Education (Inclusive of Tax Expenditures) (%)	26.1	26.1	26.1	26.1	26.1
METR on Foregone Earnings (%)	40.9	40.9	40.9	40.9	40.9
Total Annual Non-Financing Costs of Education (Direct Costs & Foregone Earnings)	32376	32376	32376	32376	32376
Education Financing Costs					
Fraction of Costs Borrowed	None	Direct Costs	All Costs	Direct Costs	All Costs
Total Amount Borrowed	0	8917	32376	8917	32376
Interest Rate (%)	NA	0.0	0.0	6.0	6.0
Annual Repayments	0	758	2752	3032	11008
Debt Finance Multiplier	1.00	0.49	0.48	1.32	1.31
Returns to Education					
Breakeven Earnings Level	282562	280864	276282	283637	286354
AETR After Education (%)	34.0	33.9	33.8	34.0	34.1
Breakeven Earnings Increment	12042	10344	5763	13118	15834
Breakeven Earnings Increment % of Previous Wage	4.5	3.8	2.1	4.8	5.9
METR Breakeven Earnings Increment (%)	40.9	40.9	40.9	40.9	40.9
Marginal Effective Tax Rate on Skills (%)	-56.0	-73.7	-89.7	-49.5	-68.3
Average Effective Tax Rate on Skills (Assumed 15% Return, %)	40.5	41.4	44.6	39.4	32.8
Average Effective Tax Rate on Skills (Return based on Labour Market Premium, %)	26.8	29.1	37.7	23.7	5.7
Government Costs and Returns					
Government Educational Costs	256274	260839	273156	253381	246078
Marginal Returns to Costs Ratio	0.09	0.10	0.17	0.08	0.07
Average Returns to Costs Ratio (Return based on Labour Market Premium)	0.59	0.58	0.55	0.59	0.61

StatLink http://dx.doi.org/10.1787/888933446846

Table C.14. Comparing Financial Incentives for Differing Savings-Financed Education Scenarios - Denmark

Single, No Children, Annual Data								Currency: DKK
Age	17	27	32	40	32	40	50	50
Income Before Education, %AW	70	100	100	100	100	100	100	100
Income During Education, %AW	25	25	25	25	95	95	25	25
Years of Education	4	1	1	1	0.05	0.05	1	1
Education is Job Related	No	No	No	No	Yes	Yes	No	Yes
Financial Costs of Up-Skilling								
Direct Costs of Education	8917	8917	8917	8917	38285	38285	8917	8917
Pre-Tax Scholarship Income	48682	48682	48682	48682	0	0	48682	0
Income Before Education	270520	386457	386457	386457	386457	386457	386457	386457
Income During Education	145296	145296	145296	145296	385490	385490	145296	96614
Pre-Tax Foregone Earnings	125223	241160	241160	241160	966	966	241160	289842
AETR Before Education (%)	33.7	36.1	36.1	36.1	36.1	36.1	36.1	36.1
AETR During Education (Exclusive of Tax Expenditures) (%)	27.4	27.4	27.4	27.4	36.1	36.1	27.4	20.7
Value of Education Tax Credits % of Direct Costs	-4.7	-4.7	-4.7	-4.7	0.0	0.0	-4.7	0.0
AETR During Education (Inclusive of Tax Expenditures) (%)	26.1	26.1	26.1	26.1	36.1	36.1	26.1	20.7
METR on Foregone Earnings (%)	40.9	41.3	41.3	41.3	42.3	42.3	41.3	41.2
Total Costs of Education (Direct Costs & Foregone Earnings)	32376	99965	99965	99965	38842	38842	99965	179315
Financial Returns to Up-Skilling								
Breakeven Earnings Level	282562	396245	396908	398500	390518	391136	402729	415645
AETR After Education (%)	34.0	36.2	36.2	36.3	36.1	36.1	36.3	36.5
Breakeven Earnings Increment	12042	9788	10451	12043	4061	4680	16272	29188
Breakeven Earnings Increment % of Previous Wage	4.5	2.5	2.7	3.1	1.1	1.2	4.2	7.6
METR Breakeven Earnings Increment (%)	40.9	42.3	42.3	42.3	42.3	42.3	42.3	42.3
Marginal Effective Tax Rate on Skills (%)	-56.0	-16.2	-16.2	-16.2	41.7	41.7	-16.2	3.9
Average Effective Tax Rate on Skills (Assumed 15% Return, %)	40.5	41.8	41.3	40.1	41.7	41.6	36.9	34.7
Government Costs and Returns								
Government Educational Costs	256274	304621	304621	304621	154919	154919	304621	273954
Marginal Returns to Costs Ratio	0.09	0.24	0.24	0.24	0.18	0.18	0.24	0.48
Average Returns to Costs Ratio (Assumed 15% Return)	1.76	2.21	2.07	1.80	0.18	0.15	1.33	1.48

StatLink http://dx.doi.org/10.1787/888933446850

Estonia

Table C.15. Comparing Financial Incentives for College Education with Different Financing Scenarios - Estonia

Single, No Children, 17 Year-Old, Four Years of Education, 70% of the Average Wage					Currency: EEK
Scenario	No Borrowing	Direct Costs Borrowed, Low Interest Rate	All Costs Borrowed, Low Interest Rate	Direct Costs Borrowed, High Interest Rate	All Costs Borrowed, High Interest Rate
Non-Financing Education Costs					
Direct Costs of Education	645	645	645	645	645
Pre-Tax Scholarship Income	133	133	133	133	133
Income Before Education	7258	7258	7258	7258	7258
Income During Education	2725	2725	2725	2725	2725
Pre-Tax Foregone Earnings	4533	4533	4533	4533	4533
AETR Before Education (%)	15.4	15.4	15.4	15.4	15.4
AETR During Education (Exclusive of Tax Expenditures) (%)	7.1	7.1	7.1	7.1	7.1
Value of Education Tax Credits % of Direct Costs	31.8	31.8	31.8	31.8	31.8
AETR During Education (Inclusive of Tax Expenditures) (%)	1.1	1.1	1.1	1.1	1.1
METR on Foregone Earnings (%)	20.4	20.4	20.4	20.4	20.4
Total Annual Non-Financing Costs of Education (Direct Costs & Foregone Earnings)	3956	3956	3956	3956	3956
Education Financing Costs					
Fraction of Costs Borrowed	None	Direct Costs	All Costs	Direct Costs	All Costs
Total Amount Borrowed	0	645	3956	645	3956
Interest Rate (%)	NA	0.0	0.0	6.0	6.0
Annual Repayments	0	55	336	219	1345
Debt Finance Multiplier	1.00	0.59	0.59	1.41	1.41
Returns to Education					
Breakeven Earnings Level	8394	8319	7932	8470	8857
AETR After Education (%)	16.1	16.1	15.8	16.1	16.3
Breakeven Earnings Increment	1137	1062	675	1212	1599
Breakeven Earnings Increment % of Previous Wage	15.7	14.6	9.3	16.7	22.0
METR Breakeven Earnings Increment (%)	20.4	20.4	20.4	20.4	20.4
Marginal Effective Tax Rate on Skills (%)	-1.5	-3.0	-1.5	-0.1	-1.5
Average Effective Tax Rate on Skills (Assumed 15% Return, %)	16.1	17.4	22.7	14.7	3.0
Average Effective Tax Rate on Skills (Return based on Labour Market Premium, %)	12.4	14.7	24.6	9.8	-12.1
Government Costs and Returns					
Government Educational Costs	4534	4796	6143	4272	2926
Marginal Returns to Costs Ratio	0.22	0.23	0.28	0.22	0.25
Average Returns to Costs Ratio (Return based on Labour Market Premium)	0.61	0.58	0.45	0.65	0.95

StatLink http://dx.doi.org/10.1787/888933446864

Table C.16. **Comparing Financial Incentives for Differing Savings-Financed Education Scenarios - Estonia**

Single, No Children, Annual Data								**Currency: EEK**
Age	17	27	32	40	32	40	50	50
Income Before Education, %AW	70	100	100	100	100	100	100	100
Income During Education, %AW	25	25	25	25	95	95	25	25
Years of Education	4	1	1	1	0.05	0.05	1	1
Education is Job Related	No	No	No	No	Yes	Yes	No	Yes
Financial Costs of Up-Skilling								
Direct Costs of Education	645	645	645	645	992	992	645	645
Pre-Tax Scholarship Income	133	133	133	133	0	0	133	0
Income Before Education	7258	10368	10368	10368	10368	10368	10368	10368
Income During Education	2725	2725	2725	2725	10342	10342	2725	2592
Pre-Tax Foregone Earnings	4533	7643	7643	7643	26	26	7643	7776
AETR Before Education (%)	15.4	16.9	16.9	16.9	16.9	16.9	16.9	16.9
AETR During Education (Exclusive of Tax Expenditures) (%)	7.1	7.1	7.1	7.1	16.9	16.9	7.1	6.4
Value of Education Tax Credits % of Direct Costs	31.8	31.8	31.8	31.8	21.0	21.0	31.8	21.0
AETR During Education (Inclusive of Tax Expenditures) (%)	1.1	1.1	1.1	1.1	14.9	14.9	1.1	1.2
METR on Foregone Earnings (%)	20.4	20.4	20.4	20.4	20.4	20.4	20.4	20.4
Total Costs of Education (Direct Costs & Foregone Earnings)	3956	6432	6432	6432	804	804	6432	6698
Financial Returns to Up-Skilling								
Breakeven Earnings Level	8394	10849	10888	10987	10433	10445	11298	11336
AETR After Education (%)	16.1	17.1	17.1	17.1	16.9	16.9	17.2	17.2
Breakeven Earnings Increment	1137	481	520	619	65	77	930	968
Breakeven Earnings Increment % of Previous Wage	15.7	4.6	5.0	6.0	0.6	0.7	9.0	9.3
METR Breakeven Earnings Increment (%)	20.4	20.4	20.4	20.4	20.4	20.4	20.4	20.4
Marginal Effective Tax Rate on Skills (%)	-1.5	-0.9	-0.9	-0.9	-0.7	-0.7	-0.9	-0.1
Average Effective Tax Rate on Skills (Assumed 15% Return, %)	16.1	15.5	15.1	14.0	7.2	4.6	10.9	10.9
Government Costs and Returns								
Government Educational Costs	4534	5169	5169	5169	3527	3527	5169	5036
Marginal Returns to Costs Ratio	0.22	0.32	0.32	0.32	0.06	0.06	0.32	0.34
Average Returns to Costs Ratio (Assumed 15% Return)	1.14	1.38	1.27	1.07	0.09	0.08	0.71	0.73

StatLink http://dx.doi.org/10.1787/888933446876

Finland

Table C.17. Comparing Financial Incentives for College Education with Different Financing Scenarios[2] - Finland

Single, No Children, 17 Year-Old, Four Years of Education, 70% of the Average Wage					Currency: EUR
Scenario	No Borrowing	Direct Costs Borrowed, Low Interest Rate	All Costs Borrowed, Low Interest Rate	Direct Costs Borrowed, High Interest Rate	All Costs Borrowed, High Interest Rate
Non-Financing Education Costs					
Direct Costs of Education	672	672	672	672	672
Pre-Tax Scholarship Income	2500	2500	2500	2500	2500
Income Before Education	28170	28170	28170	28170	28170
Income During Education	12561	12561	12561	12561	12561
Pre-Tax Foregone Earnings	15609	15609	15609	15609	15609
AETR Before Education (%)	16.3	16.3	16.3	16.3	16.3
AETR During Education (Exclusive of Tax Expenditures) (%)	5.4	5.4	5.4	5.4	5.4
Value of Education Tax Credits % of Direct Costs	-17.3	-17.3	-17.3	-17.3	-17.3
AETR During Education (Inclusive of Tax Expenditures) (%)	2.8	2.8	2.8	2.8	2.8
METR on Foregone Earnings (%)	25.2	25.2	25.2	25.2	25.2
Total Annual Non-Financing Costs of Education (Direct Costs & Foregone Earnings)	9531	9531	9531	9531	9531
Education Financing Costs					
Fraction of Costs Borrowed	None	Direct Costs	All Costs	Direct Costs	All Costs
Total Amount Borrowed	0	672	9531	672	9531
Interest Rate (%)	NA	0.0	0.0	6.0	6.0
Annual Repayments	0	57	810	229	3241
Debt Finance Multiplier	1.00	0.59	0.59	1.41	1.41
Returns to Education					
Breakeven Earnings Level	31471	31375	30109	31567	32832
AETR After Education (%)	18.3	18.3	17.6	18.4	19.0
Breakeven Earnings Increment	3301	3205	1939	3397	4662
Breakeven Earnings Increment % of Previous Wage	11.7	11.4	6.9	12.1	16.6
METR Breakeven Earnings Increment (%)	35.3	35.3	35.3	35.3	35.3
Marginal Effective Tax Rate on Skills (%)	6.4	5.6	6.4	7.3	6.4
Average Effective Tax Rate on Skills (Assumed 15% Return, %)	33.6	34.0	38.7	33.2	23.9
Average Effective Tax Rate on Skills (Return based on Labour Market Premium, %)	29.7	30.3	37.7	29.0	14.1
Government Costs and Returns					
Government Educational Costs	22406	22684	26338	22129	18474
Marginal Returns to Costs Ratio	0.23	0.24	0.34	0.23	0.20
Average Returns to Costs Ratio (Return based on Labour Market Premium)	1.02	1.01	0.87	1.04	1.24

StatLink http://dx.doi.org/10.1787/888933446881

Table C.18. **Comparing Financial Incentives for Differing Savings-Financed Education Scenarios - Finland**

Single, No Children, Annual Data								**Currency: EUR**
Age	17	27	32	40	32	40	50	50
Income Before Education, %AW	70	100	100	100	100	100	100	100
Income During Education, %AW	25	25	25	25	95	95	25	25
Years of Education	4	1	1	1	0.05	0.05	1	1
Education is Job Related	No	No	No	No	Yes	Yes	No	Yes
Financial Costs of Up-Skilling								
Direct Costs of Education	672	672	672	672	4144	4144	672	672
Pre-Tax Scholarship Income	2500	2500	2500	2500	0	0	2500	0
Income Before Education	28170	40243	40243	40243	40243	40243	40243	40243
Income During Education	12561	12561	12561	12561	40142	40142	12561	10061
Pre-Tax Foregone Earnings	15609	27682	27682	27682	101	101	27682	30182
AETR Before Education (%)	16.3	22.2	22.2	22.2	22.2	22.2	22.2	22.2
AETR During Education (Exclusive of Tax Expenditures) (%)	5.4	5.4	5.4	5.4	22.2	22.2	5.4	3.5
Value of Education Tax Credits % of Direct Costs	-17.3	-17.3	-17.3	-17.3	17.5	17.5	-17.3	0.0
AETR During Education (Inclusive of Tax Expenditures) (%)	2.8	2.8	2.8	2.8	20.4	20.4	2.8	3.5
METR on Foregone Earnings (%)	25.2	29.9	29.9	29.9	36.5	36.5	29.9	28.5
Total Costs of Education (Direct Costs & Foregone Earnings)	9531	17265	17265	17265	3483	3483	17265	22265
Financial Returns to Up-Skilling								
Breakeven Earnings Level	31471	41873	41997	42302	40584	40642	43175	44037
AETR After Education (%)	18.3	22.9	22.9	23.0	22.3	22.4	23.4	23.7
Breakeven Earnings Increment	3301	1630	1754	2059	341	399	2932	3794
Breakeven Earnings Increment % of Previous Wage	11.7	4.1	4.4	5.1	0.8	1.0	7.3	9.4
METR Breakeven Earnings Increment (%)	35.3	38.7	38.8	39.0	36.5	36.5	39.4	39.6
Marginal Effective Tax Rate on Skills (%)	6.4	8.2	8.3	8.7	22.6	22.6	9.2	16.3
Average Effective Tax Rate on Skills (Assumed 15% Return, %)	33.6	33.7	33.3	32.2	24.7	22.7	28.9	28.9
Government Costs and Returns								
Government Educational Costs	22406	26746	26746	26746	16418	16418	26746	24246
Marginal Returns to Costs Ratio	0.23	0.41	0.41	0.41	0.12	0.12	0.42	0.60
Average Returns to Costs Ratio (Assumed 15% Return)	1.70	2.08	1.93	1.65	0.14	0.12	1.17	1.29

StatLink http://dx.doi.org/10.1787/888933446893

Greece

Table C.19. Comparing Financial Incentives for College Education with Different Financing Scenarios - Greece

Single, No Children, 17 Year-Old, Four Years of Education, 70% of the Average Wage — Currency: EUR

Scenario	No Borrowing	Direct Costs Borrowed, Low Interest Rate	All Costs Borrowed, Low Interest Rate	Direct Costs Borrowed, High Interest Rate	All Costs Borrowed, High Interest Rate
Non-Financing Education Costs					
Direct Costs of Education	20	20	20	20	20
Pre-Tax Scholarship Income	6	6	6	6	6
Income Before Education	16374	16374	16374	16374	16374
Income During Education	5854	5854	5854	5854	5854
Pre-Tax Foregone Earnings	10519	10519	10519	10519	10519
AETR Before Education (%)	10.1	10.1	10.1	10.1	10.1
AETR During Education (Exclusive of Tax Expenditures) (%)	1.5	1.5	1.5	1.5	1.5
Value of Education Tax Credits % of Direct Costs	6.4	6.4	6.4	6.4	6.4
AETR During Education (Inclusive of Tax Expenditures) (%)	1.4	1.4	1.4	1.4	1.4
METR on Foregone Earnings (%)	14.9	14.9	14.9	14.9	14.9
Total Annual Non-Financing Costs of Education (Direct Costs & Foregone Earnings)	8967	8967	8967	8967	8967
Education Financing Costs					
Fraction of Costs Borrowed	None	Direct Costs	All Costs	Direct Costs	All Costs
Total Amount Borrowed	0	20	8967	20	8967
Interest Rate (%)	NA	0.0	0.0	6.0	6.0
Annual Repayments	0	2	762	7	3049
Debt Finance Multiplier	1.00	0.60	0.60	1.40	1.40
Returns to Education					
Breakeven Earnings Level	19233	19230	18099	19235	20367
AETR After Education (%)	12.4	12.4	11.6	12.4	13.2
Breakeven Earnings Increment	2859	2857	1725	2862	3993
Breakeven Earnings Increment % of Previous Wage	17.5	17.4	10.5	17.5	24.4
METR Breakeven Earnings Increment (%)	25.8	25.8	25.8	25.8	25.8
Marginal Effective Tax Rate on Skills (%)	12.9	12.9	12.9	12.9	12.9
Average Effective Tax Rate on Skills (Assumed 15% Return, %)	27.5	27.6	33.2	27.5	15.9
Average Effective Tax Rate on Skills (Return based on Labour Market Premium, %)	19.9	19.9	31.8	19.8	-4.7
Government Costs and Returns					
Government Educational Costs	5682	5689	9238	5674	2125
Marginal Returns to Costs Ratio	0.55	0.55	0.56	0.55	1.05
Average Returns to Costs Ratio (Return based on Labour Market Premium)	1.19	1.19	0.73	1.20	3.19

StatLink http://dx.doi.org/10.1787/888933446900

Table C.20. Comparing Financial Incentives for Differing Savings-Financed Education Scenarios - Greece

Single, No Children, Annual Data								Currency: EUR
Age	17	27	32	40	32	40	50	50
Income Before Education, %AW	70	100	100	100	100	100	100	100
Income During Education, %AW	25	25	25	25	95	95	25	25
Years of Education	4	1	1	1	0.05	0.05	1	1
Education is Job Related	No	No	No	No	Yes	Yes	No	Yes
Financial Costs of Up-Skilling								
Direct Costs of Education	20	20	20	20	1573	1573	20	20
Pre-Tax Scholarship Income	6	6	6	6	0	0	6	0
Income Before Education	16374	23391	23391	23391	23391	23391	23391	23391
Income During Education	5854	5854	5854	5854	23333	23333	5854	5848
Pre-Tax Foregone Earnings	10519	17537	17537	17537	58	58	17537	17543
AETR Before Education (%)	10.1	14.8	14.8	14.8	14.8	14.8	14.8	14.8
AETR During Education (Exclusive of Tax Expenditures) (%)	1.5	1.5	1.5	1.5	14.8	14.8	1.5	1.5
Value of Education Tax Credits % of Direct Costs	6.4	6.4	6.4	6.4	2.5	2.5	6.4	1.0
AETR During Education (Inclusive of Tax Expenditures) (%)	1.4	1.4	1.4	1.4	14.6	14.6	1.4	1.4
METR on Foregone Earnings (%)	14.9	19.3	19.3	19.3	25.8	25.8	19.3	19.3
Total Costs of Education (Direct Costs & Foregone Earnings)	8967	14171	14171	14171	1577	1577	14171	14184
Financial Returns to Up-Skilling								
Breakeven Earnings Level	19233	24860	24974	25279	23536	23569	26494	26497
AETR After Education (%)	12.4	16.3	16.3	16.5	14.9	14.9	17.1	17.1
Breakeven Earnings Increment	2859	1469	1583	1888	145	178	3103	3106
Breakeven Earnings Increment % of Previous Wage	17.5	6.3	6.8	8.1	0.6	0.8	13.3	13.3
METR Breakeven Earnings Increment (%)	25.8	40.0	39.1	37.1	25.8	25.8	34.6	34.6
Marginal Effective Tax Rate on Skills (%)	12.9	25.7	24.5	22.0	23.3	23.3	19.0	19.0
Average Effective Tax Rate on Skills (Assumed 15% Return, %)	27.5	30.8	30.4	29.2	24.3	23.9	24.9	24.9
Government Costs and Returns								
Government Educational Costs	5682	7495	7495	7495	4163	4163	7495	7488
Marginal Returns to Costs Ratio	0.55	1.26	1.21	1.11	0.13	0.13	1.00	1.00
Average Returns to Costs Ratio (Assumed 15% Return)	2.96	3.54	3.24	2.63	0.21	0.17	1.54	1.54

StatLink http://dx.doi.org/10.1787/888933446919

Hungary

Table C.21. Comparing Financial Incentives for College Education with Different Financing Scenarios - Hungary

Single, No Children, 17 Year-Old, Four Years of Education, 70% of the Average Wage					Currency: HUF
Scenario	No Borrowing	Direct Costs Borrowed, Low Interest Rate	All Costs Borrowed, Low Interest Rate	Direct Costs Borrowed, High Interest Rate	All Costs Borrowed, High Interest Rate
Non-Financing Education Costs					
Direct Costs of Education	349237	349237	349237	349237	349237
Pre-Tax Scholarship Income	160703	160703	160703	160703	160703
Income Before Education	1851998	1851998	1851998	1851998	1851998
Income During Education	822131	822131	822131	822131	822131
Pre-Tax Foregone Earnings	1029868	1029868	1029868	1029868	1029868
AETR Before Education (%)	12.5	12.5	12.5	12.5	12.5
AETR During Education (Exclusive of Tax Expenditures) (%)	2.7	2.7	2.7	2.7	2.7
Value of Education Tax Credits % of Direct Costs	11.6	11.6	11.6	11.6	11.6
AETR During Education (Inclusive of Tax Expenditures) (%)	0.0	0.0	0.0	0.0	0.0
METR on Foregone Earnings (%)	20.3	20.3	20.3	20.3	20.3
Total Annual Non-Financing Costs of Education (Direct Costs & Foregone Earnings)	987276	987276	987276	987276	987276
Education Financing Costs					
Fraction of Costs Borrowed	None	Direct Costs	All Costs	Direct Costs	All Costs
Total Amount Borrowed	0	349237	987276	349237	987276
Interest Rate (%)	NA	0.0	0.0	6.0	6.0
Annual Repayments	0	29684	83916	118738	335666
Debt Finance Multiplier	1.00	0.59	0.59	1.41	1.41
Returns to Education					
Breakeven Earnings Level	2129652	2089137	2015120	2171304	2262827
AETR After Education (%)	13.5	13.4	13.1	13.7	14.6
Breakeven Earnings Increment	277653	237139	163121	319306	410828
Breakeven Earnings Increment % of Previous Wage	15.0	12.8	8.8	17.2	22.2
METR Breakeven Earnings Increment (%)	20.3	20.3	20.3	20.6	23.9
Marginal Effective Tax Rate on Skills (%)	1.7	-1.5	1.7	4.4	6.1
Average Effective Tax Rate on Skills (Assumed 15% Return, %)	26.6	29.0	32.5	23.6	14.4
Average Effective Tax Rate on Skills (Return based on Labour Market Premium, %)	24.8	26.5	29.1	22.7	16.1
Government Costs and Returns					
Government Educational Costs	1490241	1634302	1897493	1346181	1082990
Marginal Returns to Costs Ratio	0.17	0.18	0.23	0.17	0.20
Average Returns to Costs Ratio (Return based on Labour Market Premium)	1.69	1.54	1.33	1.87	2.33

StatLink http://dx.doi.org/10.1787/888933446922

Table C.22. **Comparing Financial Incentives for Differing Savings-Financed Education Scenarios - Hungary**

Single, No Children, Annual Data								Currency: HUF
Age	17	27	32	40	32	40	50	50
Income Before Education, %AW	70	100	100	100	100	100	100	100
Income During Education, %AW	25	25	25	25	95	95	25	25
Years of Education	4	1	1	1	0.05	0.05	1	1
Education is Job Related	No	No	No	No	Yes	Yes	No	Yes
Financial Costs of Up-Skilling								
Direct Costs of Education	349237	349237	349237	349237	262409	262409	349237	349237
Pre-Tax Scholarship Income	160703	160703	160703	160703	0	0	160703	0
Income Before Education	1851998	2645712	2645712	2645712	2645712	2645712	2645712	2645712
Income During Education	822131	822131	822131	822131	2639098	2639098	822131	661428
Pre-Tax Foregone Earnings	1029868	1823581	1823581	1823581	6614	6614	1823581	1984284
AETR Before Education (%)	12.5	17.6	17.6	17.6	17.6	17.6	17.6	17.6
AETR During Education (Exclusive of Tax Expenditures) (%)	2.7	2.7	2.7	2.7	17.6	17.6	2.7	0.0
Value of Education Tax Credits % of Direct Costs	11.6	11.6	11.6	11.6	0.0	0.0	11.6	0.0
AETR During Education (Inclusive of Tax Expenditures) (%)	0.0	0.0	0.0	0.0	17.6	17.6	0.0	0.0
METR on Foregone Earnings (%)	20.3	24.3	24.3	24.3	35.6	35.6	24.3	23.5
Total Costs of Education (Direct Costs & Foregone Earnings)	987276	1546501	1546501	1546501	266671	266671	1546501	1867906
Financial Returns to Up-Skilling								
Breakeven Earnings Level	2129652	2784645	2794934	2820311	2671443	2675819	2892819	2944175
AETR After Education (%)	13.5	18.5	18.6	18.7	17.8	17.8	19.1	19.4
Breakeven Earnings Increment	277653	138933	149222	174599	25731	30107	247107	298463
Breakeven Earnings Increment % of Previous Wage	15.0	5.3	5.6	6.6	1.0	1.1	9.3	11.3
METR Breakeven Earnings Increment (%)	20.3	35.6	35.6	35.6	35.6	35.6	35.6	35.6
Marginal Effective Tax Rate on Skills (%)	1.7	16.2	16.2	16.2	35.0	35.0	16.2	19.5
Average Effective Tax Rate on Skills (Assumed 15% Return, %)	26.6	28.8	28.5	27.5	35.0	34.9	24.9	24.9
Government Costs and Returns								
Government Educational Costs	1490241	1724730	1724730	1724730	1100765	1100765	1724730	1564028
Marginal Returns to Costs Ratio	0.17	0.49	0.49	0.49	0.13	0.13	0.49	0.66
Average Returns to Costs Ratio (Assumed 15% Return)	1.34	1.80	1.67	1.43	0.14	0.12	1.01	1.11

StatLink http://dx.doi.org/10.1787/888933446931

Iceland

Table C.23. Comparing Financial Incentives for College Education with Different Financing Scenarios - Iceland

Single, No Children, 17 Year-Old, Four Years of Education, 70% of the Average Wage					Currency: ISJ
Scenario	No Borrowing	Direct Costs Borrowed, Low Interest Rate	All Costs Borrowed, Low Interest Rate	Direct Costs Borrowed, High Interest Rate	All Costs Borrowed, High Interest Rate
Non-Financing Education Costs					
Direct Costs of Education	100495	100495	100495	100495	100495
Pre-Tax Scholarship Income	0	0	0	0	0
Income Before Education	3939600	3939600	3939600	3939600	3939600
Income During Education	1407000	1407000	1407000	1407000	1407000
Pre-Tax Foregone Earnings	2532600	2532600	2532600	2532600	2532600
AETR Before Education (%)	23.3	23.3	23.3	23.3	23.3
AETR During Education (Exclusive of Tax Expenditures) (%)	0.0	0.0	0.0	0.0	0.0
Value of Education Tax Credits % of Direct Costs	0.0	0.0	0.0	0.0	0.0
AETR During Education (Inclusive of Tax Expenditures) (%)	0.0	0.0	0.0	0.0	0.0
METR on Foregone Earnings (%)	36.2	36.2	36.2	36.2	36.2
Total Annual Non-Financing Costs of Education (Direct Costs & Foregone Earnings)	1715684	1715684	1715684	1715684	1715684
Education Financing Costs					
Fraction of Costs Borrowed	None	Direct Costs	All Costs	Direct Costs	All Costs
Total Amount Borrowed	0	100495	1715684	100495	1715684
Interest Rate (%)	NA	0.0	0.0	6.0	6.0
Annual Repayments	0	8542	145830	34167	583318
Debt Finance Multiplier	1.00	0.58	0.58	1.42	1.42
Returns to Education					
Breakeven Earnings Level	4554037	4538987	4297091	4569088	4810984
AETR After Education (%)	25.4	25.3	24.6	25.4	26.1
Breakeven Earnings Increment	614437	599387	357491	629488	871384
Breakeven Earnings Increment % of Previous Wage	15.6	15.2	9.1	16.0	22.1
METR Breakeven Earnings Increment (%)	38.6	38.6	38.6	38.6	38.6
Marginal Effective Tax Rate on Skills (%)	5.8	4.9	5.8	6.6	5.8
Average Effective Tax Rate on Skills (Assumed 15% Return, %)	32.2	32.6	39.3	31.7	18.6
Average Effective Tax Rate on Skills (Return based on Labour Market Premium, %)	27.4	28.1	39.9	26.6	3.5
Government Costs and Returns					
Government Educational Costs	1959509	2001534	2676976	1917484	1242041
Marginal Returns to Costs Ratio	0.55	0.55	0.69	0.55	0.61
Average Returns to Costs Ratio (Return based on Labour Market Premium)	1.61	1.57	1.18	1.64	2.54

StatLink http://dx.doi.org/10.1787/888933446943

Table C.24. **Comparing Financial Incentives for Differing Savings-Financed Education Scenarios - Iceland**

Single, No Children, Annual Data								Currency: ISJ
Age	17	27	32	40	32	40	50	50
Income Before Education, %AW	70	100	100	100	100	100	100	100
Income During Education, %AW	25	25	25	25	95	95	25	25
Years of Education	4	1	1	1	0.05	0.05	1	1
Education is Job Related	No	No	No	No	Yes	Yes	No	Yes
Financial Costs of Up-Skilling								
Direct Costs of Education	100495	100495	100495	100495	557721	557721	100495	100495
Pre-Tax Scholarship Income	0	0	0	0	0	0	0	0
Income Before Education	3939600	5628000	5628000	5628000	5628000	5628000	5628000	5628000
Income During Education	1407000	1407000	1407000	1407000	5613930	5613930	1407000	1407000
Pre-Tax Foregone Earnings	2532600	4221000	4221000	4221000	14070	14070	4221000	4221000
AETR Before Education (%)	23.3	27.9	27.9	27.9	27.9	27.9	27.9	27.9
AETR During Education (Exclusive of Tax Expenditures) (%)	0.0	0.0	0.0	0.0	27.9	27.9	0.0	0.0
Value of Education Tax Credits % of Direct Costs	0.0	0.0	0.0	0.0	40.2	40.2	0.0	0.0
AETR During Education (Inclusive of Tax Expenditures) (%)	0.0	0.0	0.0	0.0	23.9	23.9	0.0	0.0
METR on Foregone Earnings (%)	36.2	37.2	37.2	37.2	38.6	38.6	37.2	37.2
Total Costs of Education (Direct Costs & Foregone Earnings)	1715684	2752334	2752334	2752334	342100	342100	2752334	2752334
Financial Returns to Up-Skilling								
Breakeven Earnings Level	4554037	5881204	5898363	5939545	5661605	5666723	6048936	6048936
AETR After Education (%)	25.4	28.3	28.4	28.4	27.9	28.0	28.6	28.6
Breakeven Earnings Increment	614437	253204	270363	311545	33605	38723	420936	420936
Breakeven Earnings Increment % of Previous Wage	15.6	4.5	4.8	5.5	0.6	0.7	7.5	7.5
METR Breakeven Earnings Increment (%)	38.6	38.6	38.6	38.6	38.6	38.6	38.6	38.6
Marginal Effective Tax Rate on Skills (%)	5.8	3.6	3.6	3.6	-2.6	-2.6	3.6	3.6
Average Effective Tax Rate on Skills (Assumed 15% Return, %)	32.2	30.7	30.2	28.9	14.0	10.2	25.5	25.5
Government Costs and Returns								
Government Educational Costs	1959509	2611258	2611258	2611258	1271788	1271788	2611258	2611258
Marginal Returns to Costs Ratio	0.55	0.66	0.66	0.66	0.17	0.17	0.66	0.66
Average Returns to Costs Ratio (Assumed 15% Return)	2.82	2.95	2.76	2.39	0.28	0.25	1.77	1.77

StatLink http://dx.doi.org/10.1787/888933446956

Ireland

Table C.25. Comparing Financial Incentives for College Education with Different Financing Scenarios - Ireland

Single, No Children, 17 Year-Old, Four Years of Education, 70% of the Average Wage					Currency: EUR
Scenario	No Borrowing	Direct Costs Borrowed, Low Interest Rate	All Costs Borrowed, Low Interest Rate	Direct Costs Borrowed, High Interest Rate	All Costs Borrowed, High Interest Rate
Non-Financing Education Costs					
Direct Costs of Education	2213	2213	2213	2213	2213
Pre-Tax Scholarship Income	1600	1600	1600	1600	1600
Income Before Education	22585	22585	22585	22585	22585
Income During Education	9666	9666	9666	9666	9666
Pre-Tax Foregone Earnings	12919	12919	12919	12919	12919
AETR Before Education (%)	9.4	9.4	9.4	9.4	9.4
AETR During Education (Exclusive of Tax Expenditures) (%)	2.0	2.0	2.0	2.0	2.0
Value of Education Tax Credits % of Direct Costs	5.2	5.2	5.2	5.2	5.2
AETR During Education (Inclusive of Tax Expenditures) (%)	1.7	1.7	1.7	1.7	1.7
METR on Foregone Earnings (%)	14.9	14.9	14.9	14.9	14.9
Total Annual Non-Financing Costs of Education (Direct Costs & Foregone Earnings)	11577	11577	11577	11577	11577
Education Financing Costs					
Fraction of Costs Borrowed	None	Direct Costs	All Costs	Direct Costs	All Costs
Total Amount Borrowed	0	2213	11577	2213	11577
Interest Rate (%)	NA	0.0	0.0	6.0	6.0
Annual Repayments	0	188	984	752	3936
Debt Finance Multiplier	1.00	0.59	0.59	1.41	1.41
Returns to Education					
Breakeven Earnings Level	26139	25858	24673	26419	27605
AETR After Education (%)	11.8	11.6	10.9	11.9	12.6
Breakeven Earnings Increment	3554	3274	2088	3834	5020
Breakeven Earnings Increment % of Previous Wage	15.7	14.5	9.2	17.0	22.2
METR Breakeven Earnings Increment (%)	27.0	27.0	27.0	27.0	27.0
Marginal Effective Tax Rate on Skills (%)	14.7	13.6	14.7	15.6	14.7
Average Effective Tax Rate on Skills (Assumed 15% Return, %)	33.7	34.9	38.8	32.3	22.9
Average Effective Tax Rate on Skills (Return based on Labour Market Premium, %)	20.5	23.8	34.1	16.7	-8.3
Government Costs and Returns					
Government Educational Costs	14270	15183	19046	13357	9495
Marginal Returns to Costs Ratio	0.30	0.31	0.38	0.30	0.32
Average Returns to Costs Ratio (Return based on Labour Market Premium)	0.57	0.54	0.43	0.61	0.86

StatLink http://dx.doi.org/10.1787/888933446961

Table C.26. **Comparing Financial Incentives for Differing Savings-Financed Education Scenarios - Ireland**

Single, No Children, Annual Data								**Currency: EUR**
Age	17	27	32	40	32	40	50	50
Income Before Education, %AW	70	100	100	100	100	100	100	100
Income During Education, %AW	25	25	25	25	95	95	25	25
Years of Education	4	1	1	1	0.05	0.05	1	1
Education is Job Related	No	No	No	No	Yes	Yes	No	Yes
Financial Costs of Up-Skilling								
Direct Costs of Education	2213	2213	2213	2213	3284	3284	2213	2213
Pre-Tax Scholarship Income	1600	1600	1600	1600	0	0	1600	0
Income Before Education	22585	32264	32264	32264	32264	32264	32264	32264
Income During Education	9666	9666	9666	9666	32183	32183	9666	8066
Pre-Tax Foregone Earnings	12919	22598	22598	22598	81	81	22598	24198
AETR Before Education (%)	9.4	14.7	14.7	14.7	14.7	14.7	14.7	14.7
AETR During Education (Exclusive of Tax Expenditures) (%)	2.0	2.0	2.0	2.0	14.6	14.6	2.0	2.0
Value of Education Tax Credits % of Direct Costs	5.2	5.2	5.2	5.2	7.8	7.8	5.2	0.0
AETR During Education (Inclusive of Tax Expenditures) (%)	1.7	1.7	1.7	1.7	13.8	13.8	1.7	2.0
METR on Foregone Earnings (%)	14.9	20.1	20.1	20.1	27.0	27.0	20.1	18.9
Total Costs of Education (Direct Costs & Foregone Earnings)	11577	18643	18643	18643	3086	3086	18643	21842
Financial Returns to Up-Skilling								
Breakeven Earnings Level	26139	34123	34277	34656	32527	32572	35739	36373
AETR After Education (%)	11.8	16.1	16.3	16.6	14.8	14.8	17.6	18.1
Breakeven Earnings Increment	3554	1859	2013	2392	263	308	3475	4109
Breakeven Earnings Increment % of Previous Wage	15.7	5.8	6.2	7.4	0.8	1.0	10.8	12.7
METR Breakeven Earnings Increment (%)	27.0	41.9	42.4	43.3	27.0	27.0	44.8	45.3
Marginal Effective Tax Rate on Skills (%)	14.7	27.7	28.3	29.4	20.4	20.4	31.2	33.8
Average Effective Tax Rate on Skills (Assumed 15% Return, %)	33.7	42.2	41.9	41.1	21.6	20.7	39.0	39.0
Government Costs and Returns								
Government Educational Costs	14270	16883	16883	16883	10994	10994	16883	15284
Marginal Returns to Costs Ratio	0.30	0.80	0.81	0.84	0.10	0.10	0.89	1.18
Average Returns to Costs Ratio (Assumed 15% Return)	2.04	3.05	2.84	2.43	0.13	0.11	1.72	1.90

StatLink http://dx.doi.org/10.1787/888933446974

Israel

Table C.27. **Comparing Financial Incentives for College Education with Different Financing Scenarios - Israel**

Single, No Children, 17 Year-Old, Four Years of Education, 70% of the Average Wage					Currency: ILS
Scenario	No Borrowing	Direct Costs Borrowed, Low Interest Rate	All Costs Borrowed, Low Interest Rate	Direct Costs Borrowed, High Interest Rate	All Costs Borrowed, High Interest Rate
Non-Financing Education Costs					
Direct Costs of Education	14096	14096	14096	14096	14096
Pre-Tax Scholarship Income	2500	2500	2500	2500	2500
Income Before Education	87784	87784	87784	87784	87784
Income During Education	33851	33851	33851	33851	33851
Pre-Tax Foregone Earnings	53933	53933	53933	53933	53933
AETR Before Education (%)	4.8	4.8	4.8	4.8	4.8
AETR During Education (Exclusive of Tax Expenditures) (%)	0.0	0.0	0.0	0.0	0.0
Value of Education Tax Credits % of Direct Costs	0.0	0.0	0.0	0.0	0.0
AETR During Education (Inclusive of Tax Expenditures) (%)	0.0	0.0	0.0	0.0	0.0
METR on Foregone Earnings (%)	7.8	7.8	7.8	7.8	7.8
Total Annual Non-Financing Costs of Education (Direct Costs & Foregone Earnings)	61316	61316	61316	61316	61316
Education Financing Costs					
Fraction of Costs Borrowed	None	Direct Costs	All Costs	Direct Costs	All Costs
Total Amount Borrowed	0	14096	61316	14096	61316
Interest Rate (%)	NA	0.0	0.0	6.0	6.0
Annual Repayments	0	1198	5212	4793	20847
Debt Finance Multiplier	1.00	0.58	0.58	1.42	1.42
Returns to Education					
Breakeven Earnings Level	103461	101954	96905	105090	110729
AETR After Education (%)	6.2	6.1	5.7	6.4	7.3
Breakeven Earnings Increment	15677	14170	9121	17307	22946
Breakeven Earnings Increment % of Previous Wage	17.9	16.1	10.4	19.7	26.1
METR Breakeven Earnings Increment (%)	14.0	14.0	14.0	14.6	16.7
Marginal Effective Tax Rate on Skills (%)	8.1	7.5	8.1	9.3	10.9
Average Effective Tax Rate on Skills (Assumed 15% Return, %)	19.6	21.4	25.2	17.5	6.9
Average Effective Tax Rate on Skills (Return based on Labour Market Premium, %)	18.1	20.7	26.1	15.0	-0.3
Government Costs and Returns					
Government Educational Costs	29046	34940	54687	23151	3404
Marginal Returns to Costs Ratio	0.34	0.32	0.31	0.41	2.54
Average Returns to Costs Ratio (Return based on Labour Market Premium)	1.52	1.26	0.81	1.90	12.95

Note: The statistical data for Israel are supplied by and under the responsibility of the relevant Israeli authorities. The use of such data by the OECD is without prejudice to the status of the Golan Heights, East Jerusalem and Israeli settlements in the West Bank under the terms of international law.

StatLink http://dx.doi.org/10.1787/888933446988

Table C.28. **Comparing Financial Incentives for Differing Savings-Financed Education Scenarios - Israel**

Single, No Children, Annual Data								Currency: ILS
Age	17	27	32	40	32	40	50	50
Income Before Education, %AW	70	100	100	100	100	100	100	100
Income During Education, %AW	25	25	25	25	95	95	25	25
Years of Education	4	1	1	1	0.05	0.05	1	1
Education is Job Related	No	No	No	No	Yes	Yes	No	Yes
Financial Costs of Up-Skilling								
Direct Costs of Education	14096	14096	14096	14096	11902	11902	14096	14096
Pre-Tax Scholarship Income	2500	2500	2500	2500	0	0	2500	0
Income Before Education	87784	125405	125405	125405	125405	125405	125405	125405
Income During Education	33851	33851	33851	33851	125091	125091	33851	31351
Pre-Tax Foregone Earnings	53933	91554	91554	91554	314	314	91554	94054
AETR Before Education (%)	4.8	9.1	9.1	9.1	9.1	9.1	9.1	9.1
AETR During Education (Exclusive of Tax Expenditures) (%)	0.0	0.0	0.0	0.0	9.1	9.1	0.0	0.0
Value of Education Tax Credits % of Direct Costs	0.0	0.0	0.0	0.0	23.0	23.0	0.0	0.0
AETR During Education (Inclusive of Tax Expenditures) (%)	0.0	0.0	0.0	0.0	6.9	6.9	0.0	0.0
METR on Foregone Earnings (%)	7.8	12.5	12.5	12.5	23.0	23.0	12.5	12.1
Total Costs of Education (Direct Costs & Foregone Earnings)	61316	91737	91737	91737	9406	9406	91737	96736
Financial Returns to Up-Skilling								
Breakeven Earnings Level	103461	132134	132590	133685	126142	126254	136592	137202
AETR After Education (%)	6.2	9.8	9.9	10.0	9.2	9.2	10.2	10.3
Breakeven Earnings Increment	15677	6729	7185	8280	737	849	11187	11797
Breakeven Earnings Increment % of Previous Wage	17.9	5.4	5.7	6.6	0.6	0.7	8.9	9.4
METR Breakeven Earnings Increment (%)	14.0	23.0	23.0	23.0	23.0	23.0	23.0	23.0
Marginal Effective Tax Rate on Skills (%)	8.1	13.4	13.4	13.4	0.0	0.0	13.4	13.9
Average Effective Tax Rate on Skills (Assumed 15% Return, %)	19.6	20.4	20.3	19.8	9.5	7.4	18.7	18.7
Government Costs and Returns								
Government Educational Costs	29046	36246	36246	36246	25142	25142	36246	33747
Marginal Returns to Costs Ratio	0.34	0.76	0.76	0.76	0.11	0.11	0.76	0.86
Average Returns to Costs Ratio (Assumed 15% Return)	2.30	2.82	2.64	2.29	0.19	0.17	1.69	1.82

Note: The statistical data for Israel are supplied by and under the responsibility of the relevant Israeli authorities. The use of such data by the OECD is without prejudice to the status of the Golan Heights, East Jerusalem and Israeli settlements in the West Bank under the terms of international law.

StatLink http://dx.doi.org/10.1787/888933446993

Italy

Table C.29. Comparing Financial Incentives for College Education with Different Financing Scenarios - Italy

Single, No Children, 17 Year-Old, Four Years of Education, 70% of the Average Wage					Currency: EUR
Scenario	No Borrowing	Direct Costs Borrowed, Low Interest Rate	All Costs Borrowed, Low Interest Rate	Direct Costs Borrowed, High Interest Rate	All Costs Borrowed, High Interest Rate
Non-Financing Education Costs					
Direct Costs of Education	1943	1943	1943	1943	1943
Pre-Tax Scholarship Income	1415	1415	1415	1415	1415
Income Before Education	20210	20210	20210	20210	20210
Income During Education	8633	8633	8633	8633	8633
Pre-Tax Foregone Earnings	11577	11577	11577	11577	11577
AETR Before Education (%)	17.7	17.7	17.7	17.7	17.7
AETR During Education (Exclusive of Tax Expenditures) (%)	0.0	0.0	0.0	0.0	0.0
Value of Education Tax Credits % of Direct Costs	0.0	0.0	0.0	0.0	0.0
AETR During Education (Inclusive of Tax Expenditures) (%)	0.0	0.0	0.0	0.0	0.0
METR on Foregone Earnings (%)	31.0	31.0	31.0	31.0	31.0
Total Annual Non-Financing Costs of Education (Direct Costs & Foregone Earnings)	8518	8518	8518	8518	8518
Education Financing Costs					
Fraction of Costs Borrowed	None	Direct Costs	All Costs	Direct Costs	All Costs
Total Amount Borrowed	0	1943	8518	1943	8518
Interest Rate (%)	NA	0.0	0.0	6.0	6.0
Annual Repayments	0	165	724	661	2896
Debt Finance Multiplier	1.00	0.59	0.59	1.41	1.41
Returns to Education					
Breakeven Earnings Level	22930	22674	21808	23186	24052
AETR After Education (%)	19.2	19.1	18.6	19.3	19.7
Breakeven Earnings Increment	2720	2464	1598	2976	3842
Breakeven Earnings Increment % of Previous Wage	13.5	12.2	7.9	14.7	19.0
METR Breakeven Earnings Increment (%)	29.8	29.8	29.8	29.8	29.8
Marginal Effective Tax Rate on Skills (%)	0.3	-2.8	0.3	2.8	0.3
Average Effective Tax Rate on Skills (Assumed 15% Return, %)	28.2	29.7	34.3	26.5	16.4
Average Effective Tax Rate on Skills (Return based on Labour Market Premium, %)	23.5	25.6	32.1	21.1	6.9
Government Costs and Returns					
Government Educational Costs	10105	10906	13619	9304	6591
Marginal Returns to Costs Ratio	0.36	0.37	0.45	0.36	0.39
Average Returns to Costs Ratio (Return based on Labour Market Premium)	1.55	1.43	1.15	1.68	2.37

StatLink http://dx.doi.org/10.1787/888933447009

Table C.30. **Comparing Financial Incentives for Differing Savings-Financed Education Scenarios - Italy**

Single, No Children, Annual Data								**Currency: EUR**
Age	17	27	32	40	32	40	50	50
Income Before Education, %AW	70	100	100	100	100	100	100	100
Income During Education, %AW	25	25	25	25	95	95	25	25
Years of Education	4	1	1	1	0.05	0.05	1	1
Education is Job Related	No	No	No	No	Yes	Yes	No	Yes
Financial Costs of Up-Skilling								
Direct Costs of Education	1943	1943	1943	1943	2903	2903	1943	1943
Pre-Tax Scholarship Income	1415	1415	1415	1415	0	0	1415	0
Income Before Education	20210	28872	28872	28872	28872	28872	28872	28872
Income During Education	8633	8633	8633	8633	28800	28800	8633	7218
Pre-Tax Foregone Earnings	11577	20239	20239	20239	72	72	20239	21654
AETR Before Education (%)	17.7	21.3	21.3	21.3	21.3	21.3	21.3	21.3
AETR During Education (Exclusive of Tax Expenditures) (%)	0.0	0.0	0.0	0.0	21.2	21.2	0.0	0.0
Value of Education Tax Credits % of Direct Costs	0.0	0.0	0.0	0.0	19.0	19.0	0.0	0.0
AETR During Education (Inclusive of Tax Expenditures) (%)	0.0	0.0	0.0	0.0	19.3	19.3	0.0	0.0
METR on Foregone Earnings (%)	31.0	30.3	30.3	30.3	29.9	29.9	30.3	28.4
Total Costs of Education (Direct Costs & Foregone Earnings)	8518	14626	14626	14626	2402	2402	14626	17456
Financial Returns to Up-Skilling								
Breakeven Earnings Level	22930	30080	30169	30390	29085	29121	31079	31563
AETR After Education (%)	19.2	21.6	21.6	21.7	21.3	21.3	22.0	22.3
Breakeven Earnings Increment	2720	1208	1297	1518	213	249	2207	2691
Breakeven Earnings Increment % of Previous Wage	13.5	4.2	4.5	5.3	0.7	0.9	7.6	9.3
METR Breakeven Earnings Increment (%)	29.8	29.9	29.9	29.9	29.9	29.9	31.8	33.2
Marginal Effective Tax Rate on Skills (%)	0.3	0.5	0.5	0.5	13.2	13.2	3.1	9.7
Average Effective Tax Rate on Skills (Assumed 15% Return, %)	28.2	30.6	30.1	29.0	17.6	15.5	25.8	25.8
Government Costs and Returns								
Government Educational Costs	10105	12659	12659	12659	5676	5676	12659	11244
Marginal Returns to Costs Ratio	0.36	0.49	0.49	0.49	0.18	0.18	0.54	0.77
Average Returns to Costs Ratio (Assumed 15% Return)	2.37	2.89	2.69	2.30	0.24	0.21	1.63	1.83

StatLink http://dx.doi.org/10.1787/888933447010

Luxembourg

Table C.31. **Comparing Financial Incentives for College Education with Different Financing Scenarios - Luxembourg**

Single, No Children, 17 Year-Old, Four Years of Education, 70% of the Average Wage — **Currency: EUR**

Scenario	No Borrowing	Direct Costs Borrowed, Low Interest Rate	All Costs Borrowed, Low Interest Rate	Direct Costs Borrowed, High Interest Rate	All Costs Borrowed, High Interest Rate
Non-Financing Education Costs					
Direct Costs of Education	680	680	680	680	680
Pre-Tax Scholarship Income	2050	2050	2050	2050	2050
Income Before Education	35472	35472	35472	35472	35472
Income During Education	14719	14719	14719	14719	14719
Pre-Tax Foregone Earnings	20753	20753	20753	20753	20753
AETR Before Education (%)	8.5	8.5	8.5	8.5	8.5
AETR During Education (Exclusive of Tax Expenditures) (%)	0.0	0.0	0.0	0.0	0.0
Value of Education Tax Credits % of Direct Costs	0.0	0.0	0.0	0.0	0.0
AETR During Education (Inclusive of Tax Expenditures) (%)	0.0	0.0	0.0	0.0	0.0
METR on Foregone Earnings (%)	14.5	14.5	14.5	14.5	14.5
Total Annual Non-Financing Costs of Education (Direct Costs & Foregone Earnings)	16377	16377	16377	16377	16377
Education Financing Costs					
Fraction of Costs Borrowed	None	Direct Costs	All Costs	Direct Costs	All Costs
Total Amount Borrowed	0	680	16377	680	16377
Interest Rate (%)	NA	0.0	0.0	6.0	6.0
Annual Repayments	0	58	1392	231	5568
Debt Finance Multiplier	1.00	0.60	0.60	1.40	1.40
Returns to Education					
Breakeven Earnings Level	40791	40694	38648	40871	42991
AETR After Education (%)	10.9	10.9	10.0	10.9	11.9
Breakeven Earnings Increment	5319	5222	3176	5399	7519
Breakeven Earnings Increment % of Previous Wage	15.0	14.7	9.0	15.2	21.2
METR Breakeven Earnings Increment (%)	27.2	27.1	26.4	27.1	28.1
Marginal Effective Tax Rate on Skills (%)	13.8	13.4	12.9	13.9	14.9
Average Effective Tax Rate on Skills (Assumed 15% Return, %)	31.0	31.2	35.8	30.7	21.0
Average Effective Tax Rate on Skills (Return based on Labour Market Premium, %)	30.8	31.0	35.8	30.5	20.4
Government Costs and Returns					
Government Educational Costs	17640	17910	24135	17370	11145
Marginal Returns to Costs Ratio	0.35	0.34	0.40	0.34	0.41
Average Returns to Costs Ratio (Return based on Labour Market Premium)	2.18	2.15	1.60	2.22	3.46

StatLink http://dx.doi.org/10.1787/888933447028

Table C.32. Comparing Financial Incentives for Differing Savings-Financed Education Scenarios - Luxembourg

Single, No Children, Annual Data								Currency: EUR
Age	17	27	32	40	32	40	50	50
Income Before Education, %AW	70	100	100	100	100	100	100	100
Income During Education, %AW	25	25	25	25	95	95	25	25
Years of Education	4	1	1	1	0.05	0.05	1	1
Education is Job Related	No	No	No	No	Yes	Yes	No	Yes
Financial Costs of Up-Skilling								
Direct Costs of Education	680	680	680	680	4989	4989	680	680
Pre-Tax Scholarship Income	2050	2050	2050	2050	0	0	2050	0
Income Before Education	35472	50674	50674	50674	50674	50674	50674	50674
Income During Education	14719	14719	14719	14719	50548	50548	14719	12669
Pre-Tax Foregone Earnings	20753	35956	35956	35956	127	127	35956	38006
AETR Before Education (%)	8.5	15.3	15.3	15.3	15.3	15.3	15.3	15.3
AETR During Education (Exclusive of Tax Expenditures) (%)	0.0	0.0	0.0	0.0	15.2	15.2	0.0	0.0
Value of Education Tax Credits % of Direct Costs	0.0	0.0	0.0	0.0	39.0	39.0	0.0	0.0
AETR During Education (Inclusive of Tax Expenditures) (%)	0.0	0.0	0.0	0.0	11.4	11.4	0.0	0.0
METR on Foregone Earnings (%)	14.5	21.6	21.6	21.6	48.0	48.0	21.6	20.4
Total Costs of Education (Direct Costs & Foregone Earnings)	16377	26830	26830	26830	3109	3109	26830	30931
Financial Returns to Up-Skilling								
Breakeven Earnings Level	40791	53275	53514	54182	51008	51077	56688	57578
AETR After Education (%)	10.9	16.3	16.4	16.6	15.4	15.5	17.5	17.8
Breakeven Earnings Increment	5319	2601	2840	3508	333	403	6013	6904
Breakeven Earnings Increment % of Previous Wage	15.0	5.1	5.6	6.9	0.7	0.8	11.9	13.6
METR Breakeven Earnings Increment (%)	27.2	35.9	35.7	35.8	36.5	35.3	36.1	36.1
Marginal Effective Tax Rate on Skills (%)	13.8	17.3	17.1	17.3	-4.5	-6.6	17.6	19.7
Average Effective Tax Rate on Skills (Assumed 15% Return, %)	31.0	31.3	30.8	29.6	9.1	2.8	25.1	25.1
Government Costs and Returns								
Government Educational Costs	17640	22388	22388	22388	14590	14590	22388	20338
Marginal Returns to Costs Ratio	0.35	0.67	0.67	0.67	0.12	0.12	0.68	0.86
Average Returns to Costs Ratio (Assumed 15% Return)	2.28	2.62	2.40	1.94	0.18	0.15	1.14	1.25

StatLink http://dx.doi.org/10.1787/888933447038

Mexico

Table C.33. Comparing Financial Incentives for College Education with Different Financing Scenarios - Mexico

Single, No Children, 17 Year-Old, Four Years of Education, 70% of the Average Wage					Currency: MXN
Scenario	No Borrowing	Direct Costs Borrowed, Low Interest Rate	All Costs Borrowed, Low Interest Rate	Direct Costs Borrowed, High Interest Rate	All Costs Borrowed, High Interest Rate
Non-Financing Education Costs					
Direct Costs of Education	19719	19719	19719	19719	19719
Pre-Tax Scholarship Income	2458	2458	2458	2458	2458
Income Before Education	63710	63710	63710	63710	63710
Income During Education	25211	25211	25211	25211	25211
Pre-Tax Foregone Earnings	38499	38499	38499	38499	38499
AETR Before Education (%)	0.4	0.4	0.4	0.4	0.4
AETR During Education (Exclusive of Tax Expenditures) (%)	-14.3	-14.3	-14.3	-14.3	-14.3
Value of Education Tax Credits % of Direct Costs	6.9	6.9	6.9	6.9	6.9
AETR During Education (Inclusive of Tax Expenditures) (%)	-19.0	-19.0	-19.0	-19.0	-19.0
METR on Foregone Earnings (%)	10.1	10.1	10.1	10.1	10.1
Total Annual Non-Financing Costs of Education (Direct Costs & Foregone Earnings)	50680	50680	50680	50680	50680
Education Financing Costs					
Fraction of Costs Borrowed	None	Direct Costs	All Costs	Direct Costs	All Costs
Total Amount Borrowed	0	19719	50680	19719	50680
Interest Rate (%)	NA	0.0	0.0	6.0	6.0
Annual Repayments	0	1676	4308	6704	17231
Debt Finance Multiplier	1.00	0.59	0.59	1.41	1.41
Returns to Education					
Breakeven Earnings Level	77407	74809	71600	79451	82661
AETR After Education (%)	3.4	2.5	2.1	3.6	3.9
Breakeven Earnings Increment	13697	11099	7890	15741	18951
Breakeven Earnings Increment % of Previous Wage	21.5	17.4	12.4	24.7	29.7
METR Breakeven Earnings Increment (%)	17.1	14.1	15.4	16.3	15.4
Marginal Effective Tax Rate on Skills (%)	8.8	3.8	7.0	9.0	6.9
Average Effective Tax Rate on Skills (Assumed 15% Return, %)	19.0	22.3	25.8	14.5	3.8
Average Effective Tax Rate on Skills (Return based on Labour Market Premium, %)	18.9	21.5	24.2	15.5	7.3
Government Costs and Returns					
Government Educational Costs	48133	56267	69039	39999	27227
Marginal Returns to Costs Ratio	0.22	0.18	0.23	0.21	0.24
Average Returns to Costs Ratio (Return based on Labour Market Premium)	1.28	1.09	0.89	1.54	2.26

StatLink http://dx.doi.org/10.1787/888933447044

Table C.34. **Comparing Financial Incentives for Differing Savings-Financed Education Scenarios - Mexico**

Single, No Children, Annual Data								Currency: MXN
Age	17	27	32	40	32	40	50	50
Income Before Education, %AW	70	100	100	100	100	100	100	100
Income During Education, %AW	25	25	25	25	95	95	25	25
Years of Education	4	1	1	1	0.05	0.05	1	1
Education is Job Related	No	No	No	No	Yes	Yes	No	Yes
Financial Costs of Up-Skilling								
Direct Costs of Education	19719	19719	19719	19719	8994	8994	19719	19719
Pre-Tax Scholarship Income	2458	2458	2458	2458	0	0	2458	0
Income Before Education	63710	91014	91014	91014	91014	91014	91014	91014
Income During Education	25211	25211	25211	25211	90787	90787	25211	22754
Pre-Tax Foregone Earnings	38499	65803	65803	65803	228	228	65803	68261
AETR Before Education (%)	0.4	7.9	7.9	7.9	7.9	7.9	7.9	7.9
AETR During Education (Exclusive of Tax Expenditures) (%)	-14.3	-14.3	-14.3	-14.3	7.8	7.8	-14.3	-16.5
Value of Education Tax Credits % of Direct Costs	6.9	6.9	6.9	6.9	44.7	44.7	6.9	5.3
AETR During Education (Inclusive of Tax Expenditures) (%)	-19.0	-19.0	-19.0	-19.0	3.4	3.4	-19.0	-21.1
METR on Foregone Earnings (%)	10.1	16.3	16.3	16.3	13.5	13.5	16.3	16.0
Total Costs of Education (Direct Costs & Foregone Earnings)	50680	71122	71122	71122	5170	5170	71122	76037
Financial Returns to Up-Skilling								
Breakeven Earnings Level	77407	95912	96275	97169	91397	91462	99725	100328
AETR After Education (%)	3.4	8.3	8.3	8.4	7.9	7.9	8.6	8.6
Breakeven Earnings Increment	13697	4898	5260	6155	382	447	8711	9313
Breakeven Earnings Increment % of Previous Wage	21.5	5.4	5.8	6.8	0.4	0.5	9.6	10.2
METR Breakeven Earnings Increment (%)	17.1	15.9	15.9	15.9	15.9	15.9	15.9	15.9
Marginal Effective Tax Rate on Skills (%)	8.8	1.8	1.8	1.8	-49.9	-49.9	1.8	2.7
Average Effective Tax Rate on Skills (Assumed 15% Return, %)	19.0	12.5	12.3	11.6	-11.7	-16.5	9.6	9.6
Government Costs and Returns								
Government Educational Costs	48133	54996	54996	54996	44647	44647	54996	52538
Marginal Returns to Costs Ratio	0.22	0.25	0.25	0.25	0.02	0.02	0.25	0.27
Average Returns to Costs Ratio (Assumed 15% Return)	1.00	0.93	0.87	0.74	0.05	0.04	0.53	0.55

StatLink http://dx.doi.org/10.1787/888933447057

Netherlands

Table C.35. Comparing Financial Incentives for College Education with Different Financing Scenarios - Netherlands

Single, No Children, 17 Year-Old, Four Years of Education, 70% of the Average Wage					Currency: EUR
Scenario	No Borrowing	Direct Costs Borrowed, Low Interest Rate	All Costs Borrowed, Low Interest Rate	Direct Costs Borrowed, High Interest Rate	All Costs Borrowed, High Interest Rate
Non-Financing Education Costs					
Direct Costs of Education	2212	2212	2212	2212	2212
Pre-Tax Scholarship Income	1869	1869	1869	1869	1869
Income Before Education	32401	32401	32401	32401	32401
Income During Education	13441	13441	13441	13441	13441
Pre-Tax Foregone Earnings	18960	18960	18960	18960	18960
AETR Before Education (%)	6.1	6.1	6.1	6.1	6.1
AETR During Education (Exclusive of Tax Expenditures) (%)	0.8	0.8	0.8	0.8	0.8
Value of Education Tax Credits % of Direct Costs	14.4	14.4	14.4	14.4	14.4
AETR During Education (Inclusive of Tax Expenditures) (%)	0.5	0.5	0.5	0.5	0.5
METR on Foregone Earnings (%)	9.8	9.8	9.8	9.8	9.8
Total Annual Non-Financing Costs of Education (Direct Costs & Foregone Earnings)	17405	17405	17405	17405	17405
Education Financing Costs					
Fraction of Costs Borrowed	None	Direct Costs	All Costs	Direct Costs	All Costs
Total Amount Borrowed	0	2212	17405	2212	17405
Interest Rate (%)	NA	0.0	0.0	6.0	6.0
Annual Repayments	0	188	1479	752	5917
Debt Finance Multiplier	1.00	0.59	0.59	1.41	1.41
Returns to Education					
Breakeven Earnings Level	39008	38667	36325	39348	41690
AETR After Education (%)	12.0	11.7	9.9	12.2	13.8
Breakeven Earnings Increment	6607	6266	3924	6948	9289
Breakeven Earnings Increment % of Previous Wage	20.4	19.3	12.1	21.4	28.7
METR Breakeven Earnings Increment (%)	41.0	41.0	41.6	40.9	40.7
Marginal Effective Tax Rate on Skills (%)	34.5	34.2	35.2	34.8	34.2
Average Effective Tax Rate on Skills (Assumed 15% Return, %)	39.8	40.7	44.6	38.9	29.4
Average Effective Tax Rate on Skills (Return based on Labour Market Premium, %)	37.9	39.2	45.1	36.6	22.2
Government Costs and Returns					
Government Educational Costs	14100	15012	21279	13187	6920
Marginal Returns to Costs Ratio	0.86	0.85	0.99	0.87	1.22
Average Returns to Costs Ratio (Return based on Labour Market Premium)	2.20	2.06	1.46	2.35	4.48

StatLink http://dx.doi.org/10.1787/888933447063

Table C.36. **Comparing Financial Incentives for Differing Savings-Financed Education Scenarios - Netherlands**

Single, No Children, Annual Data								**Currency: EUR**
Age	17	27	32	40	32	40	50	50
Income Before Education, %AW	70	100	100	100	100	100	100	100
Income During Education, %AW	25	25	25	25	95	95	25	25
Years of Education	4	1	1	1	0.05	0.05	1	1
Education is Job Related	No	No	No	No	Yes	Yes	No	Yes
Financial Costs of Up-Skilling								
Direct Costs of Education	2212	2212	2212	2212	4590	4590	2212	2212
Pre-Tax Scholarship Income	1869	1869	1869	1869	0	0	1869	0
Income Before Education	32401	46287	46287	46287	46287	46287	46287	46287
Income During Education	13441	13441	13441	13441	46171	46171	13441	11572
Pre-Tax Foregone Earnings	18960	32846	32846	32846	116	116	32846	34715
AETR Before Education (%)	6.1	16.4	16.4	16.4	16.4	16.4	16.4	16.4
AETR During Education (Exclusive of Tax Expenditures) (%)	0.8	0.8	0.8	0.8	16.3	16.3	0.8	0.8
Value of Education Tax Credits % of Direct Costs	14.4	14.4	14.4	14.4	42.0	42.0	14.4	1.2
AETR During Education (Inclusive of Tax Expenditures) (%)	0.5	0.5	0.5	0.5	12.1	12.1	0.5	0.5
METR on Foregone Earnings (%)	9.8	22.7	22.7	22.7	40.1	40.1	22.7	21.6
Total Costs of Education (Direct Costs & Foregone Earnings)	17405	25669	25669	25669	2730	2730	25669	29407
Financial Returns to Up-Skilling								
Breakeven Earnings Level	39008	48767	48951	49404	46570	46618	50697	51339
AETR After Education (%)	12.0	17.6	17.7	17.9	16.5	16.6	18.4	18.7
Breakeven Earnings Increment	6607	2480	2664	3117	283	331	4410	5052
Breakeven Earnings Increment % of Previous Wage	20.4	5.4	5.8	6.7	0.6	0.7	9.5	10.9
METR Breakeven Earnings Increment (%)	41.0	40.1	40.1	40.1	40.1	40.1	40.1	40.1
Marginal Effective Tax Rate on Skills (%)	34.5	22.5	22.5	22.5	-3.3	-3.3	22.5	24.7
Average Effective Tax Rate on Skills (Assumed 15% Return, %)	39.8	35.8	35.5	34.6	13.5	9.0	32.2	32.2
Government Costs and Returns								
Government Educational Costs	14100	19722	19722	19722	12309	12309	19722	17853
Marginal Returns to Costs Ratio	0.86	0.87	0.87	0.87	0.15	0.15	0.87	1.10
Average Returns to Costs Ratio (Assumed 15% Return)	3.40	3.29	3.06	2.62	0.24	0.21	1.85	2.04

StatLink http://dx.doi.org/10.1787/888933447073

New Zealand

Table C.37. Comparing Financial Incentives for College Education with Different Financing Scenarios - New Zealand

Single, No Children, 17 Year-Old, Four Years of Education, 70% of the Average Wage					Currency: NZD
Scenario	No Borrowing	Direct Costs Borrowed, Low Interest Rate	All Costs Borrowed, Low Interest Rate	Direct Costs Borrowed, High Interest Rate	All Costs Borrowed, High Interest Rate
Non-Financing Education Costs					
Direct Costs of Education	5581	5581	5581	5581	5581
Pre-Tax Scholarship Income	2829	2829	2829	2829	2829
Income Before Education	34577	34577	34577	34577	34577
Income During Education	15178	15178	15178	15178	15178
Pre-Tax Foregone Earnings	19399	19399	19399	19399	19399
AETR Before Education (%)	13.2	13.2	13.2	13.2	13.2
AETR During Education (Exclusive of Tax Expenditures) (%)	11.0	11.0	11.0	11.0	11.0
Value of Education Tax Credits % of Direct Costs	13.8	13.8	13.8	13.8	13.8
AETR During Education (Inclusive of Tax Expenditures) (%)	8.5	8.5	8.5	8.5	8.5
METR on Foregone Earnings (%)	14.8	14.8	14.8	14.8	14.8
Total Annual Non-Financing Costs of Education (Direct Costs & Foregone Earnings)	18896	18896	18896	18896	18896
Education Financing Costs					
Fraction of Costs Borrowed	None	Direct Costs	All Costs	Direct Costs	All Costs
Total Amount Borrowed	0	5581	18896	5581	18896
Interest Rate (%)	NA	0.0	0.0	6.0	6.0
Annual Repayments	0	474	1606	1897	6425
Debt Finance Multiplier	1.00	0.59	0.59	1.41	1.41
Returns to Education					
Breakeven Earnings Level	39709	39084	37592	40334	41826
AETR After Education (%)	13.7	13.7	13.5	13.8	13.9
Breakeven Earnings Increment	5133	4507	3015	5758	7250
Breakeven Earnings Increment % of Previous Wage	14.8	13.0	8.7	16.7	21.0
METR Breakeven Earnings Increment (%)	17.5	17.5	17.5	17.5	17.5
Marginal Effective Tax Rate on Skills (%)	3.3	1.3	3.3	4.8	3.3
Average Effective Tax Rate on Skills (Assumed 15% Return, %)	23.2	25.1	28.6	20.8	11.6
Average Effective Tax Rate on Skills (Return based on Labour Market Premium, %)	12.3	17.4	26.3	6.1	-17.4
Government Costs and Returns					
Government Educational Costs	16227	18529	24021	13925	8432
Marginal Returns to Costs Ratio	0.25	0.25	0.28	0.26	0.34
Average Returns to Costs Ratio (Return based on Labour Market Premium)	0.56	0.49	0.38	0.66	1.09

StatLink http://dx.doi.org/10.1787/888933447083

Table C.38. **Comparing Financial Incentives for Differing Savings-Financed Education Scenarios - New Zealand**

Single, No Children, Annual Data								**Currency: NZD**
Age	17	27	32	40	32	40	50	50
Income Before Education, %AW	70	100	100	100	100	100	100	100
Income During Education, %AW	25	25	25	25	95	95	25	25
Years of Education	4	1	1	1	0.05	0.05	1	1
Education is Job Related	No	No	No	No	Yes	Yes	No	Yes
Financial Costs of Up-Skilling								
Direct Costs of Education	5581	5581	5581	5581	4940	4940	5581	5581
Pre-Tax Scholarship Income	2829	2829	2829	2829	0	0	2829	0
Income Before Education	34577	49395	49395	49395	49395	49395	49395	49395
Income During Education	15178	15178	15178	15178	49272	49272	15178	12349
Pre-Tax Foregone Earnings	19399	34217	34217	34217	123	123	34217	37046
AETR Before Education (%)	13.2	15.9	15.9	15.9	15.9	15.9	15.9	15.9
AETR During Education (Exclusive of Tax Expenditures) (%)	11.0	11.0	11.0	11.0	15.8	15.8	11.0	10.5
Value of Education Tax Credits % of Direct Costs	13.8	13.8	13.8	13.8	0.0	0.0	13.8	0.0
AETR During Education (Inclusive of Tax Expenditures) (%)	8.5	8.5	8.5	8.5	15.8	15.8	8.5	10.5
METR on Foregone Earnings (%)	14.8	18.0	18.0	18.0	30.0	30.0	18.0	17.7
Total Costs of Education (Direct Costs & Foregone Earnings)	18896	30427	30427	30427	5026	5026	30427	36085
Financial Returns to Up-Skilling								
Breakeven Earnings Level	39709	51911	52098	52557	49841	49917	53871	54703
AETR After Education (%)	13.7	16.6	16.6	16.7	16.0	16.0	17.0	17.2
Breakeven Earnings Increment	5133	2516	2703	3162	446	522	4476	5308
Breakeven Earnings Increment % of Previous Wage	14.8	5.1	5.5	6.4	0.9	1.1	9.1	10.7
METR Breakeven Earnings Increment (%)	17.5	30.0	30.0	30.0	30.0	30.0	30.0	30.0
Marginal Effective Tax Rate on Skills (%)	3.3	15.0	15.0	15.0	29.5	29.5	15.0	17.3
Average Effective Tax Rate on Skills (Assumed 15% Return, %)	23.2	26.2	25.9	25.2	29.5	29.5	23.2	23.2
Government Costs and Returns								
Government Educational Costs	16227	19514	19514	19514	10180	10180	19514	16685
Marginal Returns to Costs Ratio	0.25	0.67	0.67	0.67	0.21	0.21	0.67	0.93
Average Returns to Costs Ratio (Assumed 15% Return)	1.96	2.62	2.44	2.09	0.23	0.20	1.48	1.73

StatLink http://dx.doi.org/10.1787/888933447091

Norway

Table C.39. **Comparing Financial Incentives for College Education with Different Financing Scenarios - Norway**

Single, No Children, 17 Year-Old, Four Years of Education, 70% of the Average Wage					Currency: NOK
Scenario	No Borrowing	Direct Costs Borrowed, Low Interest Rate	All Costs Borrowed, Low Interest Rate	Direct Costs Borrowed, High Interest Rate	All Costs Borrowed, High Interest Rate
Non-Financing Education Costs					
Direct Costs of Education	5815	5815	5815	5815	5815
Pre-Tax Scholarship Income	29732	29732	29732	29732	29732
Income Before Education	343708	343708	343708	343708	343708
Income During Education	152485	152485	152485	152485	152485
Pre-Tax Foregone Earnings	191223	191223	191223	191223	191223
AETR Before Education (%)	18.3	18.3	18.3	18.3	18.3
AETR During Education (Exclusive of Tax Expenditures) (%)	9.9	9.9	9.9	9.9	9.9
Value of Education Tax Credits % of Direct Costs	-22.3	-22.3	-22.3	-22.3	-22.3
AETR During Education (Inclusive of Tax Expenditures) (%)	6.4	6.4	6.4	6.4	6.4
METR on Foregone Earnings (%)	25.0	25.0	25.0	25.0	25.0
Total Annual Non-Financing Costs of Education (Direct Costs & Foregone Earnings)	114108	114108	114108	114108	114108
Education Financing Costs					
Fraction of Costs Borrowed	None	Direct Costs	All Costs	Direct Costs	All Costs
Total Amount Borrowed	0	5815	114108	5815	114108
Interest Rate (%)	NA	0.0	0.0	6.0	6.0
Annual Repayments	0	494	9699	1977	38796
Debt Finance Multiplier	1.00	0.58	0.58	1.42	1.42
Returns to Education					
Breakeven Earnings Level	378556	377813	363983	379298	393129
AETR After Education (%)	19.2	19.2	18.9	19.2	19.5
Breakeven Earnings Increment	34848	34105	20275	35591	49421
Breakeven Earnings Increment % of Previous Wage	10.1	9.9	5.9	10.4	14.4
METR Breakeven Earnings Increment (%)	28.0	28.0	28.0	28.0	28.0
Marginal Effective Tax Rate on Skills (%)	-5.6	-6.3	-5.6	-4.9	-5.6
Average Effective Tax Rate on Skills (Assumed 15% Return, %)	28.6	28.9	33.6	28.3	18.9
Average Effective Tax Rate on Skills (Return based on Labour Market Premium, %)	17.8	18.5	29.9	17.1	-5.4
Government Costs and Returns					
Government Educational Costs	245037	247469	292755	242605	197319
Marginal Returns to Costs Ratio	0.18	0.18	0.26	0.18	0.16
Average Returns to Costs Ratio (Return based on Labour Market Premium)	0.60	0.59	0.50	0.60	0.74

StatLink http://dx.doi.org/10.1787/888933447108

Table C.40. **Comparing Financial Incentives for Differing Savings-Financed Education Scenarios - Norway**

Single, No Children, Annual Data								**Currency: NOK**
Age	17	27	32	40	32	40	50	50
Income Before Education, %AW	70	100	100	100	100	100	100	100
Income During Education, %AW	25	25	25	25	95	95	25	25
Years of Education	4	1	1	1	0.05	0.05	1	1
Education is Job Related	No	No	No	No	Yes	Yes	No	Yes
Financial Costs of Up-Skilling								
Direct Costs of Education	5815	5815	5815	5815	48732	48732	5815	5815
Pre-Tax Scholarship Income	29732	29732	29732	29732	0	0	29732	0
Income Before Education	343708	491011	491011	491011	491011	491011	491011	491011
Income During Education	152485	152485	152485	152485	489783	489783	152485	122753
Pre-Tax Foregone Earnings	191223	338526	338526	338526	1228	1228	338526	368258
AETR Before Education (%)	18.3	21.6	21.6	21.6	21.6	21.6	21.6	21.6
AETR During Education (Exclusive of Tax Expenditures) (%)	9.9	9.9	9.9	9.9	21.6	21.6	9.9	8.0
Value of Education Tax Credits % of Direct Costs	-22.3	-22.3	-22.3	-22.3	0.0	0.0	-22.3	0.0
AETR During Education (Inclusive of Tax Expenditures) (%)	6.4	6.4	6.4	6.4	21.6	21.6	6.4	8.0
METR on Foregone Earnings (%)	25.0	26.9	26.9	26.9	37.0	37.0	26.9	26.1
Total Costs of Education (Direct Costs & Foregone Earnings)	114108	218383	218383	218383	49506	49506	218383	277847
Financial Returns to Up-Skilling								
Breakeven Earnings Level	378556	510591	511918	515102	495750	496472	523561	532424
AETR After Education (%)	19.2	22.2	22.2	22.3	21.7	21.8	22.5	22.8
Breakeven Earnings Increment	34848	19580	20907	24091	4739	5461	32550	41413
Breakeven Earnings Increment % of Previous Wage	10.1	4.0	4.3	4.9	1.0	1.1	6.6	8.4
METR Breakeven Earnings Increment (%)	28.0	37.0	37.0	37.0	37.0	37.0	37.0	37.0
Marginal Effective Tax Rate on Skills (%)	-5.6	9.2	9.2	9.2	36.4	36.4	9.2	15.2
Average Effective Tax Rate on Skills (Assumed 15% Return, %)	28.6	31.5	31.1	30.2	36.4	36.4	27.8	27.8
Government Costs and Returns								
Government Educational Costs	245037	288065	288065	288065	162561	162561	288065	258333
Marginal Returns to Costs Ratio	0.18	0.45	0.45	0.45	0.18	0.18	0.45	0.63
Average Returns to Costs Ratio (Assumed 15% Return)	1.68	2.23	2.09	1.81	0.19	0.16	1.34	1.50

StatLink http://dx.doi.org/10.1787/888933447110

Poland

Table C.41. Comparing Financial Incentives for College Education with Different Financing Scenarios - Poland

Single, No Children, 17 Year-Old, Four Years of Education, 70% of the Average Wage					Currency: PLN
Scenario	No Borrowing	Direct Costs Borrowed, Low Interest Rate	All Costs Borrowed, Low Interest Rate	Direct Costs Borrowed, High Interest Rate	All Costs Borrowed, High Interest Rate
Non-Financing Education Costs					
Direct Costs of Education	3982	3982	3982	3982	3982
Pre-Tax Scholarship Income	1860	1860	1860	1860	1860
Income Before Education	27112	27112	27112	27112	27112
Income During Education	11543	11543	11543	11543	11543
Pre-Tax Foregone Earnings	15569	15569	15569	15569	15569
AETR Before Education (%)	5.9	5.9	5.9	5.9	5.9
AETR During Education (Exclusive of Tax Expenditures) (%)	1.9	1.9	1.9	1.9	1.9
Value of Education Tax Credits % of Direct Costs	-22.8	-22.8	-22.8	-22.8	-22.8
AETR During Education (Inclusive of Tax Expenditures) (%)	6.1	6.1	6.1	6.1	6.1
METR on Foregone Earnings (%)	8.8	8.8	8.8	8.8	8.8
Total Annual Non-Financing Costs of Education (Direct Costs & Foregone Earnings)	16796	16796	16796	16796	16796
Education Financing Costs					
Fraction of Costs Borrowed	None	Direct Costs	All Costs	Direct Costs	All Costs
Total Amount Borrowed	0	3982	16796	3982	16796
Interest Rate (%)	NA	0.0	0.0	6.0	6.0
Annual Repayments	0	338	1428	1354	5710
Debt Finance Multiplier	1.00	0.59	0.59	1.41	1.41
Returns to Education					
Breakeven Earnings Level	31241	30837	29537	31644	32944
AETR After Education (%)	6.3	6.3	6.1	6.3	6.4
Breakeven Earnings Increment	4129	3725	2426	4533	5832
Breakeven Earnings Increment % of Previous Wage	15.2	13.7	8.9	16.7	21.5
METR Breakeven Earnings Increment (%)	8.8	8.8	8.8	8.8	8.8
Marginal Effective Tax Rate on Skills (%)	4.0	3.5	4.0	4.4	4.0
Average Effective Tax Rate on Skills (Assumed 15% Return, %)	7.9	9.5	12.7	6.0	-3.1
Average Effective Tax Rate on Skills (Return based on Labour Market Premium, %)	8.1	9.4	11.8	6.6	-0.3
Government Costs and Returns					
Government Educational Costs	16054	17697	22983	14412	9126
Marginal Returns to Costs Ratio	0.10	0.10	0.12	0.10	0.13
Average Returns to Costs Ratio (Return based on Labour Market Premium)	0.69	0.63	0.49	0.77	1.22

StatLink http://dx.doi.org/10.1787/888933447127

Table C.42. **Comparing Financial Incentives for Differing Savings-Financed Education Scenarios - Poland**

Single, No Children, Annual Data								**Currency: PLN**
Age	17	27	32	40	32	40	50	50
Income Before Education, %AW	70	100	100	100	100	100	100	100
Income During Education, %AW	25	25	25	25	95	95	25	25
Years of Education	4	1	1	1	0.05	0.05	1	1
Education is Job Related	No	No	No	No	Yes	Yes	No	Yes
Financial Costs of Up-Skilling								
Direct Costs of Education	3982	3982	3982	3982	3856	3856	3982	3982
Pre-Tax Scholarship Income	1860	1860	1860	1860	0	0	1860	0
Income Before Education	27112	38731	38731	38731	38731	38731	38731	38731
Income During Education	11543	11543	11543	11543	38634	38634	11543	9683
Pre-Tax Foregone Earnings	15569	27188	27188	27188	97	97	27188	29048
AETR Before Education (%)	5.9	6.8	6.8	6.8	6.8	6.8	6.8	6.8
AETR During Education (Exclusive of Tax Expenditures) (%)	1.9	1.9	1.9	1.9	6.8	6.8	1.9	0.6
Value of Education Tax Credits % of Direct Costs	-22.8	7.8	7.8	7.8	0.0	0.0	7.8	0.0
AETR During Education (Inclusive of Tax Expenditures) (%)	6.1	0.5	0.5	0.5	6.8	6.8	0.5	0.6
METR on Foregone Earnings (%)	8.8	8.8	8.8	8.8	8.8	8.8	8.8	8.8
Total Costs of Education (Direct Costs & Foregone Earnings)	16796	26740	26740	26740	3944	3944	26740	30461
Financial Returns to Up-Skilling								
Breakeven Earnings Level	31241	40429	40555	40865	39000	39046	41751	42172
AETR After Education (%)	6.3	6.9	6.9	6.9	6.8	6.8	6.9	7.0
Breakeven Earnings Increment	4129	1698	1824	2134	269	315	3020	3441
Breakeven Earnings Increment % of Previous Wage	15.2	4.4	4.7	5.5	0.7	0.8	7.8	8.9
METR Breakeven Earnings Increment (%)	8.8	8.8	8.8	8.8	8.8	8.8	8.8	8.8
Marginal Effective Tax Rate on Skills (%)	4.0	0.1	0.1	0.1	8.6	8.6	0.1	1.2
Average Effective Tax Rate on Skills (Assumed 15% Return, %)	7.9	6.9	6.8	6.4	8.7	8.7	5.4	5.4
Government Costs and Returns								
Government Educational Costs	16054	17730	17730	17730	13309	13309	17730	15869
Marginal Returns to Costs Ratio	0.10	0.15	0.15	0.15	0.03	0.03	0.15	0.19
Average Returns to Costs Ratio (Assumed 15% Return)	0.53	0.67	0.62	0.53	0.04	0.04	0.38	0.42

StatLink http://dx.doi.org/10.1787/888933447135

Portugal

Table C.43. Comparing Financial Incentives for College Education with Different Financing Scenarios - Portugal

Single, No Children, 17 Year-Old, Four Years of Education, 70% of the Average Wage					Currency: EUR
Scenario	No Borrowing	Direct Costs Borrowed, Low Interest Rate	All Costs Borrowed, Low Interest Rate	Direct Costs Borrowed, High Interest Rate	All Costs Borrowed, High Interest Rate
Non-Financing Education Costs					
Direct Costs of Education	1347	1347	1347	1347	1347
Pre-Tax Scholarship Income	708	708	708	708	708
Income Before Education	11346	11346	11346	11346	11346
Income During Education	4760	4760	4760	4760	4760
Pre-Tax Foregone Earnings	6586	6586	6586	6586	6586
AETR Before Education (%)	5.7	5.7	5.7	5.7	5.7
AETR During Education (Exclusive of Tax Expenditures) (%)	0.0	0.0	0.0	0.0	0.0
Value of Education Tax Credits % of Direct Costs	0.0	0.0	0.0	0.0	0.0
AETR During Education (Inclusive of Tax Expenditures) (%)	0.0	0.0	0.0	0.0	0.0
METR on Foregone Earnings (%)	9.8	9.8	9.8	9.8	9.8
Total Annual Non-Financing Costs of Education (Direct Costs & Foregone Earnings)	6580	6580	6580	6580	6580
Education Financing Costs					
Fraction of Costs Borrowed	None	Direct Costs	All Costs	Direct Costs	All Costs
Total Amount Borrowed	0	1347	6580	1347	6580
Interest Rate (%)	NA	0.0	0.0	6.0	6.0
Annual Repayments	0	114	559	458	2237
Debt Finance Multiplier	1.00	0.59	0.59	1.41	1.41
Returns to Education					
Breakeven Earnings Level	13369	13196	12524	13542	14214
AETR After Education (%)	8.9	8.7	7.7	9.2	10.1
Breakeven Earnings Increment	2023	1850	1179	2196	2868
Breakeven Earnings Increment % of Previous Wage	17.8	16.3	10.4	19.4	25.3
METR Breakeven Earnings Increment (%)	27.1	27.0	26.5	27.2	27.4
Marginal Effective Tax Rate on Skills (%)	20.0	19.2	19.3	20.6	20.3
Average Effective Tax Rate on Skills (Assumed 15% Return, %)	26.2	27.6	31.2	24.6	15.2
Average Effective Tax Rate on Skills (Return based on Labour Market Premium, %)	27.2	28.3	31.1	26.0	18.7
Government Costs and Returns					
Government Educational Costs	5501	6057	8215	4945	2787
Marginal Returns to Costs Ratio	0.45	0.44	0.49	0.46	0.63
Average Returns to Costs Ratio (Return based on Labour Market Premium)	2.72	2.47	1.82	3.02	5.37

StatLink http://dx.doi.org/10.1787/888933447141

Table C.44. **Comparing Financial Incentives for Differing Savings-Financed Education Scenarios - Portugal**

Single, No Children, Annual Data								Currency: EUR
Age	17	27	32	40	32	40	50	50
Income Before Education, %AW	70	100	100	100	100	100	100	100
Income During Education, %AW	25	25	25	25	95	95	25	25
Years of Education	4	1	1	1	0.05	0.05	1	1
Education is Job Related	No	No	No	No	Yes	Yes	No	Yes
Financial Costs of Up-Skilling								
Direct Costs of Education	1347	1347	1347	1347	1759	1759	1347	1347
Pre-Tax Scholarship Income	708	708	708	708	0	0	708	0
Income Before Education	11346	16208	16208	16208	16208	16208	16208	16208
Income During Education	4760	4760	4760	4760	16167	16167	4760	4052
Pre-Tax Foregone Earnings	6586	11448	11448	11448	41	41	11448	12156
AETR Before Education (%)	5.7	12.3	12.3	12.3	12.3	12.3	12.3	12.3
AETR During Education (Exclusive of Tax Expenditures) (%)	0.0	0.0	0.0	0.0	12.2	12.2	0.0	0.0
Value of Education Tax Credits % of Direct Costs	0.0	0.0	0.0	0.0	2.7	2.7	0.0	0.0
AETR During Education (Inclusive of Tax Expenditures) (%)	0.0	0.0	0.0	0.0	11.9	11.9	0.0	0.0
METR on Foregone Earnings (%)	9.8	17.4	17.4	17.4	28.0	28.0	17.4	16.4
Total Costs of Education (Direct Costs & Foregone Earnings)	6580	10098	10098	10098	1740	1740	10098	11513
Financial Returns to Up-Skilling								
Breakeven Earnings Level	13369	17020	17080	17228	16358	16384	17652	17854
AETR After Education (%)	8.9	13.0	13.1	13.2	12.4	12.4	13.6	13.7
Breakeven Earnings Increment	2023	812	872	1020	150	176	1444	1646
Breakeven Earnings Increment % of Previous Wage	17.8	5.0	5.4	6.3	0.9	1.1	8.9	10.2
METR Breakeven Earnings Increment (%)	27.1	28.0	28.0	28.0	28.0	28.0	28.0	28.0
Marginal Effective Tax Rate on Skills (%)	20.0	13.8	13.8	13.8	25.5	25.5	13.8	15.6
Average Effective Tax Rate on Skills (Assumed 15% Return, %)	26.0	24.0	24.0	24.0	26.0	25.0	22.0	22.0
Government Costs and Returns								
Government Educational Costs	5501	6845	6845	6845	4207	4207	6845	6137
Marginal Returns to Costs Ratio	0.45	0.57	0.57	0.57	0.16	0.16	0.57	0.73
Average Returns to Costs Ratio (Assumed 15% Return)	2.05	2.29	2.13	1.82	0.17	0.15	1.29	1.44

StatLink http://dx.doi.org/10.1787/888933447154

Slovak Republic

Table C.45. Comparing Financial Incentives for College Education with Different Financing Scenarios - Slovak Republic

Single, No Children, 17 Year-Old, Four Years of Education, 70% of the Average Wage					Currency: EUR
Scenario	No Borrowing	Direct Costs Borrowed, Low Interest Rate	All Costs Borrowed, Low Interest Rate	Direct Costs Borrowed, High Interest Rate	All Costs Borrowed, High Interest Rate
Non-Financing Education Costs					
Direct Costs of Education	641	641	641	641	641
Pre-Tax Scholarship Income	640	640	640	640	640
Income Before Education	6714	6714	6714	6714	6714
Income During Education	3038	3038	3038	3038	3038
Pre-Tax Foregone Earnings	3677	3677	3677	3677	3677
AETR Before Education (%)	6.4	6.4	6.4	6.4	6.4
AETR During Education (Exclusive of Tax Expenditures) (%)	-1.7	-1.7	-1.7	-1.7	-1.7
Value of Education Tax Credits % of Direct Costs	0.0	0.0	0.0	0.0	0.0
AETR During Education (Inclusive of Tax Expenditures) (%)	-1.7	-1.7	-1.7	-1.7	-1.7
METR on Foregone Earnings (%)	13.0	13.0	13.0	13.0	13.0
Total Annual Non-Financing Costs of Education (Direct Costs & Foregone Earnings)	3200	3200	3200	3200	3200
Education Financing Costs					
Fraction of Costs Borrowed	None	Direct Costs	All Costs	Direct Costs	All Costs
Total Amount Borrowed	0	641	3200	641	3200
Interest Rate (%)	NA	0.0	0.0	6.0	6.0
Annual Repayments	0	54	272	218	1088
Debt Finance Multiplier	1.00	0.60	0.60	1.40	1.40
Returns to Education					
Breakeven Earnings Level	7600	7528	7243	7671	7957
AETR After Education (%)	7.6	7.5	7.1	7.6	8.0
Breakeven Earnings Increment	885	814	528	957	1242
Breakeven Earnings Increment % of Previous Wage	13.2	12.1	7.9	14.3	18.5
METR Breakeven Earnings Increment (%)	16.5	16.5	16.5	16.5	16.5
Marginal Effective Tax Rate on Skills (%)	4.0	2.9	4.0	4.9	4.0
Average Effective Tax Rate on Skills (Assumed 15% Return, %)	14.4	15.6	19.0	13.0	4.6
Average Effective Tax Rate on Skills (Return based on Labour Market Premium, %)	14.4	15.6	19.1	13.0	4.5
Government Costs and Returns					
Government Educational Costs	4316	4574	5606	4057	3025
Marginal Returns to Costs Ratio	0.15	0.15	0.19	0.14	0.15
Average Returns to Costs Ratio (Return based on Labour Market Premium)	0.88	0.83	0.68	0.94	1.26

StatLink http://dx.doi.org/10.1787/888933447167

Table C.46. **Comparing Financial Incentives for Differing Savings-Financed Education Scenarios - Slovak Republic**

Single, No Children, Annual Data								Currency: EUR
Age	17	27	32	40	32	40	50	50
Income Before Education, %AW	70	100	100	100	100	100	100	100
Income During Education, %AW	25	25	25	25	95	95	25	25
Years of Education	4	1	1	1	0.05	0.05	1	1
Education is Job Related	No	No	No	No	Yes	Yes	No	Yes
Financial Costs of Up-Skilling								
Direct Costs of Education	641	641	641	641	966	966	641	641
Pre-Tax Scholarship Income	640	640	640	640	0	0	640	0
Income Before Education	6714	9592	9592	9592	9592	9592	9592	9592
Income During Education	3038	3038	3038	3038	9568	9568	3038	2398
Pre-Tax Foregone Earnings	3677	6554	6554	6554	24	24	6554	7194
AETR Before Education (%)	6.4	9.4	9.4	9.4	9.4	9.4	9.4	9.4
AETR During Education (Exclusive of Tax Expenditures) (%)	-1.7	-1.7	-1.7	-1.7	9.4	9.4	-1.7	-2.1
Value of Education Tax Credits % of Direct Costs	0.0	0.0	0.0	0.0	0.0	0.0	0.0	0.0
AETR During Education (Inclusive of Tax Expenditures) (%)	-1.7	-1.7	-1.7	-1.7	9.4	9.4	-1.7	-2.1
METR on Foregone Earnings (%)	13.0	14.5	14.5	14.5	16.5	16.5	14.5	13.2
Total Costs of Education (Direct Costs & Foregone Earnings)	3200	5604	5604	5604	986	986	5604	6883
Financial Returns to Up-Skilling								
Breakeven Earnings Level	7600	9997	10031	10121	9669	9685	10415	10603
AETR After Education (%)	7.6	9.7	9.7	9.8	9.5	9.5	10.0	10.1
Breakeven Earnings Increment	885	405	439	529	77	93	823	1011
Breakeven Earnings Increment % of Previous Wage	13.2	4.2	4.6	5.5	0.8	1.0	8.6	10.5
METR Breakeven Earnings Increment (%)	16.5	16.5	16.5	16.5	16.5	16.5	16.5	16.5
Marginal Effective Tax Rate on Skills (%)	4.0	2.3	2.3	2.3	16.1	16.1	2.3	4.9
Average Effective Tax Rate on Skills (Assumed 15% Return, %)	14.4	13.5	13.2	12.5	16.2	16.1	10.4	10.4
Government Costs and Returns								
Government Educational Costs	4316	4789	4789	4789	3201	3201	4789	4150
Marginal Returns to Costs Ratio	0.15	0.23	0.23	0.23	0.06	0.06	0.23	0.33
Average Returns to Costs Ratio (Assumed 15% Return)	0.89	1.09	1.01	0.84	0.08	0.06	0.54	0.62

StatLink http://dx.doi.org/10.1787/888933447177

Slovenia

Table C.47. Comparing Financial Incentives for College Education with Different Financing Scenarios - Slovenia

Single, No Children, 17 Year-Old, Four Years of Education, 70% of the Average Wage					Currency: EUR
Scenario	No Borrowing	Direct Costs Borrowed, Low Interest Rate	All Costs Borrowed, Low Interest Rate	Direct Costs Borrowed, High Interest Rate	All Costs Borrowed, High Interest Rate
Non-Financing Education Costs					
Direct Costs of Education	646	646	646	646	646
Pre-Tax Scholarship Income	1589	1589	1589	1589	1589
Income Before Education	12161	12161	12161	12161	12161
Income During Education	5932	5932	5932	5932	5932
Pre-Tax Foregone Earnings	6229	6229	6229	6229	6229
AETR Before Education (%)	8.3	8.3	8.3	8.3	8.3
AETR During Education (Exclusive of Tax Expenditures) (%)	0.0	0.0	0.0	0.0	0.0
Value of Education Tax Credits % of Direct Costs	0.0	0.0	0.0	0.0	0.0
AETR During Education (Inclusive of Tax Expenditures) (%)	0.0	0.0	0.0	0.0	0.0
METR on Foregone Earnings (%)	16.3	16.3	16.3	16.3	16.3
Total Annual Non-Financing Costs of Education (Direct Costs & Foregone Earnings)	4273	4273	4273	4273	4273
Education Financing Costs					
Fraction of Costs Borrowed	None	Direct Costs	All Costs	Direct Costs	All Costs
Total Amount Borrowed	0	646	4273	646	4273
Interest Rate (%)	NA	0.0	0.0	6.0	6.0
Annual Repayments	0	55	363	220	1453
Debt Finance Multiplier	1.00	0.59	0.59	1.41	1.41
Returns to Education					
Breakeven Earnings Level	13277	13209	12823	13346	13731
AETR After Education (%)	8.7	8.7	8.5	8.7	8.8
Breakeven Earnings Increment	1116	1048	663	1185	1570
Breakeven Earnings Increment % of Previous Wage	9.2	8.6	5.4	9.7	12.9
METR Breakeven Earnings Increment (%)	12.5	12.5	12.5	12.5	12.5
Marginal Effective Tax Rate on Skills (%)	-8.3	-9.6	-8.3	-7.1	-8.3
Average Effective Tax Rate on Skills (Assumed 15% Return, %)	17.2	17.9	21.1	16.4	9.1
Average Effective Tax Rate on Skills (Return based on Labour Market Premium, %)	20.3	20.8	23.0	19.7	14.7
Government Costs and Returns					
Government Educational Costs	8150	8413	9887	7887	6413
Marginal Returns to Costs Ratio	0.07	0.08	0.10	0.07	0.07
Average Returns to Costs Ratio (Return based on Labour Market Premium)	1.64	1.59	1.35	1.70	2.09

StatLink http://dx.doi.org/10.1787/888933447187

Table C.48. **Comparing Financial Incentives for Differing Savings-Financed Education Scenarios - Slovenia**

Single, No Children, Annual Data								Currency: EUR
Age	17	27	32	40	32	40	50	50
Income Before Education, %AW	70	100	100	100	100	100	100	100
Income During Education, %AW	25	25	25	25	95	95	25	25
Years of Education	4	1	1	1	0.05	0.05	1	1
Education is Job Related	No	No	No	No	Yes	Yes	No	Yes
Financial Costs of Up-Skilling								
Direct Costs of Education	646	646	646	646	1737	1737	646	646
Pre-Tax Scholarship Income	1589	1589	1589	1589	0	0	1589	0
Income Before Education	12161	17373	17373	17373	17373	17373	17373	17373
Income During Education	5932	5932	5932	5932	17329	17329	5932	4343
Pre-Tax Foregone Earnings	6229	11441	11441	11441	43	43	11441	13029
AETR Before Education (%)	8.3	11.3	11.3	11.3	11.3	11.3	11.3	11.3
AETR During Education (Exclusive of Tax Expenditures) (%)	0.0	0.0	0.0	0.0	11.3	11.3	0.0	0.0
Value of Education Tax Credits % of Direct Costs	0.0	0.0	0.0	0.0	0.0	0.0	0.0	0.0
AETR During Education (Inclusive of Tax Expenditures) (%)	0.0	0.0	0.0	0.0	11.3	11.3	0.0	0.0
METR on Foregone Earnings (%)	16.3	17.2	17.2	17.2	21.0	21.0	17.2	15.1
Total Costs of Education (Direct Costs & Foregone Earnings)	4273	8532	8532	8532	1772	1772	8532	11710
Financial Returns to Up-Skilling								
Breakeven Earnings Level	13277	18015	18067	18200	17517	17544	18616	19079
AETR After Education (%)	8.7	11.7	11.7	11.8	11.4	11.4	12.0	12.2
Breakeven Earnings Increment	1116	642	695	828	144	172	1243	1706
Breakeven Earnings Increment % of Previous Wage	9.2	3.7	4.0	4.8	0.8	1.0	7.2	9.8
METR Breakeven Earnings Increment (%)	12.5	21.0	21.0	21.0	21.0	21.0	21.0	21.0
Marginal Effective Tax Rate on Skills (%)	-8.3	2.8	2.8	2.8	20.6	20.6	2.8	7.8
Average Effective Tax Rate on Skills (Assumed 15% Return, %)	17.2	17.7	17.4	16.7	20.7	20.6	14.5	14.5
Government Costs and Returns								
Government Educational Costs	8150	9103	9103	9103	5557	5557	9103	7514
Marginal Returns to Costs Ratio	0.07	0.25	0.25	0.25	0.08	0.08	0.25	0.42
Average Returns to Costs Ratio (Assumed 15% Return)	1.02	1.35	1.25	1.05	0.10	0.09	0.70	0.85

StatLink http://dx.doi.org/10.1787/888933447194

Spain

Table C.49. **Comparing Financial Incentives for College Education with Different Financing Scenarios - Spain**

Single, No Children, 17 Year-Old, Four Years of Education, 70% of the Average Wage					**Currency: EUR**
Scenario	No Borrowing	Direct Costs Borrowed, Low Interest Rate	All Costs Borrowed, Low Interest Rate	Direct Costs Borrowed, High Interest Rate	All Costs Borrowed, High Interest Rate
Non-Financing Education Costs					
Direct Costs of Education	1742	1742	1742	1742	1742
Pre-Tax Scholarship Income	750	750	750	750	750
Income Before Education	17861	17861	17861	17861	17861
Income During Education	7128	7128	7128	7128	7128
Pre-Tax Foregone Earnings	10732	10732	10732	10732	10732
AETR Before Education (%)	12.0	12.0	12.0	12.0	12.0
AETR During Education (Exclusive of Tax Expenditures) (%)	0.0	0.0	0.0	0.0	0.0
Value of Education Tax Credits % of Direct Costs	0.0	0.0	0.0	0.0	0.0
AETR During Education (Inclusive of Tax Expenditures) (%)	0.0	0.0	0.0	0.0	0.0
METR on Foregone Earnings (%)	20.0	20.0	20.0	20.0	20.0
Total Annual Non-Financing Costs of Education (Direct Costs & Foregone Earnings)	9583	9583	9583	9583	9583
Education Financing Costs					
Fraction of Costs Borrowed	None	Direct Costs	All Costs	Direct Costs	All Costs
Total Amount Borrowed	0	1742	9583	1742	9583
Interest Rate (%)	NA	0.0	0.0	6.0	6.0
Annual Repayments	0	148	815	592	3258
Debt Finance Multiplier	1.00	0.59	0.59	1.41	1.41
Returns to Education					
Breakeven Earnings Level	20631	20423	19488	20839	21775
AETR After Education (%)	13.4	13.3	12.9	13.5	13.9
Breakeven Earnings Increment	2770	2562	1627	2978	3914
Breakeven Earnings Increment % of Previous Wage	15.5	14.3	9.1	16.7	21.9
METR Breakeven Earnings Increment (%)	22.5	22.5	22.5	22.5	22.5
Marginal Effective Tax Rate on Skills (%)	5.2	3.7	5.2	6.4	5.2
Average Effective Tax Rate on Skills (Assumed 15% Return, %)	21.8	23.1	27.7	20.4	9.7
Average Effective Tax Rate on Skills (Return based on Labour Market Premium, %)	18.1	20.5	28.9	15.4	-4.2
Government Costs and Returns					
Government Educational Costs	10090	10809	14043	9371	6137
Marginal Returns to Costs Ratio	0.28	0.28	0.34	0.28	0.32
Average Returns to Costs Ratio (Return based on Labour Market Premium)	0.83	0.78	0.60	0.90	1.37

StatLink http://dx.doi.org/10.1787/888933447208

Table C.50. **Comparing Financial Incentives for Differing Savings-Financed Education Scenarios - Spain**

Single, No Children, Annual Data								**Currency: EUR**
Age	17	27	32	40	32	40	50	50
Income Before Education, %AW	70	100	100	100	100	100	100	100
Income During Education, %AW	25	25	25	25	95	95	25	25
Years of Education	4	1	1	1	0.05	0.05	1	1
Education is Job Related	No	No	No	No	Yes	Yes	No	Yes
Financial Costs of Up-Skilling								
Direct Costs of Education	1742	1742	1742	1742	2522	2522	1742	1742
Pre-Tax Scholarship Income	750	750	750	750	0	0	750	0
Income Before Education	17861	25515	25515	25515	25515	25515	25515	25515
Income During Education	7128	7128	7128	7128	25452	25452	7128	6379
Pre-Tax Foregone Earnings	10732	18387	18387	18387	64	64	18387	19136
AETR Before Education (%)	12.0	15.7	15.7	15.7	15.7	15.7	15.7	15.7
AETR During Education (Exclusive of Tax Expenditures) (%)	0.0	0.0	0.0	0.0	15.7	15.7	0.0	0.0
Value of Education Tax Credits % of Direct Costs	0.0	0.0	0.0	0.0	0.0	0.0	0.0	0.0
AETR During Education (Inclusive of Tax Expenditures) (%)	0.0	0.0	0.0	0.0	15.7	15.7	0.0	0.0
METR on Foregone Earnings (%)	20.0	21.8	21.8	21.8	26.2	26.2	21.8	20.9
Total Costs of Education (Direct Costs & Foregone Earnings)	9583	15376	15376	15376	2569	2569	15376	16875
Financial Returns to Up-Skilling								
Breakeven Earnings Level	20631	26722	26811	27032	25732	25769	27661	27870
AETR After Education (%)	13.4	16.2	16.2	16.3	15.8	15.8	16.5	16.6
Breakeven Earnings Increment	2770	1207	1296	1516	217	253	2146	2355
Breakeven Earnings Increment % of Previous Wage	15.5	4.7	5.1	5.9	0.8	1.0	8.4	9.2
METR Breakeven Earnings Increment (%)	22.5	26.2	26.2	26.2	26.2	26.2	26.2	26.2
Marginal Effective Tax Rate on Skills (%)	5.2	7.0	7.0	7.0	25.7	25.7	7.0	8.7
Average Effective Tax Rate on Skills (Assumed 15% Return, %)	21.8	21.7	21.3	20.5	25.8	25.7	18.1	18.1
Government Costs and Returns								
Government Educational Costs	10090	11952	11952	11952	7216	7216	11952	11202
Marginal Returns to Costs Ratio	0.28	0.46	0.46	0.46	0.13	0.13	0.46	0.54
Average Returns to Costs Ratio (Assumed 15% Return)	1.59	1.93	1.80	1.54	0.15	0.13	1.09	1.16

StatLink http://dx.doi.org/10.1787/888933447214

Sweden

Table C.51. Comparing Financial Incentives for College Education with Different Financing Scenarios - Sweden

Single, No Children, 17 Year-Old, Four Years of Education, 70% of the Average Wage					Currency: SEK
Scenario	No Borrowing	Direct Costs Borrowed, Low Interest Rate	All Costs Borrowed, Low Interest Rate	Direct Costs Borrowed, High Interest Rate	All Costs Borrowed, High Interest Rate
Non-Financing Education Costs					
Direct Costs of Education	331	331	331	331	331
Pre-Tax Scholarship Income	19935	19935	19935	19935	19935
Income Before Education	263416	263416	263416	263416	263416
Income During Education	114012	114012	114012	114012	114012
Pre-Tax Foregone Earnings	149404	149404	149404	149404	149404
AETR Before Education (%)	15.4	15.4	15.4	15.4	15.4
AETR During Education (Exclusive of Tax Expenditures) (%)	7.4	7.4	7.4	7.4	7.4
Value of Education Tax Credits % of Direct Costs	-15.3	-15.3	-15.3	-15.3	-15.3
AETR During Education (Inclusive of Tax Expenditures) (%)	4.8	4.8	4.8	4.8	4.8
METR on Foregone Earnings (%)	21.5	21.5	21.5	21.5	21.5
Total Annual Non-Financing Costs of Education (Direct Costs & Foregone Earnings)	94720	94720	94720	94720	94720
Education Financing Costs					
Fraction of Costs Borrowed	None	Direct Costs	All Costs	Direct Costs	All Costs
Total Amount Borrowed	0	331	94720	331	94720
Interest Rate (%)	NA	0.0	0.0	6.0	6.0
Annual Repayments	0	28	8051	113	32204
Debt Finance Multiplier	1.00	0.59	0.59	1.41	1.41
Returns to Education					
Breakeven Earnings Level	290452	290392	279297	290482	301658
AETR After Education (%)	16.0	16.0	15.7	16.0	16.2
Breakeven Earnings Increment	27035	26976	15881	27066	38242
Breakeven Earnings Increment % of Previous Wage	10.3	10.2	6.0	10.3	14.5
METR Breakeven Earnings Increment (%)	21.5	21.4	21.5	21.5	21.6
Marginal Effective Tax Rate on Skills (%)	-7.6	-7.7	-7.6	-7.6	-7.4
Average Effective Tax Rate on Skills (Assumed 15% Return, %)	29.5	29.5	34.4	29.5	19.9
Average Effective Tax Rate on Skills (Return based on Labour Market Premium, %)	15.6	15.7	25.8	15.6	-4.4
Government Costs and Returns					
Government Educational Costs	219390	219526	258462	219253	180318
Marginal Returns to Costs Ratio	0.12	0.12	0.17	0.12	0.10
Average Returns to Costs Ratio (Return based on Labour Market Premium)	0.48	0.48	0.41	0.48	0.59

StatLink http://dx.doi.org/10.1787/888933447228

Table C.52. **Comparing Financial Incentives for Differing Savings-Financed Education Scenarios - Sweden**

Single, No Children, Annual Data								Currency: SEK
Age	17	27	32	40	32	40	50	50
Income Before Education, %AW	70	100	100	100	100	100	100	100
Income During Education, %AW	25	25	25	25	95	95	25	25
Years of Education	4	1	1	1	0.05	0.05	1	1
Education is Job Related	No	No	No	No	Yes	Yes	No	Yes
Financial Costs of Up-Skilling								
Direct Costs of Education	331	331	331	331	37544	37544	331	331
Pre-Tax Scholarship Income	19935	19935	19935	19935	0	0	19935	0
Income Before Education	263416	376309	376309	376309	376309	376309	376309	376309
Income During Education	114012	114012	114012	114012	375368	375368	114012	94077
Pre-Tax Foregone Earnings	149404	262297	262297	262297	941	941	262297	282232
AETR Before Education (%)	15.4	17.9	17.9	17.9	17.9	17.9	17.9	17.9
AETR During Education (Exclusive of Tax Expenditures) (%)	7.4	7.4	7.4	7.4	17.8	17.8	7.4	5.8
Value of Education Tax Credits % of Direct Costs	-15.3	-15.3	-15.3	-15.3	31.6	31.6	-15.3	0.0
AETR During Education (Inclusive of Tax Expenditures) (%)	4.8	4.8	4.8	4.8	14.7	14.7	4.8	5.8
METR on Foregone Earnings (%)	21.5	22.4	22.4	22.4	33.6	33.6	22.4	21.9
Total Costs of Education (Direct Costs & Foregone Earnings)	94720	180982	180982	180982	26323	26323	180982	220853
Financial Returns to Up-Skilling								
Breakeven Earnings Level	290452	390140	391131	393634	378377	378781	402845	410264
AETR After Education (%)	16.0	18.1	18.1	18.1	17.9	17.9	18.6	19.1
Breakeven Earnings Increment	27035	13831	14822	17325	2068	2472	26536	33955
Breakeven Earnings Increment % of Previous Wage	10.3	3.7	3.9	4.6	0.5	0.7	7.1	9.0
METR Breakeven Earnings Increment (%)	21.5	24.2	24.1	24.0	20.8	22.5	29.8	33.0
Marginal Effective Tax Rate on Skills (%)	-7.6	-1.6	-1.8	-1.9	-15.7	-13.3	5.8	14.3
Average Effective Tax Rate on Skills (Assumed 15% Return, %)	29.5	37.5	37.2	36.3	2.9	-0.5	33.8	33.8
Government Costs and Returns								
Government Educational Costs	219390	246020	246020	246020	176536	176536	246020	226085
Marginal Returns to Costs Ratio	0.12	0.24	0.23	0.23	0.04	0.04	0.31	0.48
Average Returns to Costs Ratio (Assumed 15% Return)	1.43	2.23	2.08	1.78	0.08	0.07	1.26	1.37

StatLink http://dx.doi.org/10.1787/888933447230

Switzerland

Table C.53. Comparing Financial Incentives for College Education with Different Financing Scenarios - Switzerland

Single, No Children, 17 Year-Old, Four Years of Education, 70% of the Average Wage — **Currency: CHF**

Scenario	No Borrowing	Direct Costs Borrowed, Low Interest Rate	All Costs Borrowed, Low Interest Rate	Direct Costs Borrowed, High Interest Rate	All Costs Borrowed, High Interest Rate
Non-Financing Education Costs					
Direct Costs of Education	2705	2705	2705	2705	2705
Pre-Tax Scholarship Income	782	782	782	782	782
Income Before Education	60413	60413	60413	60413	60413
Income During Education	22358	22358	22358	22358	22358
Pre-Tax Foregone Earnings	38055	38055	38055	38055	38055
AETR Before Education (%)	8.6	8.6	8.6	8.6	8.6
AETR During Education (Exclusive of Tax Expenditures) (%)	2.8	2.8	2.8	2.8	2.8
Value of Education Tax Credits % of Direct Costs	3.5	3.5	3.5	3.5	3.5
AETR During Education (Inclusive of Tax Expenditures) (%)	2.6	2.6	2.6	2.6	2.6
METR on Foregone Earnings (%)	12.0	12.0	12.0	12.0	12.0
Total Annual Non-Financing Costs of Education (Direct Costs & Foregone Earnings)	35350	35350	35350	35350	35350
Education Financing Costs					
Fraction of Costs Borrowed	None	Direct Costs	All Costs	Direct Costs	All Costs
Total Amount Borrowed	0	2705	35350	2705	35350
Interest Rate (%)	NA	0.0	0.0	6.0	6.0
Annual Repayments	0	230	3005	920	12019
Debt Finance Multiplier	1.00	0.59	0.59	1.41	1.41
Returns to Education					
Breakeven Earnings Level	69969	69658	65985	70260	73913
AETR After Education (%)	9.8	9.7	9.3	9.8	10.2
Breakeven Earnings Increment	9556	9244	5571	9847	13499
Breakeven Earnings Increment % of Previous Wage	15.8	15.3	9.2	16.3	22.3
METR Breakeven Earnings Increment (%)	17.1	17.0	16.5	17.0	17.1
Marginal Effective Tax Rate on Skills (%)	6.2	5.8	5.5	6.5	6.3
Average Effective Tax Rate on Skills (Assumed 15% Return, %)	17.3	17.8	22.6	16.7	5.6
Average Effective Tax Rate on Skills (Return based on Labour Market Premium, %)	16.1	16.8	22.8	15.4	1.5
Government Costs and Returns					
Government Educational Costs	35786	36902	50368	34670	21204
Marginal Returns to Costs Ratio	0.20	0.20	0.24	0.20	0.24
Average Returns to Costs Ratio (Return based on Labour Market Premium)	0.90	0.88	0.64	0.93	1.53

StatLink http://dx.doi.org/10.1787/888933447243

Table C.54. Comparing Financial Incentives for Differing Savings-Financed Education Scenarios - Switzerland

Single, No Children, Annual Data								Currency: CHF
Age	17	27	32	40	32	40	50	50
Income Before Education, %AW	70	100	100	100	100	100	100	100
Income During Education, %AW	25	25	25	25	95	95	25	25
Years of Education	4	1	1	1	0.05	0.05	1	1
Education is Job Related	No	No	No	No	Yes	Yes	No	Yes
Financial Costs of Up-Skilling								
Direct Costs of Education	2705	2705	2705	2705	7741	7741	2705	2705
Pre-Tax Scholarship Income	782	782	782	782	0	0	782	0
Income Before Education	60413	86305	86305	86305	86305	86305	86305	86305
Income During Education	22358	22358	22358	22358	86089	86089	22358	21576
Pre-Tax Foregone Earnings	38055	63947	63947	63947	216	216	63947	64729
AETR Before Education (%)	8.6	11.2	11.2	11.2	11.2	11.2	11.2	11.2
AETR During Education (Exclusive of Tax Expenditures) (%)	2.8	2.8	2.8	2.8	11.2	11.2	2.8	2.6
Value of Education Tax Credits % of Direct Costs	3.5	3.5	3.5	3.5	3.0	3.0	3.5	0.5
AETR During Education (Inclusive of Tax Expenditures) (%)	2.6	2.6	2.6	2.6	11.0	11.0	2.6	2.6
METR on Foregone Earnings (%)	12.0	14.2	14.2	14.2	21.0	21.0	14.2	14.1
Total Costs of Education (Direct Costs & Foregone Earnings)	35350	56734	56734	56734	7683	7683	56734	58283
Financial Returns to Up-Skilling								
Breakeven Earnings Level	69969	90481	90776	91555	86905	87012	93734	93920
AETR After Education (%)	9.8	11.7	11.7	11.8	11.3	11.3	12.0	12.1
Breakeven Earnings Increment	9556	4176	4471	5250	600	707	7429	7615
Breakeven Earnings Increment % of Previous Wage	15.8	4.8	5.2	6.1	0.7	0.8	8.6	8.8
METR Breakeven Earnings Increment (%)	17.1	21.4	21.1	21.4	20.4	20.9	21.4	21.2
Marginal Effective Tax Rate on Skills (%)	6.2	8.7	8.4	8.7	17.5	18.1	8.7	8.8
Average Effective Tax Rate on Skills (Assumed 15% Return, %)	17.3	18.6	18.4	17.8	18.1	17.8	16.2	16.2
Government Costs and Returns								
Government Educational Costs	35786	40294	40294	40294	30651	30651	40294	39526
Marginal Returns to Costs Ratio	0.20	0.38	0.38	0.38	0.06	0.07	0.38	0.40
Average Returns to Costs Ratio (Assumed 15% Return)	1.17	1.61	1.49	1.28	0.09	0.08	0.90	0.92

StatLink http://dx.doi.org/10.1787/888933447259

Turkey

Table C.55. Comparing Financial Incentives for College Education with Different Financing Scenarios - Turkey

Single, No Children, 17 Year-Old, Four Years of Education, 70% of the Average Wage					Currency: TRY
Scenario	No Borrowing	Direct Costs Borrowed, Low Interest Rate	All Costs Borrowed, Low Interest Rate	Direct Costs Borrowed, High Interest Rate	All Costs Borrowed, High Interest Rate
Non-Financing Education Costs					
Direct Costs of Education	136	136	136	136	136
Pre-Tax Scholarship Income	472	472	472	472	472
Income Before Education	14825	14825	14825	14825	14825
Income During Education	5767	5767	5767	5767	5767
Pre-Tax Foregone Earnings	9059	9059	9059	9059	9059
AETR Before Education (%)	9.7	9.7	9.7	9.7	9.7
AETR During Education (Exclusive of Tax Expenditures) (%)	1.0	1.0	1.0	1.0	1.0
Value of Education Tax Credits % of Direct Costs	-6.4	-6.4	-6.4	-6.4	-6.4
AETR During Education (Inclusive of Tax Expenditures) (%)	0.6	0.6	0.6	0.6	0.6
METR on Foregone Earnings (%)	15.2	15.2	15.2	15.2	15.2
Total Annual Non-Financing Costs of Education (Direct Costs & Foregone Earnings)	7326	7326	7326	7326	7326
Education Financing Costs					
Fraction of Costs Borrowed	None	Direct Costs	All Costs	Direct Costs	All Costs
Total Amount Borrowed	0	136	7326	136	7326
Interest Rate (%)	NA	0.0	0.0	6.0	6.0
Annual Repayments	0	12	623	46	2491
Debt Finance Multiplier	1.00	0.60	0.60	1.40	1.40
Returns to Education					
Breakeven Earnings Level	16875	16860	16047	16891	17704
AETR After Education (%)	10.6	10.6	10.3	10.6	11.0
Breakeven Earnings Increment	2050	2035	1221	2065	2879
Breakeven Earnings Increment % of Previous Wage	13.8	13.7	8.2	13.9	19.4
METR Breakeven Earnings Increment (%)	17.7	17.7	17.7	17.7	17.7
Marginal Effective Tax Rate on Skills (%)	2.0	1.8	2.0	2.1	2.0
Average Effective Tax Rate on Skills (Assumed 15% Return, %)	14.9	15.1	20.1	14.8	4.2
Average Effective Tax Rate on Skills (Return based on Labour Market Premium, %)	11.5	11.7	23.3	11.2	-13.1
Government Costs and Returns					
Government Educational Costs	9841	9896	12803	9786	6879
Marginal Returns to Costs Ratio	0.16	0.16	0.21	0.16	0.16
Average Returns to Costs Ratio (Return based on Labour Market Premium)	0.40	0.40	0.31	0.41	0.58

StatLink http://dx.doi.org/10.1787/888933447263

Table C.56. Comparing Financial Incentives for Differing Savings-Financed Education Scenarios - Turkey

Single, No Children, Annual Data								Currency: TRY
Age	17	27	32	40	32	40	50	50
Income Before Education, %AW	70	100	100	100	100	100	100	100
Income During Education, %AW	25	25	25	25	95	95	25	25
Years of Education	4	1	1	1	0.05	0.05	1	1
Education is Job Related	No	No	No	No	Yes	Yes	No	Yes
Financial Costs of Up-Skilling								
Direct Costs of Education	136	136	136	136	2264	2264	136	136
Pre-Tax Scholarship Income	472	472	472	472	0	0	472	0
Income Before Education	14825	21179	21179	21179	21179	21179	21179	21179
Income During Education	5767	5767	5767	5767	21126	21126	5767	5295
Pre-Tax Foregone Earnings	9059	15412	15412	15412	53	53	15412	15884
AETR Before Education (%)	9.7	12.1	12.1	12.1	12.1	12.1	12.1	12.1
AETR During Education (Exclusive of Tax Expenditures) (%)	1.0	1.0	1.0	1.0	12.0	12.0	1.0	0.7
Value of Education Tax Credits % of Direct Costs	-6.4	-6.4	-6.4	-6.4	18.7	18.7	-6.4	0.0
AETR During Education (Inclusive of Tax Expenditures) (%)	0.6	0.6	0.6	0.6	10.0	10.0	0.6	0.7
METR on Foregone Earnings (%)	15.2	16.2	16.2	16.2	17.7	17.7	16.2	15.9
Total Costs of Education (Direct Costs & Foregone Earnings)	7326	12558	12558	12558	1885	1885	12558	13502
Financial Returns to Up-Skilling								
Breakeven Earnings Level	16875	22095	22172	22370	21328	21358	23014	23151
AETR After Education (%)	10.6	12.3	12.3	12.4	12.1	12.1	12.5	12.5
Breakeven Earnings Increment	2050	916	993	1191	149	179	1835	1972
Breakeven Earnings Increment % of Previous Wage	13.8	4.3	4.7	5.6	0.7	0.8	8.7	9.3
METR Breakeven Earnings Increment (%)	17.7	17.7	17.7	17.7	17.7	17.7	17.7	17.7
Marginal Effective Tax Rate on Skills (%)	2.0	1.1	1.1	1.1	-1.2	-1.2	1.1	2.3
Average Effective Tax Rate on Skills (Assumed 15% Return, %)	14.9	14.1	13.8	13.0	4.4	1.7	10.5	10.5
Government Costs and Returns								
Government Educational Costs	9841	10963	10963	10963	8405	8405	10963	10491
Marginal Returns to Costs Ratio	0.16	0.25	0.25	0.25	0.05	0.05	0.25	0.28
Average Returns to Costs Ratio (Assumed 15% Return)	0.92	1.14	1.05	0.87	0.07	0.06	0.57	0.59

StatLink http://dx.doi.org/10.1787/888933447277

United Kingdom

Table C.57. Comparing Financial Incentives for College Education with Different Financing Scenarios - United Kingdom

Single, No Children, 17 Year-Old, Four Years of Education, 70% of the Average Wage					Currency: GBP
Scenario	No Borrowing	Direct Costs Borrowed, Low Interest Rate	All Costs Borrowed, Low Interest Rate	Direct Costs Borrowed, High Interest Rate	All Costs Borrowed, High Interest Rate
Non-Financing Education Costs					
Direct Costs of Education	6031	6031	6031	6031	6031
Pre-Tax Scholarship Income	808	808	808	808	808
Income Before Education	23858	23858	23858	23858	23858
Income During Education	9329	9329	9329	9329	9329
Pre-Tax Foregone Earnings	14529	14529	14529	14529	14529
AETR Before Education (%)	13.7	13.7	13.7	13.7	13.7
AETR During Education (Exclusive of Tax Expenditures) (%)	-12.4	-12.4	-12.4	-12.4	-12.4
Value of Education Tax Credits % of Direct Costs	9.4	9.4	9.4	9.4	9.4
AETR During Education (Inclusive of Tax Expenditures) (%)	-17.6	-17.6	-17.6	-17.6	-17.6
METR on Foregone Earnings (%)	30.5	30.5	30.5	30.5	30.5
Total Annual Non-Financing Costs of Education (Direct Costs & Foregone Earnings)	14830	14830	14830	14830	14830
Education Financing Costs					
Fraction of Costs Borrowed	None	Direct Costs	All Costs	Direct Costs	All Costs
Total Amount Borrowed	0	6031	14830	6031	14830
Interest Rate (%)	NA	0.0	0.0	6.0	6.0
Annual Repayments	0	513	1261	2050	5042
Debt Finance Multiplier	1.00	0.58	0.58	1.42	1.42
Returns to Education					
Breakeven Earnings Level	27898	27206	26198	28589	29598
AETR After Education (%)	14.6	14.5	14.3	14.8	14.9
Breakeven Earnings Increment	4040	3348	2339	4731	5740
Breakeven Earnings Increment % of Previous Wage	16.9	14.0	9.8	19.8	24.1
METR Breakeven Earnings Increment (%)	20.0	20.0	20.0	20.0	20.0
Marginal Effective Tax Rate on Skills (%)	-6.6	-12.0	-6.6	-2.7	-6.6
Average Effective Tax Rate on Skills (Assumed 15% Return, %)	14.9	18.2	22.7	10.5	-1.0
Average Effective Tax Rate on Skills (Return based on Labour Market Premium, %)	12.6	17.1	22.9	7.0	-8.1
Government Costs and Returns					
Government Educational Costs	8724	11262	14966	6185	2482
Marginal Returns to Costs Ratio	0.43	0.40	0.43	0.51	1.05
Average Returns to Costs Ratio (Return based on Labour Market Premium)	1.54	1.19	0.89	2.17	5.40

StatLink http://dx.doi.org/10.1787/888933447285

Table C.58. **Comparing Financial Incentives for Differing Savings-Financed Education Scenarios - United Kingdom**

Single, No Children, Annual Data								Currency: GBP
Age	17	27	32	40	32	40	50	50
Income Before Education, %AW	70	100	100	100	100	100	100	100
Income During Education, %AW	25	25	25	25	95	95	25	25
Years of Education	4	1	1	1	0.05	0.05	1	1
Education is Job Related	No	No	No	No	Yes	Yes	No	Yes
Financial Costs of Up-Skilling								
Direct Costs of Education	6031	6031	6031	6031	3429	3429	6031	6031
Pre-Tax Scholarship Income	808	808	808	808	0	0	808	0
Income Before Education	23858	34083	34083	34083	34083	34083	34083	34083
Income During Education	9329	9329	9329	9329	33998	33998	9329	8521
Pre-Tax Foregone Earnings	14529	24754	24754	24754	85	85	24754	25562
AETR Before Education (%)	13.7	15.6	15.6	15.6	15.6	15.6	15.6	15.6
AETR During Education (Exclusive of Tax Expenditures) (%)	-12.4	-12.4	-12.4	-12.4	15.6	15.6	-12.4	-19.3
Value of Education Tax Credits % of Direct Costs	9.4	9.4	9.4	9.4	20.0	20.0	9.4	3.5
AETR During Education (Inclusive of Tax Expenditures) (%)	-17.6	-17.6	-17.6	-17.6	13.6	13.6	-17.6	-21.8
METR on Foregone Earnings (%)	30.5	26.2	26.2	26.2	20.0	20.0	26.2	27.3
Total Costs of Education (Direct Costs & Foregone Earnings)	14830	23010	23010	23010	2811	2811	23010	24417
Financial Returns to Up-Skilling								
Breakeven Earnings Level	27898	35689	35793	36040	34292	34322	36677	36835
AETR After Education (%)	14.6	15.8	15.8	15.9	15.6	15.6	15.9	15.9
Breakeven Earnings Increment	4040	1606	1710	1957	209	239	2594	2752
Breakeven Earnings Increment % of Previous Wage	16.9	4.7	5.0	5.7	0.6	0.7	7.6	8.1
METR Breakeven Earnings Increment (%)	20.0	20.0	20.0	20.0	20.0	20.0	20.0	20.0
Marginal Effective Tax Rate on Skills (%)	-6.6	-4.2	-4.2	-4.2	0.0	0.0	-4.2	-3.5
Average Effective Tax Rate on Skills (Assumed 15% Return, %)	14.9	14.3	13.9	13.0	7.7	6.0	10.8	10.5
Government Costs and Returns								
Government Educational Costs	8724	10769	10769	10769	3697	3697	10769	10170
Marginal Returns to Costs Ratio	0.43	0.53	0.53	0.53	0.19	0.19	0.53	0.60
Average Returns to Costs Ratio (Assumed 15% Return)	2.06	2.27	2.13	1.86	0.31	0.27	1.40	1.49

StatLink http://dx.doi.org/10.1787/888933447298

Notes

1. Tables for the United States are excluded given the significant differences that are difficult to statistically account for in the cost and how these costs are covered of tertiary education.
2. These results do not incorporate interest deductibility of student loans in Finland.

ANNEX D

Country Details

This discussion outlines specific skills tax expenditures (STEs) that have been added to the personal income tax (PIT) and Social Security Contribution (SSC) systems of each country's *Taxing Wages* model for 2011. Details of these models can be found in *OECD Taxing Wages* (OECD, 2014). These STEs largely offset the costs of skills investments through the PIT system. A more detailed discussion of the STEs affecting skills investments are contained in Torres (2012).

Australia

For Australia, three features of the tax system pertaining to skills have been modelled.

- The first is the tax treatment of scholarship income. Scholarships, bursaries or other educational allowances derived by a student receiving full-time education are generally exempt from taxation. However this exemption does not apply to payments received by a student on condition that the student will become or continue to be an employee of the payer.
- The second provision modelled is the deductibility of training costs. These are tax-deductible where the expenses are connected with a taxpayers' current professional activity. It is assumed that this deduction is available for 'job-related education', as discussed in Section 4.5, but not otherwise.
- The third feature is Australia's system of income-contingent loans. As discussed in Section 3.2 and 4.3, a variety of interest rates and loan amounts have been modelled in the analysis. In the Australian case, the key feature modelled is income-contingency of the repayment of student debt. If a taxpayer does not earn more than AUS 51 309, no interest or loan principal need be repaid.

Austria

For Austria, two features of the tax system pertaining to skills have been modelled.

- The first is the tax treatment of scholarship income. In Austria, scholarship income is tax exempt where it is not related to employment. Where income is related to employment, the tax exemption for scholarship income is not available. It is assumed in this study that this deduction is not available for 'job-related education', as discussed in Section 4.5, but is available otherwise.
- The second provision modelled is the deductibility of training costs. These are tax-deductible where the expenses are connected with a taxpayers' current professional activity. This provision is modelled in the opposite way to the scholarship income provision; it is assumed that it is available for 'job-related education', but not otherwise.

Belgium

For Belgium, four features of the tax system pertaining to skills have been modelled.

- The first provision modelled is the deductibility of training costs. These are tax-deductible where these expenses are connected with a taxpayers' current professional activity. It is assumed that this deduction is available for 'job-related education', as discussed in Section 4.5, but not otherwise.
- The second provision is the tax treatment for students who work less than 23 days per year. In these cases normal SSC rates do not apply; rather a reduced employees' SSC rate of 2.71% applies, as does a reduced employers' SSC rate of 5.42%. This is assumed to only be available to college students, as discussed in Sections 4.2 and 4.3.
- The third provision is the tax exemption of scholarship income. This is assumed to be available to all kinds of scholarship income.
- The fourth provision is the tax treatment of student debt. As discussed in Section 3.2 and 4.3, a variety of interest rates and loan amounts have been modelled in the analysis. In Belgium interest on student debt is assumed to be tax-deductible.

Canada

For Canada, three features of the tax system pertaining to skills have been modelled.

- The first is the exemption of scholarship income from taxation. Scholarships in respect of non-research degrees that lead to a diploma or degree are exempted. Where the scholarship received is pertaining to education that is part-time, the scholarship exemption is limited to the value of tuition costs plus the costs of program-related materials. In this study, it is assumed that scholarship income is exempt from taxation where education is full-time. Otherwise, the amount of the deduction is limited to the value of the direct costs of education (which in the model, are assumed to be tuition fees).
- The second provision modelled is the Tuition Tax Credit. At federal level, this credit provides a 15% non-refundable tax credit of the costs of tuition. There is also a 5.05% credit applied at the provincial level for the province of Ontario. These credits together comprised a 20.05% total credit for the costs of tuition. There is no limit on the amount of tuition that can be claimed, but claims must exceed CAD 100. In the model it is assumed that all direct educational costs paid by the student are tuition fees. The value of the credit can be carried forward until it is exhausted. It is assumed that this credit is available whether training is job-related or not.
- The third provision is the tax treatment of student debt. As discussed in Section 3.2 and 4.3, a variety of interest rates and loan amounts have been modelled in the analysis. In Canada, interest paid on student loans approved under the Canada Student Loans Program and similar provincial or territorial programs is eligible for a 15-percent non-refundable tax credit. The value of the credits can be carried forward for up to five years after interest payment have been made. It is assumed that this applies to student loans in the model.

The Education and Textbook Tax Credits are not modelled, as all the costs of education in the model are assumed to be tuition fees. Finally, the deductibility of tuition assistance received for programs that do not qualify for the Tuition Tax Credit is not modelled; it is assumed that all education is eligible for the credit.

Chile

For Chile, only the tax exemption of scholarship income is modelled. It is assumed that this tax exemption is available whether the training is job-related or not.

Czech Republic

For the Czech Republic, two features of the tax system pertaining to skills have been modelled.

- The first is the exemption of scholarship income from taxation. This exemption is available to scholarships awarded from the state budget. It is assumed that scholarship income received in this study is tax exempt. It is also assumed that this tax exemption is available whether the training is job-related or not.
- The second provision modelled is the deductibility of training expenses. It is assumed that this deductibility is available whether the training is job-related or not. This tax deduction is only available for taxpayers who are less than 26 years of age, or have dependents aged less than 26. Deductibility for dependents is not modelled, so a taxpayer must be less than 26 years of age to avail of the deduction in the model.

Denmark

For Denmark, three features of the tax system pertaining to skills have been modelled.

- The first is the tax treatment of scholarship income. In Denmark, scholarship income is normally treated as general income, and is modelled here as taxable.
- The second provision is the tax treatment of student debt. As discussed in Section 3.2 and 4.3, a variety of interest rates and loan amounts have been modelled in the analysis. In Denmark interest on student debt is assumed to be tax-deductible.

Estonia

For Estonia, three features of the tax system pertaining to skills have been modelled.

- The first is taxation of scholarship income from taxation. Scholarship income is normally treated as general income if it is received in connection with employment. However scholarships paid by public authorities are exempt from taxation.
- The second provision modelled is the deductibility of training costs when these costs relate to current professional activity. In Estonia these costs are deductible up to EUR 1 920 or 50% of the taxpayers' income. It is assumed that this deductibility is available whether the training is job-related or not. Deductibility for dependents is not modelled.
- The third provision modelled is the exemption of working students from the lump-sum social contribution of EUR 91.75 per month known as the Social Tax Minimum Obligation.

Finland

For Finland three features of the tax system pertaining to skills have been modelled.

- The first is the tax deductibility of skills spending from taxation. In Finland, work-related skills expenditure is in certain cases deductible from taxable income. It is assumed that this deduction is available for 'job-related education', as discussed in Section 4.5, but is not available otherwise.
- In addition, student grant income is generally subject to taxation, though with certain special provisions applied. An allowance is provided with respect to municipal taxation

for the value of grant income. The allowance is capped at EUR 2 600, and is also reduced by 50% of earned income less the deduction for work-related expenses.

- SSCs paid on wage income and other income from work are not paid on student grant income. On student grant income only the health insurance contribution is paid.
- Finland also allows interest on student debt to be deducted from the income tax base. This feature is not modelled in the results presented in this study.

Greece

For Greece, two features of the tax system pertaining to skills have been modelled.

- The first is the tax treatment of scholarship income. In Greece, scholarship income awarded by the Greek State is exempt from taxation. It is assumed in the model that scholarship income received is state scholarship income; it is modelled as exempt from taxation. It is assumed that this tax exemption is available whether the training is job-related or not.
- The second provision modelled is the deductibility of training costs. This deductibility is available for 10% of training costs up to a maximum of EUR 1 000.

Tax deductions available for education expenses for children are not modelled.

Hungary

For Hungary, two features of the tax system pertaining to skills have been modelled.

- The first is the tax exemption of scholarship income. In Hungary, most scholarship income is not taxable. In this study, it is assumed that scholarship income received by a student is not taxable. It is assumed that this is the case whether the training is job-related or not.
- The second is the reduced rates of employers' SSCs when a worker is below 25 or above 55 years of age. In these instances income up to HUF 1 200 000 is charged at a rate of 12.5% (lower than the standard employers' SSC rate of 27%). Income above HUF 1 200 000 is taxed at a rate of 27%.

Iceland

For Iceland, only the tax deductibility of educational expenses is modelled. It is assumed that this deduction is available for 'job-related education', as discussed in Section 4.5, but not otherwise.

Ireland

For Ireland, two features of the tax system pertaining to skills have been modelled.

- The first is the tax treatment of scholarship income. In Ireland, scholarship income is exempt from taxation. It is assumed that this tax exemption is available whether the training is job-related or not.
- The second provision modelled is tax relief available for tuition fees. This tax relief is assumed to be available for direct costs of education; however the deductible amount is net of any scholarship income received. This relief is only available for fees above EUR 2 000 for full-time students and EUR 1 000 for part-time students. The maximum amount of fees on which tax relief can be claimed is EUR 7 000 at the standard rate of 20%.[1]

Israel

For Israel[2], three features of the tax system pertaining to skills have been modelled.

- The first is the tax treatment of scholarship income. In Israel, scholarship income is exempt from taxation up to a ceiling of ILS 92 000. It is assumed that this tax exemption is available whether the training is job-related or not.
- The second provision modelled is the deductibility of training costs. These are tax-deductible where these expenses are connected with a taxpayers' current professional activity. It is assumed that this deduction is available for 'job-related education', as discussed in Section 4.5, but is not available otherwise.
- The third feature is the tax credit for education expenses. This is modelled as being available for student's basic education (being related to a profession is not required). It is assumed that it is not available for job-related training (so that taxpayers cannot claim both the credit and the allowance). The value of the credit is ILS 2 508.

Italy

For Italy, two features of the tax system pertaining to skills have been modelled.

- The first is the tax treatment of scholarship income. In Italy, scholarship income is exempt from PIT, and is subject to a special schedule for SSCs. These contributions are levied on scholarship income at a rate of 17% where the employee is paying contributions on some other income, and 26.72% where the employee is paying no other SSCs. Two-thirds of the contribution is paid by the employer, one-third by the worker. It is assumed that this PIT exemption and special SSC schedule is available whether the training is job-related or not.
- The second provision modelled is the tax credit for educational expenses. This credit provides a 19% non-refundable tax credit for the costs of education. There is no limit on the expenses that can be claimed.

The 19% tax credit related to rental expenses for students who travel to study is not modelled. This is due to data limitations on student rental income.

Luxembourg

For Luxembourg, two features of the tax system pertaining to skills have been modelled.

- The first is the tax treatment of scholarship income. In Luxembourg, scholarship income is exempt from PIT and SSCs. It is assumed that this tax exemption is available whether the training is job-related or not.
- The second provision modelled is the deductibility of training costs. It is assumed that this deductibility is available whether the training is job-related or not.

Tax deductions available for education expenses for children are not modelled; nor are exemptions for certain other forms of student income.

Mexico

For Mexico, two features of the tax system pertaining to skills have been modelled.

- The first is the tax treatment of scholarship income. In Mexico, scholarship income is partially exempt from taxation. This exemption is granted up to a limit. The sum of exempt scholarship income and other taxable work-related income (wages) should not be higher than 7 times the minimum wage (MXN 148 344). When this sum is higher, the exempt income is limited to 1 annual minimum wage. However, the sum of wage income and exempt scholarship income cannot be lower than 7 minimum wages as a result of this limit.

- The second provision modelled is the deductibility of education costs. The maximum deductible varies by type of education; it is assumed that the amount for the highest qualification (professional technical education: MXN 17 100) is available for each taxpayer.

  Tax deductions available for education expenses for children are not modelled.

Netherlands

For the Netherlands, two features of the tax system pertaining to skills have been modelled.

- The first is the tax treatment of scholarship income. In the Netherlands, scholarships are given as conditional loans: conditional on a student completing a degree in a given time period. It is assumed that all scholarships for university education are not repaid and are therefore tax exempt. For the purposes of the models in this study, it is assumed that the scholarship income received by the student is exempt from taxation if the training is not job-related (such as university education). If the training is job-related, then the scholarship income is taxable.
- The second is the deductibility of training costs. In the Netherlands this tax exemption is available whether the training is job-related or not. Deductible costs should exceed EUR 500 per year, but cannot exceed EUR 15 000 per year.

New Zealand

For New Zealand, only the tax exemption of scholarship income is modelled. Specifically, the Course Participation Allowance is exempt from taxation, as are scholarships made under the Education Act 1989. It is assumed that scholarship income received by students completing four-year degrees is exempt from taxation. It is assumed that scholarship income received by students undertaking job-related training is not tax-exempt.

Norway

For Norway, three features of the tax system pertaining to skills have been modelled.

- The first is the exemption of scholarship income from taxation where this income is not related to employment. In Norway, where scholarship income is related to employment, the tax exemption is not available. Other forms of scholarship income are exempt from taxation.
- The second provision modelled is the deductibility of training costs. These are tax-deductible where these expenses are connected with a taxpayers' current professional activity. It is assumed that this deduction is available for 'job-related education', as discussed in Section 4.5, but is not available otherwise.
- The third provision is the tax treatment of student debt. As discussed in Section 3.2 and 4.3, a variety of interest rates and loan amounts have been modelled in the analysis. In Norway interest on student debt is assumed to be tax-deductible.

Poland

For Poland, two features of the tax system pertaining to skills have been modelled.

- In Poland, normal income earned by students is subject to taxation, but scholarship income is modelled as tax-exempt. It is assumed that this tax exemption is available whether the training is job-related or not.

- The second provision modelled is reduced SSC rates for students on certain temporary contracts. Income from contracts of mandate in Poland is modelled as being exempt from most social contributions, where a student's age is less than 26. It is assumed that this provision is only available where training is non-job-related.

Portugal

For Portugal, three features of the tax system pertaining to skills have been modelled.

- The first is the tax treatment of scholarship income. In Portugal, normal income earned by students is subject to taxation, but scholarship income is modelled as tax-exempt. It is assumed that this tax exemption is available whether the training is job-related or not.
- The second provision modelled is the tax credit of 30% for education and training expenses, up to a limit of 160% of the Social Benefit Index (also known as the SBI; it was valued at EUR 475 in 2011). It is assumed that this is available only when education is not job-related: job-related expenses are tax-deductible.
- The third is the deductibility of professional training expenses. It is assumed that this deduction is available for 'job-related education', as discussed in Section 4.5, but is not available otherwise. In 2011, this deductibility is available up to a limit of 3% of 12 times the SBI. In 2010 the limit was EUR 171.

Slovak Republic

For the Slovak Republic, two features of the tax system pertaining to skills have been modelled.

- The first is the tax treatment of scholarship income. In the Slovak Republic public grants and scholarships are tax exempt. It is assumed that scholarship income is state-funded scholarship income, and so is tax-exempt. It is also assumed that this tax exemption is available whether the training is job-related or not.
- The second is reduced social security contributions for workers on temporary contracts. These students benefit from reduced SSC rates as outlined in the table below. These reduced rates are assumed to only be available to college students, as discussed in Sections 4.2 and 4.3.

	Social security contribution rates (in %)					
	Regular employment income			All temporary contracts up to 2012		
	Employee	Employer		Employee	Employer	
		PAYG	Second pillar		PAYG	Second pillar
SSC	**13.4**	**35.2/26.2***	**0.0/9.0***	**0**	**1.05/1.05***	**0.0**
Health Insurance	4.0	10		0	0	
Social Insurance of which:	9.4	25.2/16.2*	0.0/9.0*	0	0	0
Sickness	1.4	1.4		0	0	
Retirement	4.0	14.0/5.0*	0.0/9.0*	0	0	0
Disability	3.0	3		0	0	
Unemployment	1.0	1		0	0	
Guarantee fund	0	0.25		0	0.25/0.25*	
Accident	0	0.8		0	0.8/0.8*	
Reserve fund	0	4.75		0	0	

Slovenia

For Slovenia, three features of the tax system pertaining to skills have been modelled.

- The first is the tax treatment of scholarship income. Scholarship income is tax-exempt up to the level of the minimum wage (EUR 8 977). It is assumed that this tax exemption is available whether the training is job-related or not.
- The second provision modelled is reduced SSC rates for student income is not subject to the to the social security contributions levied on wage income; instead a student's employer pays a flat rate of EUR 53.52 annually.
- The third provision is modelled is a fixed tax deduction for student income. This provision was worth EUR 3 143.57 in 2011.

Spain

For Spain, only the limited tax exemption of scholarship income is modelled. In Spain, most scholarship income is treated as normal income, except for public grants and scholarships which are exempt. This exemption is capped at EUR 3 000 per year, rising to EUR 15 000 for four-year university degrees. Scholarship income is modelled as being exempt up to a value of 3 000, except for four-year long educational investments, where the exemption exists up to EUR 15 000. It is assumed that this tax exemption is available whether the training is job-related or not.

Sweden

For Sweden, two features of the tax system pertaining to skills have been modelled.

- The first is the tax treatment of scholarship income. In Sweden, normal income earned by students is subject to taxation, but scholarship income, as long as it is not paid as remuneration, is modelled as tax-exempt. It is assumed that this tax exemption is available whether the training is job-related or not.
- The second provision modelled is the deductibility of training costs. These are tax-deductible where these expenses are connected with a taxpayers' current professional activity. It is assumed that this deduction is available for 'job-related education', as discussed in Section 4.5, but is not available otherwise. As Swedish law requires a taxpayer to be receiving full or close to full payment from their employer during periods of education, it is assumed that this allowance is not available during periods of education lasting one year or more.

Switzerland

For Switzerland, two features of the tax system pertaining to skills have been modelled.

- The first is the tax treatment of scholarship income. In Switzerland, normal income earned by students is subject to taxation, but scholarship income is modelled as tax-exempt. It is assumed that this tax exemption is available whether the training is job-related or not.
- The second provision modelled is the deductibility of training costs. These are tax-deductible where these expenses are connected with a taxpayers' current professional activity. It is assumed that this deduction is available for 'job-related education', as discussed in Section 4.5, but is not available otherwise.

Turkey

For Turkey, two features of the tax system pertaining to skills have been modelled.

- The first is the tax treatment of scholarship income. In Turkey, scholarship income is exempt from taxation, except where this income is earned by apprentices. It is assumed that the training undertaken in the model is not apprenticeship training, and that the scholarship income is exempt from taxation. It is assumed that this tax exemption is available whether the training is job-related or not (it is assumed that job-related training is not specifically apprenticeship training).
- The second provision modelled is the deductibility of educational costs provided that they do not exceed 10% of the declared income. It is assumed that this is available whether the training is job-related or not.

Tax deductions available for education expenses for children are not modelled.

United Kingdom

For the United Kingdom, two features of the tax system pertaining to skills have been modelled.

- The first is the tax treatment of scholarship income. To qualify for the exemption from tax and SSCs the scholarship income must be associated with training that is unrelated to any work or employment. It is assumed that this exemption is not available for 'job-related education', as discussed in Section 4.5, but is available otherwise. Where a scholarship is paid by an employer to an employee, and certain conditions are met, a cap of GBP 15 480 applies in the United Kingdom. In this study, it is assumed that scholarships are paid by the government, and this provision is not modelled.
- The second provision modelled is the deductibility of training costs. These are tax-deductible where these expenses are integral/wholly necessary to the job with a taxpayers' current professional activity. It is assumed that this deduction is available for 'job-related education', as discussed in Section 4.5, but is not available otherwise.

United States

For the United States, five features of the tax system pertaining to skills exist.[3]

- The first is the tax treatment of scholarship income. In the United States, this income is treated as normal income. There are two exceptions. The first is where the income is used to study abroad. Here it is assumed that all education is undertaken in the country, so scholarship income remains taxable. The second is where the scholarship income is conditional on documented expenses including tuition and fees required for attendance, books, supplies, and required equipment. To account for this, it is assumed that scholarship income in excess the direct costs of education is taxable, but that scholarship income below this amount is not taxable. It is assumed that this tax exemption is available whether the training is job-related or not.
- The second provision modelled is the American Opportunity Tax Credit. This partially refundable tax credit is available for only four years per student and only for expenses associated with the first four years of post-secondary education. The student must be enrolled at least half-time in a degree program and cannot have a drug conviction. This credit is calculated as 100% of first USD 2 000 of expenses less related scholarships[4] and 25% of next USD 2 000 of expenses less related scholarships; 40% of credit (up to USD 1 000) may be refundable. For example, the maximum credit is USD 2 500 but only USD 1 000 is

refundable. There is a limit on the value of the credit; USD 180 000 if married filing jointly, which linearly phases out starting at USD 160 000. The limit begins at USD 80,000 for single, head of household or qualifying widowers, linearly phasing out at USD 90 000. For a specific student, education expenses cannot be claimed simultaneously with the Lifetime Learning Tax Credit, or with the deduction for Qualified Higher Education expenses. In addition, eligible expenses include tuition, required enrolment fees and course-related books, supplies, and equipment after deducting scholarship income used to pay the eligible expenses.

- The third provision modelled is Lifetime Learning Tax Credit. This credit is not refundable. This credit is available at a value of USD 2 000 per return, calculated as 20% of first USD 10 000 of expenses less related scholarships. There is a limit on the value of the credit; USD 122 000 if married filing jointly, which linearly phases out starting at USD 102 000. The limit begins at USD 61 000 for single, head of household or qualifying widowers, linearly phasing out at USD 51 000. The credit is available for undergraduate and graduate education as well as courses to acquire or improve job skills. Eligible education expenses include tuition, books and fees that must be paid to the educational institution after deducting scholarship income used to pay the eligible expenses. For a specific student, education expenses cannot be claimed simultaneously with the American Opportunity Tax Credit, or with the deduction for tuition and fees.
- The fourth provision modelled is the deduction for tuition and fees, an alternative to the American Opportunity Tax Credit and the Lifetime Learning Tax Credit. The maximum deductible qualified expenses are the lesser of qualifying expenses less related scholarships and USD 4 000 for taxpayers with incomes of USD 65 000 or less (USD 130 000 for married filing jointly), and the lesser of qualifying expenses less related scholarships and USD 2 000 if income does not exceed USD 80 000 (USD 160 000 if married filing jointly).
- The fifth provision is the deductibility of interest paid on student debt. This deductibility is capped at USD 2 500 per year. Where the students income does not exceed USD 75 000 (USD 150 000 if married filing jointly) for joint returns, linearly phased out starting at USD 60 000 (USD 150 000 if married filing jointly).

Notes

1. This threshold has been increased steadily: in 2016 it was available for EUR 3 000 (USD 4 173) for full-time students and EUR 1 500 for part-time students (USD 2 086.5).
2. The statistical data for Israel are supplied by and under the responsibility of the relevant Israeli authorities. The use of such data by the OECD is without prejudice to the status of the Golan Heights, East Jerusalem and Israeli settlements in the West Bank under the terms of international law.
3. There are additional tax benefits including: up to USD 5 250 of employer provided educational assistance may be excluded from income, a deduction for non-reimbursed work-related education expenses, and tax preferred education savings.
4. Scholarships can cover tuition, fees, books, supplies as well as living expenses. The portion covering living expenses would not be deducted from the expenses eligible for the credit.

ORGANISATION FOR ECONOMIC CO-OPERATION AND DEVELOPMENT

The OECD is a unique forum where governments work together to address the economic, social and environmental challenges of globalisation. The OECD is also at the forefront of efforts to understand and to help governments respond to new developments and concerns, such as corporate governance, the information economy and the challenges of an ageing population. The Organisation provides a setting where governments can compare policy experiences, seek answers to common problems, identify good practice and work to co-ordinate domestic and international policies.

The OECD member countries are: Australia, Austria, Belgium, Canada, Chile, the Czech Republic, Denmark, Estonia, Finland, France, Germany, Greece, Hungary, Iceland, Ireland, Israel, Italy, Japan, Korea, Latvia, Luxembourg, Mexico, the Netherlands, New Zealand, Norway, Poland, Portugal, the Slovak Republic, Slovenia, Spain, Sweden, Switzerland, Turkey, the United Kingdom and the United States. The European Union takes part in the work of the OECD.

OECD Publishing disseminates widely the results of the Organisation's statistics gathering and research on economic, social and environmental issues, as well as the conventions, guidelines and standards agreed by its members.

OECD PUBLISHING, 2, rue André-Pascal, 75775 PARIS CEDEX 16
(23 2017 01 1 P1) ISBN 978-92-64-26937-8 – 2017

www.ingramcontent.com/pod-product-compliance
Lightning Source LLC
Chambersburg PA
CBHW061208240926
51846CB00006B/1146